MINNESOTA ALMANAC

2000

Chris McDermid
Editor

ISBN 0-942072-05-7

John L. Brekke and Sons, Publishers

i

First edition 1976 by Robert A. Jones

Second edition
Copyright © 1981 by John L. Brekke

Third edition 1987
Fourth edition 1999

John L. Brekke and Sons, Publishers

Taylors Falls, Minnesota 55084

Printed in U.S.A.

ACKNOWLEDGEMENTS

In an effort to make this almanac useful, informative and above all accurate, many people in government and in the private sector have provided invaluable advice and encouragement and some have undertaken to write or edit sections in which they are expert. Here we wish to express our appreciation and gratitude.

Initially, contributors--Barbara Stuhler, Women in MN; Paul A. Wilson, Taxes; Bruce Watson, Meteorologist-Weather; Joel Kvamme, Welfare; Kao Ly Ilean Her, Asian Pacific Minnesotans; Mario Hernandez, Chicano/Latinos in MN; Tom Dickson and others, Department of Natural Resources for much information; Sen. Dave Kleis, Politics; Bill Moore, MN AFL-CIO; Mary Ann Grossmann, Literature; John Munger, Dance/USA. Children's Theatre Company; the public relations departments of the Minnesota Twins, Vikings, Timberwolves, Lynx, Wild, the State High School League, and University of Minnesota sports information departments. Also, Associated Press Minneapolis Bureau, KTCA-TV, Minneapolis Star-Tribune, MN Newspaper Association, MN Cable Communications Association, St. Paul Pioneer Press, MPR, Seren Innovations. Also, these offices of the State of Minnesota: Council on the Economic Status of Women; Department of Agriculture; Department of Economic Development, research division; Department of Military Affairs; Office of the adjutant general; Department of Pubic Safety; Bureau of Criminal Apprehension; Department of Human Services; Department of Transportation; Department of Veteran's Affairs; Department of Redundancy Department; Law Library staff; Legislative Reference Library staff; House of Representatives Public Information Office; Senate Information Office; Office of the State Demographer; Secretary of State's office; Governor's office; State Planning Agency; Supreme Court, Court Information Office; MNSCU, Community College System; MN Private College Council; Department of Children, Families, and Learning; Education MN; University of Minnesota, Department of University Relations. Also, the United States Census Office, United States Department of Agriculture; US Forest Service; National Park Service; Norwegian Consul General; Canadian Consulate; American Iron Ore Association, Minnesota League of Women Voters, Minnesota Taxpayers Association, Fort Snelling Restoration and Historic Area, Minnesota Historical Society, Minnesota Zoological Society, St. Paul Winter Carnival Association, University of Minnesota Center for Urban and Regional Development. Special thanks to Joe Brobst, Quark god, for his technical expertise. Our apologies to anyone who was accidentally overlooked.

Your comments and suggestions regarding this almanac are welcomed. Each succeeding almanac will try contain, to the greatest possible extent, the information you find useful, entertaining and educational.

The following pages contain many quotations from *Minnesotans Say the Darnedest Things...Notable Quotes of Memorable Minnesotans(famous, infamous, alive, departed, or adopted) Volume One.* "Some are young, some are old; some are famous, some are not. Some have spoken on serious subjects, others on the trivia that makes our lives bearable. Some are still alive, some are dead-but what they said lives on in these pages."

The Minnesota Almanac thanks Midwest Book Reviews and its editors for allowing us free use of their material to give readers of this book additional insights into what it means to be Minnesotan.

Editor Owen Oxley. Contributing Editors: Stephen Alnes, Dan Byrne, Chuck Chalberg, Carl Chrislock, Carol Connolly, Robert Evans, Michael Fedo, Jimmy Hegg, Dwayne Kinney, Cassandra L. Oxley, Richard H. Parker, Robert T. Smith, Dave Wood.

Cover: Jim Strom and Heather Swanson
Design ~ Carrie Copa, Sauk Rapids
Photos: From Bottom Clockwise
   Minnesota State Capitol ~ Minnesota Almanac Photo
   Kirby Puckett ~ Courtesy Minnesota Twins Media Relations
   Pink and White Lady Slipper ~ Esther McDermid
   LXI-186 Runabout ~ Courtesy Larson Boats, Little Falls-A Genmar Co.
   Governor Jesse Ventura ~ Courtesy Office of the Governor

TABLE OF CONTENTS

1 History 1

2 Military 15

3 Geography 31

4 Vital Statistics 49

5 Government 77

6 Law, Courts and Crime .105

7 Politics 121

8 Taxes 137

9 Education 145

10 Women in the History of Minnesota 161

11 Employment/Organized Labor 173

12 Agriculture 185

13 Poverty and Welfare 193

14 Arts and Entertainment .201

15 Business/Industry 223

16 Communications 231

17 Science/Health 265

18 Weather 275

19 Recreation 293

20 Fishing, Hunting and Wildlife 325

21 Sports 343

22 Myth, Humor and Comedy 375

Index 383

Chapter 1

History

Exploration and Territory 1654 - 1857

The earliest probable explorers to reach Minnesota were French traders Radisson and Groseilliers in 1654. And 1679 Daniel Greysolon Dulhut (Duluth) held a council with the Sioux (Dakota) near Mille Lacs Lake. He met Father Louis Hennepin at the Mississippi after traveling down the St. Croix River the following year. That same year, 1680, Father Hennepin, after being held captive in the village of the Mille Lacs Sioux, discovered the Falls of St. Anthony. On May 8, 1689, Nicholas Perrot, at Fort St. Antoine, on the Wisconsin Shore of Lake Pepin, laid formal claim to the surrounding county for France. He also built a fort on the Minnesota shore of the lake, near its outlet. Between 1689 and 1736, the French continued to develop forts and settlements in Minnesota such as Isle Pelee in 1695, Fort L'Huillier in 1700, Fort Beauharnois near Frontenac in 1727 and Forts St. Pierre and St. Charles in extreme northern Minnesota established in 1731.

In 1745 the Chippewa won the most decisive battle in the war with the Sioux at the great Sioux village of Kathio on the western shore of Mille Lacs. The Sioux were eventually driven onto the western plains by the Chippewa.

The Versailles Treaty of 1763, following the French-Indian War, ceded the French territory east of the Mississippi River to England. France had ceded its area west of the Mississippi to Spain in 1762.

Following the Revolutionary War, the North West Company became important in the fur trade and Grand Portage became its headquarters in 1784. By 1797 the Minnesota area of the Northwest Territory had been mapped by North West trader David Thompson.

In 1803 President Thomas Jefferson purchased that part of Minnesota lying west of the Mississippi River, from Napoleon Bonaparte in the Louisiana Purchase.

During the War of 1812 , the Sioux, Chippewa and Winnebago joined the English. Following the War of 1812, the United States established Fort St. Anthony (renamed Fort Snelling in 1825) in 1819 to protect the confluence of the Minnesota and Mississippi Rivers. The first steamboat arrived at Fort Snelling on May 10, 1823. In the same year American explorer Stephen H. Long visited the Minnesota River, the Red River, and the

Northern frontier. In 1832 Henry R. Schoolcraft discovered the source of the Mississippi River and named it Lake Itasca. In 1836 after Michigan became a state, Minnesota became part of the territory of Wisconsin. The same year, Joseph N. Nicollet began his explorations into Minnesota.

In 1837, Governor Dodge of Wisconsin signed a treaty at Fort Snelling with the Chippewa, by which they ceded all their pine lands on the St. Croix and its tributaries. A treaty was also signed at Washington, D.C. with representatives of the Sioux for their lands east of the Mississippi. These treaties led the way to the first settlements within the area of Minnesota. The following year, Franklin Steele established a claim at the Falls of St. Anthony (Minneapolis) and Pierre Parrant built a shanty and settled on the present site of the city of St. Paul, then called "Pig's Eye", after that unsavory character.

The "Chapel of St. Paul" was built and consecrated in 1841, giving the name to the future capitol of the state.

On August 26, 1848, after the admission of Wisconsin to the Union, the "Stillwater Convention" adopted measures calling for a separate territorial organization, and asked that the new territory be Minnesota. Two months later, on October 30, Henry Hastings Sibley was elected delegate to Congress.

Territory Established

In 1849 Minnesota was organized as a territory and the first territorial legislation assembled on September 3.

By 1850 commercial steamboating was inaugurated on the Minnesota River. The first U.S. census was taken in the Minnesota territory and recorded a population of 6,077 in 1850. In 1851 St. Paul, St. Anthony, and Stillwater were selected for the locations of capitol, university, and penitentiary.

During the 1850's a number of organizations were established to encourage the importation of blooded stock and the introduction of choice seeds, grains, and fruit trees to the territory.

In 1853 W.A. Gorman was appointed governor and the first capitol was constructed. In 1854 commercial flour milling began in Minneapolis. Large scale immigration began in the mid 1850's and a real estate boom resulted. The first bridge to span the main channel of the Mississippi River anywhere along its length was opened in Minneapolis in 1855.

1857 saw the beginning of moves to establish the state government in Minnesota. The Minnesota Enabling Act was passed by Congress on February 26. Governor Samuel Medary, who had been appointed by President James Buchanan, arrived on April 22. The legislation passed a bill to move the state capitol to St. Peter, but since the bill was stolen before it was filed with the territorial secretary of state, the move to St. Peter never came about. On July 13 the Constitution was adopted and the state officers elected on October 3, 1857. Minnesota had a population of 150,037 at this time. On May 11, 1858, Minnesota entered the Union as the 32nd state. At the time of its entry, Minnesota was the third largest state in the Union - only Texas and California were larger.

Early Statehood 1858 - 1898

At the beginning of the Civil War, Governor Alexander Ramsey wired Lt. Gov. Ignatius Donnelly to begin to organize volunteers from the state to fight in the war. On April 14, 1861, Ramsey offered President Lincoln 1,000 men giving Minnesota the distinction of being the first state to offer troops to the Union cause. The first Minnesota regiment left Fort Snelling on June 22, 1861.

On July 2, 1862, the first railroad was opened in Minnesota between Minneapolis and St. Paul. During the Sioux uprising in the late summer of 1862, a number of settlements were attacked. A military commission tried 392 Indians for murder, rape, and other charges, and 303 of them were condemned. On December 26, 1862, 38 Indians were hanged at Mankato.

At the battle of Gettysburg on July 2, 1862, the First Minnesota Regiment make its famous charge and within 15 minutes 215 of the 262 men were killed or wounded. On July 3, Chief Little Crow, Sioux leader of the Sioux Uprising, was killed near Hutchinson. At the close of the Civil and Indian Wars, the Minnesota troops totaled 21,982.

The University of Minnesota was opened in 1886 with William W. Folwell as its first president.

The development by Edmund N. LaCroix of the middlings purifier for flour helped expand the development of Minnesota, the Dakotas and western Canada.

The Legislative Amendment providing for biennial sessions was passed in 1877.

On March 1, 1881, the first state capital burned. A second state capitol was built on the same spot. The legislature moved into the second capital in January, 1883.

The first iron ore was shipped from Minnesota in 1884. The first mine was the Soudan mine on the Vermillion Range. Iron was first discovered on the Mesabi Range 6 years later in 1890 and that range shipped its first iron in 1892.

In 1893 the legislature appointed a Capitol Commission to select a site for and erect a new state capitol building.

Killer forest fires started on September 1, 1894, destroying over 400 sq. miles of area near Hinckley and Sandstone.

Three-fourths of the Red Lake Indian Reservation was opened for settlement in 1896.

The cornerstone on the new state capitol was laid on July 27, 1898. Minnesota was the first state to respond to the President's call for volunteers in the Spanish-American War. Minnesota supplied four regiments for service.

Growth and Development 1899 - 1950

During the late 19th and early 20th centuries the tide of immigration into the state swelled. The most notable origins of this movement were Germany, Sweden, Norway and Denmark. The other migrations from Southern and Eastern Europe contributed to a lesser degree to the state's population increase.

In 1909 President Theodore Roosevelt issued a proclamation establishing Superior National Forest. In 1911 the legislature ratified the proposed amendment to the U.S. Constitution allowing for the direct election of U.S. Senators.

Minnesota became the first state, in 1913, to adopt a non-partisan system of electing its legislators.

During World War I, Minnesota contributed 123,325 troops.

On October 12-13, 1918, forest fires spread over large parts of Carlton and southern St. Louis counties taking 432 lives.

In 1925 a general reorganization of the state government occurred.

In 1930 Minnesotan Frank B. Kellogg, U.S. Secretary of State, was awarded the 1929 Nobel Peace Prize for his work on the Kellogg-Briand Peace Pact signed in Paris in 1928. The purpose of the Pact was to outlaw war.

Floyd B. Olson was elected as the first Farmer-Labor governor of Minnesota in 1930. State population at this time was 2,563, 953.

In 1931 Sinclair Lewis of Sauk Centre was awarded the Novel Prize for Literature.

In the election of 1932 all nine of Minnesota's representatives were elected at large. In 1933 the legislature passed a Reapportionment Act, dividing the state into nine congressional districts.

As the depression worsened in 1933-34, federal and state projects were provided to assist the large numbers of unemployed. The Old Age Assistance Act became effective March 1, 1936.

In 1937, The Pipestone National Monument was established to protect the Indians' sacred quarry near Pipestone.

As a result of a special session of the legislature in 1944, persons in the armed forces were permitted to vote.

The 1946 value of crops in Minnesota was at a high of $683,000,000.

In 1948, for the first time, the value of manufactured products exceeded cash farm receipts in the state.

1951 - 1975

In 1951, Minnesota produced 82% of the nation's total iron ore output. That year Minnesota produced a new record - 89,564,932 tons of iron ore.

A year long centennial celebration was held in 1958 marking the first 100 years of Minnesota statehood. Grand Portage National Monument was established to protect one of the nation's foremost inland centers of 18th and 19th century for trading.

Oceanic trade began with the opening of the St. Lawrence Seaway in 1959. This significant event made Duluth accessible to ocean vessels from anywhere in the world.

In the state's closest race for governor, after more than four months of recounts, Karl F. Rolvaag was sworn in as governor on March 25, 1963. He was declared the winner by 91 votes.

Hubert H. Humphrey became the first Minnesotan to obtain national elective office when he was sworn in as President Lyndon B. Johnson's vice president on January 20, 1965.

The spring of 1965 saw the worst flooding in the state's history.

Vice-President Hubert H. Humphrey, in 1968, became the first Minnesotan nominated by a major party for President of the United States.

The state noted in 1974 the death of Charles A. Lindbergh, Jr., a native of Little Falls, who was world renowned for being the first person to fly across the Atlantic Ocean alone.

The worst blizzard of the century swept through Minnesota on January 11, 1975, with the lowest barometric pressure reading ever recorded; spring and early summer flooding, especially in the Red River Valley, caused millions of dollars in crop damage. In early July the third known earthquake in state history was recorded in a large area of west-central Minnesota. The summer of 1976 brought the worst drought in 100 years to southwestern Minnesota.

1976 - 1982

Where blizzards, floods and windstorms dealt blows to the Minnesota economy in 1975, the state was plagued by an extensive drought and forest fires in 1976 and an energy emergency early in 1977.

Walter F. Mondale became the second Minnesotan to be elected to the nation's second highest office. Seventh district congressman Bob Bergland was appointed by President-elect Jimmy Carter to the post of secretary of agriculture.

On December 29, 1976, Gov. Wendell R. Anderson resigned midway through his second term and was succeeded by Lt. Gov. Rudy Perpich. The day after Perpich succeeded to the governorship, Mondale resigned his seat in the U.S. senate and Perpich appointed Anderson to succeed him.

National attention was focused on Minnesota in January of 1978 when Sen. Hubery H. Humphrey died. He was succeeded by his widow Muriel.

The Minnesota Zoological Garden opened in Apple Valley in May.

Concern over fuel shortages lasted throughout 1978, with Gov. Quie calling out the National Guard in June to protect tank trucks from possible violence during a shutdown by independent truckers protesting rising fuel prices.

After years of controversy and sometimes violent protest, a 436-mile power line from North Dakota to Minnesota was put into operation in July. The 400,000-volt line runs from Underwood, N.D., to Delano.

1980-1989

In 1980 Minnesotans, along with the rest of the nation, awaited word of the hostages held captive in Iran. Two Minnesotans were among the 52 - U.S. Charge d'Affairs Bruce Laingen,57, of Odin, and Army Warrant Officer Joseph Hall, 31, Little Falls. (They were released with the other hostages in January of 1981.)

Concern about hazardous chemical wastes and where they are dumped spread throughout the state after residents of Spring Valley and Oakdale found that old dump sites in their areas posed a risk of contamination of wells.

The U.S. hockey team earned world attention at the Winter Olympics at Lake Placid, N.Y., defeating the Russians and winning a gold medal. Coach Herb Brooks and many of the players were from Minnesota.

A shortfall of $195 million in expected tax revenues forced Gov. Quie to order cuts in spending for state agencies, school districts and local governmental aids.

Minnesota's budget problems continued through 1981; by the end of the year the state had a revenue shortage of some $700 million. Gov. Al Quie called three special sessions during the year to resolve the cash shortage problems and the state ran short of immediate cash, missing two payments to local governments.

In the private sector housing construction fell to the lowest level since the Depression and layoffs were rampant in the Twin Cities, Duluth and the Iron Range.

More than 6,000 public school teachers in 36 districts strick for a total of 302 days in some three dozen teachers' strikes. And some 140,000 state workers, almost half of the state's employees, went on strike in July and returned to work August 11, ending the largest strike by public employees in state history.

Brighter news was made by Gerry Spiess of White Bear Lake who crossed the Pacific Ocean in his 10-foot sloop, Yankee Girl.

The last game was played at Metropolitan Stadium in Bloomington on December 20 where fans caused $400,000 in damages after the Vikings played. The Teflon-coated, fiberglass roof of the new Hubert H. Humphrey Metrodome was inflated in October.

In politics, Rudy Perpich won the governorship against Wheelock Whitney and Sen. David Durenberger withstood a well-financed challenge from Mark Dayton.

Other important 1982 events included the official opening of the Hubert H. Humphrey Metrodome in Minneapolis, trials of six members of the Cermak family of southern Minnesota accused of intra-familial abuse, a liver transplant at the University of Minnesota for 11-month-old Jamie Fiske of Massachusetts and the voyage of the Viking replica ship Hjemkomst, which sailed from its home port of Duluth to Norway.

Grim economic news continued into 1983, with the unemployment rate at 15.7 in October in Minnesota's northeastern corner. The jobless rate was due to layoffs and shutdowns at Iron Range taconite mines, the largest employer in the region.

There was another record snowfall and cold weather during November and December of 1983.

In politics, Rudy Perpich was sworn in for a second term of office as governor and visited at least a dozen foreign countries and 21 states in his role as the state's leading salesman and booster.

The continuing story in most of 1984 was the presidential candidacy of native son Walter Mondale and his historic choice of Geraldine Ferraro as the nation's first female vice-presidential candidate.

About 6,300 nurses struck 16 Twin Cities hospitals for five weeks in a walkout that began on June 1, 1984 affected some 8,000 non-nursing employees. It was the largest nurses' strike in the nation's history.

In other 1984 developments, investors in Minnesota's first pari-mutuel racetrack near Shakopee asked for controversial new financing; the sex abuse case that began in 1981 with the arrest of the Cermak family grew to implicate 35 adults in the Jordan area; C. Peter Magrath resigned after 10 years as president of the University of Minnesota to take a job at the University of Missouri; Calvin Griffith and his family ended a 65-year reign as owners of the Minnesota Twins when they sold the team to Minneapolis businessman Carl Pohlad and former Twins player Harmon Killebrew was voted into baseball's Hall of Fame.

Economic crisis for many of Minnesota's farmers, and its ripple effect on small town businesses and banks, were the top stories of 1985.

Ironically, it was also the year that Garrison Keillor put Minnesota on the map with publication of his best-selling book, "Lake Wobegon Days", which celebrates the state's rural heritage.

Minnesota lost 5,000 farms from June 1984 to June 1985; six rural banks failed, the most in any year since the Great Depression.

The state mourned for 70 people, most of them Minnesotans, who were killed in the crash of an airplane just south of Reno, Nev.

Bitterness swamped Austin as 1,500 meatpackers at the Geo. A. Hormel & Co. plant went on strike after a 10-month dispute.

In sports, Bud Grant returned as head coach of the Minnesota Vikings, University of Minnesota football head coach Lou Holtz became head coach at Notre Dame and the annual All-Star baseball game was played at the Metrodome in Minneapolis.

Other 1985 highlights included the opening of the $45 million Ordway Music Theatre in St. Paul and of the $70 million Canterbury Downs race-track in Shakopee; the selection of Kenneth Keller as president of the University of Minnesota and implantation of an artificial heart in Mary Lund, the first woman to undergo the procedure.

The Hormel strike again dominated the news in January on 1986 when the plant reopened after a five-month strike and striking meatpackers ringed the plant, blocking entrances. Gov. Perpich called out the National Guard, which stayed until February.

In politics, legislators dealt with a $734 million budget shortfall, the legal drinking age was changed to 21 and Gov. Perpich was re-elected.

Will Steger's dogsled expedition reached the North Pole, making Sunfish Lake native Anne Bancroft the first woman to cross the ice to the pole.

After four years of intense negotiations and 200 years of disunity, three major Lutheran denominations agreed to merge into the new Evangelical Lutheran Church in America.

In April, 1987, the NBA granted Minnesota a professional basketball franchise for $32.5 million. Minnesota Public Radio made the final regular broadcast of Garrison Keillor's "A Prairie Home Companion" from St. Paul's World Theater.

U of M president Kenneth Keller resigned in 1988 when the University was embarrassed by cost overruns in the remodeling of his residence. Nils Hasselmo succeeded him.

In a heartbreaker, Minnesota Hockey Gophers were defeated in the 1989 NCAA finals by Harvard, 6-3 in overtime.

Will Steger led an international 7 month expedition by dogsled across Antarctica. Back at home drought conditions caused havoc for farmers.

A wildcat strike took place in International Falls at the Boise Cascade papermill culminating in a riot on September 9th.

Jacob Wetterling, 11, of St. Joseph was abducted by a masked gunman in October setting off a nation-wide search and inspiring the Jacob Wetterling Foundation. The Foundation was instrumental in advocating the 1994 Jacob Wetterling Crimes Against Children and Violent Sex Offender Registration Act that required states to register sex offenders and allowed them to enact Community notification laws.

Nov. 3rd the NBA Timberwolves played their first regular season game losing to the Seattle SuperSonics 106-94.

1990-1999

Minnesota joined the gold rush by establishing a lottery on April 17th. Funds were earmarked for the General Fund and the Environmental Trust Fund.   In June the Twin Cities were gripped by "Gorbymania" as Mikhail Gorbachev visited the area. On December 25, 1991, he resigned as the world recognized Russia and the other former Soviet republics because the Soviet Union dissolved.

Minnesota cycling sensation, Greg LeMond, won his third Tour de France.

In business, Dayton's bought Marshall Field of Chicago for $1.4 billion.

Politicians smeared each other and the state's reputation as their dirty campaigns were featured in the national press.   Arne Carlson was elected governor in a last minute campaign when primary winner, John Grunseth, withdrew at the eleventh hour amidst allegations of scandal.
1991

According to the Associated Press the $838 million aid package for Northwest Airlines even topped the Persian Gulf War story where thousands of us served and in which 7 Minnesotans died and 1 was listed as missing.   U.S. Senator Paul Wellstone made an early impression in Washington, D.C. by opposing the Gulf War during his first months in office.

The legislature dealt with a $1.1 billion budget shortfall with spending cuts and a tax increase of over $600 million. Taxpayer lost an additional $1 billion when Midwest Federal Savings and Loan failed.
The number one sports story was the Twins coming out of the American League cellar in 1990 to win their second World Series in four years. Also in sports, Vikings football coach Jerry Burns resigned and the North Stars battled to hockey's Stanley Cup finals losing to Pittsburgh in six games.

An extra heavy winter started with two blizzards early in the season, on Halloween and Thanksgiving weekend. November dumped 46.9" of fluff on the Twin Cities, a record for any single month and nine times normal snowfall.

In January 1992, the HHH Metrodome played host to Superbowl XXVI in January and again in April to NCAA Basketball's Final Four. Also coming to Minnesota was the International Special Olympics.

Minneapolis police officer, Jerry Haaf, 53, was shot in the back as he sipped coffee in a South Minneapolis pizzeria.

The Legislature passed a subsidized health insurance program that was the most comprehensive in the country. Representative Vin Weber (I-R) retired from Congress and was succeeded by David Minge.

On June 30th, a toxic spill forced thousands to evacuate their homes in Duluth and Superior.

Weather made the headlines as a wet spring and cool summer temperatures damaged crops.

In January 1993, Alan Page, former Minnesota Viking, was sworn in as the first black member of the Minnesota Supreme Court. Later, world-famous transplant surgeon, John Najarian, was removed as chief of surgery at the U of M Hospital over irregularities involving the ALG transplant drug program.

"Phone Gate" dominated the Minnesota House as Majority Leader Alan Welle's son and nephew used and distributed an access code to rack up a $90,000 phone bill. Welle later resigned.

Major flooding took place this spring, with 57 counties declared disaster areas, and four deaths attributed to flooding. A cool, wet summer left farmers with average incomes barely above the break even point. 3 million acres were non-productive. In August, the legislature approved a disaster bill for farmers worth $5.8 billion.

Northwest Airlines averted bankruptcy by negotiating a deal with the International Association of Machinists.

In politics, Sen. Dave Durenberger announced his plans not to seek reelection after indictment over charges of falsely claiming travel reimbursement. In Minneapolis, Sharon Sayles Belton became the first black elected mayor of that city. In November, Minneapolis became the first big-city school district in the nation to turn its management over to a private company.

In December, 18 people were killed when a Northwest Airlink commuter plane smashed into a hillside in Hibbing.

Minnesota native and U.S. Supreme Court Justice, Harry Blackmun announced his retirement from the nation's highest court in 1994. He was its first black justice.

NSP got the legislature's permission to store spent nuclear fuel in casks at the Prairie Island power plant site after heated debate. Mankato businessman, Glen Taylor, bought the Minnesota Timberwolves.

In August, the Mille Lacs band of Ojibway received a ruling by a federal judge allowing them to retain hunting and fishing rights granted in an 1837 treaty.

Two police officers from St. Paul were killed when they approached a man sleeping in his car in a church parking lot. Later in the month, Soo-Line workers staged the longest rail strike in 16 years.

John Laux, Minneapolis police chief retired when police officers in his department were accused of brutality, racism, and goofing off during work hours. In November, Arne Carlson defeated John Marty in the gubernatorial race.

In a health related issue, the Schwan's ice cream plant in Marshall closed down for a month following Minnesota's largest outbreak of salmonella food poisoning.

1995

In1995 the internet and its World Wide Web went from about 3 million users in 1994 to about 18 million users this year when an estimated 60,000 web sites were created.

In business, Northern States Power and Wisconsin Energy Corp. merged. Burlington Northern Railroad acquired the Santa Fe giving them rail access from Canada to Mexico. The Dow Jones Industrial Average topped 4,000 in February and passed 5,000 on November 21st.

Metro lives were disrupted for most of October as the Amalgamated Transit Union members struck, shutting down Metro Bus service for three weeks.

A forest fire along the Gunflint Trail in northeastern Minnesota caused hundreds to evacuate.

In an effort to serve children in the state more effectively, Minnesota became the first state in the nation to combine children and family services and education into a single agency called the Department of Children, Families & Learning.

People in the news include Congressman Dave Durenburger who received a light penalty for his misuse of travel funds due to numerous pleas on his behalf. The Minnesota Orchestra named Eiji Oue (AYE-gee OH-way) as its ninth musical director. St. Paul native and U.S. Supreme Court Chief Justice Warren Burger died at age 87. Former Governor Rudy Perpich, 67, died Sept. 21.

1995 was a record breaking year for homicides with 97 victims in Minneapolis.

The University of Minnesota Hospital was purchased in 1996 by Fairview Hospital in an $87 million deal

March 17th brought the advent of a 320 area code to central Minnesota in what used to be the 612 area.

In business this year, Cray Research, super-computer manufacturer, was sold to Silicon Graphics. 3M spun of a division which became Imation.

Minnesota Twins icon, Kirby Puckett, was sidelined with glaucoma and later retired, unable to see well enough to play professional baseball, staying on with the front office of the Twins club. He is considered by some the be the best Minnesota Twin there ever was.

It was a year that began with mountains of snow and ended with a frustrating lack of it. Record flooding devastated the Red River Valley destroying hundreds of homes and businesses inspiring an organized outpouring of aid. 30-40% of the whitetail herd in Northeast Minnesota died from deep snow and bitter cold.

St. Louis Park natives, Joel and Ethan Coen, released the movie Fargo starring Francis McDormand who later won an Oscar for her performance.

Notable deaths in 1996 included, Mina Peterson, 105, the Pie Lady from Lyle's Cafe in Winthrop; Bill Goldsworthy, former North Star Hockey All-Star right wing; Peter Popovich, 75, Chief Judge of MN Supreme Court and Court of Appeals; Ed Ney, 75, brilliant U of M physicist; Michelle Carew, 18, daughter of Former MN Twin Rod Carew, of leukemia; Max Winter, 93, former president of the Vikings and Minneapolis Lakers; Meridel LeSeure, 96, writer of and for the poor and women; Tiny Tim, 64, who's signature song, "Tiptoe Through the Tulips" reached #17 in 1968.

The year 1997 started snowy but later stayed mild. The worst flooding in a century caused the destruction of much of Grand Forks, ND and East Grand Forks, MN. When dikes broke, 60,000 people had to be evacuated. Damage was in the 100's of millions.

The Stroh Brewery closed after a 132 year history eliminating jobs for hundreds of workers and suds for hundreds of swillers.

The Timberwolves signed Kevin Garnett to a $125 million contract, the largest ever for a professional athlete in a team sport.

A judge upheld the rights of the Mille Lacs Ojibway band to hunt and fish according to their 1837 treaty.

The State had a budget surplus of $2.3 billion. The legislature raised speed limits on rural interstates from 65 to 70 mph, and on urban interstates from 55-65. Also in politics, Minneapolis and St. Paul mayors were reelected. Sharon Sayles-Belton and Norm Coleman, respectively.

Mark Yudof became the 14th president of the University of Minnesota on July 1, 1997.

In January 1998 long-time WCCO personality Dave Moore died at age 73.

On March 29th tornadoes ravaged southern Minnesota destroying 75% of the homes in Comfrey leaving 100 homeless. In St. Peter, 90% of businesses and homes were damaged with 50% and 25% destroyed, respectively. Gustavus Adolphus College sustained over $60 million in damages. Two died and 38 people were injured.

Minnesota's largest civil penalty ever issued was against Koch Refining in the amount of $6.9 million for environmental violations.

In May, the tobacco industry agreed to an out-of-court settlement with the state and Blue Cross and Blue Shield of Minnesota for $6.6 billion.

Norwest Corp., one of Minnesota's largest banks merges with Wells Fargo and moves to San Francisco. Another business acquisition was the July 2nd purchase of the Minnesota Vikings by Texan Red McCombs for $250 million.

In education, Minnesota college-bound students had the second highest ACT scores in the nation.

In a November political upset, Reform Party candidate for governor, Jesse Ventura, defeated St. Paul Mayor Norm Coleman and Attorney General Skip Humphrey to win the state's highest office. Ventura is the first Reform Party member to occupy the governor's mansion in any state. Republicans took control of the house which was held by the Democrats since 1986.

A tragic natural gas explosion destroyed several buildings in downtown St. Cloud on December 11th. Four people were killed and 15 injured as workers laying fiber optic cable accidentally ruptured a line.

In 1999 business, Allied Signal purchased Honeywell Inc. in June and moved the corporate headquarters to New Jersey, losing 1,000 jobs for the Twin Cities. The Dow continued setting records by breaking the 10,000 barrier and soaring past 11,000 during the course of the year.

The winds during the July 4, 1999 storm in the Boundary Waters Wilderness Canoe Area blew more than 90 miles an hour affecting 380,000 acres. A 10-12 mile wide, 35 mile long swath from Basswood Lake to the Gunflint Trail in the BWCA Wilderness was the most heavily impacted.

Governor Ventura made headlines when he was a guest referee for the World Wrestling Federation's August 22nd SummerSlam.

Farmers are continuing to suffer as commodity prices have sunk to 30-50 year lows with little relief in sight. Many are paying more to grow the crops than they will receive for them.

The Y2K computer bug is getting constant news attention as the state prepares for possible system shut-downs due to old computer chips and programs that could misinterpret the year 2000 which was often written "00". Mistakenly thinking it is the year "1900" the computer could malfunction, miscalculate, or shut down. More importantly, our computer chip machines may function, but those in other states or countries we are networked to could cripple our functions.

Sources: Minneapolis Star and Tribune. St. Paul Pioneer Press, MPR.

St. Mary's Basilica, located in Minneapolis is the oldest Basilica in the United States. Construction began in 1907. The exterior was completed in 1914, but the interior wasn't finished until 1926. It can seat up to 3,000 people.

Chapter 2

Military

Twenty six year-old Lieutenant Zebulon Montgomery Pike arrived at the current site of Mendota on Sept. 21, 1806, and raised the Stars and Stripes, probably for the first time over Minnesota.

Under George Washington, the United States had developed and operated the "factor system", a chain of federal fur-trading posts and stores. Not motivated by profit, it was designed to serve as a deterrent to foreign traders, mostly English and Spanish, improve relations with the Indians, beef up frontier military muscle and protect the Indians from the fur traders.

Thomas Jefferson took a giant step in his dream to have America extend from the Atlantic to the Pacific when he engineered the Louisiana Purchase in 1803, buying nearly half a continent from Napoleon.

Military forts were set up in the new lands, and serious explorations conducted, with added facilities established where needed. Pike was given orders to find the headwaters of the Mississippi, conciliate the Indians, "attach them to the the United Stated" and arrange for the construction of outposts and trading houses.

His discussion with the Sioux led to a treaty (ratified by the congress in 1808) which established the site of Fort Snelling. It has served the military interests of the country in the state since 1820.

History Pre-1820s

The story of Fort Snelling is the story of the development of the Northwest (now called the Upper Midwest) from 1819 to the present.

British fur traders from Canada continued effective control of the Northwest long after it became the United States' territory as a result of the Revolutionary War (1783) and the Louisiana Purchase (1803). The Chippewa and Eastern Sioux depended upon British trade goods to feed and clothe themselves. To obtain these manufactured necessities, they delivered millions of dollars worth of fur and allied themselves with the British in the War of 1812.

After the war, the United States developed a frontier policy to eliminate British influence in the Northwest. The goals of this policy were to keep out foreign traders, protect and regulate American traders, pacify and win the good will of the tribes and extend the frontier to the Great Lakes and the Mississippi. To carry out this policy, a chain of forts and Indian Agencies was built from Lake Michigan to the Missouri River. In 1819, the 5th Regiment of Infantry was ordered to build a post at the junction of the Mississippi and St. Peter's (Minnesota) Rivers. This post, called St. Anthony, was the northwestern link in the chain of forts, it lay between the lands of the Sioux and Chippewa, it controlled traffic on both rivers and it had good water communications north, south and west.

History 1820-58

Fort St. Anthony was completed by 1825 and renamed to honor its builder and first commander, Colonel Josiah Snelling. The Indian Agent, Major Lawrence Taliaferro, established St. Peter's agency besides the fort. Taliaferro was expected to lessen friction between the tribes and between the Indians and whites by drawing boundaries, making treaties, presenting gifts, providing missions, blacksmiths and model farms and by restraining the traders' most unscrupulous activities. The garrison of Fort Snelling was the force which could be used to keep settlers out of Indian Territory, to keep liquor out of the trade and to punish Indians and whites who broke the peace or violated the laws of the frontier. For almost 30 years, Snelling, Taliaferro and their successors acted as the only police and government for 90,000 square miles. The size and strength of the fort was the symbol of their power and authority. The soldiers, traders and Indians had no love for each other, but war was avoided by impartial enforcement of laws and a balance of restraint on both traders and Indians.

When the frontier of settlement reached the Mississippi in 1837, this balance was upset. Minnesota Territory was established in 1848 and soon the land-hungry farmers and speculators demanded the Sioux lands west of the river. By the treaties of 1851, the Sioux were confined to reservations and their land opened to settlement. Forts Ripley, Ridgely and Abercrombie were built to guard the new frontier further west. The Territorial government was established in St. Paul. Fort Snelling's frontier duty was over; it served as a supply depot until 1858, when, as Minnesota achieved statehood, it was turned over to the speculators who had bought it the year before.

History 1858-1987

Although the military reservation was platted for the town site, the City of Fort Snelling was never built. During the Civil War (1861-65) the state used the fort to train its volunteer troops, and after the war the regular army repossessed and used it as headquarters for Indian war campaigns in the Dakotas. Between 1870 and the early 1900s, many new brick barracks, officer's quarters, offices, shops and stables were built, while the old stone fort was allowed to decay and was gradually demolished. After serving as a recruiting and training center in two world wars, Fort Snelling was decommissioned in 1946 and turned over to the Veteran's Administration and Army Reserve.

In 1956, the threat of a freeway through the heart of the old fort stimulated public efforts to save the remnants of the oldest buildings in Minnesota.

In 1960, Fort Snelling was designated Minnesota's first National Historic Landmark, and the following year the Legislature established Fort Snelling State Historical Park. Since 1963, the Legislature has appropriated funds to develop the 2,500 acre park and to rebuild the old fort. By the time all 18 buildings of the original fort are rebuilt, a staff acting as soldiers, cooks, laundresses, blacksmith, carpenter and armorer will show how men and women on the frontier lived and worked in the 1820's.

Description of the Fort
1820-1830

Fourteen stone and two wooden buildings and over 1500 feet of stone wall were built by the troops of the 5th Infantry in four years. Colonel Snelling selected the location on the bluff above the river junction. The traditional rectangular fort design was adapted to a diamond to fit the shape of the bluff. Because limestone was handy and there were masons in the ranks, most of the fort was built of stone. Pine logs for timbers and planks were floated from the Rum River to the army sawmill at St. Anthony Falls. Large cannon in the pentagonal (2) and hexagonal (4) towers protected all four walls. Sentries watched over the walls from elevated platforms. Small cannon on the round tower (3) looked down on the rivers. Ammunition for cannon and muskets was stored in the magazine (8).

The enlisted men slept two in a bunk and ate their common meals in the barracks, one stone (11) and one wooden (12). Officer's families shared the fourteen sets of rooms in the wooden officers quarters (14) with the theater and bachelor officers' mess. The post commander set up home and headquarters in the commandant's house (13). In the post shops (5) the blacksmith, carpenter, armorer and wheelwright built and repaired the tools, vehicles, furniture, weapons and equipment needed on the frontier. The baker turned out the daily bread ration, eighteen ounces per man, aged or toasted before issue. Foodstuffs and supplies were stored in the four-story commissary warehouse (15): flour from the fort's gristmill at St. Anthony Falls, sugar, vinegar, uniforms, shoes, harness, blankets, nails, glass, paint, tents and everything else sent upriver annually from Philadelphia, Pittsburgh and St. Louis. In the guardhouse (7) were cells for military and civilian prisoners, and quarters for the guard detail and the Officer of the Day, responsible for the peace and security of the post.

The hospital (16) included a surgery, dispensary, ward, surgeon's quarters, library and kitchen. In the school (17), children of the post worked over their sums and spelling, and on Sundays the chaplain or an officer preached a sermon. The sutler's store (10) was a combination post exchange, enlisted men's club, grocery, and general store. The sutler held a monopoly on everything not supplied by the army, but was taxed to support the band, library and the regiment's widows. Among much else, he sold provisions of the officers and extra clothing to the soldiers.

Everything needed by this community was located in the neighborhood. Down at the river landing (23) cargoes of food, supplies and firewood were unloaded from keelboats, flatboats, and steamboats, and hauled up the steep road to the fort. The wash house (24) stood handy to the river, because it was easier to carry clothes than water up the bluff. Vegetables grown in the gardens (21) on the river bottoms were stored in the cool cave-like root cellars (19) beneath the road. Fields (22) of corn, oats, and wheat were fenced off on the prairie atop the bluff. Herds of beef cattle grazed in the prairie grass. The odors of manure, cowhides, hot fat and tar,wood smoke, leather and hay filled the air around the stable (18). Draft horses and oxen drew carts loaded with wheat to the gristmill (25) at St. Anthony Falls and returned loaded with lumber from the sawmill or bricks and lime from the kilns. Occasionally a small procession marched slowly across the prairie to the cometary (20), followed by a casket carried by soldiers with black armbands.

Garrison Life

Three to six companies of the regiment, 150 to 300 men, women and children, usually lived in the fort. Their daily routines were ordered by rank: officers and enlisted men. Officers were expected to inspect, supervise and report everything, everyone and every event. Still, they had the leisure to be gentlemen and sportsmen, and their tables were spread with varieties of game and fine wines. Officers and their families were assigned to private quarters, at least two rooms and a kitchen. Their wives organized the social life of the fort: teas, dances, dinners and concerts. By 1820, most young lieutenants were graduates of West Point and took their profession of arms seriously. After 30 years commanding a company on the frontier, they learned all about human failings, military forms and seniority and forgot nearly everything else. Most of them retired as middle-aged captains.

Fort Snelling Restoration is administered by the Minnesota Historical Society; phone 612-726-1171, Monday through Friday. It is located Northeast of the intersection of Interstate 494 and highways 55, south of Minneapolis, north of the airport.

FORT SNELLING 1825-1835

This view shows the fort as it looked after completion but before major alterations were made in the 1840's; it also shows the fort as it will look when the restoration is complete.

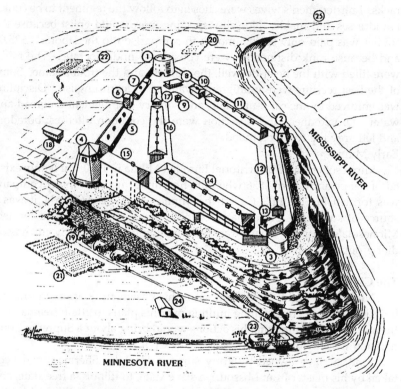

MISSISSIPPI RIVER

MINNESOTA RIVER

1. Round Tower*	13. Commandant's House
2. Pentagonal Tower*	14. Officers' Quarters
3. Semicircular Battery	15. Commissary Warehouse
4. Hexagonal Tower*	16. Hospital
5. Shops	17. School/Chapel*
6. Gate House	18. Stable
7. Guard House*	19. Root Cellars
8. Magazine*	20. Cemetery
9. Well*	21. Gardens
10. Sutler's Store*	22. Fields
11. Short Barrack	23. Landing
12. Long Barrack	24. Wash House

25. St. Anthony Falls—Sawmill Gristmill

*Restored by June, 1971

The life of the enlisted men was endless labor: building forts and roads, tending crops, cutting firewood and standing guard. Frontier duty made good farmers but rusty soldiers. Constant fatigue and guard details left no time for drill and ceremonies.

They ate regulation rations of soup, bread and coffee, with vegetables from their gardens. Enlisted families shared 17 by 20 foot rooms in the barracks. Enlisted men's wives were chosen to follow the regiment to be cooks, laundresses and maids. No self-respecting man would enlist because the soldier was paid only $6.00 a month in comparison to the laborer's $25.00 and because rank distinctions were considered undemocratic. The ranks were filled with the ne'er-do-well, the shiftless and the troublesome. Some of the best recruits were immigrants wanting to learn English. Discipline was enforced by the cat-o-nine tails and solitary confinement on bread and water. Drunkenness and desertion were the common offenses: boredom and lethargy the common mood.

Early Militia

Minnesota formed a Territorial Enrolled Militia in 1850, but it only existed of paper until April 1856 when the first uniformed, volunteer company was formed in St. Paul. Called the Minnesota Pioneer Guards, it was a source of such civic pride that soon nine other companies were formed. Minnesota's National Guard traces its beginning to these early citizen-soldier groups.

The Civil War

Night after night, Dred Scott sat in his basement quarters in officers' building No. 2 at Fort Snelling mulling over his plans to attain freeman status and little dreaming that his actions would bring about a Supreme Court decision which would, in turn, lead to the Civil War.

Scott, a slave owned by army surgeon Dr. John Sherman, had been taken by his master from Missouri, a slave state, to Illinois, a free state, and then to Minnesota territory in 1834, where slavery was prohibited by the Missouri Compromise. This was the result of a series of measures passed by congress to appease both the south and the north on the matter of slavery.

Scott married another slave at Fort Snelling and, after his master's death, sued the widow for his freedom. Scott's legal skirmishing ended up in the Supreme Court where Chief Justice Roger B. Taney handed down the controversial decision in favor of the widow Sherman, polarized the north (and the south), and resulted in the War between the States.

When the conflict started with the bombardment of Fort Sumter, Minnesota was only three years old and it was involved in it and, little more than a year later, a violent Sioux war. Minnesota Governor Ramsey by chance in Washington on April 3, 1861, learned about Fort Sumter and immediately went to Secretary of War Cameron to offer 1000 Minnesotans for federal service. President Lincoln accepted these men into federal armies, even in advance of his request for 75,000 volunteers from the entire north.

Quick to enter the fray, the First Minnesota Infantry Volunteers suffered heavy casualties in the battle of Bull Run on July 21.

All told, Minnesota provided 22,000 men-and this from a state whose total population was only 172,000. They made notable contributions at Corinth, Vicksburg, Gettysburg, Chickamauga, Chattanooga, Brice's Cross Roads and Nashville as well as clashes with Sioux at home.

The Sioux War

Four young devil-may-care Wahpeton Indians, Killing Ghost, Breaking Up, Runs Against Something When Crawling and Brown Wing, happened by the farm of Robinson Jones, whom they challenged to a friendly "turkey shoot". The friendly target practice unaccountably became violent and when the gunsmoke settled, five whites lay dead.

Learning of the incident, the outlying bands, seething because of their bad treatment at the hands of the whites, who, among other things, were late in their payments promised by treaty, gathered under Little Crow and mounted a series of surprise attacks against isolated farms, settlements and Fort Ridgely. Drained of its fighting men by the Civil War, the state quickly trained available manpower and sent units out willy-nilly to trouble spots.

After two determined assaults on Fort Ridgely and two on New Ulm were repulsed, the tide began to turn, and a militia of 1600 whites led by General Sibley brought the hostilities to an end. On September 26, his troop entered the Wood Lake Camp held by friendly Indians and were handed over 269 Sioux prisoners-107 whites and 162 half-breeds: the place is known in Sioux War history as Camp Release. It is estimated that in the widely scattered actions 486 white people were killed-360 civilians and 126 soldiers.

Captures of stray bands and voluntary surrenders brought the number of Sioux prisoners to 2,000, and a military commission sentenced 307 to death and 16 to imprisonment. President Lincoln reviewed the list and ordered Sibley to hang 39 (one of these was later reprieved) late in December in Mankato. A marker in the city indicates that spot where the 38 plunged to their deaths at the same instant on the day after Christmas.

The Spanish American War

By 1890, the dust of marching feet and battle had settled over Minnesota and the frontier forts closed. Ten years earlier, Fort Snelling was sold to one Franklin Steele, but he defaulted on his payments and later, at the urging of President Grant, Congress acted to reclaim the land and buildings, This was fortunate since they were needed to satisfy the needs of a national movement under way to reactivate a militia system. The state volunteer militia was moved into the National Guard, units of which were called out to handle state emergencies.

Meanwhile tensions were building between the United States and Spain and war broke out in the spring of 1898. Curiously, two Minnesotans were deeply involved; St. Paul's Archbishop Ireland, at the request of Pope Leo XII, had done his best to persuade President McKinley to avoid the conflict, but Senator Cushman K. Davis of St. Paul, chairman of the committee on foreign relations, steered a war resolution through the Senate.

Called by some a non-war that had been hatched by the yellow press of W. R. Hearst's *New York Journal* and Joseph Pulitzer's *New York World*, and the U.S. governments concern about the heavy losses of American investment on Cuba, it embroiled the nation.

Minnesota's adjutant general Herman Muehlberg proudly reported "The rapid mobilization resulted in our (Minnesota's) troops being the first volunteers mustered into the service of our country".

Altogether, 8,948 Minnesotans took part in the Cuban and Philippine campaigns of the war.

World War I

Minnesota, like the rest of the U.S., was caught up in the great conflict, unprepared as usual. Imperialist, economic, territorial and nationalist rivalries lit the fuse.

A collection of amateurs, jerrybuilt into a disorganized system of National Guard units, formed a cadre for a monumental military machine composed of draftees and emotional volunteers dedicated to defeating the Kaiser and making the world "safe for democracy".

Minnesotans flocked to the colors with their customary enthusiasm and distinguished themselves in every branch of the service and theater of the war. A state contingent, the 1st Battalion, 151st Field Artillery, performed with distinction with the Famed Rainbow Division under Brig. Gen. George Leach, later mayor of Minneapolis.

Of the 127,578 Minnesotans in uniform, 887 died in battle, 1,251 died of wounds suffered in combat, 5,084 were wounded and 101 were taken prisoner.

World War II

On Sunday, Dec. 7, 1941, at 3:55 a.m. Hawaiian time, the U.S. Ward was on picket duty at the entrance to Pearl Harbor. Gun crew No. 3 opened fire on a Japanese submarine, sinking it-this, four hours before Japanese bombers struck in a surprise raid on Hickam Field and the harbored fleet.

2208 military personnel were killed and 1109 wounded, along with 68 civilian deaths. The U.S. was plunged into global war.

The Ward, formerly the Gopher, was manned entirely by a St. Paul Naval Reserve group that had trained in Duluth. Known as the "First Shotters," the survivors of the unit, mostly St. Paul residents, hold a reunion each December 7.

But the struggle was not limited to the Pacific. Minnesota's famous 34th "Red Bull" division held the distinction of being the first National Guard division shipped overseas. They fought their way across North Africa from the Kasserine Pass to the Mediterranean, up the boot of Italy, through Monte Casino to the Po Valley, amassing the record for the greatest number of days in combat for any American division.

In these battles on every continent, 4,399 North Star soldiers died in battle or of wounds, 302 were listed as missing and 382 died in prison camps.

Korean and Vietnam Wars

North Korea strengthened with Communist Chinese troops invaded South Korea. 54,000 Minnesotans served their nation in the Korean war which lasted from June 25, 1950 until July 27, 1953. Eighteen years later, in 1961, following the Korean pattern, North Vietnamese troops backed by the Chinese Army surged into South Vietnam. 68,000 Minnesotans answered the call to fight in American's longest military involvement, the Vietnam conflict which dragged on until Jan. 27, 1973.

Persian Gulf War

In August, 1990, Iraq invaded Kuwait touching off the largest deployment of American combat forces since World War Two. "Operation Desert Shield," intended to protect Saudi Arabia soon became "Operation Desert Storm" when a US-led international coalition used its military might to quickly liberate Kuwait and destroy Iraq's army and air force. Approximately 32,500 Minnesotans served in the Persian Gulf War from August 2, 1990 to an undetermined date (as of July, 1999). These people included regular, reserve and National guard members. Approximately 13,200 were in the theater (war zone).

Bosnia & Kosovo

There are not yet firm figures concerning numbers of Minnesotans in these police actions partly because there is on-going involvement. See some details in the Minnesota National Guard section below.

Veterans in Minnesota

As of July, 1999, there were an estimated 457,000* former servicemen and women living in Minnesota. Approximately 149,800* Minnesota veterans had been in service during the Vietnam-era - that is after August 4, 1964. World War II veterans made up a group estimated at 113,000*.

Approximately 74,800* veterans of the Korean conflict live in the state and there are 60,000 who saw military service between the Korean conflict and the Vietnam-era (February 1, 1955 - August 4, 1964).

There are no surviving veterans of the Spanish-American War in the state.

The Minnesota National Guard

As mentioned earlier, our Guard had its roots in the state's first militias, beginning in April, 1856. The "First Minnesota" led the Union in joining the Civil War effort, while the militia at home dealt with the Sioux War. The Minnesota National Guard served in the Spanish American war as the Thirteenth Minnesota Volunteers fighting Spanish troops and Filipino insurrectionists in the Philippines from 1898-99.

During WWI, most Minnesota National Guard divisions were broken up with our soldiers reassigned to other divisions. Fortunately, Minnesota's field artillery regiment remained intact and became part of the 42nd "Rainbow" Division where it fought with great distinction in France.

In June, 1931, a 53,000-acre training site north of Little Falls was opened named Camp Ripley.

The Guard was mobilized for WWII, where some joined the 34th "Red Bull" Infantry Division. They became the first American Division to ship for Europe in January, 1942, and men of Minnesota's 175th Field Artillery fired the first American shells against the Nazis in north Africa.

During the Korean Conflict, the Minnesota National Guard was called up as a training division and many of its members were reassigned as replacement troops in Korea or Germany. Minnesota's Air Guard contributed pilots to Korea's "Mig Alley."

Though not officially mobilized during Vietnam, the Air Guard flew hundreds of supply and transport missions to Southeast Asia.

The Persian Gulf War saw 3 units and over 600 Minnesota Guard members volunteer or become activated with their units to serve.

When war broke out in Bosnia in 1996, Minnesota Guard members served support for regular Army and Air Force as well as having Battery E, 151st Field Artillery deployed to Sarajevo.

During the Kosovo Crisis in 1999, and continuing, over 300 Minnesota Air Guard members have thus far rotated on volunteer tours to provide airlifts. Many of the airlifts were to deliver humanitarian aid to refugees.

Today, there are 11,300 men and women in the Army and Air Force National Guard in the state. National Guard units are located in 60 Minnesota communities and there are two air units--one at Minneapolis-St. Paul International Airport and one at Duluth. Camp Ripley is the primary winter training site for all National Guard units in the United States with an economic impact on communities of central Minnesota of over $96 million annually. The Guard partially funds a non-profit corporation called STAR-BASE to promote youth awareness of math, science and technology by teaching about aviation and aerospace.

Source: Minnesota National Guard information largely provided by their website: www.dma.state.mn.us

Veterans Organizations

MN Department of Veterans Affairs

20 W 12th St
St. Paul, MN 55155
651-296-2562 fax 651-296-3954
www.mdva.state.mn.us

American Legion

Veterans Service Building
St. Paul, 55101
651-291-1800

The American Legion, Department of Minnesota, has 120,000 members in 590 posts. The oldest post is Minneapolis Post No. 1. Richfield Post 435, with 3,500 members, is either the second or third largest post in the nation. The American Legion began in Paris, France, in 1919. George Washington Bentley, the last living founder of the Legion passed away June 4, 1999, at the age of 101. He was a member of the Hopkins Post.

Veterans of Foreign Wars

Veterans Service Building
St. Paul, 55101
651-291-1757

The VFW has 295 posts and 74,000 members. The oldest post in Minnesota is A R Patterson Post 7 which was chartered on January 3, 1902. 1999 was the 100th anniversary of the national VFW. Richfield Post 5555 is the largest in the state with 2,300 members.

Disabled American Veterans

Veterans Service Building
St. Paul, 55101
651-291-1212

"Building better lives for American veterans." Minneapolis Chapters 1, 2, and 3 organized in 1921. Disabled American Veterans has 33 active posts; Minneapolis Chapter 1 is the largest with 5,000 members. There are 18,000 members state-wide with 2,200 in the DAV Auxiliary.

Vietnam Veterans of America
Veterans Service Building
St. Paul, MN 55155
651-224-6345, 612-970-5670

"Never again shall one generation of veterans forget another." The Vietnam Veterans of American was founded nationally in 1978. The Minnesota organization was established about 1979 with the chartering of Chapter 62 Hopkins. The VVA was chartered by Congress as a veteran's organization in 1986. Over 1000 members make up the 16 Minnesota chapters with Chapter 290 St. Cloud being the largest containing 119 members. Associates of VVA can be joined by spouses, partners, children, friends and advocates. These organizations attempt to lend aid to soldiers who returned from an unpopular war and often were scorned.

Jewish War Veterans
2044 Morgan Av
St. Paul, MN 55116
651-690-2775

Jewish War Veterans of the USA is the oldest veterans group in the nation. On July 31, 1776, Frances Salvador, a plantation owner from South Carolina, was killed in a British incited Indian skirmish. He was the first Jew killed in the Revolutionary War. In 1896, 118 years later, a group of Jewish Civil War veterans organized the Hebrew Union Veterans, an organization that was later to become the Jewish War Veterans of the USA. A study of Jewish participation in the military during World War II indicated that the Jews served in the Armed Forces beyond their numerical proportion to the general population. They received more than 52,000 awards, including the Medal of Honor, the Air Medal, the Silver Star and the Purple Heart. Today, there are 800 members in three posts, with Post 354 St. Paul being the largest having 200 members.

Amvets
Veterans Service Building
St. Paul, 55101
651-293-1212

AmVets is open to all veterans with an honorable discharge including members of all Services, Reserves, Merchant Marine, and Coast Guard. The organization was chartered nationally in 1946. Minnesota has 30 posts with 1200 members. The largest are #1 Mendota Heights and #290 Morris, each with 100 members.

Military Order of the Purple Heart
Veterans Service Building
St. Paul, 55101
651-227-4456

Military Order of the Purple Heart is a national organization composed for and of combat wounded veterans. The organization is founded upon the order issued by Gen. George Washington at Newburg, N.Y. on Aug. 7, 1782, during the Revolutionary War, when he established the Badge of Military Merit, in the figure of a heart in purple, which he directed to be a permanent one. The organization's first state chapter was founded in 1935. Today there are eight chapters in the state.

Paralyzed Veterans of America
Federal Building Room 194-B
1 Federal Drive
Fort Snelling, MN 55111-4007
612-726-6442

"Assisting and serving veterans with spinal cord injury or disease." Minnesota has one chapter with 300 members. In addition to making hospital and home visits, this group organizes activities for its members that include bowling, fishing and trap-shooting.

POW/MIA
PO Box 11782
St. Paul 55111
612-884-8756

"Help resolve the issues of missing Americans from all wars." This service organization is looking for information on the Minnesota soldiers still unaccounted for from the following wars: World War II, 645; Korean War, 153; Vietnam War, 39. The state charter was granted in 1985. POW/MIA is an outgrowth of the National League of Families, begun in 1970, who have family members that are POW's or MIA's. POW/MIA of Minnesota aids and assists Minnesota League of Families members. In April, 1999, the latest Minnesotan's remains were identified and returned from Vietnam--John Baily, MIA, 1969.

Nationally, there are more than one million POW/MIAs from five wars the U.S. has been involved in: 77,851 from WWII; 8,177 from the Korean War; 2,331 from the Vietnam War; 41 from the Persian Gulf War; and eight from the conflict in Somalia.

A 1990 law mandated that the third Friday in September be used for POW/MIA Recognition Day every year. The focus is to ensure that America remembers its responsibility to stand behind those who serve our nation and do everything possible to account for those who do not return.

Congressional Medal of Honor Winners

The Congressional Medal of Honor, established by a joint act of Congress on July 12, 1862, is awarded in the name of congress "to each person who while an officer or enlisted person of the army shall have distinguished himself or herself conspicuously by gallantry and intrepidity at the risk of his or her life above and beyond the call of duty in action involving actual conflict with the enemy."

Listed below are the Medal of Honor recipients from Minnesota:

Army-Air Force

b) State of Birth   *Posthumous Award   †Second Award

Albee, George E.
1st Lt., 41st U.S. Inf.
(Owatonna) (b. N.H.)

Barrick, Jesse
Cpl., 3rd Minn. Inf.
(Rice Co.)(b.Ohio)

Bell, Harry
Capt., 36th Inf.,
U.S. Vol.
(Minneapolis)
(b. Wisconsin)

*Bianchi, Willibald C.
1st Lt., 45th Inf.,
Philippine Scouts
(New Ulm)

Burger, Joseph
Pvt., 2nd Minn. Inf.
(Crystal Lake)
(b. Austria)

Burkard, Oscar
Pvt., Hosp. Corps,
U.S. Army
(HayCreek)(b. Germany)

Cilley, Clinton A.
Capt., 2nd Minn. Inf.
(Sasioja)(b. N.H.)

Clark, Wm, A.
Cpl., 2nd Minn. Inf.
(Shelbyville)
(b. Pennsylvania)

Colalillo, Mike
Pfc., 100th Inf. Div.
(Duluth)

†Cukela, Louis
Sgt., 5th Reg. USMC
(Minneapolis)
(b. Austria)
(Also awarded Navy
Medal of Honor)

Flannigan, James
Pvt., 2nd Minn. Inf.
(Louisville)(b. Ohio)

Hanna, Milton
Cpl., 2nd Minn. Inf.
(Henderson)(b. Ohio)

Hawks, Lloyd C.
Pfc., 3rd Inf. Div.
(Park Rapids)

Holmes, Lovilo
1st Sgt., 2nd Minn. Inf.
(Mankato) (b. N.Y.)

Huggins, Eli L.
Capt. 2nd U.S. Cav.
(b. Illinois)

Johnson, John
Pvt., 2nd Wisc. Inf.
(Rochester)(b. Norway)

Lindbergh, Charles A.
Capt., A.C. Res.,
U.S. Army
(Little Falls)(b. Mich.)

Mallon, George H.
Capt., 33rd Div.
(Minneapolis)(b. Kans.)

Morgan, George H.
2nd Lt., 3rd U.S. Cav.
(Minneapolis)

(b. Canada)

O'Brien, Henry D.
Cpl., 1st Minn Inf.
(St. Anthony Falls)
(b. Maine)

*Olson, Kenneth L.
Spec. 4, 199th Inf. Brig.
(Paynesville)

*Page, John U.D.
Lt. Col., X Corps Arty.
(St. Paul)(b. Malahi
Island, Philippines)

Pay, Byron E.
Pvt., 2nd Minn. Inf.
(Mankato)(b. N.Y.)

Pickle, Alonzo H.
Sgt., 1st Minn. Inf.
(Dover)(b. Canada)

*Pruden, Robert J.
S/Sgt., 75th Inf. Amer.
Div.
(St. Paul)

*Rabel, Laszlo
S/Sgt., 173rd Airborne
Brig.
(Minneapolis)
(b. Hungary)

Reed, Axel H.
Sgt., 2nd Minn. Inf.
(Glencoe)(b. Maine)

Rudolph, Donald E.
2nd Lt., 6th Inf. Div.
(Minneapolis)

Sherman, Marshall
Pvt., 1st Minn. Inf.
(St. Paul)(b. Vermont)

Thorsness, Leo K.
Lt. Col., 357th Tact.
Fighter Sq.
(Walnut Grove)

Tracy, John
Pvt., 8th U.S. Cav.
(St. Paul)(b. Ireland)

Vale, John
Pvt., 2nd Minn. Inf.
(Rochester)
(b. England)

*Wayrynen, Dale E.
Spec. 4, 101st Airborne
Div.
(McGregor)

Welch, Charles H.
Sgt., 7th U.S. Cav.
(Ft. Snelling)(b. N.Y.)

Wilson, William O.
Cpl., 9th U.S. Cav.
(St. Paul)(b. Maryland)

Wright, Samuel
Cpl., 2nd Minn. Inf.
(Swan Lake)
(b. Indiana)

Navy-Marine Corps

Catlin, Albertus W.
Maj., USMC
(b. N.Y.)

*Courtney, Henry A. Jr.
Maj., USMC
(Duluth)

†Cukela, Louis
Sgt., 5th Reg., USMC
(Minneapolis)
(b. Austria)
(Also awarded Army
Medal of Honor)

Dyer, Jesse F.
Capt., USMC
(St. Paul)

*Fleming, Richard E.
Capt., USMCR
(St. Paul)

*Hauge, Louis J. Jr.
Cpl., USMCR
(Ada)

*Kraus, Richard E.
Pfc., USMCR
(b. Illinois)

*LaBelle, James D.
Pfc., USMCR
(Columbia Heights)

Nelson, Oscar F.
MM1c., U.S. Navy
(Minneapolis)

*Rud, George Wm.
CMM., U.S. Navy
(Minneapolis)

Sorenson, Richard K.
Pvt., USMCR
(Anoka)

Freedom Flight III shown over Chisago Lake is the newest edition to three balloons flown and operated by Freedom Flight, Inc. It was dedicated on July 11, 1998 and is booked for several dozen events in 1999 along with its sister balloons, Freedom Flights I and II. Freedom Flight has flown in over 35 different states, Canada, France and Germany to increase public awareness of the POW-MIA issue. 320-252-7208 Photo by: Dr. Jim Tuorila

Chapter 3

Geography

Lying near the geographic center of North America, Minnesota is the northern-most of the continental United States, reaching latitidue of 49(degrees) 23'50.28" north at the tip of the Northwest Angle, that portion of Minnesota not connected to the state by land. The unique area of land came into being by virtue of an international agreement that the common boundary between Canada and the United States was to folow the natural waterways into "most northwetern point of the Lake of the Woods."

Much of the northern boundary is outlined by that lake, Rainy River, Pigeon River, Lake Superior and countless border lakes. The St. Louis, St. Croix and Mississippi rivers form most of the eastern limits. The Red River of the North, and Big Stone and Traverse lakes mark the boundary on the west. Iowa lies to the south. Minnesota is a large state, the 12th in rank in size.

The longest distance across the state is from north to south, approximately 400 miles, from latetude 43 degrees 30' on the Iowa line to a point roughly 22 miles north of the 49th parallel. While the average width is 225 miles, the greatest width is 367 miles. The narrowest dimension is 175 miles, from Goose Creek north of Taylors Falls on the east to the south tip of Big Stone Lake on the west.

Minnesota covers an area of 53,803,520 acres (84,068 square miles), with 48,836,010 of these in land and 4,967,510 of water— the greatest water area of any state. The topography is largely level of gently sloping, with only a few regions of marked elevation. Both the lowest and highest points are in the northeastern part of the state; the level of Lake Superior is the lowest at 602 feet above sea level, and the highest is Eagle Mountain in the Misquah Hills a few miles inland at 2,301 feet above sea level. The highest town is Holland in southwestern Minnesota in Pipestone County situated at 1780 feet above sea level.

The land in the state is largely level and between 1000 and 1500 feet above sea level. Elevations above 1500 feet are limited to the northwest, a fairly large reigion in Itasca County and the Leaf Hills located in the southern part of Ottertail County.

The Giant's Range is a notable elevation 50 to 500 feet above the surrounding terrain. This 100 mile long granite ridge runs northeastward from near Grand Rapids into western Lake County. South of this formation lies the iron-bearing material of the Mesabi range.

This area is part of the vast, level Laurentian rocky platform which runs from northestern Minnesota up into Canada. Some 2 billion years ago this became the first part of North America to be elevated on a permanent basis above the level of the sea, and here are to be found the oldest rocks on earth.

The Red River Lowland in northwestern Minnesota, was formed when the last of four enormous glaciers receded about 11,000 years ago, covering the area with a huge inland sea named
Glacial Lake Agassiz. The lowest points in this basin extend from the Red River eastward to Koochiching Coutny, with an average elevation today of about 760 feet.

The high and low areas of the state have been caused by stress and pressure from below and erosion by water and wind from above. These forces are of three types: 1.volcanism, a melting and eruption action; 2. diastrophism, a twisting, rumpling and uplifting of the earth's surface; and 3. gradation, a leveling-off in which high places are worn down and low places fill up by wind, water, ice and debris. Volcanism is evident along the north shore of Lake Superior where traces of the molten mineral the flowed out from fissures deep in the earth and hardened sheets of lava can be seen today.

Examination of rock layers reveals that the curmpling and tilting of sedimentary strata produced giant mountain ranges in Minnesota in the distant past. It is believed that earthqukes have had little or no effect on Minnesota - only three minor shocks have ever been noted.

The action of rivers and streams and even the waves produces erosion and deposition of particles, thus altering the earth's structure. Limestone rocks which are to be found in the state, are susceptible to erosion by ground water, thus producing undergournd caverns such as the Mystery Caves near Spring Valley.

The greatest sculptors of the state's surface have been the glaciers. These enormous ice masses developed during a long cold period and falling snow accumulated to a depth of many thousand feet. The lower layers, compacted into ice which spread out in all directions, gouged and scraped great quantities of soil and rock and incorporated them in its huge mass. Many of these glacial made basins can be seen in northern Minnesota. When the masses melted, the debris, or "drift" was strewn all over the land, in some cases foming high hilly configurations.

Rivers

Glacial activity brought about a vast water surface in Minnesota - one square mile of water to every twenty of land, and this does not include any portions of Lake Superior.

It also produced a number of massive drainage basins which gave rise to many flowing streams and rivers, the largest of which is the "Father of Waters" the mighty Mississippi.

Henry Rowe Schoolcraft in 1832 discovered the source of the river and named the modest body of water Lake Itasca; it was an accomplishment that had eluded explorers Thompson, Pike, Cass and Beltrami before him.

The principal river of the United States, it flows in every point on the compass on its 2,552 mile journey to the Gulf of Mexico. It is second in length only to its main tributary, the Missouri, with which it combines to make up the third largest river system in the world after the Nile and the Amazon. Using all its tributaries, the river drains more than 1,322,000 acres of the mid-continental are, drawing from 31 states and two Canadian provinces.

Of major economic importance, it is navigable from St. Anthony Falls in Minneapolis to the ocean by means of a series of locks and dams. The U.S. Corps of Engineers maintains a nine foot channel from Minnesota to Vicksburg, Mississippi, where channel depths of up to 40 feet are provided downstream. Access to the St. Lawrence Seaway is made possible by the Illinois waterway.

Ever since 1811, when the first steamboats travelled the river, it has had a massive impact on opening up the new frontiers, and later, on distribution of untold tons of goods and materials necessary to a burgeoning commerce on a national and international level.

Water flows out of the state through seven different river valleys: the Mississippi, the Rainy, the Red River of the North, the Cedar, The Rock, the St. Louis and the Des Moines. No water enters the state boundaries. Many other rivers and steams never leave the state, but contribute their output to the above or into Lake Superior. In addition to the lengthy Minnesota, there are historic Minnehaha Falls made famous in Longfellow's poem "Hiawatha", and colorful fast-flowing streams and falls such as Gooseberry, Temperance, Devil Track and Knife on the north shore.

Lakes

Lake Superior, the largest fresh water lake in the world, covers 31,820 square miles. At its largest dimensions, it is 351 miles long and 160 miles wide. It is also the highest (its surface elevation is 602 feet above sea level) and the deepest (1,302 ft.) of all the Great Lakes.

It receives water from many swift-flowing streams and rivers such as the Pigeon, St. Louis, Temperence, and Kaministikwia. The irregular shore line is high and rocky, with many peninsulas, inlets and large bays.

Purer than the lower lakes, it has been only locally polluted - the largest contamination is attributed by many to the large taconite plant at Silver Bay which formerly discharged 67,000 tons of waste into its waters daily.

Commercial and sport fishing contribute significantly to the economy.

Since the St. Lawrence Seaway, an international waterway 2,342 miles long, was opened in 1959, Duluth, the prinicpal Minnesota city on the lake and the furthest inland port in the world, operates a harbor visited by many large ocean-going vessels.

Probably discovered by the French explorer, Etienne Brule, the vast waters were visited by Pierre Radisson, sieur des Groseilleirs, Father Allouez, sieur Duluth, for whom the city was named, and A.M. Tracy, all hoping for deeds to increase the glory of France. The local Indians, the Algonquins, rejected the name "Lake Tracy" and retained Superior, out of their reverence for its size and the great yield of fish.

Large lakes in their order of size are:

	Acres	Miles Shoreline	Max. Depth
Red Lake	288,800	123	31
Mille Lacs	132,510	70	35
Leech Lake	109,415	154	150
Winnebegoshish	69,821	116	65
Vermillion	49,110	186	48
Cass	29,780	41	115
Kabetogoma	25,760	98	60
Pokegema	15,600	60	100

Minnesota Water Facts
- Number of Lakes 11,842 (10+ acres). 62 of these are over 5,000 acres in size.
- Minnesota's waters flow outward in three directions: North to Hudson Bay in Canada; east to the Atlantic Ocean; and south to the Gulf of Mexico.
- Voyageurs National Park is the largest water-based park in the national system.
- Rock County, in the southwestern corner of the state, is the only one of the 87 counties that does not have a natural lake.
- There are 25,000 miles of rivers and streams, as well as 90,000 miles of lake and river shoreline in Minnesota. This is more shoreline than California and Oregon together.
- Total surface water including wetlands 7,762 sq. mi.
- Five Most Popular Lake Names Mud Lake, Long Lake, Rice Lake, Bass Lake, Round Lake
- Wetlands present in 1850 18.6 million acres
- Wetlands present in 1990 7.5 million acres
- Number of natural rivers and streams 63,000 miles
- State and National Wild and Scenic Rivers 589 miles

Source: 1992 DNR Trails and Waterways brochure.

Land Use in Minnesota

Description	Acreage	Percent of state
Urban and rural development	1,472,267	2.7
Forested	14,434,482	26.7
Cultivated land	22,694,200	42.0
Water	3,211,643	5.9
Hay/pasture/grassland	4,977,451	9.2
Bog/marsh/fen	5,728,056	10.6
Brushland	1,326,796	2.5
Mining	147,175	0.3
State total	53,992,070	100.0

Source: Minnesota Department of Natural Resources
      Land Management Information Center
      658 Cedar St.
      St. Paul, MN 55155
      651-296-1211
      lmic@mnplan.state.mn.us

Minnesota Waterfalls

Name	River/Stream	Location	County
Outlet Falls	Rapid River	Mouth	L. of the Woods
Little Cascade	Little Fork River		St. Louis
Cascade	Vermillion River		St. Louis
Cascade	Vermillion River	Outlet Verm. L.	St. Louis
Cascade	Vermillion River		St. Louis
Vermillion Dalles	Vermillion River	Inlet Crane Lake	St. Louis
La Croix Cascade	Border Water	Loon Lake Inlet	St. Louis
Bottle Falls	Bottle River B.W.	Bottle L. Portage	St. Louis
Curtain Falls	Crooked Lake B.W.	Outlet Crooked L.	St. Louis
Lwr. Basswood Falls		Basswood River	Lake
Wheelbarrow Falls	Basswood River		Lake
Three Falls Cascade	North Kawishiwi		Lake
Two Lake Cascade	North Kawishiwi	Outlet Two L.	Lake
Saganaga Falls	Border Water	Inlet Saganaga L.	Cook
Granite Cascade	Granite River B.W.	Outlet Granite L.	Cook
Sea Gull Falls	Sea Gull River	Outlet Sea Gull L.	Cook
Litle Rock Falls	Pine River B.W.	Outlet Gunflint L.	Cook
Big Falls	Pigeon River		Cook
The Cascades	Pigeon River		Cook
Partridge Falls	Pigeon River		Cook

Reservation	Reservation River		Cook
	Kimball Creek		Cook
	Kadance Creek		Cook
	Arrowhead (Brule)		Cook
	Devil Track River		Cook
	Cascade River		Cook
	Poplar River		Cook
	Cross River		Cook
	Cross River	7 Falls in last 5 mi.	Cook
	Temperance River	1 mi. N.W. Hwy.	Cook
	Two Island River	4 Falls total	Cook
Manitou Falls	Manitou River		Lake
Caribou Falls	Caribou River		Lake
Cascade (High) Falls		Baptism River	Lake
Gooseberry Falls	Gooseberry River		Lake
Gooseberry Cascade	Gooseberry River		Lake
Big Falls	Cloquet River		St. Louis
Lester Park	Lester River	Lester City Park	St. Louis
Minnehaha Falls	Minnehaha Creek	Minneapolis	Hennepin
Minneopa Falls	Minneopa Creek	Minneopa State Pk	Blue Earth
Mound Falls	Mound Creek		Brown
Redwood Cascade	Redwood River	City Park	Redwood
Ramsey Falls	Ramsey Creek	City Park	Redwood
Pipestone Falls	Pipestone Creek	Pipestone	Pipestone

Minnesota's 87 Counties

Counties are governed by a board of commissioners and administrative officers elected by the people to four year terms. State law allows alternative forms of gonvernement, chiefly to allow for an elected executive, a manager, or administrator, and the option to make administrative offices appointive.

Counties are responsible for property tax assessment, tax administration, elections, record keeping, transportation, planning and zoning, solid waste management, environment, parks and water management, law enforcement, courts, and health and human services.

County	County Seat	Acreage	2000 Pop.projection
Aitkin	Aitkin 56431	1,164,502	14,010
Anoka	Anoka 55303	273,735	296,880
Becker	Detroit Lakes 56501	837,688	29,970
Beltrami	Bemidji 56601	1,608,518	38,870
Benton	Foley 56329	257,798	36,510
Big Stone	Ortonville 56278	361,501	5,660

Blue Earth	Mankato 56001	477,158	55,810
Brown	New Ulm 56073	387,266	27,750
Carlton	Carlton 55718	550,09	31,050
Carver	Chaska 55318	226,810	65,160
Cass	Walker 56484	1,302,315	25,190
Chippewa	Montevideo 56265	370,269	12,680
Chisago	Center City 55012	269,369	39,820
Clay	Moorhead 56560	668,118	53,750
Clearwater	Bagley 56621	640,689	8,390
Cook	Grand Marais 55604	936,426	4,300
Cottonwood	Windom 56101	407,635	12,440
Crow Wing	Brainerd 56401	649,083	51,770
Dakota	Hastings 55033	365,190	350,120
Dodge	Mantorville 55955	280,638	17,120
Douglas	Alexandria 56309	401,477	31,510
Faribault	Blue Earth 56013	454,723	16,010
Fillmore	Preston 55965	553,101	20,510
Freeborn	Albert Lea 56007	449,241	31,900
Goodhue	Red Wing 55066	491,465	43,050
Grant	Elbow Lake 56531	348,226	6,070
Hennepin	Minneapolis 55487	354,225	1,082,570
Houston	Caledonia 55921	364,079	19,420
Hubbard	Park Rapids 56470	596,829	17,180
Isanti	Cambridge 55008	281,302	30,260
Itasca	Grand Rapids 55744	1,729,322	42,890
Jackson	Jackson 56143	446,068	11,570
Kanabec	Mora 55051	337,535	13,630
Kandiyohi	Willmar 56201	497,292	42,430
Kittson	Hallock 56728	700,372	5,380
Koochiching	Int'l Falls 56649	1,989,188	15,620
La Qui Parle	Madison 56256	492,698	8,340
Lake	Two Harbors 55616	1,367,808	10,540
Lake of the Woods	Baudette 56649	833,821	4,440
Le Sueur	LeCentre 56057	283,692	24,840
Lincoln	Ivanhoe 56142	334,365	6,480
Lyon	Marshall 56258	453,072	25,620
McLeod	Glencoe 55336	311,488	34,960
Mahnomen	Mahnomen 56557	360,983	5,070
Marshall	Warren 56762	1,142,622	10,480
Martin	Fairmont 56031	450,521	22,330
Meeker	Litchfield 55355	382,891	21,460
Mille Lacs	Milaca 56353	365,472	20,700

Morrison	Little Falls 56345	719,593	31,150
Mower	Austin 55912	453,204	37,310
Murray	Slayton 56172	444,657	9,290
Nicollet	St. Peter 56082	280,866	30,650
Nobles	Worthington 56187	454,877	20,550
Norman	Ada 56510	558,689	7,670
Olmsted	Rochester 55901	422,400	118,730
Otter Tail	Fergus Falls 56537	1,267,003	54,340
Pennington	Thief River Falls 56701	391,606	13,400
Pine	Pine City 55063	903,366	23,400
Pipestone	Pipestone 56164	296,887	10,160
Polk	Crookston 56716	1,260,003	32,610
Pope	Glenwood 56334	426,102	10,890
Ramsey	St. Paul 55102	101,302	497,710
Red Lake	Red Lake Falls 56750	274,619	4,380
Redwood	Redwood Falls 56283	557,474	16,960
Renville	Olivia 56277	621,129	17,240
Rice	Faribault 55021	319,162	54,710
Rock	Luverne 56156	307,716	9,570
Roseau	Roseau 56751	1,073,344	16,660
St. Louis	Duluth 55802	4,043,532	199,440
Scott	Shakopee 55379	225,900	79,040
Sherburne	Elk River 55330	280,525	60,390
Sibley	Gaylord 55334	372,901	14,350
Stearns	St. Cloud 56301	864,521	134,730
Steele	Owatonna 55060	273,455	32,290
Stevens	Morris 56267	355,335	10,780
Swift	Benson 56215	475,592	11,000
Todd	Long Prairie 56374	604,286	23,390
Traverse	Wheaton 56296	363,462	4,170
Wabasha	Wabasha 55981	344,324	20,580
Wadena	Wadena 56482	341,126	13,470
Waseca	Waseca 56093	268,158	17,830
Washington	Stillwater 55082	254,868	200,830
Watonwan	St. James 56081	277,051	11,460
Wilkin	Breckenridge 56520	476,389	7,200
Winona	Winona 55987	406,320	50,060
Wright	Buffalo 55313	424,387	84,060
Yellow Medicine	Granite Falls 56241	481,686	11,240
Minnesota		84,068 sq. mi.	4,805,970

Minerals of Minnesota

The minerals preceded by an asterisk are microscopic or rare and are not normally specimens for collectors.

*Acmite-augite, a pyroxene
*Actinolite, an amphibole
*Adularia, a feldspar
*Aegirine (acmite)
*Afwillite
 Agate
 Albite, a feldspar
*Allanite, an epidote
 Almandite, a garnet
 Alum
 Amesite, a chlorite
 Amethyst (purple quartz)
 Amphibole group; actinolite, anthophyllite, asbestos, cumming tonite, glaucophane, grunerite, hornblende (green and brown), pargasite, riebeckite, tremolite, uralite
 Analcime, a zeolite
*Anatase
*Andalusite
 Anesine, a feldspar
 Ankerite
 Anorthoclase
 Anthophyllite, an amphibole
*Antigorite, a serpentine
*Apatite
*Aragonite
*Arsenopyrite
 Asbestos, an amphibole or serpen tine
 Augite (and titan-augite), a pyrox ene
*Babingtonite, a pyroxene
 Barite
*Bastite, a serpentine
 Biotite, a mica
 Bobierrite
 Bornite

*Bowlingite
 Braunite
 Bronzite, a pyroxene
*Brookite
 Bytownite, a feldspar
 Cairngorm (smoky quartz)
 Calcite
 Carnelian
 Catlinite, see pyrophyllite
*Ceylonite
 Chalcedony (agate, camelian, chert, flint, jasper sardonyx)
 Chalocite
 Chalcopyrite
 Chert
 Chlorite group: amesite, delessite, penninite, strigovite
*Chondrodite
*Chrysotile, see asbestos and sepentine
 Clay mineral group: kaolinite, monmorillonite, pyrophylite, non tronite
*Clinoenstatite, a pyroxene
 Cobalite
*Collophanite
 Columbite
 Copper
*Cordierite
*Corundum
*Covelite
*Cristobalite
*Cummingtonite, an amphibole
*Cuprite
 Cyanite, see Kyanite
 Datolite
 Delessite, a chlorite
 Diallage, a pyroxene
*Diaspore

Diopside, a pyroxene
Dolomite
Enstatite, a pyroxene
Epidote group: allanite, clizoisite,
epidote, zoisite
Fayalite, an olivine
Feldspar group: adularia, albite,
andesine, anorthoclase, bytownite,
labradorite, microcline, orthoclase,
perthite, plagioclase series, valen
cianite
Flint
Fluorite
*Fuchsite, a mica
*Galena
Garnet group: almandite, andra
dite, spessartite
Gibbsite (bauxite)
Glauconite
Goethite (limonite)
*Gold
Graphite
Greenalite
Groutite
*Grunerite, an amphibole
Gypsum
*Halite
Hermatite
Heulandite, a zeolite
** Hibbingite, an orthorhombic iron
hydroxychloride
*Hisingerite
Hornblende, green and brown—an
armphibole
Hortonolite, an olivine
Hypersthene, a pyroxene
Ice
*Iddingsite
Ilmenite
*Iolite (cordierite)
*Iron alloy (meteorite)
*Jarosite
Jasper

Kaolinite, a clay mineral
Kyanite
Labradorite, a feldspar
Laumonite, a zeolite
*Leucoxene
Limonite, see goethite
Lintonite, a zeolite
Magnetite
Malachite
*Malacon
Manganite
Manganosiderite
Marcasite
*Martite (hematite)
*Maskelynite (meteorite)
Mesotype, a zeolite
Mica group: biotite, fuchsite,
musocovite, phylogopite, sericite
Microcline, a feldspar
Minnesotaite
*Molybdenite
*Monazite
Montmorillonite, a clay mineral
(potash-montmorillonite)
Muscovite
*Nickel-iron (meteorite)
*Nontronite, a clay mineral
*Octahedrite (anatase)
Oligoclase, a feldspar
Olivine group: fayalite,hortonoite,
olivine
*Orthite (allanite, an epidote)
Orthoclase, a feldspar
*Paraffin
*Pargasite, an amphibole
*Pectolite
Penninite, a chlorite
*Pentlandite
Perthite, a feldspar
*Phlogopite, a mica
Plagioclase, a feldspar
Prehnite
Psilomelane

Pyrite
Pyrolusite
Pyrophyllite, a clay mineral
Pyroxene group: acmite (aegirine), augite, babingtonite, bronzite, cli noenstatite, diallage, diopside, enstatite, hypersthene
Pyrrhotite
Quartz (amethyst, cairngorm, milky quartz, rock crystal, smoky quartz)
Rhodochrosite
*Rhodonite
*Riebeckite
Rock crystal (quartz)
*Rutile
Sanidine (soda sanidine)
Sardonyx
Selenite (gypsum)
Sericite, a mica
Serpentine group: antigorite, bastite, chrysotile (asbestos)
Siderite
*Sillimanite
Specularite (hematite)
*Spessartite, a garnet
*Sphalerite
*Sphene

*Spherosiderite
*Spinel
Staurolite
Stilbite, a zeolite
Stilpnomelane
Strigovite, a chlorite
*Talc
*Tantalite
Thomsonite, a zeolite
*Titanite (sphene)
*Topaz
*Tourmaline
*Tremolite, an amphibole
*Tridymite (meteorite)
*Troilite (meteorite)
Uralite, an amphibole
*Valencianite, feldspar
*Vermiculite
Violarite
Vivianite
Xenotime
Xonotlite
Zeolite group: analcime, heuldite, laumontite (lintonite), mesotype, stilbite, thomsonite
*Zircon
*Zoisite, an epidote

**Hibbingite is a new mineral discovered in Minnesota in 1991. The Smithsonian approved it as a new mineral in 1994.

MINNESOTA INDEX TO CITIES FROM 1999-2000 MINNESOTA OFFICIAL HIGHWAY MAP

A

ADA 1,708	8-B
Adams 756	21-L
Adolph	10-M
Adrian 1,141	21-C
Afton (MA) 2,645	27-Z
Ah-gwah-ching	9-G
AITKIN 1,698	11-I
Akeley 393	9-G
Albany 1,548	14-G
ALBERT LEA 18,310	21-J
Alberta 136	14-C
Albertville (MA) 1,350	24-U
Alden 623	21-I
Aldrich 70	12-F
ALEXANDRIA 8,029	13-E
Almelund	15-K
Alpha 105	21-F
Altura 349	20-N
Alvarado 356	5-A
Amboy 517	20-H
Amiret	19-D
Andover (MA) 15,216	23-W
Angle Inlet	1-F
Angora	7-L
Angus	6-B
Annandale 2,054	15-H
ANOKA (MA) 17,192	16-J & 24-V
Apple Valley (MA) 34,598	28-X
Appleton 1,552	16-C
Arco 104	18-C
Arden Hills (MA) 9,199	25-X
Argyle 636	5-B
Arlington 1,886	18-H
Ashby 469	13-D
Askov 343	12-K
Atwater 1,053	16-F
Audubon 411	10-D
Aurora 1,965	7-M

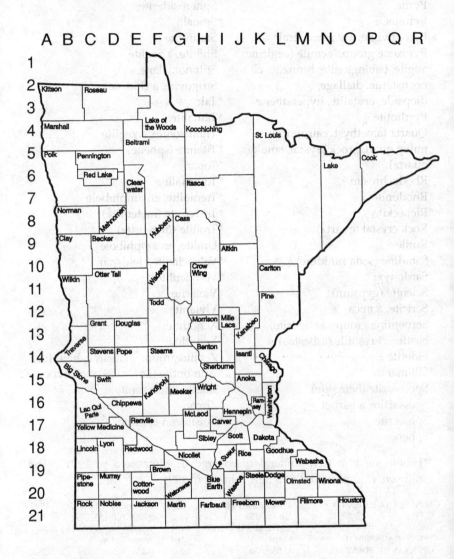

Trivia: Ramsey county is the smallest with 170 square miles. St. Louis county has the largest land area with over 6,000 square miles.

AUSTIN 21,953 . . . . 21-K
Avoca 150 . . . . 20-D
Avon 970 . . . . 14-G

B

Babbitt 1,562 . . . . 7-M
Backus 240 . . . . 10-G
Badger 381 . . . . 3-D
BAGLEY 1,388 . . . . 8-E
Baker 10-B
Balaton 737 . . . . 19-D
Ball Club 8-I
Barnesville 2,066 . . . . . . 11-C
Barnum 482 . . . . 11-L
Barrett 350 . . . . 13-D
Barry 40 . . . . 14-B
Battle Lake 698 . . . . .12-D
BAUDETTE 1,146 . . . . . 3-G
Baxter 3,695 . . . . 12-H
Bayport (MA) 3,200 . . . 26-Z
Beardsley 297 . . . . .14-B
Beaver Creek 249 . . . . . . .21-B
Beaver Bay 147 . . . . 8-O
Becker 902 . . . . 15-I
Bejou 110 . . . . 8-D
Belgrade 700 . . . . 15-F
Belle Plaine 3,149 . . . . . . 18-I
Bellechester 110 . . . . 19-L
Bellingham 247 . . . . 16-C
Beltrami 137 . . . . 7-B
Belview 383 . . . . 18-E
BEMIDJI 11,172 . . . . . . 8-F
Bena 147 . . . . 8-H
Benedict 9-G
BENSON 3,235 . . . . 15-D
Beroun 13-K
Bertha 507 . . . . 12-F
Bethel 394 . . . . 15-J
Big Falls 341 . . . . 5-I
Big Lake 3,113 . . . . 15-I
Bigelow 232 . . . . 22-D
Bigfork 384 . . . . 7-I
Bingham Lake 155 . . . . . 20-F
Birchdale 4-H
Birchwood Village
(MA) 1,042 . . . . 25-Y
Bird Island 1,326 . . . . . . 17-F
Biscay 113 . . . . 17-H
Biwabik 1,097 . . . . 7-L
Blackduck 718 . . . . 7-G
Blaine (MA) 38,975 . . . . 24-X
Blomkest 183 . . . . 17-F
Blooming Prairie 2,043 . . 20-K
Bloomington
(MA) 86,335 . . . . 27-W
BLUE EARTH 3,745 . . . . 21-H
Bluffton 187 . . . . 11-E
Bock 115 . . . . 14-J
Borup 119 . . . . 9-B
Bovey 662 . . . . 8-J

Bowlus 260 . . . . 14-G
Bowstring 7-I
Boy River 43 . . . . 9-H
Boyd 251 . . . . 17-D
Braham 1,139 . . . . 14-J
BRAINERD 12,353 . . . . 12-H
Brandon 441 . . . . .13-E
BRECKENRIDGE 3,708 . . 12-B
Breezy Point 432 . . . . . . 11-H
Brewster 532 . . . . 21-E
Bricelyn 426 . . . . 21-I
Brimson 8-N
Britt 7-L
Brook Park 125 . . . . 13-K
Brooklyn Center
(MA) 28,887 . . . . 25-W
Brooklyn Park
(MA) 56,381 . . . . 25-W
Brooks 158 . . . . 6-D
Brookston 107 . . . . 10-L
Brooten 589 . . . . 15-F
Browerville 782 . . . . 13-F
Browns Valley 804 . . . . 14-A
Brownsdale 695 . . . . . . 21-K
Brownsville 415 . . . . . . 21-O
Brownton 781 . . . . 17-H
Bruno 89 . . . . 12-L
Buckman 201 . . . . 13-H
Buffalo Lake 734 . . . . . 17-G
BUFFALO 6,856 . . . . . . 16-I
Buhl 913 . . . . 8-K
Burnsville
(MA) 51,288 . . . . 28-W
Burtrum 172 . . . . 13-G
Butterfield 509 . . . . 20-F
Buyck 5-L
Byron 2,441 . . . . 20-L

C

CALEDONIA 2,846 . . . . 21-O
Callaway 212 . . . . 9-D
Calumet 382 . . . . 8-J
CAMBRIDGE 5,130 . . . . . 14-J
Campbell 233 . . . . 12-C
Canby 1,826 . . . . 17-C
Cannon Falls 3,232 . . . . 18-K
Canton 362 . . . . 21-N
Canyon 9-L
Carlisle 12-C
Carlos 361 . . . . 13-E
CARLTON 923 . . . . 11-L
Carver (MA) 744 . . . . 28-U
Cass Lake 923 . . . . 8-G
Castle Rock 18-J
Cedar Mills 80 . . . . 17-G
Cedar 15-J
CENTER CITY 451 . . . . . 15-K
Centerville(MA) 1,633 . . 24-X
Ceylon 461 . . . . 22-G
Champlin (MA) 16,849 . . .24-V

Chandler 316 . . . . 20-C
Chanhassen (MA)
11,732 . . . . 27-U
CHASKA (MA)
11,339 . . . . 17-I & 28-U
Chatfield 2,226 . . . . 20-M
Chickamaw Beach 132 . . 10-G
Chisago City 2,009 . . . . 15-K
Chisholm 5,290 . . . . . 8-K
Chokio 521 . . . . 14-C
Circle Pines
(MA) 4,704 . . . . 24-X
Clara City 1,307 . . . . . . 17-E
Claremont 530 . . . . . . 20-K
Clarissa 637 . . . . 12-F
Clarkfield 924 . . . . . . 17-D
Clarks Grove 675 . . . 21-J
Clear Lake 315 . . . . . . 15-H
Clearbrook 560 . . . . . 7-E
Clearwater 597 . . . . . 15-H
Clements 191 . . . . 19-F
Cleveland 699 . . . . 19-I
Climax 264 . . . . 7-B
Clinton 574 . . . . 15-B
Clitherall 109 . . . . . . 12-D
Clontarf 172 . . . . 15-D
Cloquet 10,885 . . . . . . 10-L
Coates (MA) 186 . . . . . 28-Y
Cobden 62 . . . . 19-F
Cohasset 1,970 . . . . . . 8-I
Cokato 2,180 . . . . . 16-H
Cold Spring 2,459 . . 15-G
Coleraine 1,041 . . . . . 9-J
Collegeville 14-G
Cologne 563 . . . . 17-I
Columbia Heights
(MA) 18,910 . . . . . . 25-W
Comfrey 433 . . . . 19-F
Comstock 123 . . . . . . 10-B
Conger 143 . . . . 21-J
Cook 316 . . . . 6-L
Coon Rapids
(MA) 52,978 . . . . . 24-W
Corcoran (MA) 5,199 . . 25-U
Correll 60 . . . . 16-C
Cosmos 610 . . . . 17-G
Cottage Grove
(MA) 22,935 . . . . . . 28-Y
Cotton 9-L
Cottonwood 982 . . . . 18-D
Courtland 412 . . . . . 19-H
Crane Lake 5-L
Cromwell 221 . . . . . . 11-K
CROOKSTON 8,119 . . . 7-B
Crosby 2,073 . . . . 11-I
Crosslake 1,132 . . . . . 11-H
Crystal (MA) 23,788 . . 25-W
Culver 10-L
Currie 303 . . . . 20-D
Cushing 12-G

Cuyuna 172 . . . .   11-I
Cyrus 328 . . . .   14-D

D

Dakota 360 . . . .   20-O
Dalbo 14-J
Dalton 234 . . . .   12-D
Danube 562 . . . .   17-F
Danvers 98 . . . .   15-D
Darfur 128 . . . .   20-F
Darwin 252 . . . .   16-G
Dassel 1,082 . . . . 16-H
Dawson 1,615 . . . . 17-C
Dayton (MA) 5,058 . . .   24-V
De Graff 149 . . . .   15-E
Deephaven (MA) 3,653 .   26-V
Deer River 838 . . . .   8-I
Deer Creek 303 . . . . .   12-E
Deerwood 524 . . . . . .   11-I
Delano 2,709 . . . .   16-I
Delavan 245 . . . .   21-H
Delft 20-F
Delhi 69 . . . .   18-E
Dellwood (MA) 887 . . .   25-Y
Denham 36 . . . .   12-K
Dennison 152 . . . .   18-K
Dent 177 . . . .   11-D
DETROIT LAKES
7,151 . . . .   10-D
Dexter 303 . . . .   21-L
Dilworth 2,562 . . . . . .   10-B
Dodge Center 1,954 . .   20-K
Donaldson 57 . . . . . .   4-B
Donnelly 221 . . . .   14-C
Doran 78 . . . .   12-B
Dover 416 . . . .   20-M
Dovray 60 . . . .   20-D
DULUTH 85,493 . . . .   10-M
Dumont 126 . . . .   14-B
Dundas 473 . . . .   18-J
Dundee 107 . . . .   20-E
Dunnell 187 . . . .   21-F
Duquette 12-L

E

Eagan (MA) 47,409 . .   28-X
Eagle Bend 524 . . . . .   12-F
Eagle Lake 1,703 . . . .   19-I
East Bethel (MA)
8,050 . . . . .   15J & 23-W
East Gull Lake 687 . . .   12-G
East Grand Forks 8,658 .   6-A
Easton 229 . . . .   21-I
Echo 304 . . . .   18-E
Eden Prairie
(MA) 39,311 . . . . .   27-V
Eden Valley 732 . . . .   15-G
Edgerton 1,106 . . . . .   20-C
Edina (MA) 46,070 . . .   27-W
Effie 130 . . . .   6-I

Eitzen 221 . . . .   22-O
Elba 220 . . . .   20-M
ELBOW LAKE 1,186 . .   13-D
Eldred 7-B
Elgin 733 . . . .   19-M
Elizabeth 152 . . . .   11-C
ELK RIVER (MA)
11,143 . . . . .   15-I & 23-V
Elko (MA) 223 . . . . . .   30-W
Elkton 142 . . . .   21-L
Ellendale 549 . . . . .   20-J
Ellsworth 580 . . . . . .   22-C
Elmdale 130 . . . .   13-G
Elmore 709 . . . .   22-H
Elrosa 205 . . . .   14-F
Ely 3,968 . . . .   6-M
Elysian 445 . . . .   19-I
Embarrass 7-M
Emily 613 . . . .   10-I
Emmons 439 . . . .   22-J
Erhard 181 . . . .   11-C
Erskine 422 . . . .   7-D
Esko 10-L
Essig 19-G
Euclid 6-B
Evan 83 . . . .   19-F
Evansville 566 . . . . . .   13-D
Eveleth 4,064 . . . .   8-L
Excelsior (MA) 2,367 . .   27-U
Eyota 1,448 . . . .   20-M

F

Fairfax 1,276 . . . .   18-G
FAIRMONT 11,265 . . .   21-G
Falcon Heights
(MA) 5,380 . . . .   26-X
FARIBAULT 17,090 . . . .   19-J
Farmington (MA)
5,940 . . . .   29-X
Farwell 74 . . . .   14-D
Federal Dam 118 . . .   9-H
Felton 211 . . . .   9-B
FERGUS FALLS
12,701 . . . .   12-C
Fertile 853 . . . .   7-C
Fifty Lakes 299 . . . . .   10-H
Finland 8-O
Finlayson 242 . . . . . .   12-K
Fisher 413 . . . .   6-B
Flensburg 213 . . . . . .   13-G
Flom 9-C
Floodwood 574 . . . .   10-K
Florence 53 . . . .   19-C
FOLEY 1,854 . . . .   14-I
Forada 171 . . . .   14-E
Forbes 8-L
Forest Lake
(MA) 6,183 . . .   15-K & 23-Y
Foreston 354 . . . .   14-I
Fort Ripley 92 . . . . .   12-H

Fosston 1,529 . . . .   7-D
Fountain 327 . . . . . .   21-M
Foxhome 160 . . . . . .   12-C
Franklin 441 . . . .   18-F
Frazee 1,176 . . . .   10-D
Freeborn 301 . . . . . .   21-J
Freeport 556 . . . .   14-G
Fridley (MA) 28,335 .   25-W
Frontenac 18-L
Frost 236 . . . .   21-I
Fulda 1,212 . . . .   20-D
Funkley 15 . . . .   7-G

G

Garden City 20-H
Garfield 203 . . . .   13-E
Garrison 138 . . . .   12-I
Garvin 149 . . . .   19-D
Gary 200 . . . .   8-C
Gatzke 4-D
GAYLORD 1,935 . . . .   18-H
Gem Lake (MA) 439 . .   25-Y
Geneva 444 . . . . . .   21-J
Genola 85 . . . .   13-H
Georgetown 107 . . . . .   9-B
Gheen 6-K
Ghent 316 . . . .   18-D
Gibbon 712 . . . .   18-G
Gilbert 1,934 . . . .   8-L
Gilman 192 . . . .   14-I
GLENCOE 5,196 . . .   17-H
Glenville 778 . . . .   21-J
GLENWOOD 2,573 . .   14-E
Glyndon 862 . . . .   10-B
Golden Valley
(MA) 20,971 . . . . .   26-W
Gonvick 302 . . . .   7-E
Good Thunder 561 . .   20-H
Goodhue 533 . . . . .   18-L
Goodland 9-J
Goodridge 115 . . . . .   5-D
Goodview 2,878 . . .   20-N
Graceville 671 . . . . . .   14-B
Granada 374 . . . .   21-H
Grand Meadow 967 .   21-L
Grand Portage 6-S
GRAND RAPIDS 7,976 .   9-J
GRAND MARAIS 1,171 .   7-Q
Grandy 14-J
GRANITE FALLS 3,083 .   17-E
Grant (MA) 4,022 . . . . .   25-Y
Grasston 119 . . . .   14-K
Green Isle 239 . . . . .   18-H
Greenbush 800 . . . . .   3-C
Greenfield
(MA) 1,450 . .   16-I & 25-U
Greenwald 209 . . . . . .   14-F
Greenwood (MA) 614 .   27-U
Grey Eagle 353 . . . .   13-F
Grove City 604 . . . .   16-G

Grygla 220 .... 5-E
Gully 128 .... 7-E

H
Hackensack 245 ... 10-G
Hadley 94 .... 20-D
HALLOCK 1,304 .... 3-B
Halma 73 .... 3-B
Halstad 611 .... 8-B
Ham Lake (MA) 8,924 . 23-W
Hamburg 492 .... 17-I
Hamel (MA) 25-V
Hammond 205 ..... 19-L
Hampton (MA) 363 ... 30-Y
Hancock 723 ...... 15-D
Hanley Falls 246 .... 17-D
Hanover (MA) 787 .... 24-U
Hanska 443 ...... 19-G
Harding 76 .... 12-H
Hardwick 234 ...... 21-C
Harmony 1,081 ...... 21-M
Harris 843 .... 14-K
Hartland 270 ...... 21-J
HASTINGS (MA)
15,445 ...   17-K & 28-Z
Hatfield 66 .... 20-C
Hawick 15-F
Hawley 1,655 .... 10-C
Hayfield 1,283 ..... 20-K
Hayward 246 .... 21-J
Hazel Run 81 ...... 17-D
Hector 1,145 .... 17-G
Heidelberg 73 .... 18-I
Henderson 746 ..... 18-I
Hendricks 684 .... 18-B
Hendrum 309 ...... 8-B
Henning 738 .... 12-E
Henriette 78 .... 13-K
Herman 485 .... 13-C
Hermantown 6,761 .... 10-M
Heron Lake 730 ..... 21-E
Hewitt 269 .... 12-F
Hibbing 18,046 ...... 8-K
Hill City 469 .... 9-I
Hillman 45 .... 13-I
Hills 607 .... 21-B
Hilltop (MA) 749 ..... 25-W
Hinckley 948 .... 13-K
Hines 7-G
Hitterdal 242 ...... 9-C
Hoffman 576 ...... 13-D
Hokah 687 .... 21-O
Holdingford 598 ..... 14-G
Holland 216 .... 20-C
Hollandale 289 ...... 21-J
Holloway 123 .... 15-D
Holmes City 14-E
Holt 88 .... 5-C
Holyoke 11-L
Homer 20-N

Hope 20-J
Hopkins (MA) 16,534 .. 26-V
Houston 1,013 .... 21-O
Hovland 6-R
Howard Lake 1,469 ... 16-H
Hoyt Lakes 2,348 ..... 8-M
Hugo (MA) 5,223 .... 24-Y
Humboldt 74 .... 3-A
Huntley 21-H
Hutchinson 11,455 .... 17-G

I
Ihlen 101 .... 20-B
Independence
(MA) 2,822 ..   16-I & 26-U
Indus 4-I
INTERNATIONAL FALLS
8,325 .... 4-J
Inver Grove Heights
(MA) 22,477 ...... 27-X
Iona 158 .... 20-D
Iron Junction 133 ..... 8-L
Ironton 553 .... 11-I
Isabella 7-O
Isanti 1,228 .... 15-J
Island View 4-J
Isle 566 .... 12-J
IVANHOE 751 .... 18-C

J
JACKSON 3,559 .... 21-F
Jacobson 9-J
Janesville 1,969 ..... 20-I
Jasper 599 .... 20-B
Jeffers 443 .... 20-E
Jenkins 262 .... 11-H
Johnson 46 .... 14-C
Jordan (MA) 2,909 .. 29-U

K
Kanaranzi 21-C
Kandiyohi 506 .... 16-F
Karlstad 881 .... 4-C
Kasota 655 .... 19-I
Kasson 3,517 .... 20-L
Keewatin 1,118 ...... 8-K
Kelliher 348 .... 6-G
Kellogg 423 .... 19-M
Kelly Lake 8-J
Kelsey 9-K
Kennedy 337 .... 4-B
Kenneth 81 .... 21-C
Kensington 295 ..... 14-D
Kent 131 .... 11-B
Kenyon 1,552 .... 19-K
Kerkhoven 732 .... 16-E
Kerrick 56 .... 12-L
Kettle River 190 ..... 11-K
Kiester 606 .... 22-I
Kilkenny 167 .... 19-I

Kimball 690 .... 15-H
Kinbrae 18 .... 20-E
Kingston 131 .... 16-H
Kinney 257 .... 8-K
Klossner 19-G
Knife River 9-N

L
La Crescent 4,320 ... 20-O
La Prairie 441 .... 9-J
La Salle 98 .... 20-G
Lafayette 462 ...... 18-G
Lake Park 638 ...... 10-C
Lake Shore 693 ..... 11-H
Lake Lillian 229 ..... 17-F
Lake Itasca 8-F
Lake George 9-F
Lake Henry 90 .... 15-F
Lake Wilson 319 ..... 20-C
Lake Hubert 11-H
Lake Benton 693 .... 19-C
Lake Bronson 272 ... 3-B
Lake City 4,433 ..... 18-M
Lake Crystal 2,084 .... 20-H
Lake Elmo (MA) 5,876 . 26-Y
Lake St. Croix Beach
(MA) 1,078 .... 26-Z
Lakefield 1,679 ...... .21-E
Lakeland (MA) 2,000 .. 26-Z
Lakeland Shores
(MA) 291 .... 26-Z
Lakeville (MA) 33,274 .. 29-W
Lamberton 972 ...... 19-E
Lancaster 342 .... 3-B
Landfall (MA) 685 .... 26-Y
Lanesboro 858 ...... 21-N
Lansing 21-K
Laporte 101 .... 9-G
Lastrup 112 .... 13-H
Lauderdale (MA) 2,700 .. 26-X
LE CENTER 2,006 ... 19-I
Le Roy 904 .... 22-L
Le Sueur 3,714 .... 18-I
Lengby 112 .... 8-E
Leonard 26 .... 7-E
Leonidas 70 .... 8-L
Leota 20-C
Lester Prairie 1,179 ... 17-H
Lewiston 1,298 ...... 20-N
Lewisville 255 ...... 20-G
Lexington (MA) 2,279 . 24-X
Lilydale (MA) 506 .... 27-X
Lindstrom 2,476 ..... 15-K
Lino Lakes (MA) 8,807 . 24-X
Lismore 248 .... 21-C
LITCHFIELD 6,090 ... 16-G
Little Canada
(MA) 8,971 .... 26-X
LITTLE FALLS 7,232 .. 13-H
Little Fork 838 .... 4-I

Little Marais 8-O
Little Sauk 13-F
Lockhart 8-B
Loman 4-I
London 21-K
Long Beach 204 . . . . . . 14-E
Long Lake (MA) 1,984 . . 26-U
LONG PRAIRIE 2,786 . . 13-F
Longville 224 . . . . 9-H
Lonsdale 1,252 . . . . 18-J
Loretto (MA) 404 . . . . . 25-U
Louisburg 42 . . . . 16-C
Lowry 233 . . . . 14-E
Lucan 235 . . . . 18-E
Lutsen 7-P
LUVERNE 4,382 . . . . . . 21-C
Lyle 504 . . . . 22-K
Lynd 287 . . . . 19-D

M

Mabel 745 . . . . 22-N
Madelia 2,237 . . . . 20-G
Madison Lake 688 . . . . 19-I
MADISON 1,951 . . . . . . 16-D
Magnolia 155 . . . . 21-C
MAHNOMEN 1,154 . . . . 8-D
Mahtomedi (MA) 5,569 . 25-Y
Mahtowa 11-L
Makinen 8-L
Manchester 211 . . . . . . 21-J
Manhattan Beach 61 . . 10-H
MANKATO 31,419 . . . . 19-H
MANTORVILLE 874 . . . 20-L
Maple Grove
(MA) 38,736 . . . . 25-V
Maple Lake 1,394 . . . 16-H
Maple Plain (MA)
2,005 . . . . 26-U
Mapleton 1,526 . . . . . . 20-I
Mapleview 206 . . . . . . 21-K
Maplewood
(MA) 30,954 . . . . 26-Y
Marble 618 . . . . 8-J
Marcell 7-I
Margie 6-I
Marietta 211 . . . . 16-B
Marine on St. Croix
(MA) 602 . . . . 24-Z
Markville 13-L
MARSHALL 12,023 . . . . 18-D
Max 7-H
Mayer 475 . . . . 17-I
Maynard 419 . . . . 17-E
Mazeppa 722 . . . . 19-L
McGrath 62 . . . . 12-J
McGregor 376 . . . . 11-J
McIntosh 665 . . . . 7-D
McKinley 116 . . . . 8-L
Meadowlands 92 . . . . . 9-K
Medford 733 . . . . 19-J

Medicine Lake
(MA) 385 . . . . 26-V
Medina (MA) 3,096 . . . 25-U
Meire Grove 124 . . . . 14-F
Melrose 2,587 . . . . . . 14-F
Melrude 9-L
Menahga 1,076 . . . . . . 10-F
Mendota (MA) 164 . . . . 27-X
Mendota Heights
(MA) 9,431 . . . . 27-X
Mentor 94 . . . . 7-C
Merrifield 11-H
Middle River 285 . . . . . 4-C
Miesville (MA) 135 . . . . 30-Z
MILACA 2,194 . . . . 14-I
Milan 353 . . . . 16-D
Millerville 104 . . . . 13-E
Millville 163 . . . . 19-M
Milroy 297 . . . . 18-E
Miltona 181 . . . . 13-E
MINNEAPOLIS (MA)
368,383 . . . .   16-J & 26-W
Minneiska 127 . . . . 19-N
Minneota 1,417 . . . . . . 18-C
Minnesota City 258 . . . 20-N
Minnesota Lake 681 . . . 20-I
Minnetonka (MA)
48,370 . . . . 26-V
Minnetonka Beach (MA)
573 . . . . 26-U
Minnetrista (MA)
3,435 . . . .   17-I & 26-U
Mizpah 100 . . . . 6-H
MONTEVIDEO 5,499 . . 17-D
Montgomery 2,399 . . . . 18-I
Monticello 5,045 . . . . . 15-I
Montrose 1,008 . . . . . . 16-I
MOORHEAD 32,295 . . . 10-B
Moose Lake 1,206 . . . . . 11-K
MORA 2,905 . . . . 13-J
Morgan 965 . . . . 18-F
MORRIS 5,613 . . . . 14-D
Morristown 784 . . . . . . 19-J
Morton 448 . . . . 18-F
Motley 441 . . . . 12-G
Mound (MA) 9,634 . . . 26-U
Mounds View (MA)
12,541 . . . . 25-X
Mountain Iron 3,362 . . . 7-L
Mountain Lake 1,906 . . 20-F
Murdock 282 . . . . 16-E
Myrtle 72 . . . . 21-K

N

Nashua 63 . . . . 13-C
Nashwauk 1,026 . . . . . . 8-J
Nassau 83 . . . . 16-B
Nay-Tah-Waush 8-E
Nelson 177 . . . . 13-E
Nerstrand 210 . . . . . . 19-K

Nett Lake 5-K
Nevis 375 . . . . 9-F
New Auburn 363 . . . . . 18-H
New Brighton (MA)
22,207 . . . . 25-X
New Germany 353 . . . . 17-I
New Hope (MA) 21,853 . 25-V
New London 971 . . . . . 15-F
New Market 227 . . . . . 30-W
New Munich 314 . . . . . 14-G
New Prague 3,569 . . . . 18-I
New Richland 1,237 . . 20-J
New Trier (MA) 96 . . . 30-Y
NEW ULM 13,132 . . . 19-G
New York Mills 940 . . . 11-E
Newfolden 345 . . . . 5-C
Newport (MA) 3,720 . . . . 27-Y
Nicollet 795 . . . . 1 9-H
Nielsville 100 . . . . 7-B
Nimrod 65 . . . . 11-F
Nisswa 1,391 . . . . 11-H
Nopeming 10-M
Norcross 86 . . . . 13-C
North Branch 4,603 . . . . 15-K
North Mankato 10,164 . . 19-H
North Oaks (MA) 3,386 . 25-X
North St. Paul
(MA) 12,376 . . . . . . 26-Y
Northfield 14,684 . . . . . 18-K
Northome 283 . . . . 6-H
Northrop 276 . . . . 21-G
Norwood Young
America 2705 . . . . . 17-I
Noyes 2-A

O

Oak Grove (MA) 5,488 . 23-W
Oak Island 1-F
Oak Park 14-I
Oak Park Heights (MA)
3,486 . . . . 25-Z
Oakdale (MA) 18,400 . . 26-Y
Oakland 21-K
Odessa 155 . . . . 15-C
Odin 102 . . . . 20-G
Ogema 164 . . . . 9-D
Ogilvie 510 . . . . 13-J
Okabena 223 . . . . 21-E
Oklee 441 . . . . 6-D
OLIVIA 2,623 . . . . 17-F
Onamia 676 . . . . 13-I
Ormsby 159 . . . . 20-G
Orono (MA) 7,285 . . . . 26-U
Oronoco 727 . . . . 19-L
Orr 265 . . . . 6-K
ORTONVILLE 2,205 . . 15-B
Osage 10-E
Osakis 1,256 . . . . 13-F
Oslo 362 . . . . 5-A
Osseo (MA) 2,704 . . . . 25-V

Ostrander 276 . . . .   21-L
Otsego (MA) 6,639 . . . .   23-U
Ottertail 313 . . . .   11-E
Outing 10-H
OWATONNA 19,386 . . .   20-J

P

Palisade 144 . . . .   10-J
PARK RAPIDS 2,863 . . .   10-F
Parkers Prairie 956 . . .   12-E
Parkville 8-L
Paynesville 2,275 . . . .   15-G
Pease 178 . . . .   14-I
Pelican Rapids 1,886 . .   11-C
Pemberton 228 . . . .   20-I
Pencer 3-E
Pengilly 8-J
Pennington 8-G
Pennock 476 . . . .   16-F
Pequot Lakes 843 . . . .   11-H
Perham 2,075 . . . .   11-E
Perley 132 . . . .   9-B
Peterson 259 . . . .   21-N
Pierz 1,014 . . . .   13-H
Pillager 306 . . . .   12-G
PINE CITY 2,613 . . . . .   13-K
Pine Island 2,125 . . . .   19-L
Pine River 871 . . . .   10-G
Pine Springs (MA) 436 .   25-Y
PIPESTONE 4,554 . . .   20-C
Pitt 3-G
Plainview 2,768 . . . . .   19-M
Plato 355 . . . .   17-H
Pleasant Lake 79 . . . .   15-H
Plummer 277 . . . .   6-D
Plymouth (MA) 50,889 . .   26-V
Ponemah 6-F
Ponsford 9-E
Porter 210 . . . .   18-C
PRESTON 1,530 . . . . . .   21-M
Princeton 3,729 . . . . . .   14-I
Prinsburg 502 . . . .   17-E
Prior Lake (MA) 11,482 . .   28-V
Proctor 2,974 . . . .   10-M
Puposky 7-F

Q

Quamba 124 . . . .   13-J

R

Racine 288 . . . .   21-L
Radium 5-B
Ramsey (MA) 12,408 . . .   23-V
Randall 571 . . . .   13-G
Randolph 331 . . . .   18-K
Ranier 199 . . . .   4-J
Ray 4-J
Raymond 670 . . . .   16-E
Reading 21-D
Reads Landing 18-M

Red Lake 6-F
RED LAKE FALLS
1,481 . . . .   6-C
RED WING 15,145 . . . .   18-L
Redby 6-F
REDWOOD FALLS
4,859 . . . .   18-F
Regal 51 . . . .   15-F
Remer 342 . . . .   9-I
Renville 1,315 . . . .   17-E
Revere 112 . . . .   19-E
Rice 610 . . . .   14-H
Richfield (MA) 35,710 . .   27-W
Richmond 965 . . . .   15-G
Richville 121 . . . .   11-D
Richwood 9-D
Riverton 122 . . . .   11-H
Robbinsdale (MA)
14,396 . . . .   26-W
Rochert 10-D
ROCHESTER 70,997 . .   20-L
Rock Creek 1,040 . . . . 14-K
Rockford 2,667 . . . .   16-I
Rockville 579 . . . .   15-H
Rogers (MA) 711 . . . . . .   24-U
Rollag 10-C
Rollingstone 697 . . . . .   19-N
Ronneby 58 . . . .   14-I
Roosevelt 180 . . . .   3-F
Roscoe 141 . . . .   15-G
Rose Creek 363 . . . . .   21-K
ROSEAU 2,459 . . . . . .   3-D
Rosemount (MA) 8,622 . .   28-X
Roseville (MA) 33,485 . .   26-X
Ross 3-D
Rothsay 443 . . . .   11-C
Round Lake 463 . . . . .   21-E
Round Prairie 13-F
Royalton 802 . . . .   13-H
Rush City 1,508 . . . . .   14-K
Rushford 1,485 . . . .   20-N
Rushford Village 705 . .   21-N
Rushmore 381 . . . .   21-D
Russell 394 . . . .   19-D
Ruthton 328 . . . .   19-C
Rutledge 152 . . . . . .12-K

S

Sabin 495 . . . .   10-B
Sacred Heart 603 . . . . .   17-E
Saginaw 10-L
Salol 3-E
Sanborn 459 . . . .   19-F
Sandstone 2,066 . . .   12-K
Santiago 15-I
Sargeant 78 . . . .   21-K
Sartell 5,479 . . . .   14-H
Sauk Centre 3,581 . .   14-F
Sauk Rapids 7,825 . . .   14-H
Saum 6-G

Savage (MA) 9,906 .   28-W
Sawyer 11-L
Scandia (MA) 23-Z
Scanlon 878 . . . .   10-L
Schroeder 7-P
Seaforth 87 . . . .   18-E
Searles 19-G
Sebeka 662 . . . .   11-F
Sedan 63 . . . .   14-E
Shafer 368 . . . .   15-L
SHAKOPEE (MA)
11,739 . . . . .   17-J & 28V
Shelly 220 . . . .   8-B
Sherburn 1,105 . . . . . .   21-G
Shevlin 157 . . . .   7-E
Shoreview (MA)
24,587 . . . .   25-X
Shorewood (MA)
5,917 . . . .   27-U
Side Lake 7-K
Silver Bay 1,894 . . . . .   8-O
Silver Creek 15-I
Silver Lake 800 . . . . .   17-H
Skyline 272 . . . .   19-H
SLAYTON 2,147 . . . .   20-D
Sleepy Eye 3,694 . . .   19-G
Sobieski 199 . . . .   13-G
Solway 74 . . . .   8-F
Soudan 6-L
South Haven 193 . . . .   15-H
South St. Paul (MA)
20,197 . . . .   27-Y
Spicer 1,020 . . . .   16-F
Spring Grove 1,153 . .   21-N
Spring Hill 77 . . . . .   15-F
Spring Lake 7-I
Spring Lake Park (MA)
6,532 . . . .   25-W
Spring Park (MA)
1,571 . . . .   26-U
Spring Valley 2,461 . . .   21-L
Springfield 2,173 . . .   19-F
Squaw Lake 139 . . . .   7-H
St. Anthony 81 . . . .   14-G
St. Anthony
(MA) 7,727 . . . .   26-W
St. Bonifacius 1,184 . . .   17-I
St. Charles 2,642 . . . .   20-M
St. Clair 633 . . . .   20-I
ST. CLOUD 58,253 . . . .   14-H
St. Francis 2,538 . . . .   15-J
St. Hilaire 298 . . . .   6-C
ST. JAMES 4,364 . . .   20-G
St. Joseph 3,294 . . . . .   14-H
St. Leo 111 . . . .   17-C
St. Louis Park (MA)
43,787 . . . .   26-W
St. Martin 274 . . . . . .   15-G
St. Marys Point (MA)
339 . . . .   27-Z

St. Michael (MA) 5,867 . 24-U
ST. PAUL (MA)
272,235 . . . 15-K & 26-X
St. Paul Park (MA)
5,024 . . . . 27-Y
ST. PETER 9,481 . . . . 19-I
St. Rosa 75 . . . . 14-G
St. Stephen 607 . . . . . . 14-H
St. Vincent 116 . . . . 2-A
Stacy 1,081 . . . . 15-K
Stanchfield 14-J
Stanton 18-K
Staples 2,973 . . . . 12-G
Starbuck 1,141 . . . . . . 14-E
Steen 176 . . . . 22-C
Stephen 707 . . . . 4-B
Stewart 566 . . . . 17-G
Stewartville 5,032 . . . . 20-L
STILLWATER (MA)
13,972 . . . 16-K & 24-Z
Stockton 529 . . . . . 20-N
Storden 283 . . . . 20-E
Strandquist 98 . . . . 4-C
Strathcona 40 . . . . 4-C
Sturgeon Lake 230 . . 12-K
Sunburg 117 . . . . 15-E
Sunfish Lake (MA) 413 . 27-X
Svea 16-F
Swan River 9-J
Swanville 324 . . . . . . 13-G
Swatara 10-I
Swift 3-F

T

Taconite 310 . . . . 8-J
Talmoon 7-I
Tamarack 53 . . . . 10-I
Taopi 83 . . . . 21-L
Taunton 175 . . . . 18-C
Taylors Falls 694 . . . . 15-L
Tenney 4 . . . . 13-B
Tenstrike 184 . . . . 7-G
Terrace 15-E
Theilman 19-M
THIEF RIVER FALLS
8,010 . . . . 5-C
Thomson 132 . . . . 11-L
Tintah 74 . . . . 13-C
Tofte 7-P
Toivola 9-K
Tonka Bay (MA) 1,472 . 27-U
Tower 502 . . . . 7-L
Tracy 2,059 . . . . 19-D
Trail 67 . . . . 7-D
Trimont 745 . . . . 21-G
Trommald 80 . . . . 11-H
Trosky 120 . . . . 20-C
Truman 1,292 . . . . . 20-G

Turtle River 62 . . . . . 7-G
Twig 10-L
Twin Lakes 154 . . . . . 21-J
Twin Valley 821 . . . . . . 8-C
TWO HARBORS 3,651 . 9-N
Tyler 1,257 . . . . 19-C

U

Ulen 547 . . . . 9-C
Underwood 284 . . . 12-D
Upsala 371 . . . . 14-G
Urbank 73 . . . . 12-E
Utica 220 . . . . 20-N

V

Vadnais Heights
(MA) 11,041 . . . . . 25-X
Verdi 19-B
Vergas 287 . . . . 11-D
Vermillion (MA) 510 . . 29-Y
Vermillion Dam 6-L
Verndale 560 . . . . . 11-F
Vernon Center 339 . . 20-H
Veseli 18-J
Vesta 302 . . . . 18-E
Victoria (MA) 2,354 . . 27-U
Viking 103 . . . . 5-C
Villard 247 . . . . 14-E
Vining 84 . . . . 12-E
Viola 20-M
Virginia 9,431 . . . . 8-L

W

WABASHA 2,384 . . . 19-M
Wabasso 684 . . . . . 18-E
Waconia 5,309 . . . . . 17-I
WADENA 4,131 . . . . . . 11-F
Wahkon 197 . . . . 12-J
Waite Park 5,460 . . . . 14-H
Waldorf 243 . . . . 20-I
WALKER 950 . . . . 9-G
Walnut Grove 625 . . . . 19-E
Walters 86 . . . . 21-I
Waltham 170 . . . . 21-K
Wanamingo 847 . . . . 19-K
Wanda 103 . . . . 19-E
Wannaska 4-D
Warba 137 . . . . 9-J
WARREN 1,813 . . . . . 5-B
Warroad 1,679 . . . . 3-E
Warsaw 19-J
WASECA 8,385 . . . . 20-J
Waskish 5-G
Watertown 2,413 . . . . 17-I
Waterville 1,771 . . . . 19-J
Watkins 849 . . . . 15-G
Watson 211 . . . . 16-D
Waubun 330 . . . . 9-D

Waverly 600 . . . . 16-I
Wawina 9-K
Wayzata (MA) 3,806 . . 26-V
Webster 18-J
Welch 18-L
Welcome 790 . . . . . . 21-G
Wells 2,465 . . . . 21-I
Wendell 159 . . . . 13-C
West Concord 871 . . . 19-K
West St. Paul (MA)
19,248 . . . . 27-X
West Union 54 . . . . . . 14-F
Westbrook 853 . . . . . 20-E
Westport 47 . . . . 14-F
Whalan 94 . . . . 21-N
WHEATON 1,615 . . . . 13-B
Whipholt 9-H
White Bear Lake (MA)
24,704 . . . . 25-Y
White Earth 9-D
Wilder 83 . . . . 20-E
Willernie (MA) 584 . . . 25-Y
Williams 212 . . . . 3-F
WILLMAR 17,531 . . . . 16-F
Willow River 284 . . . . 12-K
Wilmont 351 . . . . 21-D
Wilton 171 . . . . 8-F
WINDOM 4,283 . . . . 20-F
Winger 167 . . . . 7-D
Winnebago 1,565 . . . 21-H
WINONA 26,286 . . . . 20-N
Winsted 1,581 . . . . . . 17-H
Winthrop 1,292 . . . . . 18-G
Winton 169 . . . . 6-N
Wirt 7-I
Withrow (MA) 25-Y
Wolf Lake 35 . . . . . . 10-E
Wolverton 158 . . . . . . 11-B
Wood Lake 406 . . . . 18-E
Woodbury (MA) 26,900 . 27-Y
Woodland (MA) 496 . . 26-V
Woodstock 159 . . . . . 20-C
WORTHINGTON 9,977 . 21-D
Wrenshall 296 . . . . . . 11-L
Wright 144 . . . . 11-K
Wykoff 493 . . . . 21-M
Wyoming (MA)
2,142 . . . . . 15-K & 23-Y

Y

Young America I-17

Z

Zemple 63 . . . . 8-I
Zim 8-L
Zimmerman 1,350 . . . . 15-I
Zumbro Falls 237 . . . . 19-L
Zumbrota 2,312 . . . . . 19-L

Chapter 4

Vital Statistics

State Seal

The Great Seal of the State of Minnesota is the insignia which the secretary of state affixes to government papers and documents to make them official. Henry H. Sibley, the first governor, is credited with selecting the motto on the seal, "L'Etoil du Nord," which, translated from French, means "The North Star." The seal was first used in 1858, our year of statehood. The picture on the seal is apparently a scene near St. Anthony Falls; a white man is plowing in the foreground while an American Indian is riding into the sunset in the background.

State Flag

The present state flag was adopted by the 1957 legislature. Pictured in the center of the flag is the state seal. Three dates are woven into a flowered wreath: 1858, the statehood year; 1819, the year Fort Snelling was established; and 1893, the year the original flag was adopted. Nineteen stars, symbolizing the fact that Minnesota was the nineteenth state to be admitted to the union after the original thirteen, were outside the center emblem on the 1893 flag. They are now included within the center emblem. The uppermost star is the largest and represents the North Star state.

State Flower

The pink and white lady slipper (Cypripedium reginae, the shoe of Venus, the queen) or showy lady slipper was adopted as the state flower in 1902. In Minnesota the lady slipper grows best in the damp shady places provided by tamarack and spruce marshes. It cannot grow without the presence of a tiny fungus which helps the flower's roots get food from the soil. The plant grows so slowly it takes from 10 to 20 years before it is old enough to bear blossoms. If it reaches full growth, from two to three feet tall, it may live to be 50 years old.

The pink and white lady slipper has become one of the state's rarest flowers, because the plant does not reproduce easily. It is illegal to pick. Since 1925 it has been protected by state law.

State Tree

The red pine (Pinus resinosa) or Norway pine is a majestic evergreen that was adopted as the official state tree in 1953 to symbolize Minnesota's history, background, and physical characteristics.

It is easy to recognize. It reaches a height of 60 to 100 feet with a straight trunk that can grow to three to five feet in diameter. The lower two-thirds of it's trunk is bare and the cone shaped crown is formed of branches that grow straight out. The scaly bark is brownish red and it's needles grow two per cluster. The tree is disease-free and insect resistant, and can live up to three hundred years. The tallest Norway pine in Minnesota is in Itasca Park. It stands 120 feet high and is over 300 years old.

State Gemstone

The Lake Superior agate, a crypto-crystalline quartz, basically white quartz with red iron deposit bands, was named official gemstone in 1969. It is found primarily in the red glacial drift areas of central and northeastern Minnesota.

Source: Art courtesy DNR by Floyd Johnson and Dan Metz.

State Grain

Wild rice (Zizania aquatica) or manomin, a staple food of Minnesota's Indians for centuries, was adopted as the official state grain in 1977. It is found in the shallow waters of lakes and rivers in the central and northern parts of the state, Minnesota was once the only place where wild rice was grown. It is still harvested the traditional way, with canoes, but in recent years it has been cultivated in paddies and harvested with specially designed combines.

State Bird

No bird better typifies Minnesota lakes, woods and the northern wilderness than the loon (Gavia immer), which knows no peer in swimming, diving, or fishing. It became Minnesota's state bird in 1961. Preferring the undisturbed isolation of the northern wilderness, it can be heard, if not often seen, through-  out the northern lake country. The common loon, or great northern diver, as it is called, has a wing span up to five feet, body lengths up to three feet, and distinctive black and white markings. Its name comes from a Norwegian word meaning "wild, sad cry." Some 12,000 loons make their homes in Minnesota.

State Fish

The walleye (Stizostedion v. vitreum) is a fitting symbol of the cool and pleasant north- land, and though found throughout Minnesota in lakes and rivers, it is most at home in the large, clear, cool lakes of Minnesota's northern forests. The state record size is 17 lbs.-8 oz. It has flesh of the highest 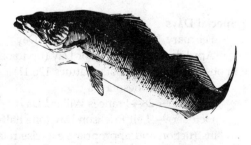 quality and is one of the most sought after fisherman's prizes. Much of the state's fishing water is managed primarily for walleye fishing.

State Song

"Hail! Minnesota" was written by Truman Rickard, a member of the class of 1904 at the University of Minnesota, for use in a class play. A second verse was written by University student Arthur Upson in 1905. In 1945, the song became the official anthem of the state of Minnesota.

Other State Symbols

In 1984, the legislature adopted the morel (Morchella esculenta) as the official state mushroom, and milk became the state drink. Minnesota ranks 5th in dairy production in the nation, producing 9.7 billion pounds of milk annually. The blueberry muffin joined the menu as the official state muffin in 1988. Blueberries are native to northeastern Minnesota, where they grow in bogs and on hillsides.

State Mottoes

"The North Star State"

"Land of 10,000 Lakes" is on Minnesota license plates. The actual number of lakes is 11,842 (over 10 acres) and we have more shoreline than California, Florida and Hawaii combined.

"The Gopher State"

Legal Holidays

January 1—New Year's Day
February, 3rd Monday—President's Day
May, last Monday—Memorial Day
July 4—Independence Day
September, 1st Monday—Labor Day
October, 2nd Monday—Columbus Day
November 11—Veteran's Day
November, 4th Thursday—Thanksgiving Day
December 25—Christmas Day

Special Days

February 15—Susan B. Anthony Day
April, last Friday—Arbor Day (up to one half school day may be spent in observance, Minnesota Statutes 126.11)
May 11—Minnesota Day
September 28—Frances Willard Day
October 9—Leif Erickson Day (one half hour, school day, may be spent in "instruction and appropriate exercise relative to and in commemoration of the life and history of the respective persons and principles and ideals they fostered." Minnesota Statutes 126.09)
January, 3rd Monday—Martin Luther King, Jr. Day

Minnesota In Profile

Name: Derived from the Dakota word Minisota meaning "sky tinted waters."
Organized as territory: March 3, 1849.

Entered union: May 11, 1858 (32nd state).

Motto: L'Etoile du Nord (The North Star)

Song: "Hail! Minnesota" (1945)

Area: 84,068 square miles (12th largest state).

Land area: 79,289 square miles. (14th largest)

Geographic center: In Crow Wing County, 10 mi. SW of Brainerd.

Counties: 87.

Inland waters: 4,779 square miles.

Width: 385 miles.

Length: 405 miles, extending from 43°30' to 49°23'4".

Circumference: 1,880 miles.

Population (July 1, 1998): 4,725,419 (20th largest state).

Density per square mile: 54.3.

Largest cities: Minneapolis 368,383; St. Paul 272,235; Bloomington 86,335; Duluth 85,495; and Rochester 70,745, Coon Rapids 62,790.

Percent urban population:78%

Percent rural population: 22%

Average mean altitude: 1,200 feet above sea level.

Highest point: Eagle Mountain (Cook County), 2,301 feet.

Lowest point: Surface of Lake Superior, 602 feet.

Three major river systems: Mississippi, Minnesota, and Red River of the North; water flows from Minnesota in three directions: Hudson Bay, Atlantic Ocean, and Gulf of Mexico; no water flows into the state.

Number of lakes: 11,842 larger than 10 acres.

Largest lake: Red Lake (451 square miles.)

Major industries: Agriculture, computers and services, health care and medical equipment, tourism, forest and forestry products, printing and publishing.

Transportation: Interstate highways I-35, I-90 & I-94. 12,011 miles of state truck highways, 130,600 miles of streets and highways, 4,652 miles of active railroad tracks, 231 miles of navigable river.

Minneapolis-St. Paul International Airport is 19th busiest in the world based on total passengers, with 29,070,480 passengers in 1997.

Sources: U. S. Bureau of the Census; State Demographer, MN Planning
MN Pocket Data Book, MN State Planning Agency, 1975
U.S. Fact Book, Grosset & Dunlap, 1975
MN Planning website: www.mnplan.state.mn.us
www.senate.gov/~grams/mnfacts.html

Minnesota and National Statistics and Ranking

	Year	State	Rank	U.S.
Population				
Resident population (1,000)				
	1990	4,376	20	248,765
	1998	4,725	20	270,299
Percent living inside metropolitan areas				
	1990	68.8	26	79.7
	1996	69.7	25	79.8
Percent under 18 years old				
	1990	26.7	17	25.7
	1997	26.7	12	26.0
Percent 65 years old and over				
	1990	12.5	28	12.5
	1997	12.3	32	12.7
Population projections (1,000)				
	2000	4,830	20	274,634
	2025	5,510	21	335,050
Vital Statistics and Health				
Infant deaths per 1,000 live births				
	1990	7.3	45	9.2
	1995	6.7	35	7.6
Births to teenage mothers, percent of total				
	1990	8.0	48	12.8
	1996	8.5	46	12.9

	Year	State	Rank	U.S.
Motor-vehicle deaths per 100 mil. vehicle miles				
	1990	1.7	44	2.2
	1996	1.3	39	1.8
Doctors per 100,000 resident population				
	1990	219	11	216
	1996	241	11	239
Education				
Public elementary-secondary schools:				
Enrollment rate \1				
	1990	91.2	29	91.3
	1995	90.8	32	91.6
Teachers' average salaries \2				
	1990	$33,126	15	$33,123
	1996	$38,281	17	$38,562
Full-time college enrollment, percent of total				
	1990	60.1	27	56.6
	1996	59.7	28	57.4

\1 Percent of persons 5 to 17 years old.
\2 For school year ending in June the following year.

Law Enforcement

	Year	State	Rank	U.S.
Violent crime rate per 100,000 population				
	1990	306	37	732
	1996	339	36	634

Year	State	Rank	U.S.
Federal & State prisoners per 10,000 population			
1990	7.2	50	31.0
1996	11.1	50	44.5

State Governments

Year	State	Rank	U.S.
General revenue per capita			
1990	$2,512	12	$2,086
1996	$3,483	9	$2,910

Labor Force

Year	State	Rank	U.S.
Percent of civilian population employed			
1990	69.5	2	62.8
1996	71.7	3	63.2
Nonfarm employment—percent in manufacturing			
1990	18.8	19	17.4
1997	17.5	15	15.2
Average annual pay			
1990	$23,121	13	$23,602
1996	$28,866	13	$28,946

Income and Poverty

Year	State	Rank	U.S.
Personal income per capita (constant 1992 dol.)			
1990	$20,857	16	$20,652
1997	$23,777	10	$22,713
Median household income (constant 1996 dol.)			
1990	$37,772	15	$35,945
1996	$40,991	6	$35,492
Percent of population below the poverty level			
1990	12.0	28	13.5
1996	9.8	40	13.7

Consumption

Year	State	Rank	U.S.
Energy consumption per capita (million BTUs)			
1990	301	29	326
1995	352	24	344
Home ownership rates (percent)			
1990	68.0	22	63.9
1997	75.4	1	65.7
Retail sales per household			
1990	$20,216	16	$19,655
1996	$25,661	22	$24,992

Source: State profile from U.S. Bureau of the Census,
Statistical Abstract of the United States, 1998.
1990 US Census Data

County Population Projections 1995 to 2025

The 1995 data is not a projection; it is the official estimate from the State Demographic Center. These projections were updated in June 1998.

County	Estimate 1995	Proj. 2000	Proj. 2005	Proj. 2010	Proj. 2015	Proj. 2020	Proj. 2025
Aitkin	13,366	14,010	14,410	14,760	15,170	15,410	15,540
Anoka	272,636	296,880	318,260	337,590	355,540	370,530	381,890
Becker	29,163	29,970	30,410	30,720	31,010	31,120	30,890
Beltrami	36,508	38,870	40,590	41,340	41,370	41,280	41,050
Benton	33,362	36,510	39,590	42,450	44,890	46,980	48,650
Big Stone	6,026	5,660	5,300	4,990	4,760	4,570	4,360
Blue Earth	55,172	55,810	56,110	56,650	56,590	56,490	56,540
Brown	27,580	27,750	27,750	27,710	27,750	27,740	27,530
Carlton	30,559	31,050	31,110	31,020	30,920	30,720	30,250
Carver	57,010	65,160	72,940	80,460	87,910	95,360	102,320
Cass	23,801	25,190	26,220	27,050	27,710	28,180	28,350
Chippewa	13,097	12,680	12,170	11,710	11,350	10,960	10,510
Chisago	36,045	39,820	43,110	46,290	49,500	52,670	55,570
Clay	52,540	53,750	54,310	54,850	54,580	54,100	53,490
Clearwater	8,452	8,390	8,260	8,170	8,130	8,070	7,970
Cook	4,166	4,300	4,360	4,400	4,420	4,440	4,420
Cottonwood	12,768	12,440	12,010	11,650	11,300	10,970	10,600
Crow Wing	48,437	51,770	54,470	56,700	58,460	59,730	60,530
Dakota	316,272	350,120	380,410	407,520	432,510	455,080	473,540
Dodge	16,680	17,120	17,350	17,530	17,760	17,950	17,970
Douglas	30,424	31,510	32,240	32,810	33,340	33,740	33,790
Faribault	16,661	16,010	15,280	14,680	14,240	13,850	13,410
Fillmore	20,906	20,510	20,040	19,720	19,600	19,500	19,290
Freeborn	32,759	31,900	31,030	30,280	29,690	29,020	28,190
Goodhue	42,477	43,050	43,600	44,490	45,940	47,290	48,170
Grant	6,242	6,070	5,810	5,560	5,380	5,220	5,060
Hennepin	1,063,631	1,082,570	1,097,610	1,106,900	1,109,570	1,103,090	1,086,950
Houston	19,123	19,420	19,520	19,590	19,690	19,740	19,660
Hubbard	16,225	17,180	17,900	18,540	19,100	19,530	19,800
Isanti	28,664	30,260	31,360	32,240	33,120	33,910	34,310
Itasca	42,446	42,890	42,930	42,920	42,950	42,780	42,340
Jackson	11,717	11,570	11,310	11,050	10,870	10,670	10,420
Kanabec	13,473	13,630	13,820	14,210	14,830	15,430	15,880
Kandiyohi	41,167	42,430	43,370	44,200	45,010	45,630	45,860
Kittson	5,572	5,380	5,170	5,010	4,910	4,830	4,730
Koochiching	15,911	15,620	15,320	15,000	14,640	14,200	13,580
Lac Qui Parle	8,717	8,340	7,850	7,370	6,950	6,600	6,260

Lake	10,473	10,540	10,420	10,230	10,000	9,720	9,340
Lake of						
the Woods	4,363	4,440	4,470	4,470	4,490	4,520	4,490
LeSueur	24,371	24,840	25,300	26,030	27,090	28,080	28,870
Lincoln	6,791	6,480	6,130	5,830	5,620	5,380	5,140
Lyon	25,211	25,620	25,850	26,010	25,740	25,740	25,610
McLeod	33,803	34,960	36,100	37,430	38,940	40,310	41,410
Mahnomen	5,127	5,070	4,980	4,950	4,990	5,010	5,030
Marshall	10,733	10,480	10,120	9,840	9,580	9,300	9,000
Martin	22,840	22,330	21,840	21,580	21,570	21,550	21,360
Meeker	21,352	21,460	21,340	21,220	21,220	21,170	20,950
Mille Lacs	19,807	20,700	21,220	21,710	22,420	23,140	23,710
Morrison	30,756	31,150	31,190	31,220	31,390	31,470	31,280
Mower	37,628	37,310	36,790	36,400	36,100	35,680	35,100
Murray	9,606	9,290	8,870	8,490	8,180	7,860	7,530
Nicollet	29,386	30,650	31,640	32,000	32,050	32,000	31,780
Nobles	20,408	20,550	20,610	20,720	20,850	20,860	20,850
Norman	7,885	7,670	7,380	7,130	6,920	6,700	6,470
Olmsted	113,968	118,730	122,490	125,440	127,840	129,490	130,000
Otter Tail	52,847	54,340	54,840	54,830	54,600	54,220	53,430
Pennington	13,391	13,400	13,370	13,390	13,410	13,370	13,230
Pine	22,816	23,400	23,920	24,650	25,650	26,550	27,230
Pipestone	10,433	10,160	9,830	9,530	9,290	9,060	8,780
Polk	2,904	32,610	32,120	31,660	31,350	30,940	30,330
Pope	10,906	10,890	10,760	10,510	10,240	9,950	9,580
Ramsey	494,674	497,710	501,780	504,920	506,390	504,290	498,460
Red Lake	4,481	4,380	4,210	4,030	3,900	3,800	3,670
Redwood	17,293	16,960	16,500	16,100	15,790	15,490	15,110
Renville	17,595	17,240	16,690	16,180	15,790	15,430	15,000
Rice	52,232	54,710	56,390	57,290	58,120	58,560	58,700
Rock	9,870	9,570	9,210	8,910	8,710	8,540	8,300
Roseau	16,025	16,660	17,150	17,600	18,060	18,490	18,820
St Louis	198,879	199,400	197,520	194,170	190,500	187,050	183,910
Scott	69,303	79,040	87,850	96,060	104,040	112,160	119,890
Sherburne	51,328	60,390	68,960	77,030	84,370	91,620	98,540
Sibley	14,584	14,350	14,180	14,170	14,360	14,590	14,700
Stearns	126,912	134,730	139,750	142,480	143,630	144,050	144,980
Steele	31,817	32,290	32,570	32,830	33,190	33,410	33,320
Stevens	10,575	10,780	10,850	10,590	10,290	10,050	9,840
Swift	11,081	11,000	10,990	11,060	11,130	11,110	11,010
Todd	23,742	23,390	22,920	22,670	22,720	22,710	22,500
Traverse	4,374	4,170	3,950	3,760	3,640	3,530	3,430
Wabasha	20,428	20,580	20,570	20,600	20,730	20,850	20,830

Wadena	13,294	13,470	13,490	13,410	13,250	13,030	12,730
Waseca	18,031	17,830	17,600	17,410	17,310	17,150	16,890
Washington	175,441	200,830	221,250	237,890	252,340	265,370	275,950
Watonwan	11,764	11,460	11,160	10,990	10,890	10,750	10,560
Wilkin	7,399	7,200	6,980	6,800	6,670	6,550	6,380
Winona	48,987	49,990	50,760	50,730	50,620	50,350	50,060
Wright	77,232	84,060	89,840	95,160	100,480	105,550	109,820
Yellow Medicine	11,613	11,240	10,790	10,360	10,020	9,700	9,310
Minnesota	4,626,514	4,805,970	4,948,720	5,066,540	5,167,870	5,243,600	5,282,840

Source: State Demographic Center, 658 Cedar St., St. Paul, MN 55155
651-296-2557 helpline@mnplan.state.mn.us www.mnplan.state.mn.us

Climate

	Twin Cities	30 year average
Annual precipitation:	29.67 inches	28.32 inches
Annual snowfall:	45.0 inches (97-98)	49.61 inches
January mean temperature:	12.2° F (99)	11.8° F
July mean temperature:	76.2° F (99)	73.6° F.
Annual mean temperature:	45.5° F	44.9° F
Average wind speed:	9.6 MPH	10.6 MPH
Hours of sunshine:	2801	4465 possible
Average last spring freeze:	May 1	—
Average first fall freeze:	October 5	—

Sources: Twin Cities Climatological Review of 1998.
National Weather Service, Minneapolis/St. Paul, Minnesota; 1998.

Minnesota's Ethnic Roots
    When Senator Stephen Douglas introduced the bill to Congress in 1849 to create the Territory of Minnesota, thirty years had passed since the first permanent white settlement at Fort Snelling. At that time, he told his colleagues that eight to ten thousand settlers lived in the territory. Most of this population was located within the protective shadow of Fort Snelling, a few miles downstream from Mendota in the emerging village of St. Paul, or a few miles upstream at the Falls of St. Anthony. The few remaining people were scattered in small clusters along the lower St. Croix and Mississippi Rivers. Later in that same year, Governor Alexander Ramsey, addressing the first territorial legislature, estimated the Indian population at 25,000, while the 1849 census counted 5,000. The Indians were spread across what is now Minnesota and the Dakotas east of the Missouri River.

By 1860, two years after statehood and establishment of Minnesota's western border at the Red River, the population had grown and spread, reaching some 172,000. From those early numbers the total population of the state rose to 2 million by 1910 and 4.5 million today, virtually all the result of immigration and subsequent natural increase of the immigrants.

Meanwhile, geographical differences in the ethnic character of the population evolved rapidly as immigrants entered the state, spread across the land, multiplied, and migrated again. American Indians were concentrated on a few reservations as treaty cessions opened most of the land to white settlement in the mid-nineteenth century.

Immigration to Minnesota was first dominated by western Europeans who established themselves on the state's best agricultural lands. Western European immigration slowed and eastern and southern European immigration increased toward the end of the nineteenth century and into the early twentieth century. These people settled on the remaining, poorer agricultural lands, on the state's iron ranges, and in the Twin Cities area. In the mid-twentieth century, black migrants from the southern United States arrived along with a second wave of eastern European immigrants. More recently, newcomers to Minnesota have included those from Mexico and southeast Asia in particular.

Less colorful but at least equally important have been Minnesota's internal population shifts. Geographical concentrations of young and elderly have evolved as people have migrated in large numbers in response to changing economic and social conditions. There are accompanying large differences in wealth, income, unemployment rates, health care, disease, housing, crime, life expectancy, and needs for welfare aids across the state. Minnesotans have adapted themselves to changing conditions and opportunities. One response is seen in the network of social organization and technology; another in the attention given to health and education—the basic requisites to guiding change.

The European Stock

Minnesota's first white settlers were New England Yankees of English, Scottish, and Irish stock who cut the trees, established the lumber mills and later the flour mills, became the early managers and professionals, and assumed political leadership in the mid-nineteenth century.

The accelerating population growth in the state in the 1860s, 70s, and 80s consisted largely of non-English-speaking European immigrants who clustered in areas of the state that were opening for settlement when they arrived. Germans, Minnesota's largest ethnic group, settled in the Lower Mississippi valley beginning in the 1850s, moving up the Mississippi and Minnesota valleys in large concentrations to within 80-100 miles of the Twin Cities area. The Swedes, Minnesota's second largest ethnic group, first

arrived in Minnesota at about the same time as the Germans, eventually filling almost solidly several counties immediately north of the Twin Cities
area and several smaller areas in west-central and western Minnesota.
Norwegians, the third largest group in Minnesota, settled first in Fillmore
County at about the same time and gradually moved across the southern
counties toward the west and northwest and are now the dominant ethnic
group in western Minnesota and the Red River valley.

Arriving slightly later,in smaller numbers and filling the gaps, were
French Canadians, Bohemians, Irish, Dutch, Flemish, Polish, Danish, Welsh,
Swiss, Luxemburgers, and Icelanders. With most of the good agricultural
lands in Minnesota already claimed, immigrant groups arriving around the
turn of the century came to the cities or were attracted by employment
opportunities in the Twin Cities and on the Iron Range. These groups
included Finnish, Russian, Austrian, Cornish, Italian, Slovakian, Morabian,
Serbian, Croatian, Hungarian, Romanian, and Greek, with important Jewish
immigration from several European countries. Many of these groups were
concentrated in small areas.

In the nineteenth and early twentieth century, these differences in
European cultural heritage were reflected in well known regional variations
in language, farming practices, and social or business affiliations. Whenever
immigrant groups settled, they brought with them their churches which
served important social and cultural, as well as religious functions. Large
variations in the architecture of church buildings and size of church membership today bear witness to that important aspect of the state's historical
geography. Today a number of festivals, restorations, and commercial enterprises display a continuing or revived interest in embellishing the legacy.

Racial Minorities
American Indians

Before white settlement, the Sioux occupied most of Minnesota, but
were concentrated in the woodland areas. Pressure from whites in eastern
North America pushed the Ojibway westward. They in turn gradually
pushed the Sioux from Minnesota's woodlands onto the prairie. The horse,
introduced by the Spanish, and adapted and bred by the Indians, provided
the Sioux with the mobility to pursue the abundant wildlife of the grass-
lands. In 1970, the Bureau of the Census recorded 23,000 Indian people living in Minnesota. This has been generally regarded as an understatement:
tribal rolls alone exceeded that number by more than 50 percent. According
to estimates, 45,000 Indians resided in Minnesota in 1975, about 24 percent
living on the state's eleven reservations. The Minnesota Indian Affairs
Council 1998 Annual Report says our state has the 12th largest American
Indian population in the country. The 1990 Census lists the state total at
49,909 with one-third living in Minneapolis and St. Paul, 15% living in the

Twin Cities suburbs, and 12,402 living on reservations. The U.S. Census Bureau projected that there would be 64,000 American Indians and Native Alaskans in the state in the year 2000.

The seven largest reservations are Ojibway, while the four smallest are Sioux. The largest reservation is Leech Lake with over 5,700 residents; the Red Lake and White Earth reservations are just slightly smaller. The four reservations in southern Minnesota have a total population of slightly over 840 Dakota Sioux (Bureau of Indian Affairs 1993 Labor Force report). At the present time, at least 90 percent of Minnesota's Indian population is Ojibway, most of the remainder are Sioux.

African Americans

The African American presence in Minnesota predates the acquisition of territorial status in 1849. One of the earliest territorial pioneers, George Bonga, was born near the site of Duluth in 1802. Bonga was influential in negotiating treaties between whites, the Sioux and Objibwe people.

Although there was a small fledgling communities of African Americans in St. Paul and St. Anthony (Minneapolis) prior to the Civil War, more significant growth occurred after the Civil War during the 1880"s. In that decade the African American population grew by 200%. Another significant period of growth was during what historians have come to call "the great migration" out of the South into the urban areas of the North between 1910 and 1920. The African American population of Minneapolis grew by 51.5% while that of St. Paul grew by only 7.3%. The Twin Cities experienced a small African American population increase during the decade of the sixties, and a more substantive increase during the 1980's where a 78% increase was recorded. According to the 1990 census approximately 96,000 resided in Minnesota with 89% living in the Twin Cities metropolitan area.

Historically, African Americans were found residing in almost every county of the state. The majority, however, are found in the three major urban areas, Minneapolis, St. Paul, and Duluth. These communities are characterized by being relatively small when compared to other major northern urban areas, very cohesive, highly educated, and very active with respect to civil/political rights. In the past the African Americans resided primarily in small enclaves located on the north and south side of Minneapolis, the Summit-University area of St. Paul and the Central Hillside neighborhood of Duluth. These neighborhoods are now somewhat diffused with approximately 20% of the African American population in the Twin Cities residing in Suburban communities.

In spite of its relatively small size, African Americans have had an important impact upon the development of Minnesota's social, economic and political institutions. They were important in the labor movement, successfully lobbied for civil rights legislation, secured passage of the first antilynching law in the United States, were influential in campaigning against discrimination in housing and employment practices, and produced five United States Ambassadors, national civil rights leaders, educators, scholars, and artists representing the visual and performing arts.   Black Minnesotans have also contributed to sustaining a vibrant African American musical tradition through such groups and artists as the Sounds of Blackness, the Twin Cities Gospel Sounds, the music of the artist formerly known as Prince, Jimmy Jam and Terry Lewis, and jazz pianist Bobby Lyles.

Chicano-Latinos

The first record of a Chicano/Latino settler in Minnesota dates back to 1886. During this year, a 19 year-old oboe player (Luis Garzon) visited Minneapolis as part of the Mexico City Orchestra. The Orchestra was scheduled to perform at a gala industrial exposition. Luis Garzon fell ill and remained behind as the orchestra left town. Thus, Luis Garzon became the first known Chicano/Latino to reside in Minnesota. By the turn of the century, Minnesota Census records reflected a population which consisted of 24 Chicano/Latinos.

During the 1910's more than 10% of Mexico's population was displaced. This was due, in part, to the Díaz rule and the revolution which ensued. Another contributing factor to the influx of Latinos was the booming meatpacking, agricultural and railroad industries in the United States. U.S. companies, including the Minnesota Sugar Company (now American Crystal Sugar), began to actively recruit Mexican workers. Due to World War I, labor shortages were also a contributing factor to the increased flow of Chicano/Latinos to Minnesota.

By 1920, an estimated 240 Chicano/Latinos lived in Minneapolis and 70 in Saint Paul.

By the early 1930's, 3,636 Chicano/Latinos were living in Minnesota. During this time, Saint Paul's west side became an established Chicano/Latino community. The first identifiable Chicano/Latino town which was established in greater Minnesota was Albert Lea. The Chicano/Latino community in this area can be traced back as early as the 1940's.

In the 1950's, despite much community opposition, the "flats" (part of Saint Paul's west side) were "rehabilitated". The $9 million development included a massive new flood wall along the Mississippi and the new Riverview Industrial Park. This construction displaced many Chicano/Latino residents and their small homes, stores, schools and churches.

In 1978, the Spanish Speaking Affairs Council (now Chicano Latino Affairs Council) and many other activist organizations were established to defend the rights of Chicano/Latinos in Minnesota.

Chicano/Latinos in the 1990's

According to the State of Minnesota Demographer's Office, 1995 Census counts show that there are an estimated 85,100 Chicano/Latinos in the state of Minnesota.

The 1995 Census estimates reflect a 56.6% increase from similar 1990 census counts. This increase makes the Chicano/Latino community the fastest growing community in Minnesota during this time period.

In addition to this group of 85,100 Chicano/Latinos, there are also an estimated 15,000 to 20,000 migrant farm workers who come to Minnesota each summer. Migrant farm worker families arrive as early as May and leave as late as September. These families primarily come from Texas.

The areas in the state with the fastest growing Chicano/Latino community are: the southwestern part of the state and the Metro Area. Chicano/Latino people have not clustered in the Twin Cities as much as other minority groups, but have spread around the state with concentrations in counties with meat packing or food processing facilities such as, Freeborn, Watonwan, Kandiyohi, and Polk. The Hispanic-origin population is projected to more than triple by 2025, becoming the state's second largest minority group. From 80,707 in 1997, their numbers are expected to reach 296,000 in 2025.

Source: Mario A. Hernandez,Greater MN Community Liaison,
Chicano Latino Affairs Council

Asian-Pacific Islanders

Telling the story of who Minnesotans are includes telling the story of Asian Pacific people. Although Asian Pacific Americans have been in Minnesota for over three generations - their history in this state spans over 150 years - there is little attention or acknowledgement of their history, diversity, and contributions.

Asian Pacific people have been in Minnesota since the late 1800's. Some migrated from other states, others were foreign exchange students who after their education stayed on for employment opportunities, and some came as foreign laborers seeking economic opportunity. The first documented arrival of Asian Pacific people to Minnesota occurred in the Spring of 1876, when two Chinese men established the Chinese Laundry in St. Paul and the Lung Wing Laundry in Minneapolis.

Source: June Drenning Holmquist, ed., They Chose Minnesota: A Survey of the State's Ethnic Groups, Minnesota Historical Society Press: St. Paul, 1981.

From 1920 to 1970, Minnesota's Asian Pacific population remained relatively small and static. The census in 1970 revealed approximately 6,000 Asian Pacific people living in Minnesota. However, in the 1970's,like the rest of the United States, Minnesota experienced an influx of refugees from

Southeast Asia. In a five year span, 21,500 Hmong, Lao, Cambodians and Vietnamese arrived in Minnesota seeking asylum. The Hmong came because they fought in the Vietnam War as soldiers in a secret army formed and funded by the Central Intelligence Agency (CIA). The Lao, Cambodians and Vietnamese came because they were employed by the U.S. government and companies in Asia.

From 1980 to 1989, Minnesota saw a 193.5% increase in the Asian Pacific population. By 1990 the Census counted a total of 77, 886. A more recent estimate puts the figure at 130,000 representing over 42 Asian Pacific ethnic groups. International immigration has been a significant factor in Minnesota's population growth within the last decade. According to the U.S. Census, the Asian Pacific population in Minnesota is one of the fastest growing racial/cultural communities in the state and is projected to increase to 229,000 by the year 2025.

This rapid expansion of the Asian Pacific American population in recent decades has created a remarkable ethnic diversification. In 1970, 96% of Asian Pacific Americans were Japanese, Filipino or Chinese. As the 21st Century approaches these three groups now number just over 50 percent of Asian Pacific Americans.

Scholars of the Asian Pacific American experience often describe and separate the experience into "three waves of immigration." The first wave spans from 1849, the start of the California "Gold Rush" to 1924 when the Immigration Act of 1924 was passed. Approximately one million people entered the United States during this period. The law then cut off immigration from Asian countries.

After a hiatus of some forty years, a second wave numbering about three and a half million people immigrated to the United States.

The third wave of Asian American people to enter the United States occurred in the years following the Vietnam War when immigration laws were removed as a response to the genocide of Southeast Asians who were friendly to democratic ideas and cause.

There are two contrasting stereotypes applied to the Asian Pacific community. One is of prosperity and the other is of poverty. Too often Asian Pacific Americans are viewed as a model minority. Data such as the following support this image. A new population bulletin, published June 1998, describes the Asian Pacific American population as active in politics 'many hold high elected office.' High levels of educational attainment, occupational status, and household incomes negate the idea of Asians as a disadvantaged minority, which is often the case with refugees from Asian Pacific countries.

The Asian Pacific community in Minnesota is vastly diverse. As a result of the "three waves of immigration," Minnesota's Asian Pacific population

generally falls into one of three socio-economic classification:
- Established second and third generation Asian Americans that tend to be relatively well established in the community as the result of good education and hard work.
- More recently arrived immigrants from around the world, often first generation; well educated, in search of improved economic opportunity for themselves and their family.
- Most recently arrived refugees from war torn areas of Southeast Asia; some fleeing political and religious persecution, many struggling in their new homeland.

Each community is different and has its share of accomplishments, contributions made to the economic strength and cultural richness of this state, and is shaped by its previous pattern of immigration history. Within the last fifty years, the landscape of Minnesota has shifted and changed due to the people that have moved here, either by choice as immigrants or by circumstances as refugees. The Twin Cities and communities in greater Minnesota have witnessed the changes for themselves in seeing Asian Pacific owned businesses emerge and become successful from the owning of the first laundromats, to technology industries, newspapers, stores, businesses, and restaurants. Asian Pacific peoples have influenced, added to, and become an integral part of Minnesota's past, present and emerging future.

Prominent Asian-Pacific Minnesotans include Representative Satveer Chaudhary, the first Asian Indian and Asian American to be elected to the Minnesota State Legislature. Supenn Harrison founded the Sawatdee restaurants. Steve Huh Architect. Jesse Kao Lee is the Executive Director of the Southeast Asian Community Council. Judge Tony N. Leung has served on the district court bench for Hennepin County since 1994 when he was appointed by Governor Arne Carlson. He is the first Asian American to be appointed judge in the State of Minnesota. David Mura: Poet, Playwright & Essayist. Vineeta Sawkar is a local reporter and fill-in anchor for KSTP, Channel 5 News. Dr. Sung Won Sohn is the Chief Economist for Norwest Corporation.

Text by: Council on Asian-Pacific Minnesotans, 200 University Avenue West, Suite 100, St. Paul, MN 55101, (651) 296-0538.
Sources: Faces of the Future, MN Population Projections 1995-2025. MN Planning. Council on Asian-Pacific Minnesotans Biennium Report (1996)

The Settlement Process

From its beginning in the southeastern part of the state during the 1850's, Minnesota's white population gradually pushed westward and northward, following the stream valleys which served as means of transportation and provided wood for building materials and fuel.

Displacement of Indians; Development of Rail Pattern

Railroad development beginning in the 1860's joined together the existing settlements across the state. White settlement gradually displaced the native Ojibway and Sioux populations and confined their reduced numbers to reservation lands. In recent years, nearly half the Indian population has shifted from these reservations to the Twin Cities area, particularly Minneapolis.

Until about the time of World War I, both the state's population and rail network advanced, then thickened in density. This was the era of resource acquisition and development. Settlers spread out to cultivate the land, harvest the timber, and later to settle the Iron Range and dig the rich ore. Towns and cities sprang up and grew to serve these economic activities, to assemble and process their output, and feed it into the mainstream of the national economy.

Tractor-Auto Age

Since the Depression and World War II, the economy of the state has become more noticeably diversified, providing a great range of services in areas like finance, education, medicine, law, business, and government. These changes in Minnesota's economy coincided with improvements in personal mobility and new machinery that allowed greater production with fewer workers. This resulted in a steady increase in farm size and a decline in farm population at the same time that employment opportunities were expanding in the urban areas of the state.

Population shifts reduced rural densities and contributed to growth in the state's cities. These urbanization trends were inhibited during the 1930's by economic stagnation and by the national emergency in the early 1940's. Beginning in the late 1940's, urbanization resumed with new vigor after being restrained for more than a decade and a half.

During the 1950's, urban growth in Minnesota, as throughout the nation, was almost explosive. Concurrently, 279,000 persons left Minnesota's farms, as the number of farms decreased and the average farm size increased rapidly. The remaining farms produced more food than ever. And the more affluent and mobile farm population was able to travel greater distances to the larger trade centers, contributing to their growth and dominance, while the smallest towns struggled to survive the competition.

The shift from natural ore mining to taconite processing on the Mesabi Range during the 1950s resulted in the emergence of several completely new communities in northeastern Minnesota.

At this time Minnesota's population increased by 431,400 persons with the urban counties increasing most rapidly in both number and percent. Meanwhile, the predominantly rural counties of the state (those without major trade centers), experienced losses in population. Notwithstanding the large urban population growth, there was a net out-migration of 98,000 persons from Minnesota, a large share of whom moved to urban centers in other states, particularly on the West Coast.

Minnesota Population, 1860-2025

Year	Population (in thousands)	Percent in 7 County Twin Cities Area
1860	172	30
1870	440	25
1880	781	24
1890	1310	31
1900	1750	28
1910	2076	31
1920	2387	32
1930	2564	36
1940	2792	36
1950	2982	40
1960	3414	45
1970	3805	49
1980	4076	49
1990	4376	53
2000 (projection)	4806	54
2005	4,949	—
2010	5,067	—
2015	5,168	—
2020	5,244	—
2025	5,283	—

Minnesota's overall population growth during the 1950s was the result of natural increase—the excess of births over deaths.   Birth rates in Minnesota, as throughout the country, experienced a continual increase during the 1950s, reaching a peak in 1959.

During the 1960s, Minnesota increased in population by 391,100 persons, while net out-migration declined to 0.7 percent of the 1960 population. Birth rates dropped steadily. The state's urban population continued to shift outward from the centers of employment toward the accessible countryside areas of lakes, trees, and hills. Population increased in the metropolitan fringe counties and in certain counties in the central part of the state with physical amenities.   During the 1960s, farm size increased and off-farm migration continued.   Many farmers living within commuting distance of alternative employment opportunities converted to part-time farming. Other farms were purchased by exurbanites and converted to recreational, hobby, or retirement farms. But in those agricultural areas of the state which were not easily accessible to expanding employment opportunities, farmers did not have the potion of securing supplemental income. The choices for many middle-aged farmers on small holdings were limited to selling out or struggling to survive—and as a result, pockets of rural poverty became evident in some areas of the state.

The cities, too, were affected by the shifting patterns of population. Two-parent middle class families with children made up most of the population spreading from the cities into suburban and nearby countryside areas. This left behind a population that was less able or less inclined to pursue the suburban lifestyle. They included the elderly, minority groups, and the socially and psychologically alienated. Certain older urban neighborhoods continued to attract transient, upwardly mobile, young adults who were seeking jobs, education, and social contacts. These population groups brought new social problems and increasing costs to the cities, and even more families left. Some persons felt trapped by their environments and unable to participate in the opportunities available to others; this brought waves of violence to American cities, including Minneapolis and St. Paul in the late 1960s.

The urban areas of Minnesota as well as the nation, have continued to grow at the expense of the rural areas through the 1970s as people moved to cities for economic reasons. In the 1980s most rural counties lost population, but in the 1990s the counties on the fringes of the suburbs have experienced a "rural renaissance" that brought returning population growth as people sought less crowded conditions outside the growing cities. These fringe counties will continue to post modest gains in the next decades.

Projections by Minnesota Planning

Nine counties, Anoka, Carver, Chisago, Dakota, Isanti, Scott, Sherburne, Washington and Wright, will account for 87 percent of the state's population growth during the 30-year period. Only a few fast-growing suburban counties are projected to show a gain in the number of children under age 15. While this has considerable implications for school enrollments, these trends could be moderated if women decide to have more children or if more young families move into the state.

At the same time, rural counties will continue to lose prime working-aged people (25-54 years of age) so that their net populations will decline over the same 30 year period. The area of the state most impacted will be the western counties. This will cause labor shortages in affected areas.

Minnesota's population age 65 and older is projected to grow 80 percent between 1995 and 2025. Much of that growth will occur in the suburbs of Minneapolis and St. Paul, where baby boomers have flocked and are now getting older. In many rural areas, the older population is projected to increase more slowly. "Middle-aged and older people tend to stay put as they age, and right now there aren't many middle-aged people living in some of our rural counties," said State Demographer Tom Gillaspy.

Minnesotans are healthier, wealthier and better educated than at the start of the decade, but the state's quality of life is under increasing pressure. That's the message from Minnesota Milestones 1998: Measures That Matter, a state assessment prepared by Minnesota Planning.

The report uses 70 progress indicators to determine whether the state has moved closer to 19 wide-ranging goals for Minnesota's people, economy, community life, government and environment. For example, progress toward the goal of health is gauged by such indicators as health insurance coverage, life expectancy, premature death and infant mortality.

The 1998 report shows that Minnesota has outpaced the nation in economic growth and standard of living, has improved academic achievement, multiplied outdoor recreational opportunities, improved the health of its people and expanded support for those in need.

However, on some goals the state has not fared as well in the 1990s. The environment, while generally of good quality, is under mounting pressure. More families are facing acute problems. The economies of some urban and rural areas remain under stress. Fewer people are exercising their right to vote.

A Sampling of Positive Trends That Show Progress and National Leadership:
- Minnesota's economy grew 22.5 percent from 1990 to 1996, adjusted for inflation, compared to 14.5 percent for the United States.
- Minnesota median family income has risen to 9 percent above the U.S. median.
- The number of counties losing population dropped from 49 in the 1980s to 19 counties thus far in the 1990s.
- Eighty-four percent of Minnesota adults are employed, the highest rate in the country.
- An estimated 28 percent of Minnesota adults had a four-year college degree in 1997, up from 22 percent in 1990.
- More households - 75 percent - own their own homes than in any other state.
- The teen pregnancy rate has fallen 17 percent since 1990.
- Infant mortality, adult smoking and urban air pollution are down.
- Nearly two-thirds of Minnesotans report doing volunteer work.
- More than 90 percent of citizens report feeling safe all or most of the time, and the rate of serious crime has declined slightly since 1992.
- Minnesotans increased recycling to 39 percent of all solid waste in 1996.

Minnesota's Indian Reservations

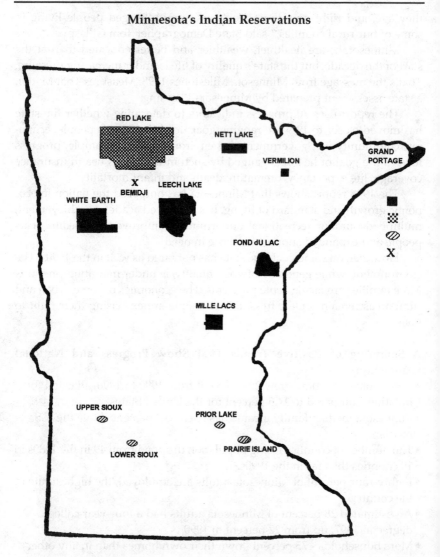

RED LAKE

NETT LAKE

VERMILION

GRAND PORTAGE

X
BEMIDJI   LEECH LAKE

WHITE EARTH

FOND dU LAC

X

MILLE LACS

UPPER SIOUX

PRIOR LAKE

LOWER SIOUX   PRAIRIE ISLAND

A Number of Indicators Show the Need to Reverse Negative Trends and Manage Growing Pressures:

- Stress on the state's lakes, rivers, forests and air quality is rising from strong economic growth, population growth and land development.
- Compared to 1990, Minnesotans are using more energy and water, driving more miles and generating more solid waste per person.
- Reports of runaway youths are up sharply and child abuse is up slightly.
- Juvenile apprehensions for serious crimes are above the national rate.

• Fewer than half of the state's African American, American Indian and Hispanic students graduate from high school on time.
• Twice as many Minnesotans are using homeless shelters as in 1990.
• Unemployment rates in northern Minnesota persist at nearly five percent age points above the Twin Cities area.

Minnesota Milestones was created in 1991 by Governor Arne H. Carlson as an early model for outcome measurement to hold government accountable for results. It is used by government agencies, businesses, non-profit organizations, local communities and individuals to understand where the state is headed. Some organizations use it for developing their own performance measurement systems.

Source: Atlas of Minnesota Resources & Settlement, 1980.
MN Planning website: www.mnplan.state.mn.us — Faces of the Future: Minnesota County Population Projection 1995-2025.
Minnesota Milestones 1998: Measures That Matter

Immigration

Immigration is accounting for about one-third of our population growth. The amount of people moving in from other states is slowing, but international in-migration is increasing. Listed in decreasing numbers are immigrant ethnic groups in Minnesota: Hispanics, Hmong, other Southeast Asians, Somalis, Russians, West Africans other East Africans, Yugoslavians, and Tibetans. The above groups are very mobile and difficult to count, so accurate numbers will not be available until after the 2000 census.

American Indians
Northwest Ordinance
Act of Congress, July 13, 1787
Section 14 Article III

"Religion, morality, and knowledge being necessary to good government and the happiness of mankind, schools and the means of education shall forever be encouraged. The utmost good faith shall always be observed towards the Indians; their lands and property shall never be taken from them without their consent; and in their property, rights and liberty they never shall be invaded or disturbed, unless in just and lawful wars authorized by Congress; but laws founded in justice and humanity shall, from time to time, be made for preventing wrongs being done to them, and for preserving peace and friendship with them."

The following Ojibway (or Chippewa) and Sioux (or Dakota) Indian reservations are located in the State of Minnesota: Fond du Lac, Grand Portage, Bois Fort (Nett Lake), Leech Lake, Mille Lacs, and White Earth.

72   The Minnesota Almanac

These six Ojibway reservations are organized and known as the Minnesota Chippewa Tribe. The following Sioux reservations are located in the southern portion of the state; Prairie Island, Lower Sioux, Upper Sioux, and some small scattered tracts of land incorporated into the city of Prior Lake which is the Shakopee Mdewakanton Sioux Reservation. This community built the Mystic Lake complex which is "the second most financially successful Indian casino operating in the United States with over 18,000 customers every day."

The only other Indian reservation is the Red Lake Chippewa Reservation in northern Minnesota. As the only "closed" reservation in the state, Red Lake maintains its own court system and police force. It also issues its own vehicle license plates.

American Indian Facts

There is no general legislative or judicial definition of "an Indian" that can be used to identify a person as an Indian. For census purposes, an Indian has been identified on a self-declaration basis. If an individual did not declare her race, the enumerator counted her as an Indian if she appeared to be a full-blooded American Indian, or if of mixed and white blood, was enrolled or was regarded as an Indian in the community in which she lived.

The Congress, on June 2, 1924, extended American citizenship to all Indians born in the territorial limits of the United States. They vote on the same basis as other citizens.

There is no automatic payment to a person because he or she is an Indian. Payments may be made to Indian tribes or individuals for losses which resulted from treaty violations or encroachments upon lands or interests reserved to the tribe by the government. Tribes or individuals may receive government checks for income from their land and resources, but only because the assets are held in trust by the Secretary of the Interior and payment for the use of the Indian resources has been collected by the federal government. Contrary to popular belief, Indians do not receive regular monthly payments from the government.

They pay local, state, and federal taxes the same as other citizens unless a treaty, agreement, or statute exempts them. Most tax exemptions which have been granted apply to lands held in trust for them and to income from such land.

Personal Statistics
Where to Apply for a Certified Copy of Birth or Death Records

Copies of records of births and deaths which occurred in any years after 1870 within the city limits of the cities of Duluth, Minneapolis, or St. Paul should be ordered from the City Health Department of that city. Copies of records of births and deaths which occurred elsewhere in Minnesota in any year may be ordered from the clerk of district court of the county where the event occurred. Checks are to be made payable to the Clerk of District Court of that county.

Copies of records of births and deaths which occurred anywhere within the state since 1900 may also be ordered from the Minnesota State Department of Health, Vital Statistics Department, 717 Delaware Street Southeast, Minneapolis, MN 55440 612-676-5120. The fee for a search of its files and a certified birth certificate is $14; a death certificate is $11. Checks are to be made payable to Treasurer, State of Minnesota, and mailed directly to the Minnesota Department of Health with your request for the record.

For birth records, the following information is required: name of child, date of birth, location of birth, and mother's and father's names.

For death records, the following information is required: name of decedent, date of death, and location of death.

For marriage records, the following information is required: name of each party, date of marriage, and place where application was made for the license. Records would be kept in the county seat where original application was made. Send requests to the Clerk of District Court of the county. The fee for a marriage certificate is $8.

Requirements of Applicants for a Marriage License

The statute requires that one of the parties of the contemplated marriage appear in person before the Director and make the application, and five days thereafter the license is issued; the marriage may take place immediately. The waiting period may be waived by a Judge of the District Court, but this is a matter between the applicants and the Judge, and when an order is issued waiving the waiting period, authority is given the Director to issue the license as soon as the application has been made and the marriage may take place immediately.

The man must be eighteen years of age and the woman eighteen. If either candidate is 16 or 17 years old, a judge may waive this requirement with the permission of the candidate's parents or guardians. A certified copy of the divorce decree is required in some, but not all, Minnesota counties if one or both of the candidates have been divorced.

The statute further provides that no nearer of kin than second cousins may marry, and "that neither of us has a spouse living; that neither of us is a mentally deficient person committed to the guardianship or conservationship of the commissioner of public welfare, and that one of the applicants is a man and the other is a woman."

Source: Application for Marriage License #045-7854 Rev. 2/93)

A medical certificate is not required. The marriage license fee is $70.

Passports

With a few exceptions, all U. S. citizens need a passport to depart from or enter the United States and to enter most foreign countries. The exceptions generally relate to travel between the United States and countries in North, South, and Central America and the Caribbean, except Cuba. However, some of these countries require a passport or other travel document for admission. For information, contact the embassy or consulate of the country to be visited. All persons are required to obtain individual passports in their own names. The following address will get you a recommended pamphlet "Know Before You Go" for Minnesotans planning to travel out of the country: Dept. of the Treasury, U. S. Customs Service, 331 2nd Av S, Suite 560, Minneapolis MN 55410 612-348-1690 www.customs.ustreas.gov

For your first passport, you must personally present a completed Passport Application (Form DSP-11) at any Federal or State court of record accepting applications; or at a post office designated by the Postmaster General.

If you have had a previous passport, you may be eligible to apply for a passport by mail.

Needed To Obtain a Passport:

- A properly completed passport application.
- A certified birth certificate must be presented if you were born in the United States.
- A Certificate of Naturalization shall be submitted if you claim citizenship by naturalization.
- A Certificate of Citizenship issued by the Immigration and Naturalization Service shall be submitted if citizenship was acquired through naturalization of a parent or parents. If such a certificate is not available, your parent's/parents' certificate(s) of naturalization and your foreign birth certificate and evidence of admission to the United States shall be submitted with the application.
- A Report of Birth Abroad of a Citizen of the United States of America, a Certificate of Birth, or a Certificate of Citizenship should be submitted if citizenship was acquired by birth abroad to a U. S. citizen parent or parents.
- Two identical unretouched photographs (2x2 in.) taken within the last 6 months.

Canada is taken from the Native American word "kanata" which means "settlement, village, home."

• Fees. The fee for a passport is $55 (plus $10 for execution of application for those 18 and older. Valid for 10 years. Under 18, cost is $30 plus $10 for execution of application. Valid for 5 years.)
• Proof of identification, such as a valid driver's license.

Entering Canada

Canadian Consulate General, 701 4th Av S, Minneapolis 612-333-4641; tourism/visa information 612-332-4314.

U.S. Consulate, 100 Wellington St., Ottawa, Ontario, Canada K1P5T1 613-238-5335

www.travelcanada.ca with links to all provinces.

Travel Manitoba 1-800-665-0040 ext. CU8 or 204-945-3777

Recorded messages for U.S. citizens 1-800-529-4410

Minnesotans can cross the U. S. - Canada border either way, usually without difficulty or delay. They do not require passports or visas but need to carry identification to establish citizenship such as a Birth Certificate and at least one ID card with a photo. Naturalized U. S. citizens should carry an original naturalization certificate. Alien permanent residents of the United States who are not American citizens must have their Alien Registration Receipt Card (U. S. Form I-151/Green Card). Rarely, Canadian immigration officials may prevent the entry of visitors who appear to pose a health risk, whom thy doubt will be able to support themselves and their dependents in Canada, whose willingness and means to return to the U.S. is in doubt, and those with a criminal record including driving while intoxicated.

Recreational Equipment

Visitors may bring into Canada sporting outfits and other equipment, for their own use, by declaring them at entry. These can include fishing tackle, portable boats, outboard motors, ice boats, motorized toboggans, snowmobiles, etc., equipment for camping, golf, tennis, and other games, radios and portable or table-model television sets used for the reception of sound broadcasting and television programs, musical instruments, typewriters and cameras (with a reasonable amount of film and flashbulbs) in their possession on arrival. Although not a requirement, it may facilitate entry if visitors have a list (in duplicate) of all durable items carried, with a description of each item, including serial numbers, where possible. All such articles must be identified and reported when leaving Canada.

While such items are normally admitted free of duty and tax, a deposit may be requested to ensure exportation. This deposit will be forwarded to the non-resident's home address by check on proof of exportation of the goods.

All pets may be brought into Canada if they are accompanied by their owners with a rabies vaccination certificate and a veterinarian signed description of the pet. Amounts of alcohol, tobacco, and certain types of firearms crossing the border either way is restricted. Minnesotans entering Canada from three locations, the Duluth airport, Grand Portage, and International Falls, may purchase spirits free of any federal and state taxes if they are taken directly across the border. Many visitors feel the savings, despite the duty and tax imposed by Canadian customs on anything over 1.14 liters of liquor, is still worthwhile.

Exemptions and Duty

American residents who spend more than 48 hours in Canada are allowed to take goods valued up to U.S. $400.00 back home duty free. You can use this exemption only once every 30 days. As of January 1998, there is no longer any duty charged on items made in Canada or the U.S. worth less than U.S. $1,400.

Car radar detectors are illegal in many provinces and can be confiscated whether in use or not.

Source: Passport and Canadian travel information taken from "Know Before You Go: Customs Regulations for U.S. Residents" and "Welcome To Our Home. Canada" The information given is of a general nature, any specific questions can be directed to the consulates and customs officials listed above.

"People are more aware of where their telephone lines are buried than where Indian burial sites are around here." -- Ev Sargent, White Earth Indian Reservation

"What a glorious new Scandinavia might not Minnesota come. The climate, the situation, the character of the scenery, agrees with our people better than that of any of the other American states, and none of them appear to me to have a greater or more beautiful future before them than Minnesota." --Frederica Bremer, author-pioneer (1853)

Chapter 5

Government

United States Senator
The U. S. Constitution provides: To qualify as senator a person must be thirty years old, a citizen of the United States nine years, and a resident of the state. Each state is allowed two senators.
Term: six years; Salary: $136,700*

Senator Paul David Wellstone
(Democratic-Farmer-Labor)
2550 University Ave. W, St. Paul 55114-1025 651-645-0323, 1-800-642-6041, fax 651-645-0704
105 Second Ave W, PO Box 281 Virginia 55792
218-741-1074, fax 218-741-8544
417 Litchfield Ave. SW, Willmar 56201
320-231-0001, fax 320-231-0006
136 Hart Senate Office Bldg., Washington, D. C. 20510-2303; phone 202-224-5641, fax 202-224-8438 TDD 202-224-4754
E-mail: senator@wellstone.senate.gov
Web site: http://www.senate.gov/~wellstone
Committees: Veterans Affairs; Foreign Relations;

Health, Education, Labor and Pension; Small Business; Select Committee on Indian Affairs.
Biography: Northfield. Born July 21, 1944, Washington, D. C. University of North Carolina (B. A. 1965, Ph.D. 1969, political science); faculty member, Carleton College (20 years); author; former director, Minnesota Community Energy Program; married, Sheila; children, David, Mark, Marcia.
Elected: 1990, 1996; Term expires: January, 2003
*Senator Wellstone has returned pay raises.

Senator Rod Grams
(Republican)
2013 Second Ave. North, Anoka 55303
612-427-5921, fax 612-427-8872, TTD/TTY 612-427-5902
257 Dirksen Senate Office Bldg., Washington, D. C. 20510; phone 202-224-3244, fax 202-228-0956, TTD/TTY 202-224-9522
E-mail: mail_grams@grams.senate.gov
Web site: http://www.senate.gov/~grams
Committees: Budget; Banking, Housing and Urban Affairs; Foreign Relations; Joint Economic Committee.
Biography: Ramsey. Born February 4, 1948, Princeton, MN. St. Francis High School; Anoka-Ramsey Junior College; Brown Institute in Minneapolis; Carroll College, Helena, Montana; U. S. Representative (1993-1994); married, Laurel; children, Michelle, Tammy, Rhiannon, Morgan.
Elected: 1994; Term Expires: January, 2001

United States Representative
The U. S. Constitution provides: To qualify as representative a person must be twenty-five years old, a citizen of the United States seven years, a resident of the state, and elected by the people.
Term: two years; Term expires: December, 1998
Salary: $133,600

Congressional District 1
Representative Gil Gutknecht (R)
Midway Office Plaza, 1530 Greenview Drive SW, Suite 108, Rochester 55902 507-252-9841; phone 1-800-862-8632 fax 507-252-9915
425 Cannon House Office Bldg., Washington, D.C. 20515 202-225-2472 fax 202-225-3246
E-mail: gil.gutknecht@mail.house.gov
Website: www.house.gov/gutknecht/
Committees: Budget; Agriculture; Science.
Biography: Rochester. Born March 20, 1951. Cedar Falls High School (1969), University of Northern Iowa (1973), Auction College (1978); Minnesota House of Representatives (1983-1994); married, Mary; children, Margie, Paul, and Emily.
Elected: 1994, 1996, 1998

Congressional District 2
Representative David Minge (DFL)
542 First St. S., PO Box 364, Montevideo 56265,
320-269-9311 1-800-453-9392
205 East Fourth St., Chaska 55318, 612-448-6567
fax 612-448-6930
P. O. Box 367, 938 Fourth Av., Windom 56101,
507-831-0115 fax 507-831-0118
1415 Longworth House Office Bldg.,
Washington, D.C. 20515; phone 202-225-2331 fax
202-226-0836
E-Mail: dminge@hr.house.gov
Website: www.house.gov/writerep
Committees: Agriculture, Science.
Biography: Montevideo, Born 1942, Clarkfield. St. Olaf College (BA 1964,
Phi Beta Kappa), University of Chicago (JD 1967); law professor, University
of Wyoming; private law practice; married, Karen Aaker Minge; sons, Erick
and Olaf.
Elected: 1992, 1994, 1996, 1998

Congressional District 3
Representative Jim Ramstad (R)
8120 Penn Av. S., Suite 152, Bloomington 55431,
612-881-4600 fax 612-881-1943
103 Cannon House Office Bldg., Washington,
D.C. 20515; phone   202-225-2871 fax 202-225-
6351
E-mail: mn03@mail.house.gov
Website: www.house.gov/ramstad/
Committee: Ways and Means.
Biography: Minnetonka. Born May 6, 1946;
University of Minnesota (BA 1968, Phi Beta
Kappa), George Washington University (JD,
1973, honors); 1st Lt., U.S.A.R. (1968-74); attorney; Minnesota Senate (1981-
90), assistant minority leader; vice-chair of Republican Freshman Caucus,
1991.
Elected: 1990, 1992, 1994, 1996, 1998

"There are not enough jails, not enough courts to enforce a law not supported by the people." --Hubert H. Humphrey, when Mayor of
Minneapolis

Congressional District 4
Representative Bruce F. Vento (DFL)
111 E Kellog Blvd, Suite 215, St. Paul 55101, 651-224-4503 fax 651-224-0575
2413 Rayburn House Office Building, Washington, D.C. 20515-2413, 202-225-6631 fax 202-225-1968
E-mail: vento@mail.house.gov
Website: www.house.gov/vento/
Committees: Banking and Financial Services; Resources.
Biography: St. Paul. Born October 7, 1940, St. Paul; Johnson HS (1958), Wisconsin State University (BS 1965, with honors); teacher, Minneapolis; Minnesota House of Representatives (1971-76); assistant majority leader (1974-76); sons, Michael, Peter, John.
Elected: 1976, 1978, 1980, 1982, 1984, 1986, 1988, 1990, 1992, 1994, 1996, 1998

Congressional District 5
Representative Martin Olav Sabo (DFL)
286 Commerce at the Crossings, 250 Second Av. S., Minneapolis 55401, 612-664-8000 fax 612-664-8004
2336 Rayburn House Office Bldg., Washington, D.C. 20515; phone 202-225-4755 fax 202-225-4886
E-mail: martin.sabo@mail.house.gov
Website: www.house.gov/sabo/
Committees: Appropriations; Standards of Official Conduct.
Biography: Minneapolis.   Born February 28, 1938; Augsburg College (BA 1959); Minnesota House of Representatives (1961-78); minority leader (1969-72), speaker of the house (1973-78); married, Sylvia; daughters, Karin, Julie.

Elected: 1978, 1980, 1982, 1984, 1986, 1988, 1990, 1992, 1994, 1996, 1998

Responding to a reporter who indicated he was not too smart following his election to the Minnesota Railroad and Warehouse Commission... "I'm no dumber than the people who voted for me." --Anonymous

"You can site a hazardous-waste dump easier than you can site an airport." --Ray Glumack, (former) Executive Director , Metropolitan Airports Commission

---

Congressional District 6
Representative William P. (Bill) Luther (DFL)
1811 Weir Dr., Suite 150, Woodbury 55125, Voice
and TTY 651-730-4949 fax 651-730-0507
117 Cannon House Office Bldg., Washington,
D.C. 20515; phone 202-225-2271 fax 202-225-3368
E-mail: bill.luther@mail.house.gov
Website: www.house.gov/luther/welcome.html
Committee: Commerce.
Biography: Stillwater. Born June 27, 1945, Fergus
Falls; University of Minnesota (BS 1967 and JD
1970, cum laude); Minnesota House of
Representatives (1975-76); Minnesota Senate
(1977-94), assistant majority leader (1983-94);
married, Darlene; children, Alex and Alicia.
Elected: 1994, 1996, 1998

Congressional District 7
Representative Collin C. Peterson (DFL)
714 Lake Av., Suite 107, Detroit Lakes 56501, 218-
847-5056 fax 218-847-5109
110 Second St. S., Suite 112, Waite Park 56387,
320-259-0559 fax 320-259-0413
MN Wheat Growers Bldg., 2603 Wheat Dr., Red
Lake Falls 56750, 218-253-4356 fax 218-253-4373
2159 Rayburn House Office Bldg., Washington,
D.C. 20515, phone 202-225-2165 fax 202-225-1593
E-mail: tocollin.peterson@mail.house.gov
Website: www.house.gov/collinpeterson/
Committees: Agriculture; Veterans' Affairs.
Biography: Detroit Lakes. Born June 29, 1944; Glyndon HS, Moorhead State
University (BA, business administration and accounting 1966); accountant;
Minnesota Senate (1976-86); divorced, sons: Sean, Jason, Elliot.
Elected: 1990, 1992, 1994, 1996, 1998

"Minnesota suffers from excellophobia, the fear of being excellent. We
think big to start with, but when we get right down to carrying out our
designs, we back off, as though it is somehow offensive to be too good."
--Curtis W. Johnson, Executive Director, Citizens League

"The climate here is worth 500 cops because of reduced crime in the
cold months." --Tony Bouza, while Minneapolis police chief

Congressional District 8
Representative James L. Oberstar (DFL)
Chisholm City Hall, 316 Lake St., Chisholm 55719, 218-254-5761.
13065 Orono Parkway, Elk River 55330, 612-241-0188 fax 612-241-0233
231 Federal Bldg., Duluth 55802, Voice and TDD 218-727-7474.
Brainerd City Hall, 591 Laurel St., Brainerd 56401, 218-828-4400 fax 218-828-1412
2366 Rayburn House Office Bldg., Washington, D.C. 20515, phone 202-225-6211 fax 202-225-0699
E-mail: oberstar@hr.house.gov
Website: www.house.gov/oberstar/welcome.html
Committees: Transportation and Infrastructure.
Biography: Chisholm. Born September 10, 1934. College of St. Thomas (BA French and Political Science, 1956), College of Europe, Belgium (MA, Comparative Government, 1957), additional studies Laval University, Quebec, and Georgetown University; civilian teacher of French, English and Creole in Haiti, U.S. Navy (1959-63), chief staff assistant to U.S. Rep. John Blatnik (1963-74), chair, Congressional Travel and Tourism Caucus and Conference of Great Lakes Congressmen; married, Jean Kurth (1993); children: Ted, Noelle, Ann-Therese, Monica, Charlie, Lindy.
Elected: 1974, 1976, 1978, 1980, 1982, 1984, 1986, 1988, 1990, 1992, 1994, 1996, 1998

Seth Huntington of Minneapolis designed the reverse side of the special Bicentennial half dollar, winning a prize of $5,000 and numismatic immortality.

Another Minnesotan, James Earle Fraser of Winona, designed a famous coin—the Inianhead and buffalo nickel. Issued in 1913, the five-cent piece bore the face of Chief Two Gun Whitecalf, who posed for the portrait.

1996 METROPOLITAN AREA CONGRESSIONAL DISTRICTS

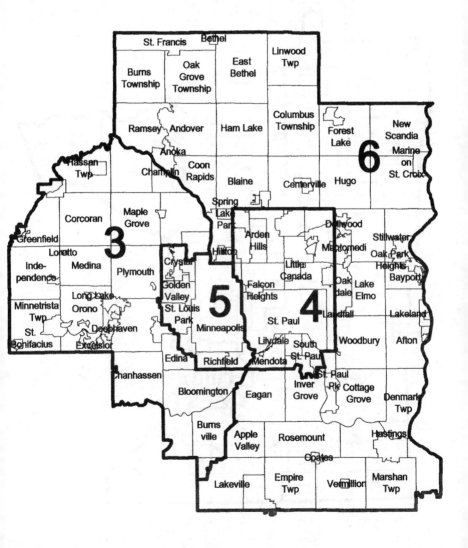

1996 MINNESOTA
CONGRESSIONAL DISTRICTS

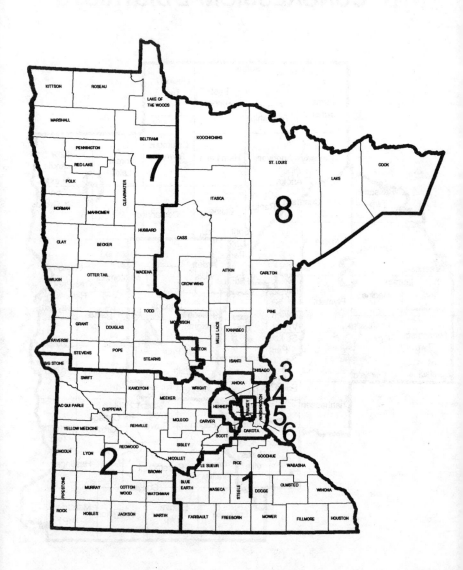

State Constitutional Officers

The Minnesota constitution defines three branches of state government: legislative, executive, and judicial. Article V establishes a six-member executive branch consisting of governor, lieutenant governor, secretary of state, auditor, treasurer, and attorney general. These constitutional officers are nominated with political party designation and elected by statewide ballot.

Office of the Governor

Jesse Ventura, 130 State Capitol, St. Paul 55155
651-296-3391, 1-800-657-3717, fax 651-296-2089
TDD 651-296-0075 or 1-800-657-3598
Constitution provides: To qualify as governor a person must be twenty-five years old, resident of the state one year, citizen of the United States, and elected by the people (Article V).
Term: four years; Salary: $114,506

Jesse Ventura
(Reform)

Biography: Maple Grove. Born James George Janos, July 15,1951, Minneapolis. Roosevelt High School, Minneapolis (1969), Navy SEAL (1969-1973), attended North Hennepin Community College. Professional wrestler (1973-1984); actor; talk show host; mayor of Brooklyn Center, MN, (1991-1995); elected Minnesota's 38th Governor in 1998 as the first Reform Party candidate ever to win a state governorship; married, Terry; children, Tyrel and Jade. Elected: 1998; Term Expires: 2003

The Chief Executive in Minnesota

The primary duties of the governor are to oversee all operations of state government and to take the lead in shaping public policy by proposing ideas to the legislature. The operation of government is carried out through more than 20 major departments whose heads are appointed by the governor. These department heads, along with the lieutenant governor, make up the governor's cabinet. The departments of revenue and finance are the governor's chief advisors on financial matters; the departments of health, human services and corrections advise the governor on various social policies; and the departments of pollution control, natural resources and waste management and others carry out the governor's environmental policies.

The governor appoints people to state boards and commissions, and appoints judges for all court systems when vacancies occur. The governor chairs the state executive council and the legislative advisory commission, both of which deal with extraordinary matters when the legislature is not in session. He also serves on the land exchange board and the state board of investments. As commander in chief of state military forces, the governor can dispatch the national guard for emergency duty.

The governor reviews all bills passed by the legislature and has the power to veto those of which he disapproves. On occasion, the governor may appear before the legislature. Because of the separation of powers required by Minnesota constitution, a governor may appear in legislative chambers only with the permission of the legislature. Only the governor has the power to call a special session of the legislature.

Office of the Lieutenant Governor
Mae A. Schunk, 130 State Capitol, St. Paul 55155
651-296-3391, 1-800-657-3717, fax 651-296-2089
TDD 651-296-0075 or 1-800-657-3598
e-mail: mae.schunk@state.mn.us
Constitution provides: That to qualify as lieutenant governor a person must be twenty-five years old, resident of the state one year, citizen of the United States, and elected by the people jointly with the governor by a single vote applying to both offices (Article V).
Term: four years; Statutory salary: $62,980

Mae A. Schunk
(Reform)
Biography: Inver Grove Heights. Born May 21, 1934, Chicago. Greenwood (WI) High School, 1952. University of Wisconsin-Eau Claire (B. S. elementary education); University of St. Thomas (M. A. gifted/talented education and educational leadership); classroom teacher; assistant principal; curriculum specialist; enrichment specialist at Phalen Lake Elementary (St. Paul); elected 45th Lieutenant Governor of Minnesota in 1998; married, William; one son.
Elected: 1998; Term expires: 2003

The Lieutenant Governor in Minnesota
The lieutenant governor serves as an extension of the governor and assists the governor in carrying out the functions of the executive branch.

She represents the governor and is prepared to act in the governor's place in the event of his absence or disability. The governor may delegate to the lieutenant governor any powers, duties, responsibilities, or functions as prescribed by law to be performed by the governor by filing a written order with the secretary of state.

Office of the Secretary of State
Mary Kiffmeyer, 180 State Office Bldg., St. Paul 55155 651-296-3266, fax 651-215-0682 E-mail: secretary.state@state.mn.us
www.sos.state.mn.us
Constitution provides: That the secretary of state is an officer in the executive department; to qualify as secretary of state a person must be a qualified voter, twenty-one years old, and elected by the people (Article V).
Term: four years; Statutory salary: $66,169

Mary Kiffmeyer
(Republican)
Biography: Big Lake. Born December 29, 1946. Pierz High School, St. Gabriel's School of Nursing, RN; co-owner of R.K. Anesthesia Services, PA; owner, Kiffmeyer Political Consulting Business. Married, Ralph; children, Christina, Patrick, James, and John.
Elected: 1998; Term expires: 2003

The Secretary of State in Minnesota
The secretary of state serves with the other constitutional officers on special state policy boards the Executive Council and the State Board of Investment. In order of gubernatorial succession the secretary of state follows the lieutenant governor, president of the senate, and speaker of the house.

Minnesota law provides that this office maintains many official records of the state, oversees the administration of elections in the state, charters and registers corporations, and maintains annual reports for foreign and domestic corporations. The office provides and administers a statewide database for voter registration, and administers a statewide database for the filing of liens under the uniform commercial code.

A statewide computerized network with county recorders is maintained so that the public may search Uniform Commercial Code records throughout the state from any filing office. Business information is also available for a fee at any county courthouse through this communications network.

As chair of the state canvassing board, the secretary of state compiles and certifies state election results. the office publishes the election law book, election judge training guides, official election results, Minnesota Legislative Manual and Minnesota Elected Officials booklet. As keeper of the great seal of the state of Minnesota, the secretary of state certifies the authenticity of official records, documents, proclamations, and executive orders of the governor, and acts of the legislature.

Divisions of the Office of the Secretary of State

Election Division--(651)296-2805--administers election responsibilities of the secretary of state and publishes election materials and information.
Business Services division--(651)296-9215--reviews, approves, and files articles of incorporation and amendments for all companies doing business in the state.

Uniform Commercial Code & Certification Division--(651)296-2434--maintains the financing records filed under the uniform commercial code.
Fiscal Operations Section--(651)297-3982--maintains a centralized system for handling all incoming mail, receipting and tracking all incoming revenue, and providing the general accounting functions for the office.
Human Resources Section--(651)296-0964--administers the office's personnel and labor relations program, and assists in the preparation of the biennial budget and annual spending plans.

Information Services Division--(651)297-2594--manages the computerized information management needs of the customer base of the Office of the Secretary of State.

Computer Services Section--(651)297-8760--provides computer programming support and manages all electronic data storage for information gathered by other divisions and sections of the Office of the Secretary of State.

Records Processing Section--(651)297-4802--is responsible for data entry from documents on businesses and processes voter registration cards for the 87 counties.

Public Information Section--(651)296-6243--is responsible for information made available to the public through the business information telephone lines and by direct access to the computer system.

Office of the State Auditor

Judith H. Dutcher, 525 Park St., #400, St. Paul 55103 (651)296-2551
Constitution provides: That the state auditor is an officer in the executive department. To qualify as state auditor a person must be a qualified voter, twenty-one years old, and elected by the people (Article V).
Term: four years; Statutory salary: $68,709

Judith H. Dutcher
(Republican)

Biography: Minnetonka. Born November 27, 1962, Alpena Michigan. Jefferson High School, Bloomington (1980); University of Minnesota (B. A. political science and English, 1984); University of Minnesota Law School (J. D., 1987); assistant city attorney, city of Minneapolis (1987-1988); Lang, Pauly & Gregerson, Ltd. (1988-1994). Married, two children.

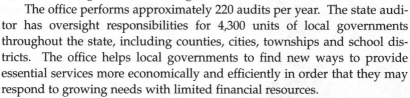

Elected: 1994, 1998; Term expires: 2003

The State Auditor in Minnesota

The Office of the State Auditor is a constitutional office which serves as a watchdog for Minnesota taxpayers and helps to assure integrity, accountability, and cost-effectiveness in government throughout the state.

The office performs approximately 220 audits per year. The state auditor has oversight responsibilities for 4,300 units of local governments throughout the state, including counties, cities, townships and school districts. The office helps local governments to find new ways to provide essential services more economically and efficiently in order that they may respond to growing needs with limited financial resources.

The state auditor serves on the State Executive Council, State board of Investment, Land Exchange Board, Public Employees Retirement Association Board, Minnesota Housing Finance Agency, Rural Finance Administration Board, and the Board of Government Innovation and Cooperation.

Divisions of the Office of the State Auditor

Audit Practice--(651)296-7003--conducts audits of local units of government to ensure the proper expenditure of public funds.

Legal Compliance--(651)297-3673--serves as a resource to review and assess whether local government expenditures have complied with Minnesota laws.

Special Investigations--(651)296-7003--determines whether or not crimes have been committed within local government.

Research and Information Division--(651)297-3682--collects, examines, and shares information on the financial condition of local governments and the financial trends affecting government at the state and local levels.

Police and Fire Relief Oversight Division--(651)296-5985--monitors financial and actuarial reporting for approximately 715 police and fire relief associations in Minnesota and ensures a financially stable retirement system for police and firefighters.

Office of the State Treasurer
Carol C. Johnson, 303 State Administration Bldg., St. Paul 55155 651-296-7091, fax 651-296-8615, E-mail: state.treasurer@state.mn.us, www.treasurer.state.mn.us/

Constitution provides: The state treasurer is an officer in the executive department; to qualify as state treasurer a person must be a qualified voter, twenty-one, and elected by the people (Article V).
Term: four years; Statutory salary: $62,980

Carol C. Johnson
(Democratic-Farmer-Labor)
Biography: Inver Grove Heights. Born Jauary 28, 1941, Jackson County, MN; Lakefield High School; Lutheran Bible Institute, Professional business Institute; dental assistant, licensed insurance agent, Chief Aide to State Treasurer; Bloomington City Council; Bloomington Planning Commission; Bloomington Crime Prevention Association; Bloomington Human Rights Commission, League of Minnesota Human Rights Commissions; Distinguished Leadership Award, National Associtation of Community Leadership (1988); children, Lisa and Scott; grandchildren, Taylor and Evan.
Elected: 1998; Term expires: 2003

The State Treasurer in Minnesota
    The state treasurer receives and issues receipts for all monies paid into the state treasury. The treasurer also transfers funds to pay warrants presented by banks. The treasurer transacts about $150 billion in receipts and disbursements annually. The treasurer's office controls funds held in state bank accounts so that the maximum daily amount can be invested by the State Board of Investment. Collateral accounts are monitored to assure the safety of state funds held by others.
    The treasurer's office maintains records, provides accounting services, and directs principal and interest payments on 150 separate bond accounts (authorizations and issues), and certificates of indebtedness. The state's vault is in the treasurer's office for safekeeping of assets.

The treasurer is a member of the Executive Council and the State Board of Investment.

Office of the Attorney General
Mike Hatch, 102 State Capitol, St. Paul 55155, (651)296-6196 or 1-800-657-3787 TTY: 651-297-7206 TTY: 1-800-366-4812
Constitution provides: That the attorney general is an officer in the executive department; to qualify as attorney general a person must be a qualified voter, twenty-one years old, and elected by the people (Articles V, VII).
Term: Four years; Statutory salary: $89,454

Mike Hatch
(Democratic-Farmer-Labor)

Biography: Burnsville. Born November 12, 1949, Des Moines, IA.   Duluth East High School (1966);   University of Minnesota-Duluth (Bachelor's Degree in political science with honors, 1970); University of Minnesota (J. D. 1973); private practice; Commissioner of Commerce (1983-1989); married, Patti, three daughters.
Elected: 1998; Term expires: 2003.

The Attorney General in Minnesota
The attorney general is the chief legal officer for the state and is the legal advisor to the governor and all of the constitutional officers.   The attorney general's duties stem from the state constitution, statutes and common law. He is the attorney for all state officers, departments, boards and commissions. He represents them in all matters related to their official duties. He interprets statutes and provides other legal services for local units of government. He enforces statutes and acts to protect the legal interests of Minnesotans. He also provides legal information and solves problems for citizens. The attorney general regularly initiates legislation to deal with public and legal policy concerns in Minnesota.

The attorney general appears for the state in all cases in the federal courts, in all civil cases in the district courts and, upon request of the governor or any county attorney, in any criminal case in the district courts.

The attorney general prosecutes all actions against persons who claim an interest adverse to the state, as well as claims of the state against the federal government. He may institute, conduct, and maintain preservation of order, and the protection of public rights. The attorney general is a member of the Executive Council, the State Board of Investment, the Pardons Board,

Governors Since Statehood

Name	P. O. address	Assumed Office
Henry H. Sibley	St. Paul	May 24, 1858
Alexander Ramsey	St. Paul	January 2, 1860
Henry A. Swift	St. Peter	July 10, 1863
Stephen Miller	Worthington	January 11, 1864
William R. Marshall	St. Anthony	January 8, 1866
Horace Austin	St. Peter	January 9, 1870
Cushman K. Davis	St. Paul	January 7, 1874
John S. Pillsbury	Minneapolis	January 7, 1876
Lucius F. Hubbard	Red Wing	January 10, 1882
A. R. McGill	St. Peter	January 5, 1887
William R. Merriam	St. Paul	January, 9, 1889
Knute Nelson	Alexandria	January 4, 1893
David M. Clough	Minneapolis	January 31, 1895
John Lind	New Ulm	January 2, 1899
Samuel R. VanSant	Winona	January 7, 1901
John A. Johnson	St. Peter	January 4, 1905
Adolph O. Eberhart	Mankato	September 21, 1909
Winfield S. Hammond	St. James	January 5, 1915
J. A. A. Burnquist	St. Paul	December 30, 1915
J. A. O. Preus	Minneapolis	January 5, 1921
Theodore Christianson	Dawson	January 6, 1925
Floyd B. Olson	Minneapolis	January 6, 1931
Hjalmar Petersen	Askov	August 24, 1936
Elmer A. Benson	Appleton	January 4, 1937
Harold E. Stassen	South St. Paul	January 2, 1939
Edward J. Thye	Northfield	April 27, 1943
Luther W. Youngdahl	Minneapolis	January 8, 1947
C. Elmer Anderson	Brainerd	September 27, 1951
Orville L. Freeman	Minneapolis	January 5, 1955
Elmer L. Anderson	St. Paul	January 2, 1961
Karl F. Rolvaag	St. Paul	March 25, 1963
Harold LeVander	South St. Paul	January 2, 1967
Wendell R. Anderson	St. Paul	January 4, 1971
Rudy Perpich	Hibbing	December 29, 1976
Al Quie	Dennison	January 4, 1979
Rudy Perpich	Hibbing	January 3, 1983
Arne Carlson	Shoreview	January 7, 1991
Jesse Ventura	Maple Grove	January 4, 1999

and the Land Exchange Board. The attorney general's office is comprised of litigation, collections, commerce, construction litigation, consumer, corrections, criminal, education, employment law, environmental protection, gambling, health, human rights, human services, labor, licensing, Medicaid fraud, natural resources, opinions, public finance, public safety, public utilities, residential utilities, tax litigation, telecommunication and energy, tort claims, and transportation.

Legislative Branch
Constitution Provides

To be elected a state senator or representative, a person must be a qualified voter, twenty-two years old, a resident of Minnesota for one year, and a resident of the legislative district for six months immediately preceding the election (article IV).

Term

Senator - four years; Representative - two years.

Compensation

$29,657 annually; round trips between home and state capital; per diem allowance for living expenses during session.

Membership and Apportionment

The state of Minnesota is divided into sixty-seven senate districts, each of which is divided into two of the one hundred and thirty-four house districts. Each senate district is entitled to elect one senate and each house district is entitled to elect one representative.

Organizations

Members of the Minnesota legislature are nominated and elected with party designation. At the November 8, 1994 general Election, Minnesota voters elected legislators affiliated with the state's two major political parties: Democratic-Farmers-Labor (DFL) and Independent-Republican (IR). The DFL caucus organized both houses of the legislature during the 1993 session, Presiding officers: Senate members elect the president of the senate from among their members. The president presides over the senate and shares with the speaker the chairmanship of the Legislative Coordinating Commission. The speaker of the house is both a voting member of the house and the presiding officer. The speaker also presides over joint sessions of the house and senate.

Committees

The speaker appoints members of the house to committees and names committee chairs. Nominated by the majority caucus, the speaker works closely with the house majority and becomes a leading spokesman for caucus policies.

In the senate, the chair of the committee on rules and administration, normally the leader of the majority group, has similar power. A senate committee names the committee members and chairs.

The committee system is a vital component of the legislative machinery. The volume of legislation pending before a single session is too great to permit all legislators to work closely with all proposals. Committees hear testimony from proponents and opponents of legislation before they make recommendations to the full legislature. A committee may decide the fate of any legislative proposal. After study, hearing, research, and deliberation, a committee may amend, recommend passage, re-refer to another committee, or table a bill.

The number of committees in each house and the number of members serving on each committees varies from session to session as state concerns and problems dictate. In addition to the standing committees which operate during each session, some committees continues to study specific problems during the legislative interim to report findings to the next legislative session.

Convening the Legislature

On the first day of a regular session both houses of the legislature convene at noon. The lieutenant governor, having already taken the oath of office, calls the senate to order and presides until a president has been elected and has taken the oath of office. The house is called to order by the secretary of state who presides over that body as its convening authority until a speaker is elected and has taken the oath of office. After convening, the oath of office is administered to all members of each house.

Special Sessions

The legislature may be called into special session at any time by the governor. Special sessions become necessary when legislative action is needed to meet emergencies or when legislative work is unfinished at the end of a regular session. The governor is the only official empowered to call a special session. The governor does not have the power to limit the length or scope of the session.

Functions and Powers

The principal legal task of the legislature is to make law by which public policy is established. Legislative activity affects a wide range of state programs and resources including agriculture, conservation, crime prevention, consumer protection, contracts, education, economic development, elections, environment, finance, forestry, health, highways, human rights, insurance, labor relations, natural resources, property, pollution control, recreation, safety, taxation, transportation, utilities, unemployment compensation, veterans' affairs, and worker's compensation.

Additional legislative functions include proposing amendments to the state constitution for approval by the electorate, electing regents of the University of Minnesota, confirming certain gubernatorial appointments (senate) and performing legislative oversight or review.

The legislature possesses a judicial function. It judges the election and qualifications of its members, may punish or expel members for contempt or disorderly behavior, and may impeach or remove from office members of the executive and judicial branches.

Each legislative body has a rules committee which directs the operating procedures of the legislature. The rules the two houses adopt, their joint rules, Minnesota Statutes, and the state constitution provide the guidelines under which the legislature conducts legislative business.

Regular Sessions

The Minnesota Legislature convenes in regular sessions each odd-numbered year on the first Tuesday after the first Monday in January. The 1972 flexible session amendment to Article IV of the constitution authorized the legislature to meet in regular session in both years of the biennium, for a total of 120 legislative days, providing that the legislature cannot meet after the first Monday following the third Saturday in May of any year.

The temporary adjournment between the session of the first year and the second year of the biennium is not a final adjournment, as the biennial session is considered to be one continuous session. For this reason the journal pages of both houses are numbered consecutively through both years and bills are numbered consecutively in order of introduction through both years.

Three tests cases were brought in district court for declaratory judgments to determine whether three bills passed on the last day of session in 1973 were valid enactments of law by the legislature. The district court ruled and the supreme court affirmed that the 1973 session and the 1974 session were technically one session separated by a temporary adjournment.

Bills which have not become law or been defeated by legislative action or vetoed by the end of the first half of the session are still available for possible action in the second half of the session. This means standing committees may hear such bills in the interim recess and make recommendations on their passage.

Passage of Laws

All revenue (tax measures) must originate in the house. All other matters may originate in either the house or the senate. There is no stated time schedule; speed is often related directly to the legislative support a proposal gathers.

Committee meetings are open to the public, and anyone wishing to speak for or against proposals being considered is given a chance to be heard. The house and senate index offices in the capitol keep a file of bills by number, and anyone may visit these offices to request and receive a copy of a bill without charge.

A Bill for an Act . . .

. . . is an idea for a new law or an idea to change or abolish an existing law. Ideas follow ten steps on their way to become Minnesota laws:

1. The Idea

Anyone can propose an idea for a bill - an individual, a consumer group, corporation, professional association, a governmental unit, the governor - but most frequently ideas come from members of the legislature.

2. Legal Form

The Office of the Revisor of Statutes and staff from other legislative offices work with legislators in putting the idea for a new law into proper legal form. The revisor also updates Minnesota Statutes to include all new laws after the legislative session.

3. The Authors

Each bill must have a legislator to introduce it in the legislature as chief author. The chief author's name appears on the bill with the bill's file number as identification while it moves through the legislative process. There may be up to four co-authors from the House and four from the Senate. Their names also appear on the bill.

4. Introduction

When introduced in the House in Representatives, a bill receives a House File number (H.F. 2312, for example); in the Senate, a Senate File number (S.F. 503, for example). These numbers indicate the bill's chronological order of introduction in each body.

5. Committee Consideration

Next the bill has its first reading (the Minnesota constitution requires three readings for all bills - on three separate days), and the presiding officer of the House or Senate refers it to an appropriate standing committee. All committee meetings are open to the public. A committee may:

- recommend passage of a bill in its original form.
- recommend passage after amendment by the committee.
- make no recommendation, in which case a bill may die when the session ends.

- refer a bill to another committee (one requiring funds to the appropriation or finance committee, for example).

After acting on a bill, the committee sends a report to the House or Senate, stating its actions and recommendations.

6. General Orders

After adoption of the committee report in the House and Senate, the bill has its second reading and goes onto General Orders of the Day. In Committee of the Whole legislators discuss bills on General Orders; they may debate the issues, adopt amendments, present arguments on the bills, and they may vote to recommend:

- that a bill "do pass".
- that a bill not pass.
- postponement.
- further committee action.

7. The Calendar

The calendar is a list of bills the Committee of the Whole recommends to pass. At this point:

- a bill has its third reading,
- amendments to the bill need the unanimous consent of the entire body.
- legislators vote on it for the final time.

By committee recommendation, bills of a noncontroversial nature can by-pass General Orders and go directly onto a "consent calendar," usually passing without debate.

Every bill requires a majority vote of the full membership of the House (68 votes) and Senate (34 votees) to pass.

Voice votes may be used in House and Senate votes until the bill is being voted on in final passage. That final vote and vote on any amendments are roll call or recorded votes.

8. Conference Committee

When the House and the Senate both pass the same version of a bill, that bill goes to the governor for his approval or disapproval. If the House and Senate do not agree, a conference committee, with members of both houses, meets to reach an agreement. If both bodies them pass the bill in compromise form, it goes to the governor.

9. Floor

The conference committee's compromise bill then goes back to the House and the Senate for another vote. If both bodies pass the bill in this form, it is sent to the governor for his or her approval or disapproval.

10. The Governor

When a bill arrives, the governor may:

- sign it and the bill becomes law.
- veto it (return it with a "veto message" stating objections) to the body where it originated within three days.

- pocket veto the bill (after final adjournment of the legislature).
- exercise the right to line veto portions of appropriations bills.
If the governor does not sign or veto a bill within three days after receiving it, while the legislature is in session, the bill becomes a law.
Source: MN Legislative Manual

Minnesota Senate 1999-2000

President of the Senate: Allan H. Spear.
Secretary of the Senate: Patrick E. Flahaven.
Senate Majority Leader: Roger Moe.
Senate Minority Leader: Dick Day.
Senate Information 651-296-0504/1-888-234-1112
E-mail: sen.firstname.lastname@senate.leg.state.mn.us
The Capitol street address is 75 Constitution Av. 55155-1606;
the State Office Building street address is 100 Constitution Av. 55155-1206.

Senator	Party	Dist.	Home Home Phone/Work Phone
Ellen R. Anderson	DFL	66	St. Paul 651-488-7403/651-296-5537
Mr. Tracy L. Beckman	DFL	26	Bricelyn 507-653-4426/651-296-5713
William V. Belanger, Jr.	R	41	Bloomington 612-881-4119/651-296-5975
Charles A. Berg	IND	13	Chokio 320-324-2506/651-296-5094
Linda Berglin	DFL	61	Minneapolis 612-822-0694/651-296-4261
Don Betzold	DFL	48	Fridley 612-571-0098/651-296-2556
Richard J. Cohen	DFL	64	St. Paul 651-699-4476/651-296-5931
Dick Day	R	28	Owatonna 507-451-0165/651-296-9457
Steve Dille	R	20	Dassel 320-398-6545/651-296-4131
Michelle L. Fischbach	R	14	Paynesville 320-243-7052/651-296-2084
Carol Flynn	DFL	62	Minneapolis 612-827-2016/651-296-4274
Leo T. Foley	DFL	49	Coon Rapids 612-757-8379/651-296-4154
Dennis R. Frederickson	R	23	New Ulm 507-359-9482/651-296-8138
Paula E. Hanson	DFL	50	Ham Lake 612-755-3533/651-296-3219
Linda I. Higgins	DFL	58	Minneapolis 612-522-2776/651-296-9246
John C. Hottinger	DFL	24	Mankato 517-388-4838/651-296-6153
Jerry R. Janezich	DFL	5	Chisholm 218-254-2246/651-296-8017
Dave Johnson	DFL	40	Bloomington 612-881-7544/651-296-9261
Dean E. Johnson	R	15	Willmar 320-235-6815/651-296-3826
Douglas J. Johnson	DFL	6	Tower 218-753-2321/651-296-8881
Janet B. Johnson	DFL	18	North Branch 651-674-8561/651-296-5419
Ember Reichgott Junge	DFL	46	New Hope 612-535-5065/651-296-2889
Steve Kelley	DFL	44	Hopkins 612-933-4107/651-297-8065
Randy C. Kelly	DFL	67	St. Paul 651-772-1114/651-296-5285
Sheila M. Kiscaden	R	30	Rochester 507-287-6845/651-296-4848

Dave Kleis	R	16	St. Cloud 320-253-9535/651-296-6455
David L. Knutson	R	36	Burnsville 612-431-6232/651-296-4120
Jane Krentz	DFL	51	May Township 651-430-2983/651-296-7061
Gary W. Laidig	R	56	Stillwater 651-439-2808/651-296-4351
Keith Langseth	DFL	9	Glyndon 218-498-2580/651-296-3205
Cal Larson	R	10	Fergus Falls 218-736-5548/651-296-5655
Arlene J. Lesewski	R	21	Marshall 507-532-3912/651-296-4125
Bob Lessard	DFL	3	International Falls 218-283-8555/296-4136
Warren Limmer	R	33	Maple Grove 612-493-9646/651-296-2159
Becky Lourey	DFL	8	Kerrick 218-496-5528/651-296-0293
John Marty	DFL	54	Roseville 651-633-8934/651-296-5645
James P. Metzen	DFL	39	South St. Paul 651-451-0174/651-296-4370
Roger D. Moe	DFL	2	Erskine 218-574-2216/651-296-2577
Steven Morse	DFL	32	Dakota 507-643-6226/651-296-5649
Steve Murphy	DFL	29	Red Wing 651-385-7649/651-296-4264
Thomas M. Neuville	R	25	Northfield 507-645-9058/651-296-1279
Steven G. Novak	DFL	52	New Brighton 651-636-7564/651-296-4334
Edward C. Oliver	R	43	Deephaven 612-474-1399/651-296-4837
Gen Olson	R	34	Minnetrista 612-472-3306/651-296-1282
Mark Ourada	R	19	Buffalo 612-682-5024/651-296-5981
Sandra L. Pappas	DFL	65	St. Paul 651-227-6032/651-296-1802
Pat Pariseau	R	37	Farmington 651-463-8496/651-296-5252
Pat Piper	DFL	27	Austin 507-433-7519/651-296-9248
Lawrence J. Pogemiller	DFL	59	Minneapolis 612-378-1006/651-296-7809
Leonard R. Price	DFL	57	Woodbury 651-735-0397/651-297-8060
Jane B. Ranum	DFL	63	Minneapolis 612-822-5081/651-297-8061
Martha R. Robertson	R	45	Minnetonka 612-545-3715/651-296-4314
Clair A. Robling	R	35	Prior Lake 612-492-2241/651-296-4123
Linda Runbeck	R	53	Circle Pines 612-784-8822/651-296-1253
Dallas C. Sams	DFL	11	Staples 218-894-3029/651-297-8063
Don Samuelson	DFL	12	Brainerd 218-829-4898/651-296-4875
Kenric J. Scheevel	R	31	Preston 507-937-3433/651-296-3903
Linda Scheid	DFL	47	Brooklyn Park 612-561-5872/651-296-8869
Sam G. Solon	DFL	7	Duluth 218-727-3997/651-296-4188
Allan H. Spear	DFL	60	Minneapolis 612-377-1735/651-296-4191
Dan Stevens	R	17	Mora 320-679-4085/651-296-8075
LeRoy A. Stumpf	DFL	1	Thief River Falls 218-681-3731/296-8660
David J. Ten Eyck	DFL	4	East Gull Lake 218-828-8874/651-296-4913
Roy Terwilliger	R	42	Edina 612-941-8258/651-296-6238
Jim Vickerman	DFL	22	Tracy 507-629-4878/651-296-5650
Deanna Wiener	DFL	38	Eagan 651-452-4980/651-297-8073
Charles W. Wiger	DFL	55	North St. Paul 651-770-0283/651-296-6820

Minnesota House of Representatives

Speaker of the House: Steve Sviggum.
Chief Clerk of the House: Edward A. Burdick.
House Majority Leader: Tim Pawlenty.
House Minority Leader: Thomas W. Pugh.
House Information 612-296-2146/1-800-657-3550.
E-mail: rep.firstname.lastname@house.leg.state.mn.us

1996 METRO AREA LEGISLATIVE DISTRICTS

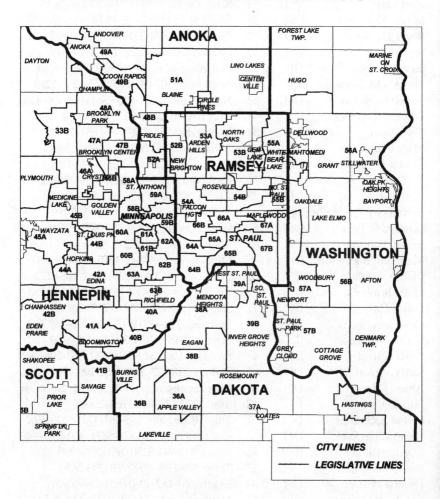

Representative	Party	Dist.	Home	Home Phone/Work Phone
Jim Abeler	R	49A	Anoka	612-245-3764/651-296-1729
Ron Abrams	R	45A	Minnetonka	612-546-5356/651-296-9934
Bruce Anderson	R	19B	Buffalo Township	612-682-1480/296-5063
Irv Anderson	DFL	3A	International Falls	218-283-2416/296-4936
Thomas Bakk	DFL	6A	Cook	218-666-5041/651-296-2190
Len Biernat	DFL	59A	Minneapolis	612-788-4923/651-296-4219
Dave Bishop	R	30B	Rochester	507-288-7733/651-296-0573
Lynda Boudreau	R	25B	Faribault	507-332-7760/651-296-8237
Mr. Fran Bradley	R	30A	Rochester	507-288-3439/651-296-9249
Sherry Broecker	R	53B	Vadnais Heights	651-429-8269/651-296-7153
Mark Buesgens	R	35B	Jordan	612-492-2992/651-296-1072
Lyndon Carlson	DFL	46B	Crystal	612-541-0525/651-296-4255
Phil Carruthers	DFL	47B	Brooklyn Center	612-535-5551/651-296-3709
George Cassell	R	10B	Alexandria	320-762-2471/651-296-4317
Satveer Chaudhary	DFL	52A	Fridley	612-571-0897/651-296-4331
James T. Clark	R	23A	Springfield	507-723-5565/651-296-9303
Karen Clark	DFL	61A	Minneapolis	612-722-7728/651-296-0294
Roxann Daggett	R	11A	Frazee	218-334-3871/651-296-4293
Gregory Davids	R	31B	Preston	507-765-2790/651-296-9278
Andy Dawkins	DFL	65A	St.Paul	612-224-6270/651-296-5158
Steve Dehler	R	14A	St. Joseph	320-363-8778/651-296-7808
Jerry Dempsey	R	29A	Hastings	651-437-5249/651-296-8635
Dan Dorman	R	27A	Albert Lea	507-377-9441/651-296-8216
John Dorn	DFL	24A	Mankato	507-388-3649/651-296-3248
Matt Entenza	DFL	64A	St. Paul	651-647-1425/651-296-8799
Ron Erhardt	R	42A	Edina	612-927-9437/651-296-4363
Sondra Erickson	R	17A	Princeton	612-389-4498/651-296-6746
Tim Finseth	R	1B	Angus	218-745-6200/651-296-9918
Betty Folliard	DFL	44A	Hopkins	612-933-4036/651-296-3964
Doug Fuller	R	4A	Bemidji	218-751-1055/651-296-5516
Chris Gerlach	R	36A	Apple Valley	612-432-4100/651-296-5506
Mark S. Gleason	DFL	63B	Richfield	612-861-4542/651-296-5375
Kevin Goodno	R	9A	Moorhead	218-236-9585/651-296-5515
Gregory Gray	DFL	58B	Minneapolis	612-377-5270/651-296-8659
Lee Greenfield	DFL	62A	Minneapolis	612-724-7549/651-296-0173
Mindy Greiling	DFL	54B	Roseville	651-490-0013/651-296-5387
Bob Gunther	R	26A	Fairmont	507-235-6154/651-296-3240
Barb Haake	R	52B	Mounds View	612-786-1022/651-296-0141
Bill Haas	R	48A	Champlin	612-421-6153/651-296-5513
Tom Hackbarth	R	50A	Cedar	612-753-3215/651-296-2439
Elaine Harder	R	22B	Jackson	507-847-3550/651-296-5373
Kris Hasskamp	DFL	12A	Crosby	218-546-7010/651-296-4333

Alice Hausman	DFL	66B	St. Paul 651-646-6220/651-296-3824
Bill Hilty	DFL	8B	Finlayson 320-233-6626/651-296-4308
Mary Liz Holberg	R	37B	Lakeville 612-435-8723/651-296-6926
Mark W. Holsten	R	56A	Stillwater 651-430-2538/651-296-3018
Larry Howes	R	4B	Hackensack 218-675-6587/651-296-2451
Thomas Huntley	DFL	6B	Duluth 218-724-6568/651-296-2228
Mike Jaros	DFL	7B	Duluth 218-727-0412/651-296-4246
Loren Geo Jennings	DFL	18B	Harris 651-674-7538/651-296-0518
Alice M. Johnson	DFL	48B	Spring Lake Park 612-786-2025/651-296-5510
Al Juhnke	DFL	15A	Willmar 320-235-4442/651-296-6206
Phyllis Kahn	DFL	59B	Minneapolis 612-378-2591/651-296-4257
Henry J. Kalis	DFL	26B	Walters 507-294-3147/651-296-4240
Margaret Anderson-Kelliher	DFL	60A	Minneapolis612-377-9836/651-296-0171
Tony Kielkucki	R	20B	Lester Prairie 320-395-2905/651-296-1534
Jim Knoblach	R	16B	St. Cloud 320-252-6179/651-296-6316
Luanne Koskinen	DFL	49B	Coon Rapids 612-427-1044/651-296-4231
Phil Krinkie	R	53A	Shoreview 651-481-8355/651-296-2907
Gary W. Kubly	DFL	15B	Granite Falls 320-564-4295/651-296-4346
William Kuisle	R	31A	Rochester 507-282-5714/651-296-4378
Peg Larsen	R	56B	Lakeland 651-436-5073/651-296-4244
Dan Larson	DFL	40A	Bloomington 612-854-8550/651-296-7158
Rob Leighton	DFL	27B	Austin 507-437-6972/651-296-4193
Ann Lenczewski	DFL	40B	Bloomington 612-881-8627/651-296-4218
Peggy Leppik	R	45B	Golden Valley 612-546-3328/651-296-7026
Bernie L. Lieder	DFL	2A	Crookston 218-281-1991/651-296-5091
Arlon Lindner	R	33A	Corcoran 612-420-3491/651-296-7806
Darlene Luther	DFL	47A	Brooklyn Park 612-560-7188/651-296-3751
Tim Mahoney	DFL	67A	St. Paul 651-776-3200/651-296-4277
Harry Mares	R	55A	White Bear Lake 651-429-7189/651-296-5363
Carlos Mariani	DFL	65B	St. Paul 651-224-6647/651-296-9714
Sharon Marko	DFL	57B	Newport 651-459-7757/651-296-3135
Betty McCollum	DFL	55B	North St. Paul 651-770-0025/651-296-1188
Dan McElroy	R	36B	Burnsville 612-890-2224/651-296-4212
Mary Jo McGuire	DFL	54A	Falcon Heights 651-644-1066/651-296-4342
Bob Milbert	DFL	39B	South St. Paul 651-451-6188/651-296-4192
Carol L. Molnau	R	35A	Chaska 612-448-3513/651-296-8872
Richard Mulder	R	21B	Ivanhoe 507-694-1539/651-296-4336
Joe Mullery	DFL	58A	Minneapolis 612-521-4921/651-296-4262
Willard Munger	DFL	7A	Duluth 218-624-4050/651-296-4282
Mary Murphy	DFL	8A	Hermantown 218-729-6399/651-296-2676
Robert Ness	R	20A	Dassel 320-275-3122/651-296-4344
Bud Nornes	R	10A	Fergus Falls 218-736-7777/651-296-4946

Name	Party	District	City Phone/State Phone
Mark Olson	R	19A	Big Lake 612-263-3500/651-296-4237
Joe Opatz	DFL	16A	St. Cloud 320-252-1138/651-296-6612
Myron Orfield	DFL	60B	Minneapolis 612-926-9205/651-296-9281
Mike Osskopp	R	29B	Lake City 651-345-5680/651-296-9236
Tom Osthoff	DFL	66A	St. Paul 651-489-9596/651-296-4224
Mary Ellen Otremba	DFL	11B	Long Prairie 320-732-6201/651-296-3201
Dennis Ozment	R	37A	Rosemount 651-423-1331/651-296-4306
Erik Paulsen	R	42B	Eden Prairie 612-949-8869/651-296-7449
Tim Pawlenty	R	38B	Eagan 651-688-6105/651-296-4128
Michael Paymar	DFL	64B	St. Paul 651-698-3084/651-296-4199
Gene Pelowski Jr.	DFL	32A	Winona 507-454-3282/651-296-8637
Doug Peterson	DFL	13B	Madison 320-769-2453/651-296-4228
Thomas W. Pugh	DFL	39A	South St. Paul 651-455-5016/651-296-6828
Ann H. Rest	DFL	46A	New Hope 612-545-8057/651-296-4176
Doug Reuter	R	28A	Owatonna 507-444-0466/651-296-5368
Jim Rhodes	R	44B	St. Louis Park 612-933-1325/651-296-9889
Michelle Rifenberg	R	32B	La Crescent 507-895-6390/651-296-1069
Jim Rostberg	R	18A	Isanti 612-444-9045/651-296-5364
Tom Rukavina	DFL	5A	Virginia 218-749-5690/651-296-0170
Leslie Shumacher	DFL	17B	Princeton 612-662-2075/651-296-5377
Alice Seagren	R	41A	Bloomington 612-835-6721/651-296-7803
Jim Seifert	R	57A	Woodbury 651-731-2331/651-296-7808
Marty Seifert	R	21A	Marshall 507-537-9794/651-296-5374
Rod Skoe	DFL	2B	Clearbrook 218-776-3420/651-296-4365
Wes Skoglund	DFL	62B	Minneapolis 612-721-1515/651-296-4330
Steve Smith	R	34A	Mound 612-472-7664/651-296-9188
Loren A. Solberg	DFL	3B	Bovey 218-245-1602/651-296-2365
Rich Stanek	R	33B	Maple Grove 612-420-4497/651-296-5502
Doug Stang	R	14B	Cold Spring 320-243-7033/651-296-4373
Julie Storm	R	24B	St. Peter 507-931-1850/651-296-7065
Steve Sviggum	R	28B	Kenyon 507-789-4673/651-296-2273
Howard Swenson	R	23B	Nicollet 507-246-5125/651-296-8634
Barbara Sykora	R	43B	Excelsior 612-474-3634/651-296-4315
Kathy Tingelstad	R	50B	Andover 612-421-2000/651-296-5369
David Tomassoni	DFL	5B	Chisholm 218-254-3430/651-296-0172
Steve Trimble	DFL	67B	St. Paul 651-7744-2096/651-296-4201
John Tuma	R	25A	Northfield 507-663-0013/651-296-4229
Jim Tunheim	DFL	1A	Kennedy 218-674-4480/651-296-9635
Henry Van Dellen	R	34B	Plymouth 612-553-9088/651-296-5511
Ray Vandeveer	R	51B	Forest Lake 651-464-7904/651-296-4124
Jean Wagenius	DFL	63A	Minneapolis 612-822-3347/651-296-4200
Linda Wejcman	DFL	61B	Minneapolis 612-827-6917/651-296-7152
Steve Wenzel	DFL	12B	Little Falls 320-632-6485/651-296-4247

Andrew Westerberg	R	51A	Blaine	612-757-5097/651-296-4226
Robert Westfall	R	9B	Rothsay	218-867-2621/651-296-6829
Torrey Westrom	R	13A	Elbow Lake	218-685-6266/651-296-4929
Tim Wilkin	R	38A	Eagan	651-994-8293/651-296-3533
Ted Winter	DFL	22A	Fulda	507-425-2664/651-296-5505
Ken Wolf	R	41B	Burnsville	612-894-3027/651-296-5185
Tom Workman	R	43A	Chanhassen	612-934-0343/651-296-5066

1996 MINNESOTA LEGISLATIVE DISTRICTS

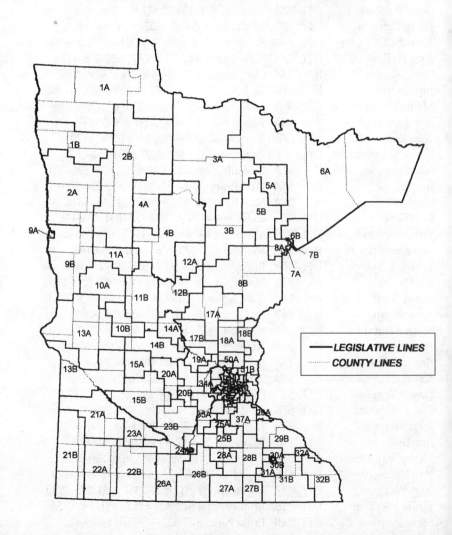

Chapter 6

Law, Courts and Crime

After Minnesota officially became a territory in March of 1849, a judicial system had to be established. The first term of the district court began on August 13, 1849 at the Stillwater Courthouse. Chief Justice Goodrich presided, assisted by Judge Cooper. The term of the court lasted one week, with 35 cases on the calendar. The large number of attorneys present, 19 the first day, was a result of the requirement, common in those days, that all attorneys be sworn in before each term of court.

One hundred and fifty years later, Minnesota's judicial system includes seven Supreme Court Justices, 16 Court of Appeals Judges, 254 District Court Judges and 22,000 attorneys. Last year, Minnesota's courts resolved nearly two million disputes. In 1998, Kathleen Blatz was appointed the first woman Chief Justice in the history of the state, and July 1, 1999, District Court Judge Leslie Metzen was elected the first woman Chair of the Conference of Chief Judges. Minnesota's Court of Appeals processes cases faster than any intermediate appellate court in the
nation and the state Supreme Court is also among the nation's most expeditious. Minnesota's trial courts are successfully implementing judicial innovations like restorative justice, community courts, drug court, teen court, family group conferencing and the opening of child protection hearings to the public.

The first jury trial held within the present boundaries of Minnesota occurred in 1840. The jury was impaneled at Marine-on-St. Croix, with Judge Brown presiding. At issue was plaintiff Philander Prescott's charge that the defendant, Charles Foote, had jumped Prescott's claim to a tract of land at the mouth of the St. Croix River. The jurors insisted on visiting the premises, and judge, jury and litigants started down the St. Croix in boats. At Lake St. Croix, the channel was so obstructed with ice that they had to continue by foot. After the premises were finally reached and viewed, the party started back, only to find that their boats had been burned. The entire return trip thus had to be made on foot. Even after all these exertions, the jury could still not agree. Justice Brown suggested a division of the land; the claimants agreed, and the case was settled.

The first criminal jury trial held in Minnesota also occurred in Stillwater, in 1847. At the time, Minnesota was not yet a territory, so the Wisconsin territorial Supreme Court Chief Justice Charles Dunn presided. An Indian Chief named Wyn ("Wind") was indicted for the murder of a whiskey seller in the area. Since there was no courthouse, the trial by jury took place in a general store. Ultimately, the jurors found the defendant not guilty.

Portions of the above text were excerpted from Sheran, Robert J. and Baland, Timothy J. "The Law, Courts and Lawyers in the Frontier Days of Minnesota: An Informal Legal History of the Years 1835-1865." 2 William Mitchell Law Review 1 (1976). www.mnbar.org

A Profile of the Judicial Branch

Introduction. For the average citizen the court system is probably the most remote and least understood branch of government. Though his attention may be drawn to the court proceedings on television, personal involvement with the courts is likely limited to a traffic violation, a divorce proceeding, or the settlement of a deceased relative's estate.

What may not be readily apparent to him is the tremendous variety and volume of business transacted in our court system. At one time or another almost every aspect of life is touched by the courts. Aside from the duty to try persons accused of criminal violations, the courts must decide civil disputes between private citizens ranging from the outline collection of an overdue charge account to the complex adjudication of an antitrust case involving many millions of dollars and months or even years of costly litigation. The courts must also act as referees between the citizens and their government by deciding what are the permissible limits of governmental power and the extent of an individual's rights and responsibilities.

A judicial system which strives for fairness and justice must be capable of first finding the truth and then deciding disputes under the rule of law. Thus, the courts are the places in which the facts are determined and the rules regulating conduct are interpreted and applied.

Constitution provides: "The judicial power of the state is vested in a supreme court of appeals, if established by the legislature, a district court and such other courts, judicial officers and commissioners with jurisdiction inferior to the district court as the legislature may establish" (Article VI, section I).

Where Does the "Law" Come From?

Judges rely on several sources of the law in making their decisions. First and foremost is the United States Constitution, as well as the Constitution of the State of Minnesota. Secondly, the courts rely on the statutes passed by the legislatures—the Minnesota legislature, the Congress, ordinances passed by city governments, and regulations made by any agencies of government, such as the Internal Revenue Service and others. Another source of the law is previous cases. Under our legal system, precedents are set by the decisions of high courts, such as the Supreme Court, and these are used as models in deciding later cases. All of the decisions of appeals courts may be found in legal books, and it is these cases that are generally referred to in briefs that lawyers write.

Source: The Minnesota Courts (Court Info. Office of the Minn. Supreme Court, 1979)

AN OVERVIEW OF THE JUDICIAL SYSTEM

CONCILIATION COURT
- Hearings in civil matters (amounts up to $7,500)

DISTRICT COURT
(10 Districts, 252 Judges)
- Trials in civil and criminal cases
- Appeals from conciliation court

COURT OF APPEALS
(16 Judges)
- Appeals from trial courts, administrative agencies,
Commissioner of Economic Security

MINNESOTA SUPREME COURT
(Seven Justices)
- Appeals from Minnesota Court of Appeals, trial courts, Tax Court,
Workers' Compensation Court of Appeals
- Oversees administration of state courts and the practice of law

Source: Minnesota Supreme Court, Court Information Office

How well the judicial branch performs the tasks we assign it depends a great deal on its organization and structure. In recent years many citizens, lawyers, legislators, and judges have complained that the judicial process has become so expensive and time-consuming that justice is denied to many citizens.

During the '90s the make-up of the court system has changed so that it more closely resembles the population as a whole by diversifying through gender, age and race.

1998 Minnesota Supreme Court.
Standing L to R: Justice Russell A. Anderson, Justice Edward C. Stringer,
Justice James H. Gilbert and Justice Joan Ericksen Lancaster.
Seated L to R: Justice Alan C. Page, Chief Justice Kathleen A. Blatz and
Justice Paul H. Anderson.

Supreme Court

Jurisdiction: The Minnesota constitution provides that the supreme
court shall have original jurisdiction in such remedial cases as are prescribed
by law, and appellate jurisdiction in all cases, but there shall be no trial by
jury in the supreme court.

Justices: The constitution provides for one chief justice and from six to
eight associate justices. Justices are elected by the people of the state to six-
year terms; vacancies are filled by governor's appointment. Justices are
elected without party designation. Candidates file for a specific judicial
office which is designated on the ballot by seat number.

Functions: The chief justice of the supreme court is the administrative
head of the judicial branch and supervises the work of all courts. A state
court administrator, supreme court administrator/clerk of the appellate
courts, and state law librarian are appointed by the court. The court has
power and duties to promote effective utilization of judicial officers and
conduct continuing study of the court system.

Court of Appeals

Jurisdiction: The court of appeals has jurisdiction of appeals from all final decisions of trial courts other than conciliation courts except for appeals in certain election contests, convictions of murder in the first degree, and from administrative agencies except appeals from the workers' compensation court of appeals and the tax court. All of these exceptions go directly to the supreme court.

Judges: The Court of Appeals has sixteen judges. Judges are elected by the voters to six-year terms; vacancies are filled by governor's appointment. Judges are elected without party designation and candidates file for a specific seat. All judges of the court are subject to statewide election, but one seat on the court is designated for each congressional district. One year's residence in the district is required for appointment or election to a congressional district seat. The governor designated one of the judges as chief judge, who, subject to the authority of the chief justice, has administrative authority for the court.

District Court

Jurisdiction: Minnesota has one district court, divided into ten judicial districts. The chief justice of the supreme court has the power to assign judges from one district to serve in another. The constitution provides that the district court has original jurisdiction as may be prescribed by law. In Hennepin and Ramsey counties the district courts have juvenile court jurisdiction.

Judges: Each district has three or more judges. Judges are elected by the voters of the district to six-year terms; vacancies are filled by governor's appointment. Judges are nominated and elected without party designation. Candidates file for a specific judgeship. (Judges of each district elect a chief judge and assistant chief judge to exercise general administrative authority over the courts of the district.)

County Court

Jurisdiction: The county court system combines probate, municipal, and justice courts into one court and in some instances combines two or more counties into a single county court district. Hennepin and Ramsey counties are excluded from the county court law.

The county court is divided into three divisions, civil and criminal, family court, and probate. The county court has civil jurisdiction where the amount in controversy does not exceed $7,500 exclusive of interest and costs. The county court has criminal jurisdiction over misdemeanor, petty misdemeanor, and preliminary hearing over which the county court has original exclusive jurisdiction and all cases arising out of or affecting the family relationship including civil commitments. The county court has concurrent jurisdiction with the district court over actions for divorce, separate maintenance, adoption, and change of name. The probate division hears all cases in law and in equity for the administration of estates of deceased persons and all guardianship and incompetency proceedings. In addition the county court may establish a traffic violations bureau and a conciliation court within the civil and criminal division.

Election: Judges are elected by the voters in their respective county court districts for six-year terms. Candidates file for a specific judgeship, and this information is stated on the ballot. Judges are nominated and elected without party designation.

Probate Court

Jurisdiction: Probate court jurisdiction is incorporated into the county court except in Hennepin and Ramsey counties which have a separate probate court with judges elected for six-year terms. The probate court has unlimited original jurisdiction in law and equity for the administration of the estates of deceased persons and all guardianship and incompetency proceedings.

Justices of the peace were abolished in Minnesota as of July, 1977.
Source: Minn. Legislative Manual, 1985-86 and 1995-96.

Supreme Court

Minnesota Judicial Center, 25 Constitution Avenue, St. Paul, MN 55155, 651-296-2581 fax 651-297-5636

Jurisdiction: The Minnesota constitution provides that the supreme court shall have original jurisdiction in such remedial cases as are prescribed by law, and appellate jurisdiction in all cases, but there shall be no trial by jury in the supreme court.

Justices: The constitution provides for one chief justice and from six to eight associate justices. Justices are elected by the people of the state to six-year terms; vacancies are filled by governor's appointment. Justices are elected without party designation. Candidates file for a specific judicial office which is designated on the ballot by seat number.

Functions: The chief justice of the supreme court is the administrative head of the judicial branch and supervises the work of all courts. A state court administrator, supreme court administrator/clerk of the appellate courts, and state law librarian are appointed by the court. The court has power and duties to promote effective utilization of judicial officers and conduct continuing study of the court system.

Salary: $118,542 chief justice; $107,765 associate justices.

Chief Justice Kathleen A. Blatz

Biography: Bloomington. Born July 22, 1954, Minneapolis. University of Notre Dame (B.A., 1976); University of Minnesota (M.S.W., 1978); University of Minnesota (J.D., 1984); state representative Minnesota House of Representatives, eight terms (1979-94); associate attorney Popham, Haik, Schnobrich & Kauffman, Ltd. (1984-88); assistant Hennepin County attorney (1992-93); Hennepin County trial court judge (1994-96). Appointed associate justice November 1, 1996; chief justice January 29, 1998.

Associate Justice Alan C. Page

Biography: Minneapolis. Born August 7, 1945, Canton, OH; University of Notre Dame, (B.A., 1967); University of Minnesota Law School (J.D., 1978); associate, Lindquist & Vennum (1979-84); special assistant attorney general, employment law division, (1985-87); assistant attorney general (1987-93); member, board of regents, University of Minnesota (1989-93); founder, Page Education Foundation (1988); married Diane Sims Page, four children; elected 1992.

Associate Justice Paul H. Anderson

Biography: Inver Grove Heights. Born May 14, 1943, Eden Prairie; Macalester College (B.A. 1965; cum laude with departmental honors in political science); University of Minnesota Law School, 1968; VISTA volunteer attorney (1968-69); special assistant attorney general (Criminal Division and Motor Vehicle Division of the Department of Public Safety, 1970; associate (1971-75) and partner (1975-92) LeVander, Gillen & Miller Law Offices, South St. Paul; Independent School District No. 199, board member and chair; member and chair of Minnesota Judicial Selection Commission (1991-92); appointed Chief Judge of the Minnesota Court of Appeals, September 1, 1992; married Jan Stadther, two children, Yovanna & Marina. Appointed July 1, 1994, elected 1996.

Associate Justice Edward C. Stringer

Biography: St. Paul. Born February 13, 1935, St. Paul. Amherst College (B.A., 1957, cum laude, American studies); University of Minnesota Law School, (J.D., 1960, cum laude, Order of the Coif); Stringer, Donnelly & Sharood (1960-69); Briggs & Morgan, partner and shareholder, manager, board of directors (1969-80); The Pillsbury Company, senior vice president and general counsel and chief administrative officer executive vice president, general counsel and chief administrative office (1983-89); secretary (1983-87); U.S. Department of Education, general counsel (1989-91); Office of the Governor, State of Minnesota, deputy chief of staff (1992); chief of staff (1992-94); married, Virginia L., four children, one stepson. Appointed September 1, 1994, elected 1996.

Associate Justice James H. Gilbert

Biography: Orono. Born March 11, 1947, Minneapolis. Meshbesher & Spence (1972-98), served as shareholder, vice president, secretary, director, head of the Business Law Department, managing partner (1984-92) and CEO (1996-97). Member and chair of Minnesota Judicial Merit Selection Commission (1992-1998). Married Mary Makepeace Gilbert; three daughters, Alison, Erica and Kristina. Appointed January 29, 1998.

Associate Justice Russell A. Anderson

Biography: Fertile. Born May 28, 1942, Bemidji. St. Olaf College (B.A., 1964); University of Minnesota Law School (J.D., 1968); George Washington University (LL.M., 1977). Judge Advocate General's Corps, U.S. Navy (1968-76); private practice (1976-1982); Beltrami county attorney (1978-82); district court judge (1982-98); chief judge (1993-95). Married Kristin Ostby Anderson; three children, Rebecca, John and Sarah. Appointed September 1, 1998.

Associate Justice Joan Ericksen Lancaster

Biography: Minneapolis. Born October 11, 1954, St. Paul. St. Olaf College (B.A., magna cum laude); Oxford University (Special Diploma in Social Studies); University of Minnesota Law School (1981). Private practice (1981-83), assistant United States attorney (civil, 1983-85; criminal 1985-93), shareholder Leonard, Street & Deinard (1993-1995), district court judge (1995-98). Married Peter Lancaster, two children, John and Claire. Appointed September 8, 1998.

Minnesota Court of Appeals

Minnesota Judicial Center, 25 Constitution Avenue, St. Paul, MN 55155, 651-297-1000

Salary: $106,619 chief judge; $101,543 judges.

Edward Toussaint, Chief Judge	Jack Davies
Harriet Lansing	Randolph W. Peterson
R. A. Randall	Roland C. Amundson
Gary L. Crippen	James C. Harten
Thomas Kalitowski	Bruce D. Willis
Robert H. Schumacher	Gordon W. Shumaker
Marianne D. Short	G. Barry Anderson
Roger M. Klaphake	Jill Flaskamp Halbrooks

District Court

Jurisdiction: Minnesota has one district court, divided into ten judicial districts. The chief justice of the supreme court has the power to assign judges from one district to serve in another. The constitution provides that the district court has original jurisdiction in civil and criminal cases and such appellate jurisdiction as may be prescribed by law. In Hennepin and Ramsey counties the district courts have juvenile court jurisdiction.

Judges: Each district has three or more judges. Judges are elected by the voters of the district to six-year terms; vacancies are filled by governor's appointment. Candidates file for a specific judgeship. Judges of each district elect a chief judge and assistant chief judge to exercise general administrative authority over the courts of the district. There are 243 judges presiding in the 10 district courts.

Salary: $100,086 chief judges; $95,320 judges.

Administrative Agencies

Board of Pardons

1450 Energy Park Dr., Suite 200, St. Paul 55108; 651-642-0284

Law provides: The board may grant pardons, commutations, and pardons extraordinary to applicants. The board consists of the governor, the chief justice of the supreme court, and the attorney general. It meets twice yearly and the meetings are open to the public. (Minnesota Statutes 638)

Board On Judicial Standards

2025 Centre Pointe Blvd., Suite 420, Mendota Heights 55120; 651-296-3999

Law Provides: The board of 10 lawyers, judges and public members investigate allegations of misconduct by Minnesota judges and recommends judicial discipline to the Supreme Court. (Minnesota Statutes 490.15)

Client Security Board

25 Constitution Ave., Suite 105, St. Paul, MN 55155, 651-296-3952; 1-800-657-3601

Law provides: that the board is established by the supreme court and funded by lawyers' registration fees. The board has four lawyer members, two none-lawyer members, and a chair. Members may serve two three-year terms. The board was established to reimburse clients who suffer a loss of money or other property from the intentional dishonesty of their attorney.

Commission On Judicial Selection

Office of the Governor, 130 State Capitol, St. Paul, MN 55155, 651-296-0013

The commission is established by the state legislature to recommend to the governor nominees for vacancies which occur in the district courts prior to a judge's elected term being completed. The nine at large and four members from each of the ten districts who meet when a vacancy occurs in their specific district. Judges who are appointed must run for election beyond one year of their swearing-in date.

Lawyers Professional Responsibility Board
Judicial Center, Suite105, 25 Constitution Ave., St. Paul 55155, 651-296-3952
Court rules provide: The board oversees the Office of the Lawyers Professional Responsibility, which investigates complaints of alleged misconduct and disability involving lawyers, and prosecutes disciplinary actions against lawyers.

Minnesota Sentencing Guidelines Committee
Meridian National Bank Bldg., 205 Aurora Ave., Suite 205, St. Paul 55103, 651-296-0144
Law provides: The office is responsible for the conduct of rulemaking and contested case hearings for state agencies pursuant to the Administrative Procedures Act, certain child support enforcement hearings, hearings for political subdivisions, and workers' compensation trials pursuant to the Workers' Compensation Law, issuance of reports and orders, and preparation of the record of the proceedings. (Minnesota Statutes 14 and 176)

State Board of Public Defense
625 4th Ave. S., #1425, Minneapolis 55145, 612-349-2565
Law provides: The seven member board approves and recommends a budget to the legislature and establishes procedures for distribution of state funding for the board, the office of state public defender, the judicial district public defenders, and the public defense corporations. The board approves standards for the offices of the state and district public defenders and for the conduct of all appointed counsel systems as established by the state public defender. The board also appoints the state public defender and all judicial district public defenders. (Minnesota Statutes 611.215)

State Public Defender
Law School, University of Minnesota, Minneapolis 55455, 651-625-5008
Law provides: that the state public defender has responsibility for criminal cases on appeal to the Minnesota supreme court and court of appeals; post-conviction proceedings in the district courts throughout the state and appeals there from; parole revocation proceedings for juveniles and adults; in conjunction with these responsibilities. (Minnesota Statutes, Section 611.215).

Tax Court
Judicial Center, 2nd Fl., 25 Constitution Ave., St. Paul 55155, 651-296-2806.

Law provides: The court is composed of three members, to which tax-payers may file appeals related to any state or local tax, except for special assessments. (Minnesota Statutes 271)

Workers' Compensation Court of Appeals
Judicial Center, 4th Fl., 25 Constitution Ave., St. Paul 55155-1500, 651-296-6526

Law provides: The five member court reviews all appealed questions of law and fact concerning workers compensation claims. (Minnesota Statutes 175A and 176)

Department of Corrections
1450 Energy Park Dr., Suite 200, St. Paul MN 55108-5219, 651-642-0200
www.corr.state.mn.us

The Department of Corrections ensures that the sanctions and services of the criminal justice system are designed and delivered to create a safer Minnesota. The department operates 10 correctional facilities, including seven for adults, two for juveniles and one for adults and juveniles. Department agents supervise more than 12,500 offenders on probation, supervised release and parole.

Sentencing reform has led to more violent, repeat offenders going to prison for longer periods, which has helped swell the prison population. The number of adults in Minnesota correctional facilities increased from 3,178 in January 1991, to 5,327 in January, 1998. $93.6 million has been spent in that time for expanded facilities. Other measures taken include a "boot-camp" type program in 1992, and the Sentencing to Service program where thousands of offenders do community service instead of being incarcerated.

Department of Public Safety
1000 NCL Tower, 445 Minnesota St., St. Paul, MN 55101, 651-296-6642
www.dps.state.mn.us

The Department is in charge of alcohol and gambling enforcement, the state fire marshal, driver and vehicle service, and pipeline safety. In addition, the State Patrol in 1977 responded to more than 22,000 traffic accidents, made about 227,000 arrests, assisted 148,000 motorists and had in excess of 754,000 contacts with motorists. Anne Beers was appointed as the first female chief in 1997, only the second woman nationwide to hold such a post.

Emergency management in the '90s took place during 12 declared disasters, including the Red River Valley Floods in 1977 and the March, 1998 tornado in the St. Peter area. The Bureau of Criminal Apprehension was instrumental in 1997 in organizing the Statewide Gang Strike Force, one of the first multi-jurisdictional efforts in the nation aimed at combating growing gang violence.

For full information, contact the Minnesota Crime Victims Reparations Board. 1-888-622-8799; 651-282-6256; TTY 651-205-4827
245 E 6th St Suite 705, St Paul MN 55101

If You Are the Victim of a Crime...
...you may be eligible for compensation from the State of Minnesota.

It is the purpose of the Minnesota Crime Victims Reparations Law to "reduce the economic impact of violent crime on victims and their families by providing direct financial assistance; and to hold criminal offenders accountable for the costs of crime through improved collections of restitution and civil awards."

Victims of a crime committed in Minnesota may file a reparations claim with the Board for reimbursement of medical costs, counseling, lost wages, and other crime related expenses. Loss of personal property is not covered. Family members of homicide victims may also be eligible for benefits including funeral expenses, loss of financial support, and counseling.

To be eligible, victims must have reported the crime to the police within 30 days, except for sexual assault or domestic child abuse; victims must cooperate FULLY with the police; and claim forms must be submitted within two years of the victim's injury or death, with the exception of domestic child abuse.

The reparations law is funded from state general revenues. There are 27 such programs in the United States; Minnesota was the 13th to pass this legislation in 1974. The Board in 1977 reimbursed more than $2.86 million in medical and counseling expenses, lost wages, funeral expenses, and loss of support. 35% of that total was paid to families of homicide victims. In the same year more than $200,000 was collected from offenders and others liable for injuries to crime victims.

In addition, the Department of Public Safety created the Crime Victim and Witness Advisory Council in 1985 to be a statewide advocate for all crime victims and witnesses. The Council provides training and technical assistance, information, and legislative and policy development on behalf of crime victims. The listed phone numbers will reach both the Board and the Council.

The Crime Victims Ombudsman can be called by victims of crime who believe their rights have been violated at 1-800-247-0390 or 651-282-6258.

Referring to a career criminal... "He's an excessive consumer of police services." --District Court Judge Neil A. Riley (retired)
Source: *Minnesotans Say the Darnedest Things*

Felony Case Process

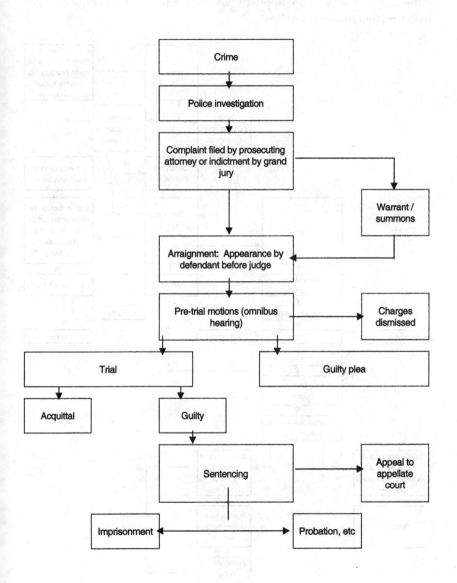

Source: "I'll See You In Court"
State Court Information Office

Juvenile Court Procedure

(Offender only - does not apply to cases of adoption, child abuse or other issues related to social services)

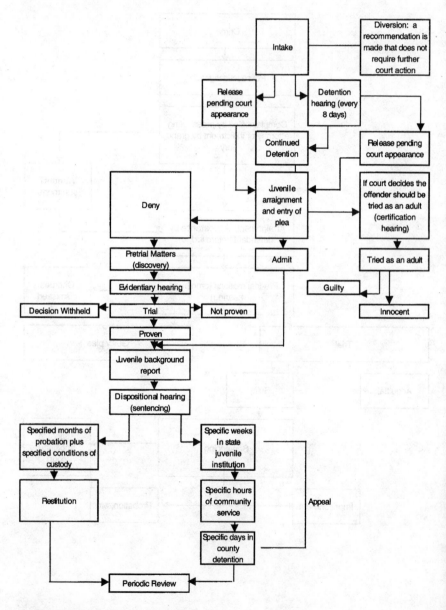

Source: "I'll See You In Court"
State Court Information Office

Narcotic Arrest Information

Narcotic arrest information for the state in 1998 involved 22,004 arrest situations with 18,774 males and 3,230 females arrested. Persons aged 18 comprise the greatest portion of the arrests (1,875), persons aged 17 were the next highest with 1,833 arrests. Race information reveals that 73 percent of the narcotics arrests were for persons of the white race. Compared with the 1997 figures for narcotic arrests (19,072), the 1998 amount indicates a 15 percent increase. Since 1989 there has been a 205 percent increase in the number of narcotic arrests within the state.

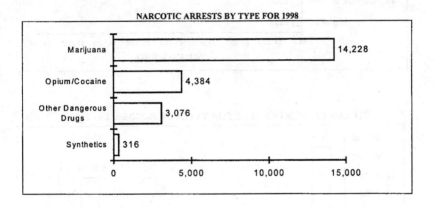

NARCOTIC ARRESTS BY TYPE FOR 1998

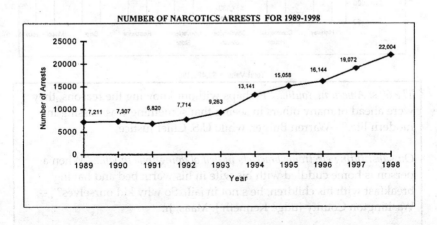

NUMBER OF NARCOTICS ARRESTS FOR 1989-1998

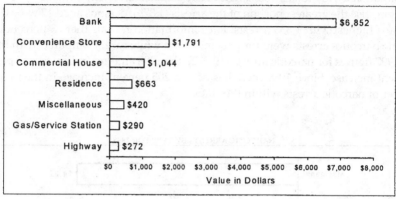

AVERAGE STOLEN PROPERTY LOSS PER ROBBERY TYPE FOR 1998

Type	Value
Bank	$6,852
Convenience Store	$1,791
Commercial House	$1,044
Residence	$663
Miscellaneous	$420
Gas/Service Station	$290
Highway	$272

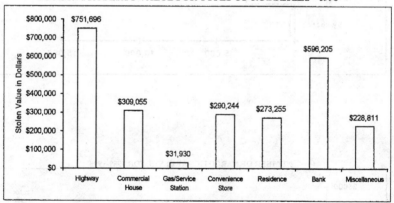

STOLEN PROPERTY VALUE FOR TYPES OF ROBBERIES - 1998

Type	Stolen Value in Dollars
Highway	$751,696
Commercial House	$309,055
Gas/Service Station	$31,930
Convenience Store	$290,244
Residence	$273,255
Bank	$596,205
Miscellaneous	$228,811

Total Value = $2,481,196

The 60's: American Youth... "Perhaps without knowing the reasons, they were ahead of many others in seeing that something was missing in modern life." --Warren Burger, while U.S. Chief Justice

On substituting electronic bracelets in lieu of doing time in jail... "When a person is home cuddled with his wife in his warm bed and having breakfast with his children, he's not in jail. So why kid ourselves?" -- Washington County Judge Kenneth J. Maas, Jr.

Source: *Minnesotans Say the Darnedest Things...*

Chapter 7

Politics

Cato, the great Roman political philosopher, couldn't have had Minnesota in mind in the year 194 B.C. when he said, "Some have said it is not the business of private men to meddle with government,—a bold and dishonest saying, which is fit to come from no mouth but that of a tyrant or a slave. To say that private men have nothing to do with government is to say private men have nothing to do with their own happiness or misery; that people ought not to concern themselves whether they be naked or clothed, fed or starved, deceived or instructed, protected or destroyed."

Certainly not many, if any, Minnesota pioneers had time to read and absorb Cato's wisdom. As private citizens however, concerned with their government, they shared the great Roman's political philosophy. Today this great state can look back on 123 years and challenge any of the 50 states in the Union to match its records of vigorous and socially productive politics.

Reform Mentality

Both the Republican and Democratic parties and later the Farmer-Labor and Democratic-Farmer-Labor parties (the Democrats and Farmer-Labor fused in 1944) have experienced control of the state's political offices, Not, however, without confrontations with a strong tradition of reformist protest. The political mix has produced many major protest groups—the Grange, the Greenbackers, the Anti-Monopolists, the Farmers' Alliance, the Populists, the Prohibitionists, and the Nonpartisan League. This "mix" provided the original impetus to, and eventual implementation into law of, the numerous reforms that the more conservative parties enacted when the time for their acceptance by the public arrived.

Minnesota's constitution is one of the oldest in the nation. In fundamental principle and framework it hasn't changed much since it was first ratified by Congress in 1858 when Minnesota joined the Union as the thirty-second state. While conservative in its governmental institutions, at times the people of Minnesota have often been liberal, occasionally radical, in their politics, as has been pointed out previously. It presents a study in contrasts equaled by few other states. Over the years the reform movements initiated have undergone frequent rebirths, all attention to the prolonged distress that came along with the transition from a simple frontier community to a complex, interdependent economy.   Agriculture—Minnesota's mainstay—was the dominant factor in the state's maturing. If farm prices were depressed—farmers took to the warpath. Populism, which represented the strong protests of Minnesota wheat farmers, grew strong and felt no decline until wheat prices began to climb after McKinley was elected President in 1896. However, profitable years were the exception and farmers eked out a living and some kept even with their debts. Farmers' woes were blamed on the railroads, the banks and terminal grain elevators. Not without some justification, as these firms did exact a disproportionate tribute for their services. The wheat farmers never diversifies, insisting on raising wheat exclusively, when the times called for diversification.

Many of the farmers were forced by poor wheat crop to adjust their operations to include livestock raising and dairying which eventually brought a modicum of success—never for long, however.

Third Parties

Third parties in Minnesota didn't always confine their interests to farmers' welfare exclusively.   The prohibition party in 1872 came out for women's suffrage. "Give women the vote," was their battle cry. In 1879 the Greenbackers advocated a graduated and equitable income tax and a vociferously worded platform plank for the outright end to employment of children under fourteen. In 1888 the Farm and Labor party made demands for the Australian ballot, the eight-hour work day, employer liability for workmen injured on the job and a sizable number of other reforms.

Thirty-four men have occupied the governor's chair since Henry Sibley, a Democrat, was the first to be elected in 1858. Twenty five of those were Republicans, four were Democrats, two were Farmer-Laborites and four belonged to the hyphenated Democratic-Farmer-Labor Party.

One fact stands out in going over the political annals of Minnesota—Minnesotans don't like to be bossed—they have inherited a stiff independence from sturdy forebears of various stocks. Attempts to crank up political machines have never worked out. Leaders with that thought in mind were quickly shunted aside. It became harder to build a working political organization at the turn of the century, all party lines were wiped out except for state and congressional offices. With civil service laws, much of the incentive for doing grass roots political word vanished—there were no more "spoils" to be dished out.

National Status

Minnesota has produced a number of public figures who attained national status. They were Ignatius Donnelly. John Lind, John A. Johnson,

Arthur C. Townley, Frank B. Kellogg. Floyd B. Olson. Harold Stassen. Hubert H. Humphrey. Eugene J. McCarthy, and Walter F. Mondale. While obscured by the exploits of his son, Charles Jr., Charles A. Lindbergh, Sr., as a Congressman played a significant role in the development of Minnesota and American political reforms.

Ignatius Donnelly was one of the most colorful personalities associated with third parties in Minnesota. He was brilliant. cantankerous and a man of wide-ranging interests in social and literary pursuits. He was often referred to as the "universal genius of the prairies." While he initially led the People's Party (commonly known as the "Populists") he was eventually elected lieutenant governor and to the U.S. House of Representatives as a Republican. In his later years Donnelly spent much of his time as an editor and his last public office was as a member of the legislature in 1897. His fame rests more on his literary achievements than on his political successes. He was too much of a "loner."

Turn-of-the-Century

John Lind was the state's outstanding Democrat at the turn of the century. He had served a term in Congress as a Republican but crossed swords with that party over the tariff and quit as a Representative. Lind was a deadly serious man and his dour dignity was taken by many as a sign of ability and rectitude. Scandinavian voters preferred stuffiness in their candidates and frowned on levity in a public man. Lind"s stern bearing accommodated them. Lind held the distinction of being the only one armed man ever to enter the United States Army. He was given a commission in the Minnesota National Guard when the Spanish-American was broke out. He served one term as governor, refusing to run a second time. Named personal representative by President Woodrow Wilson, he was assigned to go to Vera Crez, Mexico and observe the country's internal problems. He once said that Pancho villa was the hope of Mexico. It was not John Lind's recommendation that U.S. Army and never happened. Villa died in bed, unfettered and uncaught, years later.

Johnson

John A. Johnson, editor of the St. Peter Herald, the Democratic governor from 1904 to 1910, was the embodiment of the "rags to riches" tradition in a Horatio Alger era. Born on a farm near St. Peter, Johnson's early life was a struggle. His alcoholic father deserted the family, forcing his mother to take in washing. He was thirteen at the time and took various jobs to supplement the family's income. Successful as a journalist (he was elected president of the Minnesota newspaper Association at age 32) Johnson won his first political victory in 1898 when he was voted in as a senator in the state legislature. His political acumen and vigorous campaigning attracted the attention of state Democratic leaders and he became their gubernatorial candidate in 1904. A "reform" governor, he drew strength from Minnesota's liberal third parties. He was a devoted conservationist, went after the railroads for their abuses, protected the public against utility privileges and never failed to defend the exploited and downtrodden. He was responsible for enacted codes to regulate insurance companies. Inheritance taxes were tightened, railroads prohibited from giving free passes to office holders, and cities were empowered to own and operate public utilities.

Johnson's achievements eventually brought him a national reputation. He was the first Minnesotan to receive serious consideration for Presidency. To Democrats who thought William Jennings Bryan was too radical, Johnson seemed an attractive alternative. Several Johnson-for-President clubs sprang up around the country but by the time of the national Democratic convention Bryan had most of the delegates sewed up. Then in 1909, following abdominal surgery for a cancer, he died. A statue of John A. Johnson looks down on the capitol plaza in St. Paul. It is a fitting tribute to one of the best loved men in Minnesota history.

Nonpartisan League

Arthur C. Townley and his lieutenants descended on Minnesota in 1917 bringing the gospel of the Nonpartisan League. Specially trained organizers came in droves to canvas rural areas under the direction of local farmers' committees. Townley preached public ownership of certain essential farm services and facilities—flour mills, packing houses and grain terminal elevator. "Nonpartisan" in principle, the League was originally not another political party but was to work for its chosen candidates within the established parties. Nevertheless, despite its neutral sounding mane the Nonpartisan league played a big part in politics, first in its own way and finally as the "father" of the Farmer-Labor Party in 1920. Townely gained national prominence and certainly gave the solidly entrenched Republicans in Minnesota some uneasy moments.

Kellogg

Frank B. Kellogg was an outstanding Minnesota lawyer but not mush of a politician. Elected to the U.S. Senate in 1922, he lasted only one term. However, from the ashes of political defeat he went on to become ambassador to Great Britain, Secretary of state, a judge in the World Court, and gave his name to the Kellogg-Briand treaty which gave an illusive promise of lasting universal peace. He was a friendly, folksy person with an extremely nervous manner. His Washington nickname was "Nervous Nellie." He was awarded the Nobel Peace Prize in 1929.

First Third Party Governor

Floyd B. Olson first came into prominence in Minnesota when he led the old Nonpartisan League and labor unions to a victory that set the Farmer-Labor Party in a seat of political power for eight turbulent years. He was the first 3rd-party candidate to win the governorship of Minnesota. He was a political genius with a gift for taming the party's "wild men." He had a winning personality and a saving sense of humor. He headed a one-state party, but if he had lived, he certainly would have represented Minnesota in the U.S. Senate and been a national figure with Presidential possibilities. Olson was headed for Tom Schall's senate seat. They were destined, it was thought, to meet in head-on clash in 1936—both were loaded for bear. However, Schall, who was blind, was killed by an automobile just before Christmas in Washington, and the battle-of-the-century never came off. Olson died the following August in Rochester as the result of an inoperable cancer. To all intents and purposes the Farmer-Labor party died with him.

Stassen

In 1938 Harold Stassen was elected governor by the sweeping majority of almost 300,000 votes. Minnesota was ripe for a change when Harold E. Stassen, a young South St. Paul attorney, 31 years old, took over the governor's office. He went in with a program to reorganize state government, centralize responsibility and to install a civil service system. The legislature backed them. Although Stassen was a three term governor, he had served only four months of his third term when he resigned and accepted a commission in the U. S. Navy. After VJ day Stassen became a delegate to the United Nations' conference in San Francisco.

Harold E. Stassen made a greater impact on national affairs than any previous son of Minnesota. He was a contender for the Republican Presidential nomination making his first serious bid in 1948. He lost out to Tom Dewey and spent the next four years as president of the University of Pennsylvania. From the national platform such a position afforded, he prepared for the 1952 Republican convention. He couldn't contend with the power of war hero, Dwight D. Eisenhower, however, and his second bid for the nomination floundered when his own Minnesota delegation switched allegiance from him to Eisenhower. He finally lost his Minnesota image as the "Boy Wonder" but continued to serve in a cabinet-ranked -post in the Eisenhower administration. He never made a political comeback and the Administration never made the most of his talents.

DFL Created

Democrats merged with the Farmer-Labor party for the 1944 gubernatorial election. Their candidate, Byron Allen, lost to Republican Edward Thye by over 250,000 votes.

Orville Freeman, another Minnesotan in politics, was elected governor in 1954 and went on to become Secretary of Agriculture in John F. Kennedy's administration.

Humphrey

By far Minnesota's top vote-getter and most prominent political personality was Hubert H. Humphrey. In 1943 he was 32 years old and lost his first bid for political office when he was defeated in the Minneapolis mayoralty race. Undaunted, he came back and ran again in 1945 and was elected. An effective administrator, he proved to be a strong mayor and cracked down on vice, gambling and corruption. He used citizens' volunteer committees to study and make recommendations on housing, veterans' affairs, fair employment practices and law enforcement. He was aided in the latter by an outstanding police chief, Ed Ryan. In 1948 he took on Joe Ball for the United States Senate as the first Democratic-Farmer-Labor candidate and won after a masterful campaign. He received nearly 60 percent of the Minnesota vote.

Humphrey first captured national attention while mayor of Minneapolis when he established the city's Fair Employment Practices Commission. At the 1948 Democratic convention he was accorded national acclaim for his civil rights stand.

"To those who say that this civil rights program is an infringement on states' rights," Humphrey asserted, "I say this. The time has arrived in America for the Democratic party to get out of the shadow of states' rights and to walk forthrightly into the bright sunshine of human rights."

After Humphrey was elected to a second term in the Senate in 1954 he became a powerful and controversial member of the Senate's inner council. His legislative activities and interests were wide-ranging—foreign policy, social welfare, agriculture and government reform.

His nimble mind and articulate tongue, his tremendous energy and unbridled ambition coupled with great personal warmth made him a formidable candidate in any political campaign and a continuing force on the national political scene. He proved this contention in 1964 when he was elected Vice President and again in 1968 when as the Democratic nominee for President he lost in a whisker finish to Richard M. Nixon. He almost swung it but the specter of riots at the Chicago Democratic convention and the lackluster support he received from other highly ranked Democrats put him in the loser's corner for the second time in his political career. He was reelected to the Senate and died in 1978.

Following Humphrey's death, his wife, Muriel, was appointed to fill his vacancy. Later, Governor Wendell Anderson appointed himself as U.S. Senator.

Republican Return to Power— and Independence

Also in 1978, a Republican Governor, Al Quie, was elected. His party hadn't had a governor since Elmer Anderson in 1956.

After Nixon's Watergate Scandal, Minnesota Republicans added "Independent" to their party name to distance themselves from that political fiasco. They dropped "independent" from their name in 1998.

Political Highlights

Other Minnesotans who have etched their names on the political wall are Eugene McCarthy, member of the House of Representatives and U.S. Senate. a Presidential contender in 1968, and an independent candidate for president in several states in 1976.

Walter F. Mondale, former Minnesota Attorney General and Minnesota's senior senator since 1966—he was appointed to the Senate in 1964 and elected in 1966 and 1972. With a distinguished liberal record he was encouraged to enter the presidential race for 1976, but "after considerable thought and study" declined to run in order to devote full time to his Senate responsibilities. But when Jimmy Carter Offered him the opportunity to be his Vice Presidential running mate he accepted. Following his Vice Presidency, he was Ambassador to Japan under President Clinton.

In 1990, candidate Jon Grunseth withdrew from the governor's race amidst allegations of scandal. Arne Carlson, who had lost to Grunseth in the primary again entered the gubernatorial race with only days until the election and won.

The 1998 race for governor was unique in several ways. Three former governors had a son who ran for the office in 1998; Walter Mondale (Ted), Hubert Humphrey (Skip), and Orville Freeman (Mike).

Republican candidate, Skip Humphrey, insisted that reform Party candidate, Jesse Ventura, be included in all debates. Democrat candidate and St. Paul mayor, Norm Coleman said, "A vote for Ventura is a vote for Humphrey."

Apparently, each major party candidate felt that a vote for Ventura would take away from their opponent. But when late polls showed the three candidates in almost a dead heat, citizens knew their votes would count and the rest is history. Jesse Ventura is the first Reform Party candidate ever elected to the governorship of a state.

Minnesotan Frank Billings Kellogg was appointed Secretary of State on March 5, 1915 by Calvin Coolidge.

"Minneapolis is not mentioned in the Bible." -- Lawrence Cohen, Former Mayor of St. Paul on the difference between Minneapolis and St. Paul. Source: *Minnesotans Say the Darnedest Things*

Abbreviations of Political Parties

A	Alliance	IR	Independent-Republican
AM	American Party of MN	L	Libertarian
Am	American	M-Pop	Midroad-Populist
C	Communist	N	National
D	Democratic	Peo	People's
DFL	Democratic-Farmer-Labor	Pro	Prohibition
D-Peo	Democratic People's	Prog	Progressive
FL	Farmer-Labor	Ref	Reform
G	Greenback	R	Republican
GPM	Green Party Member	S	Socialist
HG	Honest Government 87	SA	Savings Account
I	Independent	SD	Socialist Democrat
In	Industrial	SIn	Socialist Industrial
InG	Industrial Government	SL	Socialist Labor
InGSL	Industrial Government (Socialist Labor)	SW	Socialist Workers
		TPC	The People's Champion
InL	Industrial Labor	WC	Workers Communist
IProg	Independent Progressive	WL	Workers League

Minnesota Vote For Governor Since 1857

1857
Henry H. Sibley (D)   17,790
Alexander Ramsey (R)   17,550
                        35,340

1859
Alexander Ramsey (R)   21,335
George L. Becker (D)   17,582
                        38,917

1861
Alexander Ramsey (R)   16,274
E.O. Hamblin (D)   10,448
                    26,722

1963
Stephen Miller (R)   19,628
Henry T. Welles (D)   12,739
                       32,367

1865
William R. Marshall (R)   17,318
Henry M. Rice (D)   13,842
                     31,160

1867
William R. Marshall (R)   34,874
Charles E. Flandrau (D)   29,502
                           64,376

1869
Horace Austin (R)   27,348
George L. Otis (D)   25,401
Daniel Cobb (Pro)   1,764
                     54,513

1871
Horace Austin (R)   46,950
Winthrop Young (D)   30.376
Samuel Mayall (Pro)   846
                       78,172

1873
Cushman K. Davis (R)   40,741
Ara Barton (D)   35,245
Samuel Mayall (Pro)   1,036
                       77,022

1875		
John S. Pillsbury (R)	45,073	
D. L. Buell (D)	35,275	
R. F. Humiston (Pro)	1,669	
	84,017	
1877		
John S. Pillsbury (R)	57,071	
William L. Banning (D)	39,147	
William Meigher (G)	2,396	
Austin Willey (Pro)	1,421	
	100,035	
1879		
John S. Pillsbury	57,524	
Edmund Rice (D)	41,524	
W. W. Satterlee (Pro)	2,868	
William Meigher (G)	4,264	
	106,180	
1881		
Lucius F. Hubbard (R)	65,025	
Richard W. Johnson (D)	37,168	
C. H. Roberts (G)	2,676	
Isaac C. Stearns (Pro)	708	
	105,577	
1883		
Lucius F. Hubbard (R)	72,462	
Adolph Biermann (D)	58,251	
Charles E. Holt (Pro)	4,924	
	135,637	
1886		
Andrew R. McGill (R)	107,064	
Albert A Ames (D)	104,464	
James E. Childs (Pro)	9,030	
	220,558	
1888		
William R. Merriam (R)	1324,355	
Eugene M. Wilson (D)	110,251	
Hugh Harrison (Pro)	17,026	
	261,632	
1890		
William R. Merriam (R)	88,111	
Thomas Wilson (D)	85,844	
Sidney M. Owen (A)	58,513	
James P. Pinkham (Pro)	8,424	

	240,892
1892	
Knute Nelson (R)	109,220
Daniel W. Lawler (D)	94,600
Ignatius Donnelly (Pro)	39,863
William J. Dean (Pro)	12,239
	255,021
1894	
Knute Nelson (R)	147,043
George L. Becker (D)	53,584
Sidney M. Owen (Peo)	87,890
Hans S. Hilleboe (Pro)	6,832
	296,249
1896	
David M. Clough (R)	165,806
John Lind (D-Peo)	162,254
William J. Dean (Pro)	5,154
A. A. Ames (I)	2,890
W. B. Hammond (S)	1,125
	337,229
1898	
William H. Eustis (R)	111,796
John Lind (D-Peo)	131,980
George W. Higgins (Pro)	5,299
William B. Hammond (SL)	1,685
Lionel C. Long (M-Pop)	1,802
	252,562
1900	
Samuel R. VanSant (R)	153,905
John Lind (D-Pro)	150,651
Bernt B. Haugan (Pro)	5,430
Sylvester M. Fairchild (M-Pop)	663
Thomas H. Lucas (SD)	3,546
Edward Kriz (SL)	886
	314,181
1902	
Samuel R. Van Sant (R)	155,849
Leonard A. Rosing (D)	99,362
Thomas J. Meighen (Peo)	4,821
Charles Scanlon (Pro)	5,765
Jay E. Nash	2,521
Thomas Van Lear (SL)	2,570
	270,888

1904

Robert C. Dunn (R)	140,130
John A. Johnson (D)	149,992
Charles W. Dorsett (pro)	7,577
Jay E. Nash (PO)	5,910
A. W. M. Anderson (SL)	2,293
	303,802

1906

A. L. Cole (R)	96,162
John A. Johnson (D)	168,480
Charles W. Dorsett (Pro)	7,223
O. E. Loftus (PO)	4,646
	276,511

1908

Jacob F. Jacobson (R)	147,997
John A. Johnson (D)	175,136
George D. Haggard (Pro)	7,024
Beecher Moore (PO)	6,515
William W. Allen (I)	593
	337,266

1910

Adolph O. Eberhart (R)	164,185
James Gray (D)	103,779
J. F. Heiberg (Pro)	8,960
George E. Barrett (PO)	11,173
C. W. Brandborg (SL)	6,510
	295,627

1912

Adolph O. Eberhart (R)	129,688
Peter M. Ringdalh (D)	99,659
David Morgan (PO)	25,769
Engebret E. Lobeck (Pro)	29,876
Paul V. Collins (Prog)	33,455
	318,447

1914

William E. Lee (R)	143,730
Winfield S. Hammond (D)	156,304
Thomas J. Lewis (S)	17,225
Willis G. Calderwood (Pro)	18,582
Hugh T. Halbert (Prog)	3,553
Herbert Johnson (InL)	3,861
	343,255

1916

J. A. A. Burnquist (R)	245,841
Thomas P. Dwyer (D)	93,112
J. O. Bentall (S)	26,306
Thomas J. Anderson (pro)	19,884
John P. Johnson (InL)	5,476
	390,619

1918

J. A. A. Burnquist (R)	166,515
Fred E. Wheaton (D)	76,793
L. P. Berot (S)	7,794
Olaf O. Stageberg (N)	6,648
David H. Evans (FL)	111,948
	369,698

1920

Jacob A. O. Preus (R)	415,805
Henrik Shipstead (I)	281,402
L. C. Hodgson (D)	81,293
Peter J. Sampson (S)	5,124
	782,624

1922

Jacob A. O. Preus (R)	309,756
Magnus Johnson (FL)	295,479
Edward Indrehus (D)	79,903
	685,138

1924

Theodore Christianson (R)	406,692
Floyd B. Olson (FL)	366,029
Carlos Avery (D)	49,353
Oscar Anderson (SIn)	3,876
Michael Ferch (IProg)	9,052
	835,002

1926

Theodore Christianson (R)	395,779
Magnus Johnson (FL)	266,845
Alfred Jaques (D)	38,008
	700,632

1928   1,257,491
Theodore Christianson (R)   549,857   1942
Ernest Lundeen (FL)   227,193   Harold E. Stassen (R)   409,800
Andrew Nelson (D)   213,734   Hjalmer Petersen (FL)   299,917
Harris A. Brandborg (In)   3,279   John D. Sullivan (D)   75,151
J. O. Bentall (WC)   5,760   Martin Mackie (C)   5,082
                             999,823   Harris A. Brandborg (InG)   4,278
                                                                     794,228
1930
Raymond P. Chase (R)   289,528   1944
Floyd B. Olson (FL)   473,154   Edward J. Thye (R)   701,785
Edward Indrehus (D)   29,109   Byron G. Allen (DFL)   430,132
Karl Reeve (C)   5,594   Gerald M. York (InG)   7,151
                             797,385   1,138,468
1932   1946
Earle Brown (R)   334,081   Luther W. Youngdahl (R)   519,067
Floyd B. Olson (FL)   522,438   Harold H. Barker (DFL)   349,565
John E. Regan (D)   169,859   Rudolph Gustafson (InGSL)   11,716
William Schneiderman (C)   4,807   880,348
John P. Johnson (In)   1,824   1948
                           1,033,009   Luther W. Youngdahl (R)   643,572
                                        Charles L. Halsted (DFL)   545,766
1934   Rudolph Gustafson (InGSL)   6,598
Floyd B. Olson (FL)   468,812   Orville E. Olson (Prog)   14,950
Martin A. Nelson (R)   369,359   1,210,886
John E. Regan (D)   176,928   1950
Samuel K. Davis (C)   4,334   Luther W. Youngdahl (R)   635,800
Arthur C. Townley (I)   4,454   Harry H. Peterson (DFL)   400,637
                           1,050,887   Vernon G. Campbell (InGSL)   10,195
1936   1,046,632
Elmer A. Benson (FL)   680,342
Martin A. Nelson (R)   421,841   1952
Earl Stewart (In)   7,996   C. Elmer Anderson (R)   785,125
                           1,120,179   Orville L. Freeman (DFL)   624,480
                                        Martin Fredrickson (Prog)   5,227
1938   Eldrid H. Bauers (InGSL)   4,037
Elmer A. Benson (FL)   387,263   1,418,869
Harold E. Stassen (R)   678,839
Thomas Gallagher (D)   65,875   1954
John William Castle (In)   899   C. Elmer Anderson (R)   538,865
                           1,132,876   Orville L. Freeman (DFL)   607,099
                                        Ross Schelin (InG)   5,453
1940   1,151,417
Harold E. Stassen (R)   654,686
Hjalmer Petersen(FL)   459,609
Edward Murphy (D)   140,021
John William Castle (In)   3,175

1956

Orville L. Freeman (DFL)	731,180
Anchor Nelson (R)	685,196
Rudolph Gustafson (InG)	<u>5,785</u>
	1,422,161

1958

Orville L. Freeman (DFL)	658,326
George MacKinnon (R)	490,731
Arne Anderson (InG)	<u>10,858</u>
	1,159,915

1960

Orville L. Freeman (DFL)	760,934
Elmer L, Andersen (R)	783,818
Rudolph Gustafson (InG)	<u>5,518</u>
	1,550,265

1962

Karl F. Rolvaag (DFL)	
Elmer L. Andersen (R)	619,751
William Braatz (InG)	<u>7,234</u>
	1,246,827

1966

Karl R. Rolvaag (DFL)	607,043
Harold LeVander (R)	680,593
Kenneth Sachs (InG)	<u>6,522</u>
	1,295,058

1970

Wendell R. Anderson (DFL)	737,921
Douglas M. Head (R)	621,780
Karl Heck (InG)	4,781
Jack Kirkham (write-in votes)	<u>961</u>
	1,365,443

1974

Wendell R. Anderson (DFL)	786,787
John W. Johnson (R)	367,722
Jane VanDeusen (SW)	8,232
Erwin Marquit (C)	3,570
Harry M. Pool (Am)	20,454
Richard R. Kleinow (L)	2,115
Genevieve Gunderson (InG)	2,720
James G. Miles (I)	<u>60,150</u>
	1,252,750

1978

Al Quie (IR)	830,019
Rudy Perpich (DFL)	718,244
Richard Pedersen (AM)	21,244
Jill Lakowske (SW)	6,287
Tom McDonald (HG)	4,254
Robin E. Miller (L)	3, 689
Edwin C. Pommerening (SA)	<u>2,043</u>
	1,585,594

1982

Rudy Perpich (DFL)	1,049,104
Wheelock Whitney (IR)	711,796
Kathy Wheeler (SW)	10,332
Tom McDonald (HG)	7,984
Franklin Haws (L)	<u>6,323</u>
	1,785,539

1986

Rudy Perpich (DFL)	790,138
Cal Ludeman (IR)	606,755
W. Z. "Bill" Brust (WL)	4,208
Tom Jaax (SW)	3,151
Joseph A. Rohner III (L)	<u>3,852</u>
	1,408,104

1990

Arne Carlson (IR)	895,988
Rudy Perpich (DFL)	836,218
Heart Warrior Chosa (ER)	21,139
Ross S. Culverhouse (GRP)	17,176
Wendy Lyons (SW)	6,701
Jon Grunseth (IR)	<u>10,941</u>
	1,788,163

1994

Arne Carlson (IR)	1,094,165
John Marty (DFL)	589,344
Will Shetterly (GRP)	20,785
Jon Hillson (SWP)	3,022
Eric Olson (LIB)	15,467
Leslie Davis (NRA)	<u>4,611</u>
	1,727,394

1998	
Jesse Ventura (Ref)	773,403
Norm Coleman (R)	716,880
Hubert (Skip) Humphrey (DFL)	587,060
Frank Germann (LIB)	1,932
Chris Wright (Grass Roots Party)	1,727
Thomas Fiske (SW)	787
Fancy Ray McCloney (TPC)	919
Ken Pentel (GPM)	7,034
	2,105,984

Elections

Where do elections begin?

Constitutions and charters provide the basic framework for elections by defining the qualification for voting and the offices to be elected and the qualifications and terms for each.

Statutes, ordinances, and rules spell out details for administering these elections.

In Minnesota, statutes defines political parties and regulate the conduct of primary elections for partisan and nonpartisan offices.

Who is eligible to vote?

Any citizen of the United States who will be eighteen years old by the date of the next election, who has resided in Minnesota for twenty days, and who is registered to vote is eligible.

Who is not eligible to vote?

The following are not eligible to vote in Minnesota: anyone who is convicted of treason or a felony and not yet restored to civil rights; anyone under guardianship over her/his person; anyone adjudicated mentally incompetent; anyone not properly registered.

Registration

All voters are required to register before they can vote. Registration in areas where preregistration is allowed will be accepted at all times except 20 days before an election. In areas that do not have preregistration, registration will only be accepted on election day. You may also register as you vote on election day at all polling places in Minnesota. Should you decide to register on election day you will be asked to prove your residency by producing a valid drivers license, a non-qualification card, or have a registered voter of your precinct swear to your residency. Your registration is permanent once you register, provided you vote at least once every four years. You may register by mail by requesting a registration form from your county auditor. You must cancel any previous registration if you change your address and register in a new community.

If you will be away from your voting residence on election day, you may still participate in the election process by casting an absentee ballot. Your county auditor will provide you with a form to apply for an absentee ballot. Application must be made not more than 45 days nor less than one day before an election.

Members of the armed forces may request ballots from their county auditor. All servicemen who are not already registered will be required to register before they will be allowed to vote. When a serviceman applies for an absentee ballot. He may return the registration form in the same envelope as his absentee ballot.

Parties, Caucuses and Elections

What is a political party?

Minnesota law defines "political party" as an organization presenting candidates in the last preceding general election one or more of whom has been voted for in each county in the state and shall have received not less than five percent of the total vote cast for all candidates in such election.

Who joins a party?

Since Minnesota voters do not register with a declaration of political party, they may choose to affiliate with a party in a variety of ways, including attending its precinct caucus and declaring intent to support that party's candidates in the next election.

What is a precinct caucus?

The legal process of the general election year beings with political party precinct caucuses the fourth Tuesday evening in February.

A precinct is an election area which has one polling place. Each of the 4,200 precincts will elect delegates to represent their residents directly and indirectly at county, district, state, and national conventions.

What is a primary election?

In Minnesota, the purpose of a primary election is to nominate political party candidates to the general election ballot and to reduce the number of candidates for a nonpartisan office to no more than twice the number to be elected in the general election.

Partisan candidates, therefore, run among themselves in such an election, and the choice of candidates is within each party. Voters must vote in the primary election of only one political party, and no write-in votes are allowed.

How are other parties' candidates nominated?

Other parties, groups, or individuals may place a candidate on the general election ballot by nominating petitions signed by the required number of voters in the district to be represented by that office.
What is a general election?

All candidates nominated either in the primary election or by petition appear on the ballot at the general election on the first Tuesday after the first Monday in November, every even-numbered year. A candidate who did not win nomination in the primary election may not run in the general election. In a general election, voters may write in names of persons for whom they wish to vote which do not appear on the ballot.

U of M Alumni Prominent in Law, Politics and Public Affairs

- Janet Benshoof, president, Center for Reproductive Law and Policy.
- Warren Burger (deceased), retired U.S. Supreme Court chief justice.
- Donald Fraser, former Minneapolis mayor.
- Orville Freeman, former Minnesota governor and agriculture commissioner in President Kennedy's administration.
- Rod Grams, U.S. Senator (R-Minnesota).
- Hubert Humphrey (deceased), former vice president of U.S. Walter Mondale, former vice president of U.S.
- Norman Ornstein, political consultant, TV analyst.
- Jim Ramstad, U.S. House of Representatives (R-Minnesota).
- Patricia Schroeder, U.S. House of Representatives (D-Colorado).
- Harold Stassen, former Minnesota governor and assistant to President Eisenhower on disarmament.
- Carl Stokes (deceased) former Cleveland mayor, first black mayor of major U.S. city.
- Y.S. Tsiang (M.S. 1940, Ph.D. 1942), Secretary General to President of Taiwan, regarded as architect of Taiwanese Economic Miracle.
- Roy Wilkins (deceased), civil rights leader, former president of the NAACP.

"Being in politics is like being a football coach. You have to be smart enough to understand the game and dumb enough to believe it's important." --Eugene J. McCarthy

"How could I win (the mayoral election), with the Star and Tribune throwing insinuendoes at me?" --Charles Stenvig

"Under current law, it is a crime for a citizen to lie to a public official, but not for a government official to lie to the people." --Donald M. Fraser, Former Mayor of Minneapolis

The Volstead Act

Andrew Volstead, a back-bencher from Goodhue County in Minnesota lent his name to the act passed by Congress which led to the Eighteenth Amendment, prohibiting the manufacture, sale and transportation of alcoholic beverages. In 1919, this ushered in an era of illegal moonshining, bootlegging and the organization of the worst and most powerful criminal elements in the nation's history.

The "noble experiment" failed in its aim to stamp out the hated saloons and legislate morality. Though federal agents raided stills and speakeasies, the demon rum continued to be made and sold everywhere—Minnesota 13 from Stearns county was sought after as a quality product—and arrests in Minneapolis for drunkenness rose from 2456 in 1902 to 7294 in 1925.

All this came to an end when the Twenty-First Amendment was repealed in 1933.

In a memo on how to campaign... "Walk behind your car; don't ride. Rush over to shake some hand at the curb (with spouse). Stop every hundred yards and conspicuously wipe the sweat off your brow." --Senator Rudy Boschwitz

Asked by Augsburg faculty wives if he was a booze-hound and woman-chaser, the guest speaker replied... "Ah, yes, Mrs. Knutson, that's a cross I have to bear." --Floyd B. Olson, Governor

Seeking self-improvement... "I'm into the CCC thing--confidence, communication, and ...trust." --Senator Clarence Purfeerst, Faribault

"The St. Paul Pioneer Press contains 200 lies to the square inch. Read it for an hour and it makes you want to get up and steal something. The devil himself might well paper the walls of hell with its editorials." --Ignatius Donnelly, legislator, author, gadfly

On being a member of the minority party... "You like to swear after the day is over." --William Schreiber, House Minority Leader

"The impersonal hand of government can never replace the helping hand of a neighbor." --Hubert H. Humphrey

"Above all, Hubert (Humphrey) was a man with a good heart... he taught us how to hope, how to win and how to lose. He taught us how to live and, finally, he taught us how to die." --Walter Mondale
Source: *Minnesotans Say the Darnedest Things*

Chapter 8

Taxes

In 1996, state and local governments collected over $14 billion in taxes, or about $3,100 per capita. Three-tenths of this total was collected by local governments (primarily property taxes); seven-tenths was collected in state taxes. Total state and local tax collections were fairly evenly divided among income taxes (35 percent), sales and excise taxes (31 percent), and property taxes (34 percent).

Minnesota taxes are higher than the national average, whether measured per capita or as a percent of personal income. Table 1 compares Minnesota state and local taxes with national averages in 1996 (the latest year for which comparable local government data is available for all states). Minnesota ranked 8th highest in per capita taxes and 5th highest in taxes as a percent of personal income. In per capita terms, Minnesotan's personal income tax collections exceeded the national average by over 50 percent; Minnesotan's property and corporate income tax collections were 10 and 25 percent above the national average respectively, while sales and excise tax collections equaled the national average. In 1999, income taxes were cut by almost 10 percent. This may reduce Minnesota's income tax rank shown below.

Table 1.

Minnesota State and Local Taxes Compared to Other States
(1996 fiscal year)

Type of Tax	Tax Collections Per Capita			Tax Collections as % of Income		
	Minn.	Rank	Nat. Ave.	Minn.	Rank	Nat. Ave.
Personal Income	$ 888	5th	$554	3.7%	5th	2.4%
Corporate Income	$151	11th	$121	0.6%	11th	0.5%
Sales & Excise	$990	13th	$939	4.2%	23rd	4.1%
Property Tax	$884	15th	$789	3.7%	19th	3.4%
Other Taxes	$215	18th	$195	0.9%	20th	0.9%
All Taxes	$3,128	8th	$2,597	13.2%	5th	11.3%

Minnesota collects 70% of its tax revenues at the state level, with only 30% collected by local governments. The state share in Minnesota is higher than in most states. In 1996, Minnesotans state share of total taxes exceeded that of 32 other states (with 85 percent of the U.S. population). As a result, Minnesotans total state taxes ranked 5th highest in the nation (40 percent higher than the national average), while Minnesotans local taxes ranked 25th (almost 10% below the national average).

A relatively high proportion of Minnesotans state tax collections is used to provide state aid to local governments. In 1996, state aid to local governments equaled 64 percent of state taxes. State aids exceeded local tax collections. For every dollar collected in local taxes, local governments and school districts received more than $1.30 in state aids.

Table 2.

State Aids to Local Government	($millions in 1996 fiscal year)
Education Aids	$2,253
Human Service Aids	
Medicaid	$1,188
Other	$479
Local Government Aids	$1,049
Transportation Aids	$487
Total State Aids	$6,196
Total Local Taxes	$4,747
Total State Taxes	$9,990

Property Taxes in Minnesota

Minnesotans property tax system is complex. Unlike most states, Minnesota has a classified property tax system, which means that equal-valued properties face different tax rates based on the nature of the property. As a result, the tax on business property is substantially higher than the tax on homes of equal value. In addition, homes with market value under $76,000 are taxed at a lower rate than higher-valued homes. Table 3 shows estimated 2000 property taxes for various types of property in a community with tax rates equal to the 1998 state-wide average.

> "Taxes are not high enough in this country. Our educational system has gone to hell–the sewers, the streets, water systems are dilapidated... there's the Godawful drug problem. It all adds up to a declining America." –William C. Norris, Founder of Control Data
> From *Minnesotans Say the Darnedest Things*

Table 3.
Estimated Average 2000 Property Tax as Percent of Market Value/1

Type of Property	Property Tax as Percent of Market Value
Homeowners	
$75,000 home	1.27%
$150,000 home	1.68%
$300,000 home	1.89%
Rented Homes	
$75,000 value	1.52%
$150,000 value	1.81%
Apartments	3.05%
Commercial/Industrial	
$150,000 value	3.05%
$1,000,000 value	4.13%

1 Includes only the value of land and buildings. Estimates shown here include the impact of law changes enacted in 1999. Average state-wide tax rate is for 1998.

Table 1 showed Minnesota ranking 19th among all states in property taxes as a percent of personal income. This overall property tax ranking fails to capture the complex impact of Minnesotans class rate system, which reduces relative taxes on homeowners and raises relative taxes on most businesses. In 1998, commercial and industrial property accounted for only 14 percent of total property value, but they paid 32 percent of total property taxes. In contrast, homesteads accounted for 57 percent of market value, but paid only 42 percent of total property taxes. A recent comparison of 1998 property taxes in all 50 states concluded that Minnesotans homeowner property taxes were below the national average for lower-valued homes, and slightly above the national average for higher-valued homes. In contrast, Minnesotans property tax on apartments was twice the national average, and Minnesotans property tax on commercial property was among the highest in the nation.

Minnesota also reduces the burden of residential property taxes on many lower-income renters and homeowners by refunding a portion of their property taxes. In 1996, homeowners received $82 million in property tax refunds; renters received $89 million. Refunds are targeted to those whose property taxes are large relative to their incomes. In 1996, refunds were generally available only for those with income below $38,000 for renters and $65,000 for homeowners.

Other Minnesota Taxes

Minnesota enacted the state income tax in 1933. Today, Minnesotans personal income tax uses the same personal exemptions and standard deductions as the federal income tax. In 1999, a married family of four (with no itemized deductions) will pay no tax on the first $18,200 of gross income. Income tax rates range from 5.5 percent to 8 percent. Minnesotans working family credit and dependent care credit are targeted toward lower-income working families. In 1996, the working family credit provided over $42 million of tax relief to over 215,000 low-income working households; the dependent care credit provided another $12 million in tax relief to over 37,000 low-income households. Unlike many states, Minnesota local governments levy no income taxes.

Minnesotans corporate income tax was also enacted in 1933. In 1999, Minnesota taxable income is taxed at a flat 9.8 percent.

Minnesotans state sales tax is 6.5 percent. Unlike most states, Minnesota levies no sales tax on clothing. Other major exemptions include food consumed at home, prescription drugs, residential heating fuels, vehicle repairs, and motor fuels. The sales tax base was significantly expanded in the late 1980s, when many services became taxable for the first time. Local sales taxes are less important in Minnesota than in most states. In 1996, only 9 cities and one county levied local sales taxes, with rates of one-half or one percent.

The state gasoline tax, first adopted in 1925 at a rate of 2 cents per gallon, has been levied at 20 cents per gallon since 1988. The cigarette tax was first levied in 1947, at 3 cents per pack. The tax rate has been 48 cents per pack since 1992. Since 1987, excise tax rates on alcoholic beverages have been $2.40 per barrel of 3.2 percent beer and $4.60 for strong beer, $5.03 per gallon of liquor, and from $0.30 (under 14 percent) to $3.52 (over 24 percent alcohol) per gallon of wine.

Beginning in 1993, Minnesota has financed a special system of health care subsidies for low-income uninsured households. In 1999, this MinnesotaCare program is financed by a 1.5 percent tax on medical care. This tax is levied on the gross revenues of hospitals and health care providers. Sales of prescription drugs are also subject to this tax. Nursing homes and home health care services are exempt from tax, as are payments by Medicare, medical assistance, and the MinnesotaCare program.

The Distribution of Minnesota's Tax Burden by Income Level

The Minnesota system of state and local taxes is roughly proportional; typical households at all income levels pay about the same portion of their income in tax. The progressive income tax and property tax refunds largely offset the regressivity of other state and local taxes. According to the 1999 Minnesota Tax Incidence Study, typical households at almost most income levels paid between 12 and 13 percent of their income in state and local taxes. (See Table 4.)   In contrast, most other states have regressive tax systems, taking a larger share of income from low-income than from higher-income households.

Table 4.

Minnesota State and Local Tax Burden in 1996 as Percent of
Total Cash Income

Population Decile 1	Income Range	Tax as Percent of Income
First	$6,817 & Under	17.8%
Second	$6,817 - $11,166	12.0%
Third	$11,166 - 15,828	12.2%
Fourth	$15,828 - 21,634	12.5%
Fifth	$21,634 - 27,866	13.0%
Sixth	$27,866 - 35,486	13.1%
Seventh	$35,486 - 45,144	13.1%
Eighth	$45,144 - 57,697	13.0%
Ninth	$57,697 - 78,618	13.0%
Tenth	$78,618 & Over	12.2%
Total		12.7%

1 Each decile includes 10 percent of all Minnesota households.

Three Years of Tax Rebates and Permanent Income Tax Cuts

Minnesota's healthy economy created substantial budget surpluses in 1997, 1998, and 1999.   Over $2.2 billion of these surpluses - about $500 per person - was returned to taxpayers as property tax rebates (1997 and 1998) and a sales tax rebate (1999).   Starting in 1999, income tax rates have been reduced, cutting future income tax revenues by an average of 9 percent.

Federal Taxes Paid by Minnesotans

The Tax Foundation estimates that Minnesotans paid an average of $5,563 per capita in federal taxes in 1996, only slightly above their estimate for the nation as a whole ($5,365).   They also estimate the magnitude of federal expenditures in each state, and they claim that Minnesota only receives 76 cents in federal expenditures for every dollar Minnesotans pay in federal taxes.   Only four states are estimated to have lower ratios of federal expenditures to federal taxes.

State and Local Government Expenditures

Minnesotans government expenditures per capita, like its tax revenues per capita, rank it high among the 50 states.   Table 5 shows per capita expenditures in 1996 for several major categories of state and local spending, along with Minnesotans rank.   With the exception of police and corrections,

Minnesotans per capita expenditures rank higher than tenth. At $5,306 per capita, total state and local expenditures exceeded those in all but six other states.

Table 5.

Minnesota State and Local Expenditures Compared to Other States
(1996 Fiscal Year)
Per Capita Expenditures

Expenditure Category	Dollars	State Rank	Share of Total Expenditures
Education (includes higher education)	$1,772	8th	33.4%
Health and hospitals	$484	10th	9.1%
Police and corrections	$238	32nd	4.5%
Highways	$418	13th	7.9%
Welfare	$1,003	5th	18.9%
Other/1	$1,391	13th	26.2%
Total general expenditures/2	$5,306	7th	100.0%

1 Includes interest payments ($262 per person), natural resources and parks ($181), air transportation ($33), fire protection ($44), sewers and solid waste ($170), housing and community development ($106), judicial and legal ($74), administration and other ($521).

2 General expenditures exclude municipal utilities and social insurance trust funds (workers compensation, unemployment compensation, and employee retirement).

Source: Paul A. Wilson, Fiscal Analyst, Minnesota House of Representativc. 328 State Office Building, 100 Constitution Ave., St. Paul, MN 55155

Sales Tax Rebate of 1999 Will Add to Future State Tax Revenues

The $1.3 billion sales tax rebate will provide a small but significant, one time boost to Minnesota's economy. The total amount to be rebated is less than 1 percent of both gross state product ($150 billion in 1997) and personal income ($133 billion in 1998), but it will be more than 2 percent of retail sales.

The average rebate was more than $650, and everyone eligible received a check for at least $200. Most Minnesota families received between $600 and $1000. If the rebate were spent in exactly the same way as current consumer spending patterns, an additional $26 million would be added to sales tax receipts.

Source: MN Department of Revenue website.

Table 6.

Minnesota - General Fund Forecasted Revenues Fiscal Years 2000 & 2001
(All numbers in thousands)
Based on February 1999 forecast

Corporate Income	$1,383,500	5.2%
FY 99 Balance Forward	$1,495,900	5.6%
Individual Income	$11,940,200	45.0%
Investment Income	$234,000	0.9%
Liquor/Tobacco	$475,692	1.8%
Motor Vehicle Excise (MVET)	$916,200	3.5%
Tobacco Settlement	$760,606	2.9%
Other	$1,980,981	7.5%
Sales Tax	$7,344,339	27.7%
	$26,531,418	100.0%

Other includes:

Inheritance, Estate, Gift	$94,000	0.4%
Iron Ore Occupation	$300	0.0%
Taconite Occupation	$4,000	0.0%
Taconite Production	$0	0.0%
Deed & Mortgage Registration	$252,200	1.0%
Insurance Gross Earnings & Fire Marshal	$350,400	1.3%
Controlled Substance Tax	$280	0.0%
Other Gross Earnings	$90	0.0%
Lawful Gambling	$126,692	0.5%
Health Care Provider	$244,614	0.9%
Income Tax Reciprocity	$81,336	0.3%
Illegal Sports Bookmaking Tax	$20	0.0%
Motor Vehicle Registration	$1,750	0.0%
Other Excise and All Other	$0	0.0%
All Other Refunds	($46,662)	-0.2%
DHS RTC Collections	$41,672	0.2%
Other Non-Dedicated Revenue	$144,000	0.5%
All Other Refunds	($200)	-0.0%
Dedicated Revenues	$237,320	0.9%
Transfers In	$428,969	1.6%
Prior Year Adjustments	$20,200	0.1%
Subtotal - Other	$1,980,981	7.5%

Balance forward from 1999 adjusted for 1999 Session actions
Revenues are prior to tax reductions enacted in the 1999 Legislative
session for FY 2000 & 2001
Source: Minnesota House Fiscal Staff 5/99

Table 7.

General Fund Appropriations - Budget Base - Fiscal Year 2000-2001
By Budget Function
Based on February 1999 Forecast

(Dollars in thousands) Base	FY 00-01	% of total
Education, Children & Families	$7,271,466	26.1%
Higher Education	$2,376,392	8.5%
Property Tax Aids & Credits	$3,058,105	11.0%
Tax Reform Account	$200,000	0.7%
Other Major Local Assistance	$1,094,808	3.9%
Health Care	$3,623,017	13.0%
Family Support	$499,366	1.8%
State Operated Institutions	$932,760	3.3%
Legislative, Judicial and Constitutional	$516,293	1.9%
State Agencies	$1,651,573	5.9%
Debt Service	$521,419	1.9%
Reserves/Other	$1,085,105	3.9%
Uncommitted Revenue*	$4,055,678	14.5%
Dedicated Expenditures	$221,551	0.8%
Inflation in Planning Estimates	$797,230	2.9%
Total	$27,904,763.	100.0%

*The uncommitted revenue includes $1,235,304,000 carried over from FY 1998-99.

Source: Minnesota House Fiscal Staff 2/99

Minnesota mentions in the *Guinness Book of Records*

Largest Hanging One Gallows

The most people hanged from one gallows were 38 Sioux Indians, executed by William J. Duly outside Mankato, MN, on December 26, 1862, for the murder of a number of unarmed citizens.

Driving In Reverse

The highest average speed attained in any non-stop reverse drive exceeding 500 miles (805km) is 36.30 mph (58.42km/h) was achieved by John Smith, who drove a 1983 Chevrolet Caprice Classic 501 miles (806.2km) in 13 hr. 48 min. at the I-94 Speedway, Fergus Falls, MN, on August 11, 1996.

Source: Guinness Media, Inc. printed with permission.

Chapter 9

Education

Minnesota was a rough and sparsely populated wilderness at the outer limits of the Northwest frontier when Harriet Bishop opened the first public school in St. Paul in 1848. Ox-carts and riverboats provided the only access, but settlers made their way to the region and established schools in the early settlements of St. Paul, Stillwater, and St. Anthony.

When Minnesota achieved statehood in 1857, provisions for public education were made official. The constitutional convention made the state legislature responsible for establishing a public school system and providing ongoing support. Legislators established what was then the largest permanent school fund in the nation. By 1862, it totaled $242,531 and yielded an annual income of $12,308.

Education on the Frontier

Who were these pioneers who valued public education? In 1861, the young state of Minnesota had 171,196 settlers, according to the census, and 17,000 Native American residents. Of the settlers, more than 98 percent were white, more than a third were foreign-born, and another 47 percent had recently immigrated from the East. Although most could read and write, less than 15 percent had attended school within the year.

The obligation to educate Minnesota's children was widely accepted. However, the definition of education fell far short of today's standards. In the agrarian society of pioneer Minnesota, an educated person was one who had completed elementary school. Anyone who could read, write, and do simple arithmetic had all the education necessary to succeed in life. Besides, older children needed to work in the fields or at home to help their families survive. Most Minnesotans believed a boy's further education was his family's responsibility. Additional education for girls was rarely even considered.

Early Educators in Minnesota

Most schools in pioneer days were rough, one-room shelters. Children warmed themselves at a pot-bellied stove, drank from a tin cup at the water barrel, and used a nearby outhouse. One teacher instructed children of all ages in the basics-reading, spelling, writing, and arithmetic-with some U.S.

history and grammar added for the more "advanced" pupils.

In the midst of these sparse surroundings, a typical teacher was a mere servant, accepting poor pay and severe personal restrictions without complaint. Without the need for professional qualifications, most teachers were hired because they were related to a school board member or simply willing to work cheap. In exchange for their positions, they were expected to be devout and morally upright-and rules regarding smoking, drinking, courting, and church attendance were strictly enforced. Some school districts even denied teachers the right to leave town without permission.

Despite these hardships, women in the teaching profession enjoyed more autonomy and acceptance than virtually any other group of women in the nineteenth century. What they often sacrificed, however, was the freedom to marry and raise children of their own. Authorities at the time considered women, marriage, and teaching an unacceptable combination.

But not everyone taught in a one-room schoolhouse. As early as the 1850s, colleges were springing up in river towns.

Minnesota Normal schools were named State Teachers Colleges in 1921, then State Colleges in 1957. They were founded as follows:

State Colleges	Year Founded
Winona	1858
Mankato	1868
St. Cloud	1869
Moorhead	1888
*Duluth	1902
*Bemidji	1913

Minnesota's first junior colleges were founded in the early twentieth century:

Junior Colleges	Year Founded
Rochester	1915
Hibbing	1916
Eveleth	1918

*Duluth became a branch of the University of Minnesota in 1947.
*Bemidji didn't open until 1919 due to World War I.

Educational Issues

- The College of Education, endorsed by the MEA, was established at the University of Minnesota in 1905.
- The notion of standards for teachers was first voiced in the 1860s.
- In 1877, the Minnesota Legislature granted women the right to vote on all school questions and serve on school boards.

- A 1914 article...revealed...the average annual salary paid to U.S. teachers was $485, carpenters made $802, coal miners earned $600, factory workers averaged $550, and even common laborers made $513.
- By 1928, the MEA endorsed two years of professional training beyond high school for elementary teachers. In 1936, four years were recom mended.

World War II

After World War II, soldiers returned home and entered college on the GI Bill. Women left their jobs to return home and raise children. A growing Baby Boom generation would bring 33 million students to America's public schools in the 1950s. There was an acute shortage of classroom teachers throughout the nation, but there were far too many school districts.

Through school district reorganization law, passed in 1947, districts were encouraged to consolidate. By 1963, the number of Minnesota school districts had dropped from 7,606 to 2,150.

In many districts, women were still forced to make the choice between family and teaching. Even in the 1950s, some districts refused to employ married women. Other districts allowed marriage, but refused to employ women with children under the age of eighteen. But throughout Minnesota, the fourth month of pregnancy put an end to a teacher's employment. If those teachers got their jobs back, their prior experience was voided and they began at entry level pay.

In reaction to the Russian launch of Sputnik on October 4, 1957, schools across Minnesota and across the country began to actively promote the study of mathematics and sciences.

In 1961, four years of preparation for teachers was signed into law. In 1962, 90 percent of rural elementary school teachers and 14 percent of city elementary teachers still had fewer than three years of college training.

In 1964, the MEA launched its Teacher of the Year award to recognize teaching excellence. Minnesota is one of only two states (along with California) to have four National Teachers of the Year. They are: 1967-Roger Tenney, Owatonna; 1975-Bob Heyer, Mounds View; 1986-Guy Doud, Brainerd; and 1996-Mary Beth Blegen, Worthington.

The late 1960s and through the 1980s were times of teacher organizing punctuated by strikes for more autonomy, higher wages and benefits.

Between 1957 and 1979:
- Student population in the U.S. increased from 33 million to 43 million, 30 %
- Elementary school enrollment grew from 24 million to 25 million, 4 %
- High school enrollment skyrocketed from 10 million to 18 million, 80 %

Social Change

When a deep recession hit the nation in 1981, public education suffered major financial cutbacks. Minnesota schools endured program reductions, students saw dramatic increases in class size, and 6,000 teachers were laid off.

In the early 1980s the changes in society dramatically affected schools. Rising divorces and out-of-wedlock births led to a proliferation of single-parent families. In most two-parent families, economic pressures made it necessary for both parents go work. A growing drug problem emerged among the nation's youth and a wave of immigrants brought more non-English speaking children into schools.

In 1983, " Nation at Risk" made public education a permanent issue on the national political agenda. Business also joined the crusade, demanding that schools provide a better-trained work force to compete in the growing global economy. The public rallied around the "excellence" issue, and called for new approaches to education.

The Minnesota Business Partnership, an organization of the chief executive officers of Minnesota's largest corporations, advocated changes in state public schools and called for increased student choice and open enrollment policies. Honeywell Corporation even started a school on company property where disadvantaged teens, often with children of their own, could be encouraged to finish their education and become employable citizens. Parents demanded a return to the system they had experienced in their school days and a return to the basics.

By 1988, student enrollment was back on a growth curve after years of decline in the early to mid-1980s. A dozen school districts, primarily in the urban areas, accounted for 70% of the growth from the baby boomlet. many districts were stable at best and others continued to decline. The 1980s also brought the advent of technology to schools. An ever increasing number of computers found their way into schools so that by the end of the decade, many schools had computer labs and students were learning in different ways.

A continuing wave of school consolidation had also reduced the number of Minnesota school districts to 434 in the early 1980s. By 1998 the number shrunk to 347.

1990s

Schools in the 1990s were not the ones many of us older people remember. Children in Minnesota classrooms were more diverse in terms of race, culture, and nationality. Many were recent immigrants who didn't speak English when they enrolled in school. Some had serious emotional problems from exposure to drugs, alcohol, or abuse. Physically and mentally challenged children, who previously attended special schools or none at all, were now mainstreamed into the public education system. Although special needs students made up only 10 percent of the student population, their education placed an enormous demand on school resources. The amount of paperwork was enormous. .

Children also made up a disproportionate share of the poor. Many lived below the official poverty line and 27 percent qualified for free or reduced-price meals. Poor children who came to school hungry weren't prepared to meet their learning potential. Poor families also moved frequently, a problem that Minneapolis public schools identified as the single biggest obstacle to student success.

Meanwhile, school enrollments increased while public education's share of financial support from the state declined. In the 1960s the main state priorities were schools and highways. Half the state budget went to K-12—now it's about one-third. And special education costs and enrollment increases have gobbled up almost every new dollar coming into the system.

On September 1, 1998, there was a merger of the two teacher unions in the state, the Minnesota Educators Association and the Minnesota Federation of Teachers. It became a 65,000 member organization named Education Minnesota. The note of confusion bound to occur is that the October teacher conferences people know as MEA will now be called "EM".

Standards and Accountability

After years of debate, the Minnesota Legislature approved and adopted graduation standards for Minnesota high school students in 1996. Students who began ninth grade in 1996 will be required to pass basic tests in reading and math before receiving their high school diplomas. A writing requirement was added for those students who began ninth grade in 1997. Tests in science, government, physical health and safety, and geography will be added for subsequent classes. Testing begins in eighth grade.

When the basic standards tests were instituted in 1996, only 53% of eighth graders received a passing grade. By 1998, that figure had risen to about 70%, a dramatic improvement.

In spite of these challenges, Minnesota's public schools consistently produce highly successful students. Minnesota ties with Iowa for the second highest average ACT scores in the nation and Minnesota's average SAT scores place it among the top three states. Minnesota's high school graduation rate of 89.1% ranks second nationally, and 65% of graduates pursue post-secondary education within two years of graduation.

In addition to excellent student achievement, in both 1996 and 1997, the National Commission of Teaching and America's Future rated Minnesota's teachers the best in the United States. Minnesota ties with California for the most National Teachers of the Year. The state ranks fourth in the nation for the number of National Board-certified teachers.

Source: Minnesota Education Association: 137 Years Proud
Children, Families and Learning website www.cfl.state.mn.us

Education Statistics Summary

Number of Public Operating Elementary and Secondary School District
(July 1998) 347

Public

Number of Schools 1998-99 1,752
    Area Learning Centers (ALC's) 145
    K-12 Schools 16
    Elementary 975
    Middle 154
    Secondary 462
    Jr. High 71
    Sr. High. 196
    Combined Jr. & Sr. High 195

    PK-12 Enrollment (Fall 1997) 844,410
    Kindergarten 62,126
    Elementary 382,659
    Secondary 399,625

    Graduates (1996) 52,205

Administrators (Superintendent & Principals
(F.T.E.) full time equivalent (fall 1997) 2,097
Teachers (F.T.E.) full time equivalent (fall 1997) 52,481

Nonpublic

Number of Schools 1997-98 524
Enrollment (fall 1997) 85,100
    Kindergarten 8,895
    Elementary 47,586
    Secondary 28,619

Source: Minnesota Department of Children, Families & Learning
Information: (651) 582-8200

Children, Families and Learning

    The Minnesota Department of Children, Families & Learning works to
help communities to measurably improve the well-being of children
through programs that focus on education, community services, prevention,
and the preparation of young people for the world of work. All

department efforts emphasize the achievement of positive results for children and their families.

Through this integration of its programs at the state level, the department encourages state education professionals and social services advocates to work together to meet the needs of Minnesota's children and families.

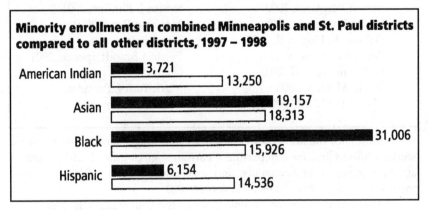

Minority enrollments in combined Minneapolis and St. Paul districts compared to all other districts, 1997 – 1998

American Indian: 3,721 / 13,250
Asian: 19,157 / 18,313
Black: 31,006 / 15,926
Hispanic: 6,154 / 14,536

Post-Secondary Education

The University of Minnesota was born in 1851 when a charter was passed and signed by the governor of the territory to authorize an institution of higher learning, but it was 1869 before college classes were finally begun. A major factor in the early success of the college was due to passage of the Morrill Act, signed into law by President Lincoln in 1862. This "land grant act" gave each state a parcel of land within its borders. The income from the sale of this land was to be used to provide education for people in the state, especially in the areas of agriculture and mechanic arts.

In 1867, the preparatory school opened its doors. Following a major reorganization in 1868, the university finally got underway as an institution of higher learning in 1869. The first class that fall numbered 18 students; the faculty numbered nine.

From these faltering origins, the university has grown to become one of the largest and most comprehensive universities in the country with full-time enrollment of 51,835 on its four state campuses. That total grows to 66,129 if one includes continuing education and extension courses.

The University of Minnesota, Twin Cities, is a classic Big Ten campus in the heart of Minneapolis and St. Paul. It is made up of 19 colleges, offers 161 bachelor's degrees, 218 master's, 114 doctoral degrees, and five professional degrees.

The University was among the top 10 among public institutions in the U. S. and the top 20 among all public and private institutions according to a

National Academy of Sciences ranking of arts and sciences done in the mid-1990's (The ranking does not include professional schools or agricultural-related fields).

Current Regents and the year their terms expire:

Anthony R. Baraga, 2005	William R. Peterson, 2005
Robert Bergland, 2003	Jessica J. Phillips, 2001
Dallas Bohnsack, 2005	Maureen Reed, 2003
William E. Hogan II, 2005	Vice Chair
Warren C. Larson, 2001	Patricia Brandt Spence, 2001
H. Bryan Neel III, 2003	Chair
David Metzen, 2003	Mark Yudof, President
Michael O'Keefe, 2001	ex officio member

Funding for the university comes from state and federal appropriations; student tuition and fees, department earnings; gifts, grants, and contracts; auxiliary services; endowments, and investment income. The total from these sources for 1995-1996 was $1,466,426,000.

A 12-member Board of Regents governs the University. The legislature chooses one regent from each of Minnesota's eight congressional districts and four from the state at large. One at-large regent must be a university student at the time of election. Regents serve without pay for six year terms. The president of the University is ex officio president of the Board of Regents.

Besides campuses in Minneapolis and St. Paul, the university has campuses in Duluth, part of the university system since 1947; in Morris, opened in 1960; and Crookston, opened 1966. A campus in Waseca, which opened in 1971, was closed in 1992.

Duluth offers 11 bachelor's degrees in 70 majors; Morris offers the baccalaureate degree in 27 majors and course work in seven preprofessional areas; and Crookston offers 19 technical bachelor's and 11 associates' degrees.

Tuition varies, but a typical lower division College of Liberal Arts student on the Twin Cities or Duluth campus taking 12 credits would pay tuition of $1854 or $1692 respectively per semester plus the student services fee for 1999-2000. Out-of-state tuition is almost three times higher. In 1999-2000, the U of M will switch from a quarter system (three academic quarters per year) to a two semester system.

University of Minnesota Facts
• There are about 370,000 living U of M alumni.
• University graduates and faculty have founded more than 3,000 compa-

nies that employ more than 350,000 people worldwide. 1,500 of them are technology companies that employ 100,000 Minnesotans and contribute $30 billion to our economy annually.

• Five alumni have won the Nobel prize.

• Approximately 80 percent of the state's doctors and dentists are trained at the University of Minnesota.

• The U library has more than 48,000 subscriptions to periodicals and jour- nals and 5.5 million volumes on the Twin Cities campus alone. It lends more books and journal articles to other libraries than any other academic library in the nation.

• School colors, maroon and gold, were chosen by English instructor Augusta Norwood Smith sometime between 1876 and 1880. The colors were not officially approved by the regents until March 1940.

• School Songs:

"Hail! Minnesota" was written by Truman Rickard, a member of the class of 1904, for use in a class play. A second verse was written by University student Arthur Upson in 1905. In 1945, the song became the official anthem of the state of Minnesota. The "Minnesota Rouser," sung at most University athletic events, was written by Floyd M. Hutsell in 1909 in response to a contest sponsored by the Minneapolis Tribune. Hutsell, a Minneapolis choir director and voice teacher, won $100 in the contest to choose a fight song for the University.

• The U of M is a thriving center for culture and the arts. The Twin Cities campus boasts the 4,800-seat Northrop Auditorium, the Weisman Art Museum ("Five of the most gorgeous galleries on earth."-New York Times), and the Ted Mann Concert Hall, with possibly the best acoustics in the Twin Cities.

MnSCU

Minnesota's public post-secondary educational system also includes MnSCU (pronounced MINN-skew). It means community colleges, state uni- versities, technical colleges, and comprehensive community and technical colleges organized into a statewide system of 53 college and university cam- puses in 46 communities plus a campus in Akita, Japan. The Minnesota State Colleges and Universities serve about 145,000 students and produce about 30,000 graduates each year.

MnSCU Admission

At Minnesota' state two-year technical and community colleges, the basic requirement is a high school diploma or a General Equivalency Diploma (GED). This can be waived in some cased if the applicant can demonstrate potential for being a successful college student.

Four-year degrees are available from Minnesota state universities. Admission is generally granted to students who have graduated in the upper half of their high school graduating class or who have obtained at least a score of 21 on the ACT or a combined score of 1000 on the SAT standardized tests. Some of the state universities have even stricter requirements. Students planning to enroll in a state university should complete the following preparatory curriculum or its competency equivalent while in high school:

English: 4 years. Courses in composition, literature and speech.

Math: 3 years. Two years of algebra, including intermediate or advanced algebra, and one year of geometry.

Science: 3 years. One year each of a biological science and a physical science, and all three courses with lab experience.

Social Sciences: 3 years. One year each of geography and U. S. history, along with other courses in the social sciences.

The Arts or World Culture: 1 year.

World Language: 2 years of a single world language.

In addition, some programs may require special preparation for enrollment.

Tuition and Fees

Costs vary among schools, but here's a look at the approximate amounts for a full year for full-time students:

	State Universities	Comm. & Tech.
Tuition (15 cr/sem)	$2,525	$1,995
Room & board	$2,975	$2,500*
(dbl. occup.)		
Fees (98-99 average)	$485	$223
Books, supplies, travel, etc.	$2,500-3,500	$2,500-3,500
	$8,485-9,485	$7,218-8,218

* Estimate. Many community and technical colleges have nearby housing but most don't have college-style dormitories. Check with the college you're interested in.

Financial Aid

Reciprocity allows residents of North Dakota, South Dakota, Wisconsin, and Manitoba to attend Minnesota colleges and universities at special tuition rates that are lower than the tuition usually charged to out-of-state residents. The Midwest Student Exchange Program also allows some students from Kansas, Michigan, Missouri, and Nebraska to receive 150% tuition. Out-of-state tuition is double the Minnesota residents' tuition rate.

Minnesota provides more financial aid to college students than most states. About two-thirds of students at Minnesota State Colleges and

Universities receive financial aid to help pay for tuition, fees, room and board and other costs. A number of grants and loan programs are available to students with financial aid need; students or their parents also may qualify for student loans that are not based on need. Many Minnesota State Colleges and Universities also provide assistance to students in finding local part-time jobs while in school. To apply for financial aid, or to learn more about it, contact your high school counselor or the financial aid office of the college or university you wish to attend.

University of Minnesota Enrollment

Enrollment (fall quarter 1998)	Men	Women	Total
Twin Cities	19,374	20,221	39,595
Duluth	3,941	3,890	7,831
Crookston	1,111	1,318	2,492
Morris	774	1,143	1,917
Total U of M	25,200	26,635	51,835
Continuing Ed & Extension			14,294
Grand Total			66,129
Grand Total in 1971			44,082
Minority Enrollment (fall quarter 1998)			
Asian or Pacific Islander:			3,065
African American:			1,479
Hispanic:			898
American Indian or Alaskan:			535
All Campuses:			5,977

Degrees Granted

Students may earn undergraduate and graduate degrees in more than 373 fields of study. Total degrees awarded through June 1998: 526,525 (including 24,070 Ph.D.s). 1997-98 10,646 degrees (including 679 Ph.D.s).

Information

Location	College	Phone Number
University Of Minnesota:		
Twin Cities		(612)625-5000
		(800)752-1000
Duluth		(218)726-8000
Morris		(320)589-2211
Crookston		(218)281-6510
MnSCU:		(651)296-8012
www.mnscu.ed		(888)MnSCU-4-U

Akita, Japan	Japan's MN State University in Akita	(651)649-5758
Albert Lea	Riverland Community College	(507)379-3300 (800)333-2584
Alexandria	Alexandria Technical College	(320)762-0221 (888)234-1222
Anoka	Anoka-Hennepin Tech College	(612)576-4700 (800)247-5588
Austin	Riverland Community College	(507)433-0600 (800)247-5039
Bemidji	Bemidji State University	(218)755-2000 (800)475-2001
Bemidji	Bemidji Technical College	(218)755-4270 (800)942-8324
Bloomington	Normandale Community College	(612)832-6000
Brainerd	Central Lakes College	(218)855-8000 (800)933-0346
Brooklyn Park	Hennepin Technical College	(612)550-3112 (800)345-4655
Brooklyn Park	North Hennepin Com College	(612)424-0702
Cambridge	Anoka-Ramsey Com College	(612)689-7000
Canby	Southwestern Tech College	(507)223-7252 (800)658-2535
Cloquet	Fond du Lac Tribal & Com Coll	(218)879-0800 (800)657-3712
Coon Rapids	Anoka-Ramsey Com College	(612)427-2600
Detroit Lakes	Northwest Technical College	(218)847-1341 (800)492-4836
Duluth	Lake Superior College	(218)733-7600 (800)432-2884
East Grand Forks	Northwest Technical College	(218)773-3441 (800)451-3441
Eden Prairie	Hennepin Technical College	(612)944-2222 (800)345-4655
Ely	Vermillion Community College	(218)365-7200 (800)657-3608
Eveleth	Mesabi Range Com & Tech Col	(218)744-3302 (800)345-2884
Fairbault	South Central Technical College	(507)334-4965 (800)422-0391
Fergus Falls	Fergus Falls Community College	(218)739-7500
Grand Rapids	Itasca Community College	(218)327-4460 (800)996-6-ICC

Granite Falls	Southwestern Technical College	(320)564-4511
		(800)657-3247
Hibbing	Hibbing Community College	(218)262-7200
		(800)224-4422
Hutchinson	Ridgewater College	(320)234-0225
		(800)222-4424
International Falls	Rainy River Community College	(218)285-7722
		(800)456-3996
Inver Grove Heights	Inver Hills Community College	(651)450-8500
Jackson	Southwestern Technical College	(507)847-3320
		(800)658-2522
Mankato	South Central Technical College	(507)389-7200
		(800)722-9359
Mankato	Mankato State University	(507)389-6767
		(800)722-0544
Marshall	Southwest State University	(507)537-7021
		(800)642-0684
		x 6268
Minneapolis	Metropolitan State University	(612)341-7250
Minneapolis	Minneapolis Community & Tech	(612)341-7000
	(800)247-0911	
Moorhead	Moorhead State University	(218)236-2161
		(800)593-7246
Moorhead	Northwest Technical College	(218)236-6277
		(800)426-5603
Pine City	Pine Technical College	(320)629-6764
		(800)521-7463
Pipestone	Southwestern Technical College	(507)825-5471
		(800)658-2330
Red Wing	Red Wing-Winona Technical Col	(612)385-6300
		(800)657-4849
Rochester	Rochester Community & Tech	(507)285-7210
		(800)247-1296
Rochester	Winona State University-Roch	(507)285-7100
Rosemount	Dakota County Technical Coll	(651)423-8301
		toll free
		(877)YES-DCTC
St. Cloud	St. Cloud State University	(320)255-0121
		(800)369-4260
St. Cloud	St. Cloud Technical College	(320)654-5000
		(800)222-1009
St. Paul	Metropolitan State University	(651)772-7777

St. Paul	St. Paul Technical College	(651)221-1300
		(800)227-6029
Staples	Central Lakes College	(218)904-2051
		(800)247-6836
Thief River Falls	Northland Community & Tech	(218)681-0701
		(800)959-6282
Virginia	Mesabi Range Community & T	(218)749-0314
		(800)657-3860
Wadena	Northwest Technical College	(218)-631-3530
		(800)247-2007
White Bear Lake	Century College	(651)779-3200
Willmar	Ridgewater College	(320)231-6067
		(800)722-1151
Winona	Red Wing-Winona Technical Co	(507)453-2700
		(800)372-8164
Winona	Winona State University	(507)457-5000
		(800)DIALWSU
Worthington	Worthington Community College	(507)372-2107
		(800)657-3966

Comprehensive Fees For 1999-2000 at Minnesota's Private Colleges

College/University	Tuition & Fees	Room & Board	Comprehensive Fees
Augsburg College	$15,250	$5,240	$20,490
612-330-1001; 1-800-788-5678			
Bethel College	$15,300	$5,410	$20,710
651-638-6242; 1-800-255-8706			
Carleton College	$23,469	$4,761	$28,230
507-663-4190; 1-800-995-2275			
College of St. Benedict	$16,441	$5,025	$21,466
320-363-5308; 1-800-544-1489			
College of St. Catherine	$15,578	$4,550	$20,128
651-690-6505; 1-800-945-4599			
College of St. Scholastica	$15,510	$4,760	$20,270
218-723-6046; 1-800-447-5444			
Concordia College-Moorhead	$13,340	$3,760	$17,100
218-299-3004; 1-800-699-9897			
Concordia College-St. Paul	$13,840	$4,962	$18,802
651-641-8230; 1-800-333-4705			
Gustavus Adolphus College	$17,480	$4,320	$21,800
507-933-7676; 1-800-GUSTAVUS			
Hamline University	$15,574	$5,138	$20,933
651-641-2207; 1-800-753-9753			

Macalester College 651-696-6357; 1-800-231-7974	$20,688	$5,760	$26,448
Minneapolis College of Art and Design 612-874-3760, 1-800-874-6223	$18,266	$4,376	$22,642
St. John's University 320-363-2196; 1-800-245-6467	$16,441	$4,930	$21,371
St. Mary's University of Minnesota 507-457-1700; 1-800-635-5987	$13,645	$4,420	$18,065
St. Olaf College 507-646-3025; 1-800-800-3025	$18,250	$4,320	$22,570
University of St. Thomas 651-962-6150; 1-800-328-6819	$16,340	$5,180	$21,520
AVERAGE	$16,588	$4,807	$21,395

NOTE: Charges apply to new entering students only. Several colleges have differential tuition for upper-level students, housing cost freezes for returning students or other policies that result in price variation.

About 70 percent of Minnesota private college students recieve financial aid to help pay for their tuition and fees. The average financial package (grants, work-study and loans) is more than $9.200, including more than $6,500 in grant aid that does not have to be repaid.

Private Colleges
• Private colleges and universities award one-third of all four-year degrees in Minnesota. In addition, each Minnesota student who chooses to attend a private college or university saves state taxpayers up to $4,500 per year in public tuition subsidies.
• All courses are taught by experienced professors, not graduate students.
• Students of color represent 7.5% of all private college undergraduates, compared to 4.2% at Minnesota state universities and 10.7% at the University of Minnesota.
• Enroll 28% of Minnesota's undergraduate students and 44% of all graduate and professional students. Award:
    50% of all science degrees
    51% of all mathematics degrees
    49% of economics degrees
    36% of business degrees
    27% of alumni start new businesses.
    47% of alumni go on to earn advanced degrees in medicine, business, science and other fields.

- Enrollment: 47,900 undergraduate and graduate students.
- Faculty-to-student ratio: 1 professor for every 13 students. 15 students in the average science lab.
- Percent of students who receive financial aid: 70%
- Average student financial aid package: $9,200 (includes grants, loans and work-study). 20% of Minnesota private college students are from families who earn $20,000 of less per year; half are from families with annual incomes under $40,000.
- Percentage of students who graduate in four years: 57% (compared to 20% at the University of Minnesota).
- Percent of graduates who go on to earn advanced degrees: 47%

Source: MN Private College Council
651-228-9061 E-mail: colleges@mnprivco.org; www.mn-colleges.org/

Tax Benefits
There are several new tax benefits that are available to help families meet the costs of postsecondary education.

Hope Scholarship Credit
A student is eligible for the Hope Scholarship Credit if: (1) for at least one academic period (e.g., semester, trimester, quarter) beginning during the calendar year, the student is enrolled at least half-time in a program leading to a degree, certificate, or other recognized educational credential and is enrolled in one of the first two years of postsecondary education.

Lifetime Learning Credit
An individual paying qualified tuition and related expenses at a postsecondary educational institution may claim the credit, provided the institution is an eligible educational institution. Unlike the Hope Scholarship Credit, students are not required to be enrolled at least half-time in one of the first two years of postsecondary education.
Consult your tax advisor or the IRS for details.

Minnesota's Univesities Facts

Hamline University, founded in 1854 in Redwing, was Minnesota's first university. It later moved to St. Paul.

Winona State University was founded in 1858 as the first public teacher-training institution west of the Mississippi.

Chapter 10
Women in the History of Minnesota

Women were long invisible, or nearly so to American historians. Traditionally concerned with power and the powerful, scholars either ignored women or discussed only those who were associated with "women's rights" and consequently impinged on power and politics, or those who were sufficiently colorful or notorious to provide good anecdotal material. The historical profession, interested in change over time, assumed that women were immutable and changeless and therefore of little relevance or interest.

In recent decades, however, there has been great interest among both professional historians and the general public in women and their place not only in the past but in the present.

Minnesota, because of its diversity, offers a particularly rich field of exploration for women's history. Since the territorial days of the 1850s it has been both urban and rural, industrial and agricultural. It has been populated by a wide variety of people of several races (however small their numbers) and by many ethnic groups. Because it is impossible to compress in a few pages the whole story of women in Minnesota, a few areas have been singled out for emphasis: a quick overview of women in the past, women winning the vote, the second wave of the women's movement, the status of women today in business, politics and government, women in sports, and some individual leaders and organizations that have advanced the cause of women.

The First Minnesota Women

In earliest times, American Indian women contributed significantly to the survival of the tribes: they processed skins and hides needed for shelter, clothing and later for the fur trade. Women also made pottery; they wove baskets and mats, gathered fuel, preserved wild foods, and cooperated with men in fishing, harvesting wild rice, and building canoes and houses. French traders and trappers of the Great Lakes region depended upon Native American women as guides and mediators, and the French and Indians often intermarried.

The first white women in the Minnesota territory were wives of missionaries and of farmers. By 1850 Minnesota was fundamentally agricultural, and the Grange, initially a brotherhood of farmers known as the Patrons of Husbandry, began to admit women.   In such settings women found companionship, shared problems, and made significant educational and social contributions to the organization.

Both the Indian and white women served as "culture bearer," in their tribes and communities. The first white teacher, Harriet Bishop, came to St. Paul, Minnesota in 1849, one of many sent by the New England Popular Education Society to fertilize the pioneering territories with education. As education became officially structured around 1858, women were ignored and left out of decision-making as men took control of the system. Although women were the teachers, they could not vote for school board members or run for election to that board. After many years of campaigning, women finally succeeded in their quest. The affirmative vote by male voters on an amendment to the Minnesota constitution in the 1875 election repaired this obvious injustice. Almost immediately, women were successful in their contests for election to the school boards and as county superintendents!

The Middle Period

Towards the end of the nineteenth century, doctors and lay people alike became concerned that too much education would hurt females, either physically or mentally. So educators decided to teach women "appropriate" skills that they could use in their own sphere of influence — the home. Needless to say, these teachers of domestic arts received less pay than the men who taught manual arts. In 1910 Minneapolis women teachers formed their own organization to serve as a lobbying and pressure group, and, in early meetings of the Minnesota Education Association, women secured a commitment to the principle of equal pay.

Despite the controversy about "overeducated" women, they became a familiar sight on college campuses by the late 1890s. Even though women had been admitted to the University of Minnesota from the time it opened its doors in 1869, their numbers were small. The experience of middle class women in "literary societies" that could be found in communities across the nation informed them of the value and excitement of education. Their work in the WCTU and the suffrage movement was another spur to support the idea that daughters as well as sons should go to college. Many fathers, sensing the inequity of educating boys and not girls, were also supportive.   In 1905 the sisters of St. Joseph of Carondelet founded the College of St. Catherine in St. Paul, the nation's first fully accredited Catholic women's college, and the first to have a chapter of Phi Beta Kappa.

During the Depression of the 1930s, women who wanted professional employment in education were told they were taking men's jobs. Many school systems established regulations forbidding married women to teach. Despite these restrictions, women continued in the teaching profession often in one-room school houses and with declining salaries. Not until 1972 did the Minnesota State Department of Education issue guidelines eliminating sex discrimination.

In their roles as "culture bearers," women helped support all the arts. In 1852 Episcopalian women in St. Paul raised money for the first church organ in the territory. Women organized the Schubert Club in 1882 and the Thursday Musicale in 1892. In 1898 — thanks largely to the efforts of the state Federation of Women's Clubs — voters approved an amendment permitting women to vote and serve on library boards. After the turn of the century, the Federation also played a part in the formation of a state arts commission .

In the nineteenth century services for the elderly, the poor, and the sick were provided by private social agencies and staffed, more often than not, by women. Helping the less fortunate was regarded as an acceptable activity for women outside the home. In 1887 Dr. Martha Ripley founded Maternity Hospital in Minneapolis to care for indigent women and unwed mothers. The hospital's articles of incorporation stipulated that the medical department was to be the responsibility of female physicians. Catheryne Cooke Gilman founded the Women's Cooperative Alliance, an organization that was especially prominent in the 1920s. It was designed to protect young women and children in Minneapolis from the evils of the city and to confront prejudices of the male-dominated legal system, especially in its treatment of prostitutes. Other important women in the world of social services included Gertrude Brown, first director of the Phyllis Wheatley House in Minneapolis and In St. Paul, Myrtle Carden of the Hallie Q. Brown House, Constance Currie of Neighborhood House, and Sister Giovanni were outstanding leaders on behalf of the African-American, immigrant, and Hispanic communities.

In 1890 nearly 34 percent of Minnesotans lived in cities. Urbanization provided jobs in factories, mill, offices, and stores to young women who previously had been hired as maids or as teachers. By 1900 more than twelve percent of Minnesota's working women were employed as garment makers or seamstresses. But they were not paid a living wage. Eva Valesh used her considerable talents as a communicator in both speech and print to in efforts to improve the lot of nineteenth century working women, In the mid-1930s Nellie Stone Johnson organized a local of the hotel and restaurant employees union. Twin Cities laundry workers were organized in 1934, and St. Paul schoolteachers formed one of the nation's earliest and strongest locals of the American Federation of Teachers.

Women Win the Vote

One of the most significant advances for women was winning the vote in 1920 (Minnesota became the fifteenth state to ratify the Nineteenth Amendment in September 1919). With the right to vote and to hold office, women began to make their move. In 1922 Anna Dickey Olesen of Cloquet became Minnesota's first Democratic committeewoman and the first female candidate for the U.S. Senate endorsed by a major party. She came in third behind the Republican incumbent and winner Henrik Shipstead who swept to power with the rise of the Farmer-Labor party. In that same year, four women were elected to the Minnesota Legislature. Myrtle Cain, called the "flapper legislator" because of her youth, attractiveness, and progressive ideas, was an agent for the Telephone Operators Union and, once in office, she championed a bill "Granting Equal Rights, Privileges and Immunities to Both Sexes." After her defeat in 1924, she remained active in labor politics and lived long enough to testify on behalf of the Equal Right Amendment and see it ratified by the Legislature in 1973. Sue Dickey Hough, an early advocate of gun control, was a Minneapolis businesswoman who also served only one term although she continued to seek reelection in 1924, 1926, 1930. and 1934 before changing careers to work with the Minneapolis Department of Public Welfare. By contrast, Hannah Kempfer and Mabeth Hurd Paige served fourteen and twenty years respectively, and each had distinguished careers. Laura Naplin was the first woman state senator, initially appointed in 1927 to fill out the unexpired term of her late husband but subsequently elected in her own right.

The Second Wave of the Women's Movement

In the 1960s, prompted by their participation in the civil rights movement, young American women became acutely conscious that they, like African-Americans, suffered from unjust discrimination. At about the same time women of all ages identified with the wasted lives described by Betty Friedan in The Feminine Mystique, and the second wave of the women's movement erupted in a turbulent era of advocacy, protest, and counter-cultures. Women's lives would never be the same, and women's progress was spurred by national and state inquiries into the status of women, legislation, by judicial rulings that resulted in a new legal identity for women, and by the beginning of attitudinal changes about women's roles. In many respects, Minnesota was in the forefront of those changes.

Minnesota sent a well-prepared delegation to the historic International Women's Year meeting in Houston, Texas in 1977. The Minnesota group was the only one to have met several times before the IWY meeting to hammer out a list of resolutions they hoped would be accepted by the conference. Feeling that their voices had not been heard at the prior Minnesota

Women's meeting in St. Cloud,   black, Native American, Asian, and Hispanic women established their own caucus, Women of Color, in June 1976. They carried a separate agenda to Houston, condemning racism in the women's movement.   Racism remains an issue for all Americans, but Minnesota (as well as other states) can point to unpublicized efforts by women to address some of those issues That they do not always succeed suggests how difficult they are to overcome.   One promising effort, a dialogue between African-American and Jewish women spawned a number of meetings, conferences, and other groups. They did succeed in creating an environment of trust where they could articulate many of the things that separated them. As one participant put it, " that trust, however, did not survive the heart of the issue." Although they stayed friends, the formal dialogue dissolved after five years.

Minnesota Women Today

Perhaps the most striking development of the last part of the twentieth century has been the entry of women into fields heretofore occupied almost exclusively by men.   There are women rabbis and ministers as well as women serving in key paid and volunteer leadership positions within church and synagogue. Women journalists are commonplace in all media forms; women in television, however, are more often than their male counterparts to be subject to discrimination on the basis of age and thus experience a shorter professional life-span. Women have become indispensable in maintaining the military establishment. Women design and build homes and offices. They wear hard hats and operate cranes and tractors. They run businesses large and small. They tend bar and care for the elderly. They provide medical and legal services. There are now women doctors and male nurses (turnabout is fair play). Even as women have less to point to by way of achieving some measure of equality in the fields of engineering and science, they are in the pipeline and soon will be making their marks. Occupational diversity is clearly the name of the game

Enrollments at the University of Minnesota document these changes: in 1996, 69 percent of the students in pharmacy and veterinary medicine were women (in 1960 comparable figures were 14 percent and two percent). Comparing the same years, women accounted for 44 percent of the enrollments in law and medicine compared with one percent and five percent; 43 percent in management compared with two percent; 21 percent in technology compared with one percent, and 38 percent in dentistry compared with zero percent.   Women are earning more degrees in higher education at every level save the doctorate and first professional (e.g., law, medicine, etc.)

Women in Business

It does not follow from these extraordinary figures that all is well in the world of women. A glass ceiling hangs over the heads of women in business. In Minnesota just over ten percent of the top jobs of Minnesota's 200 largest companies are held by women; only a fraction more than six percent serve on the boards of those same companies. There may be cracks in the glass ceiling but it is still firmly in place. One consequence of this barrier has been the emigration of corporate women to positions as consultants or as entrepreneurs. For many of these women, programs to establish parental leave for both sexes, to provide flexible scheduling and child care have been too little and too late. Women entrepreneurs have built new business with new ways of managing. Most of the women-owned businesses in Minnesota (nearly 35 percent) are located in the Twin Cities — 104,000 of them providing jobs for 240,000 people and generating annual revenues of $31 billion.

Equal pay for equal work remains the number one priority of 94 percent of working women. In 1977, women were paid at the rate of 47 cents for every dollar earned by men. Twenty years later the rate of pay was a tad under 75 cents for every dollar. That figure is down, however, from a high of 77 cents in 1993, Economists tend to agree that this decline may not reflect a resurgence of pay discrimination so much as the fact that greater numbers of welfare women are entering the workforce in unskilled, low-paying jobs. The AFL-CIO, recognizing that the recruitment of women into labor unions is essential for its survival, has changed its tune, bringing women into important leadership positions and initiating recruitment campaigns that appeal to working women's concerns — equal pay, child care, and better benefits.

The 1977-79 strike of the Willmar 8 — bank women who finally rebelled at the expected practice of training their male successors and then becoming their subordinates — called nationwide attention to injustices that had been taken for granted as long as anyone could remember. The American Banker noted "The Willmar incident has become an almost legendary illustration of the movement toward equal opportunity and equal rights in the United States." Minnesota was the first state to address wage and salary inequities in public employment with legislation enacted in the 1980s.

Women in Politics and Government

While Minnesota has always had a high rate of female employment and a high rate of female education, it was only with the onset of the second wave of the women's movement that women began to make their mark with increasing number and efficacy on the politics and public policy of Minnesota. In Minnesota the rate of increase in the number of women legislators went from six percent in 1979 to 28 percent in 1999. While that figure represents a drop from sixth place before the 1998 election, Minnesota's rank in eleventh place nationally is way ahead of its neighboring states. Of these four, Wisconsin comes closest and is in twenty-fourth place. Four of the state's six constitutional officers are women. Marlene Johnson was the first Lieutenant Governor, serving with Governor Rudy Perpich from 1983 to 1991. She was followed by Joanelle Dyrstad and Joanne E. Benson in the first and second terms of Governor Arne H. Carlson. and by May Schunk in 1999 who serves with Reform Party Governor Jesse Ventura.   Joan Anderson Growe served 22 years as Secretary of State. Her successor is Mary Kiffmeyer. Judith H. Dutcher made her successful political debut in the race for state auditor in 1996, and Carol Johnson was elected state treasurer in 1998.   For a few years beginning in 1991, four women and three men served on the Minnesota Supreme Court. Rosalie Wahl was the first woman to serve, beginning in 1977, and Kathleen Blatz became the first woman Chief Justice with her appointment by Governor Carlson in 1998. Women can now be found on the Appeals Court (19%) and on district courts (23%).

There have been failures as well. No woman from Minnesota has been elected to the U.S. House of Representatives since Coya Knutson, from the old Ninth District, served two terms in the late 1950s.   Despite vigorous efforts by Joan Growe in 1984 and by Ann Wynia in 1994, no woman from Minnesota has been elected to the U.S. Senate.

Almost fifteen percent of the mayors of Minnesota are women, including Sharon Sayles Belton, Minneapolis, who was elected mayor of the state's largest city in 1993 and reelected in 1997. All told, almost 15 percent of women serve as mayors.   In other local offices, 17 percent of the 447 county commissioners are women; they hold almost one-third of the 2,593 school board seats, and nearly 25 percent of the 3,477 city council seats..

Women's organizations have also made their mark on the political scene. The League of Women Voters of Minnesota, founded in 1919 as the successor to the state suffrage association, has long served as an advocate for legislation in the public interest, as a provider of nonpartisan information to voters, and as a training ground for women in public office. In 1971 the bipartisan Minnesota Women's Political Caucus was started. In 1982 the Minnesota Women's Campaign Fund was formed to fund pro-choice women candidates; it has since become the largest state organization of its kind in the country.   Three years later, the Campaign Fund and the Minnesota Women's Consortium worked together to initiate a Woman Candidate Development Coalition to recruit women candidates for local and state offices.

Minnesota women have also been prominent on the national political scene. Eugenie Anderson of Red Wing was the first American woman with the rank of Ambassador, serving in Denmark from 1949-53 and subsequently in Bulgaria from 1962-64. St. Paul native, Roxanne Ridgway, served as Ambassador to Finland, and Geri Joseph of Minneapolis as Ambassador to the Netherlands. Koryne Horbal and Arvonne Fraser, both stalwarts of the women's movement in Minnesota, served as U.S. delegates to the United Nations Commission on Women.

Women in Sports

The exceptionally large increase of women in sports throughout the nation has to be attributed to the enactment of Title IX in which barred sex discrimination in educational institutions that receive federal funds. The legislation was greeted with early hostility by key groups like the National Collegiate Athletic Association (NCAA), challenged in court by individual colleges and universities, and beleaguered by feeble enforcement on the part of the Office of Civil Rights. Nevertheless, it endured and changed the landscape of women's sports. While it has not leveled the playing field (most men's athletic programs still consume more dollars than women's programs), participation has gone up in Minnesota high schools from 2,406 varsity teams in ten sports in 1977 to 2,821 varsity teams in 15 sports in 1997 At the University of Minnesota in 1997, 375 men participated in 11 teams (106 in football); 239 women participated in the same number of teams (47 in track and field). With the addition of rowing, women's' teams will number 12, and the number of participants will increase accordingly. The showing of the American women in the 1996 Olympic games, winning in basketball, softball, and soccer —and the subsequent winning of the world cup by the women's soccer team in 1999— help to achieve visibility and motivate participation by young girls and women. Not only are more women doing more sports in high school and college, but professional opportunities in basketball, fast pitch (baseball), and soccer have been established or soon will be.. Data from the University of Minnesota indicates that women student athletes have excelled at academics with 62 percent earning grade point averages of 3.0 or above and more than fifty of those posting straight A grades. Participation in sports brings out qualities of teamwork and leadership. Not surprisingly, 80 percent of women identified as key leaders in Fortune 500 companies credited their sports backgrounds as contributing to their success,

Individual Minnesota Women of Today

So many women have made their mark on the Minnesota scene that it is impossible to mention them all. A small and very arbitrary selection may serve, however, to represent their numbers and their diversity. Distinguished women artists and writers have been and continue to be an important part of Minnesota life, among them Margaret Culkin Banning, Grace Flandreau, Maud Hart Lovelace, Grace Lee Nute, and Martha

Ostenso. Of more recent vintage are Carol Bly, Judith Guest, Tami Hoag, Patrticia Hample, LaVyrle Spencer, and Susan Allen Toth. Many of the distinguished small publishing houses in the state have women at the helm — Emilie Buchwald (Milkweed), Joan Drury (Spinsters Ink), Vicki Lanski (The Book Peddlers), and Fiona McCrae (Graywolf). Anne DeCoster, Janti Visscher, and Phyllis Weiner are among the multitude of prominent Minnesota women artists at work today. Dancers Loyce Houlton and Nancy Hauser led nationally known and respected companies.

Marge Anderson, Chief Executive of the Mille Lacs Band of Ojibway, and Winona LaDuke, founder of the White Earth Land Recovery Project and the Indigenous Women's Network, have become well-known leaders in the Minnesota Indian community. Black women like Reatha Clark King, president of the General Mills Foundation, Mary Thornton Phillips on the St. Paul School Board, Dorothea Burns, assistant director of Hallie Q. Brown/Martin Luther King Multi Service Center in St. Paul are only a few of the many African-American women in important leadership positions.

Martha Boessing, dramatist, organized At the Foot of the Mountain, a company of women actors. Ann Bancroft has traveled on an otherwise all-male dog-sled expedition to the North Pole and led an all-woman ski expedition to the South Pole. Sara M. Evans of the University of Minnesota received high praise for her book, Born for Liberty: A History of Women in America. and is a Distinguished McKnight University Professor.

Women's Organizations in Minnesota

There have been institutional developments as well. Women's Advocates, the first battered women's shelter in the nation, opened in St. Paul in 1974. Organizations like Working Opportunities for Women and WomenVenture have trained women, some of them on welfare, some displaced homemakers — all searching for job and entrepreneurial skills. The Melpomene Institute for Women's Health Research, founded by Executive Director Judy Mahle Lutter in 1982, is a unique organization researching and disseminating information about physically active girls and women. The Minnesota Women's Consortium, formed in 1980, is a confederation of over 170 women's groups that has served as a focal point for informing and activating women. Women, leafing through the biennial directory, can find organizations to serve their needs or organizations to be served through volunteer activity. Old women, young women, women of color, lesbian women, women interested in social change, in politics, in economic policy, in the arts, in health, in athletics — they are all there, ready and welcoming. The Minnesota Women's Press celebrated its 15th anniversary in 1999 and, to the great surprise of skeptics, has proved to be a resounding success. The Commission on the Economic Status of Women, established by the Minnesota Legislature in 1976, has provided valuable research data over the years and endorsed legislation designed to benefit women at work and women in the home.

The story of Minnesota women is rich in history, varied in content, and diverse in personalities. As more and more people have become acquainted with their achievements, they have come to recognize that women merit more than just a passing reference in a text book. These last few decades have witnessed a veritable explosion in scholarship by women about women. There is now ample documentation to affirm the proposition that the remarkable changes in women's lives will be writ large as the most significant social reform in twentieth century America.

Edited and enlarged by: Barbara Stuhler
Source: Barbara Stuhler and Gretchen Kreuter, Women of Minnesota: Selected Biographical Essays. St. Paul: Minnesota Historical Society Press, St. Paul, 1997; revised edition 1998.

Legislative Commission on the Economic Status of Women
85 State Office Building
St. Paul, MN 55155   651-296-8590 or 1-800-657-3949 E-mail: lcesw@commissions.leg.state.mn.us

Minnesota Women in the 20th Century 1900-1990
The Commission collected statistical data about the changing culture for women in this century. Highlights of the report include:
• Current marital status patterns resemble those in the state in the first part of the century. The number of divorces tripled in the past 30 years.
• Women are almost half of the paid labor force, and almost two-thirds of women participate in the paid labor force.
• The educational attainment of women has increased. The percentage of women age 25 and over with at least a college degree increased more than fivefold between 1940 and 1990.
• The number of female-headed households and families has increased.
• There has been a progressive decrease in the income of female-headed families as a percentage of the income of married-couple families between 1960 and 1990.
• The age group with the highest percent increase in number of women between 1980 and 1990 was women age 40 to 44, reflecting the aging of the baby boom generation.
• Women continue to outlive men and the gap between them has increased over time.
Source: Minnesota Women In the Twentieth Century 1900-1990, Legislative Commission on the Economic Status of Women.

Marital Status of Women From 1900 to 1990

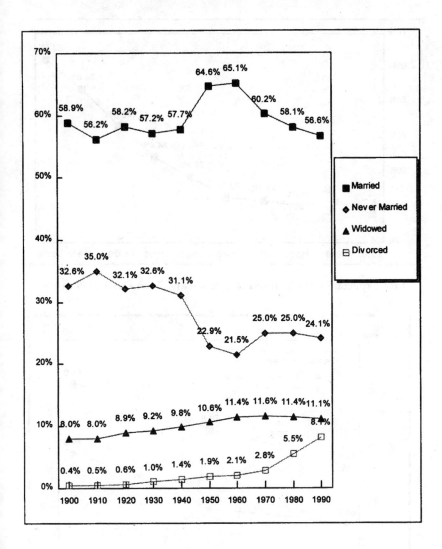

During his arrest and after being thrashed by alleged victim Emma Korbel, 87, while trying to steal her handbag... "I don't care what you do to me, but keep me away from that old lady!" --An accused purse snatcher

Labor Force Participatiion of Minnesota Women From 1900 to 1990

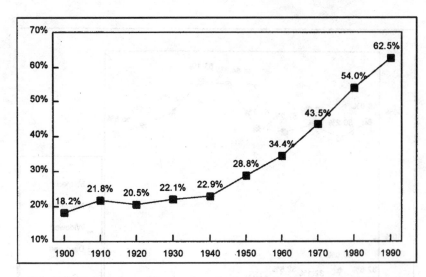

Life Expectancy for Minnesota Women and Men From 1950 to 1990

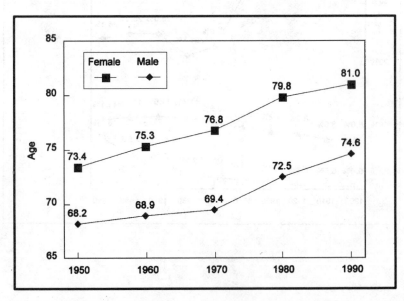

Source: Minnesota Women In the Twentieth Century 1900-1990, Legislative Commission on the Economic Status of Women.

Chapter 11
Employment/Organized Labor

The beginnings of the Minnesota labor movement, 1854-1900, were marked with success and adversity.

The first newspaper report of a Minnesota strike was in October, 1854. The strikers were journeyman tailors of St. Paul and the outcome is not known, but the strikers probably lost.

In 1856, the Typographical Union was formed in St. Paul. Today, it is known as Local Union No. 30 of the International Typographical Union and is the oldest existing labor organization in the state.

Post-Civil War—1880s

In the post-Civil War period labor was in the doldrums.

Three laboring groups, however, were organized in 1867. Plasterers of St. Paul first organized that year. The Journeyman Tailors Self-Help Protective Society was incorporated as a result of an earlier strike and German immigrants in Minneapolis established a Workingman's Society to find jobs for all society members.

St. Paul Journeyman Cigar Makers' Union was organized by "tramp" members from other cities in 1868.

At least seven strikes can be traced through newspapers in 1870. Strikers wanted higher wages, a shorter workday, improvements in working conditions, promotion of state intervention on behalf of workers, and promotion of the dignity of labor.

Also in 1870, the Brotherhood of Locomotive Engineers at Austin was formed. It is now the state's oldest labor union with continuous existence.

The Depression of 1873-1879 not only limited union growth, but ruined most unions.

But in 1873, the Custom Tailors Benevolent Union was formed in Minneapolis, and by 1874 the Miller's Union was holding regular meetings in Minneapolis.

A local assembly of Knights of Labor was formed in Minneapolis in 1878 and the following year another one arose in St. Paul. That same year Great Lakes sailors organized.

1880-1900

Prosperity and growth of industry were boons to the organized labor movement in the 1880s.

The Federal Census of 1880 recorded Minnesota as having 21 unions out of a total of 2,440 in the entire nation. Nine of these were railroad brotherhoods and the remainder manufacturing and craft groups.

During this period tradesmen, particularly in the Twin Cities, became union conscious. Unions grew rapidly, despite the need for utmost secrecy because of workers' fears that their union activities would become known to employers.

During the decade working conditions improved, wages rose and hours fell. The Twin Cities were recognized as two of the best-organized cities in the United States.

In 1882 the St. Paul Trades and Labor assembly, the first such body in Minnesota, was founded with the assistance of the Knights of Labor Assembly. In 1883 the Minneapolis Trades Assembly was organized. Its name changed several times and finally the Minneapolis Central labor Union Council was accepted.

Knights of Labor experienced a rapid growth in Minnesota during the 1880s. Besides the Twin Cities it had local assemblies in Duluth, Still water, Albert Lea and Rochester. By 1883 it claimed 85 local assemblies within the state with 6,500 members.

The Knights stimulated workers to make demands for what they considered to be their rightful place in society. But by 1887 the Knights' decline was beginning and skilled workers were finding the new craft-conscious American Federation of Labor more appealing.

In 1886 joint political state conventions were held in St. Paul by Knights of Labor and the Farmers Alliance. (This was one of the first of many efforts which would lead, in the 20th century, to establishment of the Farmer-Labor Party.)

By the end of the 1880s, trade unionism had spread over a larger part of the state. As membership increased, so did strikes.

In 1885, for instance, only three strikes were recorded. But in 1888 there were 16 and in 1890 there were 20.

The 1890s saw growth of organized labor and the winning of concessions from factory, mill and mine owners.

The Minnesota State Federation of Labor was formed in 1890, proclaiming the following principles: an 8-hour day, contracts for convict labor should be abolished, wages should have first lien on all products, employees should be paid once a week, there should be state inspection of mines and factories, employees should be able under law to recover damages for loss of life or limb at work (a suggestion that was a forerunner of workman's compensation), the state should own and control railroads, telegraph and telephones and textbooks should be supplied free to all school children.

In 1893, the State Board of Labor Statistics was renamed the Bureau of labor, with enlarged powers.

Nationally-known socialist and union organizer Eugene V. Debs in 1894 directed the successful American Railway Union 18-day tie-up of the great Northern railway after James J. Hill ordered a wage cut.

Union members got their own newspapers in 1896 when both the Minnesota Union Advocate in St. Paul and The Duluth Labor World were started.

1900-1930

In the years between 1900 and 1930 labor experienced both advances and reverses in Minnesota.

By its militant unionism, labor reflected the influence of radial populism in the early 1900s. But organized labor in Minneapolis experienced serious setbacks.

Strong anti-union sentiments of flour milling companies proved to be a powerful threat to unionism and gave rise to labor strife.

In 1902 and 1903 there was a general strike against the three largest flour companies in Minneapolis. Workers demanded an 8-hour day to replace the 12-hour one, with no reduction in pay.

In those same years unionism was threatened by the formation of the Citizens Alliance, an organization of employers which fought every major strike in the city for more than 30 years. Its existence made Minneapolis well known nationally among employers as an "open shop" city and among labor as "one of the worst scab cities in the country."

Despite these adversities, the labor movement gained momentum through organization, slowly-won economic gains and a gradual increase in political power.

Between 1900 and 1903 Boot and Shoe workers, Ice Wagon Drivers, St. Paul butchers, Stillwater sawmill workers and St. Paul brewery workers were all organized.

A new, dynamic force on the state labor obscene is first mentioned in the early 1900s—the Industrial Workers of the World (IWW). The IWW offered a militant, radical form of industrial unionism that sprang from the socialist-anarchist tradition.

By 1911, the IWW was involved in street fights in Duluth and Minneapolis over the question of the union organizers' right to speak in public.

The two biggest IWW strikes in Minnesota erupted in 1916. The first significant strike in the timber industry involved at one time an estimated

4,000 strikers who demanded an 8-hour day and increased pay. In the mining industry, from 12,000 to 15,000 Iron Range miners struck, also demanding an 8-hour day.

In 1913, Minnesota became only the second state in the nation to pass a workmen's Compensation law, doing so after a decade of struggle.

But in 1917 labor suffered a severe setback when the legislature voted near dictatorial powers to a seven-man Public Safety Commission. The commission barred strikes, forbade moves to extend unionization and used its powers to cripple the IWW and any other unions they considered "subversive."

1930-1940

By 1930 the effects of the deepening Depression were obvious in Minnesota, with 18.5 per cent of state union members unemployed. By 1932 the number had risen to 30 per cent unemployed with 17 per cent working part-time.

Labor activity increased dramatically in 1933, largely as a result of the National Industrial Recovery Act, legislation designed to get the nation's economy moving again.

America's first "sit down" strike also took place in 1933 at the Hormel Company in Austin.

The year 1934 was a banner one for labor unions.

The first bakers Union contract in the Twin Cities covering a machine producer of baked goods was signed. State employees in the Highway Department organized and Twin Cities newsmen organized. Their union became the foundation for the American Newspaper Guild. The first Minnesota contract was was by International Ladies Garment Workers Union and some Twin Cities filling stations were organized.

The 1934 truck drivers' strike in Minneapolis was perhaps the most violent, and yet the most significant, in the state's labor history.

In May a strike for recognition resulted in a pitched battle between pickets and an employers' "army." Gov. Floyd B. Olson intervened and brought about a tentative agreement. But in July a more violent strike erupted when some employers reneged on the May settlement and martial law was invoked.

Four strikes were killed and scores injured until Gov. Olson again intervened and helped the Teamsters win the strike. The Citizens Alliance was finally defeated.

After the strike the Minneapolis labor movement emerged from a period of official hostility and public antagonism to one of acceptance and began to grow to its present strength. (Today Minneapolis is one of the most highly organized cities in the U.S.)

The middle and late 1930s were years of significant labor developments. Unemployment compensation, long sought by the State Federation, was adopted. The Steel Workers Organizing Committee organized the Mesabi range, the Minnesota State Federation of Teachers was established and state locals participated in the formation of the American Federation of State, County and Municipal Employees.

Long-sought goals were attained in 1937. A Twin Cities-wide contract was won by the Hotel and Restaurant Employees and Bartenders Union, the International Power Company, the Twin Cities paperbox and carton industry was organized and the Twin Cities "waterfront" was finally organized.

Greyhound bus line employees organized and the Minnesota State CIO Council representing an estimated 40,000 workers was formed.

In 1939, Gov. Harold Stassen succeeded in having the legislature pass a state labor relations act to apply to intra-state commerce. The bill anticipated many features of the later national Taft-Hartley Act.

1940-1980

Labor played a prominent role in the merging of the Democratic and Farmer-Labor parties in 1944.

As the state entered the post-World War II era in 1946 the all-time national record for labor unrest was reflected in Minnesota.

Five thousand members of the National Maritime Union on the Great Lakes struck against the 7-day, 56-hour work week. St. Paul teachers began the first organized teachers' strike in the nation's history.

The issue of communism and how to handle it had risen by 1946. In 1947 a strongly anti-communist executive board was formed by the Minnesota Federation of Labor, the DFL party and farm groups to work with the CIO.

In 1951 a strike by Minneapolis schoolteachers during the legislative session provided Conservatives in the legislature an argument to finally enact a law prohibiting strikes by public employees.

But in 1954 a liberal turn in Minnesota politics resulted in favorable labor legislation and other developments. Many measures supported by the AFL State Federation of Labor were passed, including the Fair Employment Practices Act, improvements in workmen's and unemployment benefits and in old age assistance and increased state school aids.

The state's first comprehensive medical care program was negotiated that same year by the Duluth building trades.

In 1956 the AFL and CIO held a state merger convention in Rochester and formed the new Minnesota AFL-CIO Federation of Labor.

A strike in 1959 at Wilson Company meat packing plant in Albert Lea resulted in the worst violence since 1934 when Wilson attempted to reopen the plant with strike breakers. The dispute ended in arbitration.

In 1967 the legislature enacted a "meet and confer" law for teachers, restricting the rights of teachers to genuine negotiations. This law was the chief cause for making 1969 one of the most turbulent years for public education in Minnesota annals.

In 1970 the Minneapolis Federation of teachers voted to strike pointing up the deficiencies of the "meet and confer" and "no strike" laws. The "meet and confer" law was repealed in 1971 and new rights were conferred on the state's 230,000 public employees. 390 locals elected the MN Education Association (MEA) as their representative and 50 locals elected the MN Federation of Teachers (MFT) as their representative.

The beginning of the 1970s found Minnesota's labor movement numerically strong and financially stronger. Traditionally, mining contributed the largest number of union members followed by manufacturing.

1980-Present

However, new challenges awaited labor in the 1980s. Among them were automation, the shift from a manufacturing to a service oriented economy, organizing white collar clerical workers and continued recruitment of minorities and women. In addition, a deep recession in 1981 cut into union power as workers focused on keeping jobs.

For teachers, a modified right to strike law was enacted by the legislature in 1981 allowed strikes at any point during negotiations. In a show of solidarity in the face of school board foot dragging during negotiations in the 1981 season, 380 locals in 434 school districts filed intent to strike notices. Of these, 35 MEA locals went out on strike.

On the Iron Range, the collapse of the steel industry in 1981 and 1982 lead to restructuring. United Steelworker locals fought a losing battle against retrenchments, concessions and downsizing.

Fed up after years of wage freezes, concessions speed-ups and rising injury rates, United Food and Commercial Workers (UFCW) Local P-9 members at Austin-based Hormel, struck in 1985, after the company had cut wages 23 percent and offered a contract that nullified many work rules, grievance procedures and seniority rights. The strike pitted Hormel workers against both their company and their international union, in one of the most complex labor management struggles in state history.

In 1988 Boise Cascade of International Falls brought in contractors from the southern U.S. for upgrading and expansion of their mill. BE&K, the prime contractor attempted to operate on an "open shop" basis, a move that was fiercely resisted by construction trades union locals in the state.

Minnesota union members, environmentalists and other concerned citizens mobilized against Congressional passage of the North American Free

Trade Agreement (NAFTA), in 1993, because it lacked safeguards for workers and the environment.

In 1998, the state's two teacher unions, the Minnesota Education Association and the Minnesota Federation of Teachers merged into Education Minnesota.

Diversity in the workforce became a demographic as well as a social issue. The number of traditional job holders in many businesses and industries (men, especially white) was shrinking due to retirements, and the expansion of business began forcing employers to actively recruit minority and women workers.

Workers' Compensation Reform Laws

The Department of Labor and Industry oversaw reforms to the workers' compensation system in 1992 and 1995 that resulted in reduced litigation, more oversight of insurance rates, greater safety incentives, cost controls on benefits and increased compliance provisions for insurers and employers. By contrast, the Minnesota AFL-CIO says cuts in injured workers' benefits enacted in 1995 are a 1/3 reduction. The statement that the legislation resulted in "reduced litigation," is also inaccurate, and meaningful oversight of insurance rates increased only nominally, if at all.

Union Membership

From the mid 1980's to the mid 1990's union membership in private employment fluctuated from 237,000 members to a high in 1992 of 259,000 and dropping back to 236,000 members in 1996. As a percentage, union numbers declined from 14.6% to 12.9% in that period.

Minnesota Workers and Their Jobs

Minnesota currently has one of the hottest economies in the nation. We've had the lowest unemployment rate in the country (2.6% in June, 1999) for the last 20 months in a row. Minnesotans also rank near the top in wages earned, placing 11th in the nation in per capita personal income at $27,510. Minnesota had the seventh highest median income for a four-person family, at $60,577 in 1997, while the U.S. median was $53,350.

In 1998, Minnesota had an average of 2,613,454 people in the workforce, 2,545,162 of whom were employed and 68,292 of whom were unemployed. Once again, the Twin Cities area counties had the lowest levels of unemployment and the northern counties had the highest unemployment.

Most sectors remained stable from 1986 to 1997. Notably, manufacturing shrank from 20.1% to it's present 17.9% of employees. Fiscal responsibility as well as a robust economy reduced government employment from 16.2% to 13.6%. The largest gain was in the service sector which grew by approximately 4%

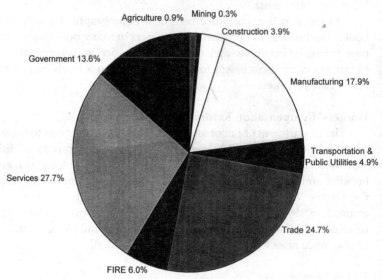

1997 Minnesota Employment Distribution by Industry

Agriculture 0.9%   Mining 0.3%
Construction 3.9%
Government 13.6%
Manufacturing 17.9%
Services 27.7%
Transportation & Public Utilities 4.9%
Trade 24.7%
FIRE 6.0%

Source: Minnesota Department of Economic Security/Covered Employment and Wages (ES 202)

The Future

With a decade long economic boom in the national economy, Minnesota is situated well for further growth, even though our present rate is non-sustainable. The following table and graph depict past and projected growth in broad segments of our economy. The strong trend of service sector growth will continue into the millennium with trade and manufacturing showing modest growth. Agriculture, forestry and fishing are expected to decline but not as sharply as they did from the mid 1980s to the mid-1990s.

Source: Reprinted from the March 1999 issue of MN Economic Trends, MN Department of Economic Security, Research and Statistics Office. Analysis by Dave Senf, Long Term Projections Unit.

Individual occupations that are expected to top the growth charts for the next decade reflect our culture where we depend increasingly on technology and have an aging population. Opportunities are available in these and other fast growth occupations for individuals with all levels of education.

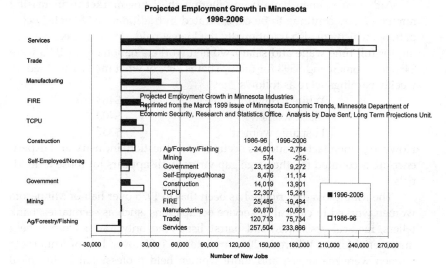

This chart is reprinted from the March 1999 issue of Minnesota Economic Trends, Minnesota Department of Economic Security, Research and Statistics Office. Analysis by Dave Senf, Long Term Projections Unit.

Top 10 Fastest Growing Occupations and Hourly Wages

Rank	Occupation	Projected Growth	1997 Median
1	Computer Engineers	141%	$28.03
2	Computer Programmer	98%	20.79
	Systems Analysts	98%	24.50
3	Desktop Publishing Specialists	93%	16.93
4	Computer Support Specialists	81%	16.09
5	Database Administrators	76%	22.76
6	Personal and Home Care Aides	75%	7.37
7	Occupational Therapy Assistants & Aides	73%	13.43
8	Physical and Corrective Therapy	73%	11.75
9	Home Health Aides	69%	7.71
10	Human Service Workers	66%	10.56

Source: Employment Projections, Occupational Employment Statistics, MN Dept. of Economic Security.

Chapter sources: Compare Minnesota 1998/1999: MN Department of Trade and Economic Development. www.dted.state.mn.us
State Rankings, 1999. Minnesota Workforce Facts, April, 1999. Department of Economic Security www.MNWorkForceCenter.org/lmi

Working Women

Although women have been entering the labor market in increasing numbers, they continue to be concentrated in traditionally "female" occupations, which are also traditionally the lowest paid. Median weekly earning for full time wage and salary women workers nationally in 1998 were $456 for women and $598 for men. That is 76% of what men earn. Median weekly earnings were as follows:

White women	$468
Black women	$400
Hispanic women	$337

However, when factors such as occupation, education, industry and experience are accounted for, the wage gap virtually disappears for those individuals.

The Minnesota experience has been that in 1975 over half of Minnesota women worked in clerical or service occupations such as secretaries, bank tellers, medical assistants, and hairstylists. And only 5% of women held managerial jobs. Whereas, 20 years later in 1995, over 11% of Minnesota women were managers, and more women held professional or technical jobs (such as accounting, research, and social work) than jobs in the service sector. Women represented 23% of Minnesota's directors and 15% of Minnesota's executives in 1995.

The percentage of women who work in our state was second highest nationally in 1966 at 68.7%. That figure rose to 85.5% when considering only women ages 25 to 54. With so many women working, child care is an important issue. Nearly 40% of employers with more than 5 employees offer services that range from referral to on-site day care. Additionally, we have the fourth highest ratio of licensed daycares in the country. Minnesota has 53 licensed child care centers per 1,000 children under age 5 compared with 19 centers per 1,000 as a national average.

Source: Text by Carrie Conaway, State of Minnesota.

Employed Women by Occupational Group, 1998 (in thousands)

Occupation	Employed	Percent
Managerial and professional specialty	19,070	31.4
Technical, sales, and administrative support	24,728	40.7
Service occupations	10,614	17.5
Precision, production, craft, and repair	1,203	2.0
Operators, fabricators, and laborers	4,487	7.4
Farming, forestry, and fishing	668	1.1
Total	60,771	100.0

Source U.S. Dept. of Labor, Bureau of Labor Statistics, Employment & Earnings, January 1999.

Women In the Trades (WIT)

Historically, women have had a difficult, if not impossible, time trying to gain equal access to employment opportunities in non-traditional fields. In addition, women who have managed to break into non-traditional occupations frequently experience isolation, a lack of role models, sexual discrimination, and various forms of harassment on the jobsite. Nontraditional jobs for women are jobs where women make up less than 25% of the total number of workers

In 1939 the state approved the Minnesota Apprenticeship Program. Since that time over 93,000 people have gone through the program. A 1979 survey by the Council on the Economic Status of Women found there were 7,521 active apprenticeships in Minnesota. Apprentice means a person engaged in study and on-the-job training for a skilled trade and enrolled in a program which is registered with the Apprenticeship Division of the Minnesota Department of Labor and Industry. Of these active apprenticeships, 91, or 1.2%, were women.

Minnesota ranked well below the national average in the proportion of its apprentices who were women. In June, 1978, the state ranked 48th of the 54 states and territories in this respect. One reason may be that other states, but not Minnesota, recognized apprenticeships in cosmetology, a trade which accounted for 12% of registered female apprentices nationally.

The legislature instituted the Labor Education Advancement Program (LEAP) "to combat the residual effect of racial and gender discrimination" in apprenticeship programs in 1996. This was in addition to a plan begun in 1978 under the requirements of Title 29 entitled Minnesota Plan for Equal Employment Opportunity In Apprenticeship.

July 1999 figures stand at 260 women out of a total 6113 apprenticeships, or 4.2%. Participation by minority groups including both sexes is 534 , or 9.5%.

Write to the Division of Apprenticeship, 443 Lafayette Road N., St. Paul, MN 55155; Call (651) 296-2371 or 1-800-657-3607

Women in the Trades (WIT) is a non-profit organization whose primary purpose is to help women find and keep well paying jobs with good benefits in non-traditional occupations. In this way, WIT hopes to bridge the pay gap that exists between men and women and to enable women to live financially independent and economically stable lives. WIT also seeks to make all workplaces truly diverse and receptive to all peoples regardless of race or gender. WIT seeks to bring awareness of construction trades as viable careers to young women who are still forming their plans as well as women in the workforce who are looking for better employment. For this WIT offers, monthly orientation sessions are held to explore possibilities, consulting, referrals, a job hotline, newsletter, and speakers bureau.

WIT are cooperating in two initiatives to promote more diverse construction company employees:

The F.A.C.T. Project (Future for All in the Construction Trades) funded by the MN Dept. of Transportation and managed by WIT, Minneapolis Urban League, and Women Venture began a three phase process in 1996.

1) Identify existing barriers and solutions to enhance the recruitment and retention of minorities and women in the construction trades.

2) Based on findings from Phase One, design a collaborative work plan with representatives of community organizations, educational institutions, government agencies, industry, and labor to assist minorities and women into the construction industry. Phase two was begun in April 1997.

3) Implement the workplan designed in Phase Two.

Construction Employment Diversity Assistance (CEDA) is a joint partnership of the Minneapolis Urban League, MN Building and Construction Trades Council (unions), MN American Indian Employment Rights Office, MN Women in the Trades, and WomenVenture. This partnership works "to increase the numbers of people of color and women employed and retained in the construction trades."

According to spokespersons at WIT, jobsites with some success in recruitment and retention of women have been due to community involvement and having a site liaison. Examples are the Federal Courthouse in 1995-96 where 5.6% women worked and the Science Museum from 1997-99 with 8.7% women working on the crew. It is still a struggle on most other projects to rise above the U.S. Department of Labor report of 2% women working in the trades.

Women In the Trades: 651-228-9955.

The Viking ship, Hjemkomst, built in Hawley, MN, by Robert Asp, successfully sailed 6,100 miles to Berge, Norway, May 11-July 19, 1982. Photo by Gjert Jahnsen, courtesy Hjemkomst Interpretive Center, Moorhead, MN.

Chapter 12

Agriculture

Minnesota has been an agricultural state since the first white settlers came from Scandinavia and Germany in the 19th century to break the virgin prairie soil with hand-made plows. The state's farmers have fed the nation through a depression and two world wars and our culture is permeated with the values of rural life, including strong family ties, hard work, regular church attendance, and Populist-based politics.

Until 1950, most Minnesotans lived in rural areas rather than in cities. That is why there has been so much concern about the "Farm Crisis," the loss of small, family operated farms that began at the beginning of the 1980s. Besides sympathy for the families who have lost their homes and jobs, Minnesotans also seem to sense that the end of family farming as a way of life is a loss for us all.

The national agricultural scene has been on the decline for the last half century. The peak of land in farms was 1,206 million acres in 1954 which declined to 968 million acres in 1997, a loss of 238 million acres. By comparison, Minnesota's land in farms was 28.9 million acres in 1998, down 1.5 million acres since 1984.

The number of farms also decreased during the same time from 101,000 to 80,000. From 1984-1985 alone, Minnesota recorded a drop of 5,000 farms, the largest year-to-year drop for any state in the nation. While the number of farms decreased, the average size of farms has increased from 301 in 1984 to 364 acres in 1998. This change reflects the trend of small, family operated farms selling to neighbors who were rounding out existing operations as well as to corporate farms. The number of farms in the U.S. in 1997 was estimated at 2,057,910.

Land values peaked in 1981, then declined. State average price per acre was $515 in 1986. Prices rose so that in the mid 1990s the per acre price passed $900 and settled at $916 state-wide in 1997. Prices ranged from a mean average of $471 per acre in the Northwest up to $1,839 in South Central Minnesota in 1998.

Statewide there were 1,746 sales reported during 1998 with an average value of $1,011 per acre, up $72 per acre from the average of the previous year.

Minnesota's major crops, ranked in the top five nationally, are sugarbeets, green peas, soybeans, dry edible beans, oats, spring wheat, sunflowers, flax, sweet corn, corn for feed, barley, cultivated wild rice, and rye. Sugarbeets are primarily grown in the Red River Valley, corn and soybeans mostly in southern Minnesota, wheat in the northwest corner, and oats on a diagonal line running from the northwest to the southeast corner of the state.   Minnesota is also a leader, nationally, in the production of milk, cheese, butter, ice cream, turkeys, mink pelts, pork, and honey.

From 1997-1998, the number of cattle operations dropped 2,000 to 31,000 while hog operations dropped 500. Beef cow operations dropped 200 to 15,800, while milk cow operations fell 800 to 9,700 and sheep operations dropped 300 to 2,600.   Combined value of all livestock and poultry on Minnesota farms was over $2.0 billion at the end of 1998.   All cattle and calves, valued at $1.7 billion, were 6% above a year earlier. The value of hogs was $291 million, down 40 %; all sheep and lambs, $15.9 million, down 8 %; all chickens, $28.0 million, up slightly; and turkeys, $359.7 million, down 9%.

The current farm crisis has its roots in international financial problems, historic price supports and U.S. Department of Agriculture "set aside" programs. The government purchased surplus grain supplies to affect the market's supply and demand by withholding or releasing stored grain at any given time.   Set aside programs such as the 1960s "Land Bank" and "Conservation Reserve" in the early 1980s paid farmers to keep land out of production, which led to smaller crops and, therefore, higher prices. Developing countries reconfigured their agricultural aims to capture some of these artificially high prices and in the case of Brazil, is poised to overtake U.S. domination in the worldwide production of soybeans.

The "Freedom to Farm" bill enacted in 1996 reduced government supports for diverted acres, so those acres were planted with crops. Additional acres in production, bigger and more efficient machinery, lower exports, plus favorable weather the last two years has given the U.S. a grain surplus that has lowered commodity prices to levels not seen in decades.

Minnesota's Rank Among States

Item	National Rank
Cash Receipts, 1997:	
Total	6
Livestock and Livestock Products	8
Crops	6
Crop Production, 1997:	
Corn	4
Soybeans	3

All Wheat 10
Spring Wheat 3
Oats 3
Barley 5
All Sunflowers 4
Dry Edible Beans 5
All Hay 7
All Potatoes 7
Sugarbeets 1
Flax 3
Rye 5
Sweet Corn for Processing 1
Green Peas for Processing 1
Cultivated Wild Rice 1* 2
Livestock, Dairy, Poultry:
Red Meat Production,1997 6
Cattle/Calves, 1/98 2* 11
Milk Cows, 1/98 5
Cattle/Calves Marketed, 1997 3* 14
Cattle/Calves on Feed, 1/98 10
Hogs, 12/97 3
Pig Crop, 1997 3
Hogs Marketed, 1997 3
Breeding Sheep & Lambs, 1/98 4* 12
Lamb Crop, 1997 4* 12
All Chickens, 12/97 5* 11
Eggs Produced, 1997 9
Turkeys Raised, 1997 2
Milk Production, 1997 5
Dairy Products Manufactured, 1997:
    Total Cheese 3
    American Cheese 1
    Italian Cheese 5
    Butter 5
    Ice Cream 4
Mink Pelts Produced, 1996 3
Honey Produced, 1997 6
Agricultural Exports, Fiscal 1997: 7
Fertilizer Consumption (year ending 6/30/86) 7

Source for whole chapter: Minnesota Agricultural Statistics 1998, information from Minnesota Department of Agriculture and U. S. Department of Agriculture website www.nass.usda.gov/mn

Number of Farms, Land in Farms, and Average Size

Year	Number	1,000 Acres	Ave. Farm Acres
1984	97,000	30,400	313
1985	96,000	30,400	317
1986	93,000	30,000	323
1987	92,000	30,000	326
1988	92,000	30,000	326
1989	90,000	30,000	333
1990	89,000	30,000	337
1991	88,000	30,000	341
1992	88,000	29,800	339
1993	86,000	29,700	345
1994	84,500	29,500	349
1995	83,000	*29,400	354
1996	82,000	29,200	356
1997	81,000	29,100	359
1998	80,000	28,900	364

A farm is any establishment from which $1,000 or more of agricultural products were sold or would normally be sold during the year.
* The increase in farm numbers is mainly due to a change in definition that includes places with 5 or more horses.

Exports

Minnesota ranked 7th in farm exports for fiscal year 1998. The value of the state's exports came to $2.28 billion versus $2.56 billion in 1997. This is a decrease of $275.0 million.

Agricultural Exports	(valued in millions of dollars.)	
Commodity	1986	1998
Feed grains & products	$389.0	$556.9
Soybeans & products	424.9	857.0
Wheat and products	152.9	60.0
Live animals & meat (no poultry)	39.3	231.1
Vegetables & preparations	44.0	169.5
Feeds & fodder	47.8	105.5
Dairy products	51.1	76.2
Hides & skins	40.7	50.7
Poultry & products	8.7	61.5
Sunflower seed & oil	12.9	10.0
Fats, oils & greases	14.6	25.5
Seed	9.5	24.3
Other	33.5	55.2
Total	$1,268.9	$2,283.3

Cultivated Wild Rice

Wild rice is the only cereal grain native to the United States. In 1977, the State Legislature designated wild rice as Minnesota's official state grain.

The cultivated crop is grown in the northern one-third of the state on an estimated 18,500 acres in the counties of Aitkin, Beltrami, Cass, Clearwater, Crow Wing, Itasca, Koochiching, Lake of the Woods, Polk, and Pennington. In 1998, cultivated wild rice production was 5.8 million processed pounds, down 6% from 1997.

Source: Minnesota Cultivated Wild Rice Council and MN Agricultural Statistics, 1998.

Farm Income

Total gross income for Minnesota farms amounted to $9.6 billion, the cost of production decreased 1% from 1997 to 8.3 billion so total net farm income for 1998 was $1,260.4 million dollars, compared to $953.8 million in 1997. This is compared to the $2,262.4 million in 1996.

The "average" Minnesota farm had gross farm income of $119,420 in 1998. Expenses used up $103,665 of the income, leaving the typical farm with $15,754 of net farm income in 1998, compared with $11,776 in 1997 and $27,590 in 1996, $12,161 in 1995 and $1,108 in 1993.

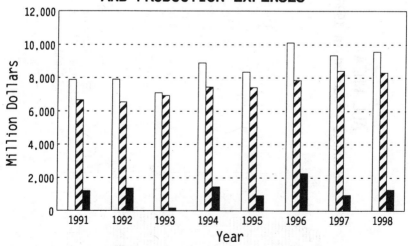

MINNESOTA FARM INCOME AND PRODUCTION EXPENSES

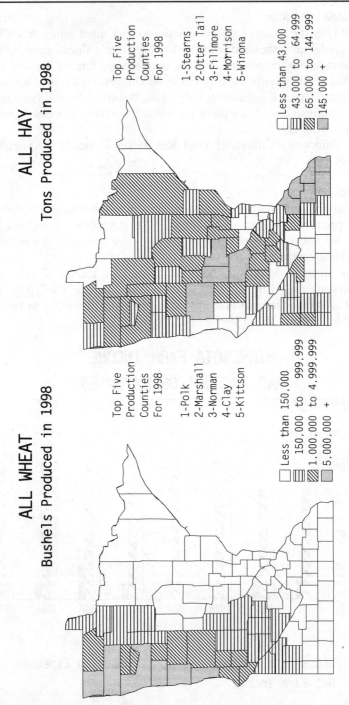

ALL WHEAT
Bushels Produced in 1998

Top Five
Production
Counties
For 1998

1-Polk
2-Marshall
3-Norman
4-Clay
5-Kittson

☐ Less than 150,000
▥ 150,000 to 999,999
▨ 1,000,000 to 4,999,999
▩ 5,000,000 +

ALL HAY
Tons Produced in 1998

Top Five
Production
Counties
For 1998

1-Stearns
2-Otter Tail
3-Fillmore
4-Morrison
5-Winona

☐ Less than 43,000
▥ 43,000 to 64,999
▨ 65,000 to 144,999
▩ 145,000 +

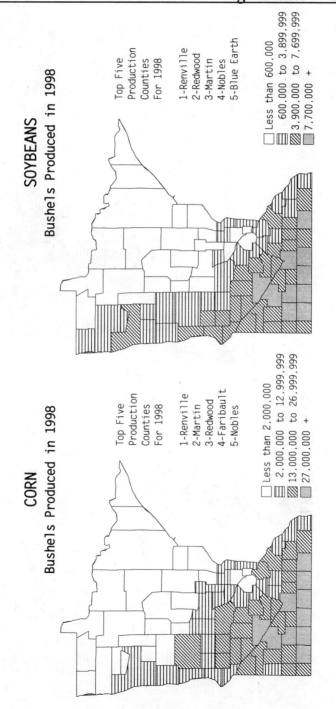

CORN

Bushels Produced in 1998

Top Five
Production
Counties
For 1998

1-Renville
2-Martin
3-Redwood
4-Faribault
5-Nobles

Less than 2,000,000
2,000,000 to 12,999,999
13,000,000 to 26,999,999
27,000,000 +

SOYBEANS

Bushels Produced in 1998

Top Five
Production
Counties
For 1998

1-Renville
2-Redwood
3-Martin
4-Nobles
5-Blue Earth

Less than 600,000
600,000 to 3,899,999
3,900,000 to 7,699,999
7,700,000 +

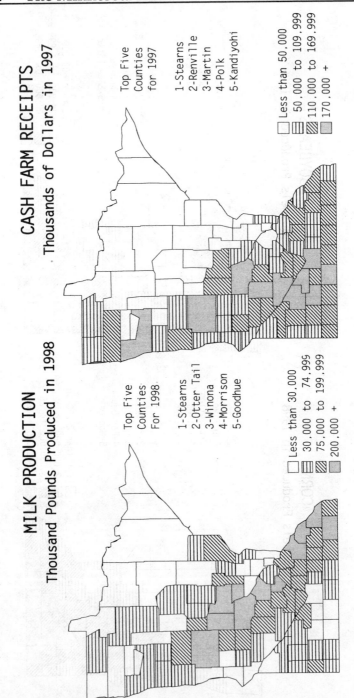

CASH FARM RECEIPTS
Thousands of Dollars in 1997

Top Five
Counties
for 1997

1-Stearns
2-Renville
3-Martin
4-Polk
5-Kandiyohi

Less than 50,000
50,000 to 109,999
110,000 to 169,999
170,000 +

MILK PRODUCTION
Thousand Pounds Produced in 1998

Top Five
Counties
For 1998.

1-Stearns
2-Otter Tail
3-Winona
4-Morrison
5-Goodhue

Less than 30,000
30,000 to 74,999
75,000 to 199,999
200,000 +

Chapter 13

Poverty and Welfare

Summary of Minnesota Welfare Reform

The effort to reform welfare for families with children in Minnesota had its beginnings in 1986. A legislative deadlock over a proposal to reduce the AFDC assistance standard was resolved by establishing a Commission on Welfare Reform. The commission issued a report in December 1996, that called for far reaching changes in Minnesota's approach to financial assistance. These changes would require waiver of federal law. The Minnesota Department of Human Services developed a design for a new program based on the principles recommended by the commission. After obtaining the legislature's endorsement in 1989, the department secured changes in federal law late in 1989 that authorized the granting of waivers to Minnesota for field trials of this new strategy, the Minnesota Family Investment Program (MFIP).

Field trials began in April, 1994. In 1997 the independent evaluation firm published interim findings that MFIP substantially increased employment among welfare families and lifted a substantial number of families out of poverty. This evidence provided support for a decision by the legislature in 1997 to implement MFIP statewide as Minnesota's program of reform under the TANF block grant that federal welfare reform had created to replace the AFDC program.

The MFIP program has two primary goals:
- reduction of dependency and
- reduction of poverty.

The program represents a contract with a family. If the parent "does her/his best" to support the family, the program will ensure that the economic outcome is positive. If only a low wage job can be obtained, the program will supplement the income from the job. A family loses the last dollar of cash support from MFIP when family income reaches about 120% of the federal poverty level.

The final evaluation report on MFIP in early 2000 will provide a large amount of information on the program's longer term impacts, including a special study of the effects upon children. As support for reform was based, in part, on a concern for the well-being of thousands of children living in poverty and dependency in the old welfare system, the information about the effects of reform on the well-being of children is awaited with interest.

The following graph shows a July 1998 caseload total of 47,533 which is subsequently reduced by 3,179 cases in 10 months. The following graph shows that by the end of the same time period 56.9% of those eligible were working. In a larger historical context, the change is more pronounced when you consider that the AFDC case load in 1994 was over 64,000 with only 9.9% working. Part of the reduction was due to changes brought about by federal welfare reform. So, there has been a substantial decline in case load and an increase in working cases.

Source: Text by Joel Kvamme, Evaluation Coordinator, Minnesota Department of Human Services, 1999.

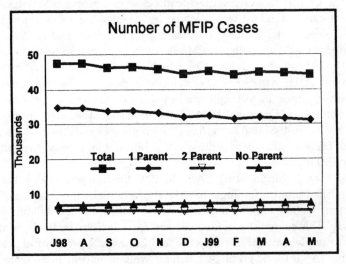

What is the Average MFIP Payment?

Month	Cash	Food	Total
December 1998	$386.75	$229.76	$616.51
January 1999	381.97	230.22	612.18
February	385.70	229.99	615.69
March	389.49	231.32	620.81
April	386.75	230.77	617.52
May	386.43	230.49	616.92

On the decision not to require government financing of abortions... "There is another world out there, the existence of which the (Supreme) Court, I suspect, either chooses to ignore or fears to recognize. And so the cancer of poverty will continue to grow." -- Justice Harry Blackmun Source: *Minnesotans Say the Darnedest Things*

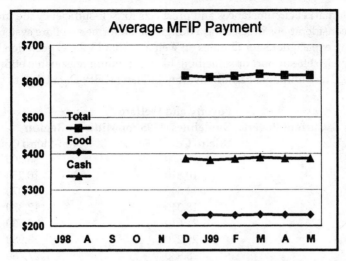

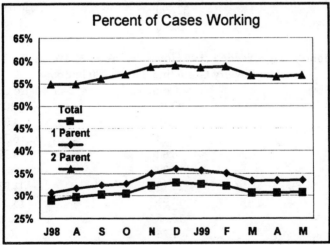

Trends

Nation-wide, real hourly wages have declined singe the early 1970's.

The most conservative measurement may be the calculations by Kosters and Ross (The Public Interest, Winter, 1988), who report a decline in real hourly wages of 4% between 1972 and 1981 Others, using different methods, announce a 11% decline.

This labor market trend supplies special meaning to the trends in family circumstances and their relevance to welfare reform.

- The combination of the decline in real wages and the increase in single parent families creates a special problem. Single parents lack the main device used by married couple families to offset wage erosion - another worker.

• Labor market circumstances and prospects for self-sufficiency are important considerations in selecting a design for a reformed welfare system and
setting expectations for families on welfare. Should the expectation be
complete self-support or something like "maximum reasonable effort"?
Source: The Minnesota Family Investment Plan (MFIP) Data Digest

Poverty and Welfare
Current Poverty Guidelines, 1998 for Midwest Region

Family Size	Metro Counties*	Non-Metro Counties
1	$6,600	$6,260
2	10,810	10,250
3	14,840	14,070
4	18,310	17,370
5	21,610	20,500
6	25,270	23,980
7	28,930	27,460
8	32,590	30,940
Additional	3,660	3,480

Total Hourly Wage Needed at 40 Hours Per Week, 52 Weeks Per Year to
Meet Poverty Guideline Base (2,080 hours):

Family Size	Metro Counties*	Non-Metro Counties
1	$3.17	$3.01
2	5.20	4.93
3	7.13	6.76
4	8.80	8.35
5	10.39	9.86
6	12.15	11.53
7	13.91	13.20
8	15.67	14.88
Additional	1.76	1.67

*Metro counties include Anoka, Benton, Carver, Chisago, Clay, Dakota,
Hennepin, Houston, Isanti, Olmsted, Polk, Ramsey, Scott, Sherburne, St.
Louis, Stearns, Washington, and Wright.
Source: Minnesota Workforce Facts. Federal Register, U.S. Dept. of Health
and Human Services; Federal Register, U.S. Dept. of Labor.

Minnesota had the 12th lowest poverty rate nationally, at 9.7 % in 1996/97.
The national poverty rate was 13.5% in the same period.
Source: State Rankings, 1999. MN Dept. of Economic Security, Research and
Statistics Office.

In the U.S., 18 percent or 12.9 million families were maintained by women. Fourteen percent of white families, 47 percent of black families, and 24 percent of Hispanic families were maintained by women in 1997. Large numbers of women work for low pay and are the sole providers for their families. It is no surprise that nearly a third of all families maintained by women are living below the poverty level.

Department of Human Services (DHS)

The Department of Human Services provides health care, economic assistance, and social services to people who do not have the resources to meet their basic needs. DHS works first to prevent reliance on government assistance and next to help those on government assistance become self suf- ficient as quickly as possible. DHS also ensures that a strong, but limited, safety net is in place for the most vulnerable Minnesotans. As Minnesota's largest state agency, DHS has an annual budget of more than $6 billion (all funds; over $5 billion is state funds) and 6,700 employees statewide.

1999 Legislative Session at a Glance

How human services legislation fared.
Tobacco Settlement.

Nine hundred sixty-eight million dollars of the tobacco lawsuit settle- ment will be invested as endowments with interest used to fund tobacco prevention, medical research and public health programs.
Senior Drug Program

The Legislature appropriated $19 million to fully fund the Senior Drug Program, which helps low-income seniors pay for prescription drugs.
Health care workers' salary hikes

The Legislature allocated $99 million for the biennium to provide cost of living adjustments for staff who provide continuing care services for people who are disabled or elderly (4% on July 1, and 3% on July 1, 2000.)
Rate increases for health care services

To ensure needed access to primary health care providers, rates for physicians, dentists, inpatient and outpatient hospitals participating in Medical Assistance (MA or Medicaid), General Assistance Medical Care and MinnesotaCare will increase by $21 million.
Disabilities and employment.

The Legislature removed some financial rules that keep people with disabilities from seeking employment for fear of losing their MA benefits.
MinnesotaCare

Legislators this session voted to retain the 1.5 percent tax on medical fees that finances MinnesotaCare.
Developmental Disabilities Funding

The Legislature approved $12 million to expand three programs that provide services to persons with developmental disabilities.

State operated services

The Legislature agreed to shift some state operated services that are funded through the general fund to fee-supported activities.

Children with emotional disturbance

Efforts to help children with severe emotional disturbance and their families connect with community resources and therapeutic assistance received $3.4 million in funding for the biennium. The goal is to prevent removal of the child from the family home.

Permanency planning

The Legislature approved $9.3 million for the biennium for the continuation of concurrent permanency planning for children in the child welfare system. The goal is to place children in permanent homes.

Adoption Assistance

Adoption assistance for children with special needs was increased by $3.7 million, helping an additional 1,000 children in the next biennium.

Employment help for welfare recipients

The Legislature voted to use more than $24 million to reduce job counselors' caseloads so they can move welfare recipients into jobs and off assistance before the 60-month national lifetime limit on welfare takes effect.

Public housing benefits

The Legislature delayed until Jan. 1, 2001, a provision to count a portion of public housing subsidies as income when determining MFIP benefits.

Welfare exit levels

The income level at which families leave the MFIP was increased to be consistent with current federal poverty guidelines.

Food assistance

Legislation passed this session allows legal noncitizens to continue to receive state-funded food assistance after July 1, 1999.

Child support expedited process

The Legislature replaced the administrative process for establishing and modifying child support orders to comply with state Supreme Court ruling.

Recreational licenses

The Legislature authorized the suspension of certain recreational licenses issued by the Department of Natural Resources for those parents who fail to pay child support or enter into a payment agreement.

Food Stamps

Federal program—state has virtually no control.

96,000 households, or 220,000 individuals—5 percent of the state's population used food stamps in an average month during 1998.

Ave. benefits—$140 a month per household or $61 a month per person.

Statewide annual expenditures—$161 million.

Eligibility determined by income and household size.

Work requirement for able-bodied adults ages 18-50 without children.
General Assistance (GA)
An average of 13,000 recipients a month use the state-funded program. Cases are at the lowest number in the past 10 years. Maximum monthly benefit for a single adult with no other income is $203.

Most recipients are single, unemployable adults without children. These include people who are: elderly, ill, injured or otherwise incapacitated. Most also receive General Assistance Medical Care.
Supplemental Security Income (SSI)
A federally funded program for the aged, blind or disabled. A monthly average of 63,300 Minnesotans. Average monthly benefit is $353.
Minnesota Supplemental Aid (MSA)
A state-funded program for the aged, blind or disabled to supplement SSI. A monthly average of 24,100 people. Average monthly benefit is $81.
Emergency Assistance
Provides one-time help with emergency needs, such as rent and utility bills. An average of 1,400 cases or 4,800 people a month received Emergency Assistance in 1998. 1998 yearly payments were $11.5 million.
Child Support Enforcement Services
Help more than 200,000 children collect child support payments. Families receiving public assistance must cooperate with child support efforts. County and state offices collected $396 million in 1998.
Child Support in Minnesota: Facts and Figures
County and state child support offices provide services for more than 200,000 children. Both custodial and noncustodial parents can receive services. With welfare reform, child support continues to be a key component to help many families to financial independence.
Child Support Services
Locating noncustodial parents. Establishing paternity. Establishing, enforcing and modifying child and medical support orders.
1998 Collections
$396 million in child support, a 9 percent increase from 1997, was collected and disbursed in state fiscal year 1998.

Public assistance, including MFIP, collections were $61 million, a 14 percent decrease from 1997; nonpublic assistance collections were $335 million, a 15 percent increase from 1997.

Collections for current support totaled $296 million.

Arrears, or past due support, collected totaled $100 million.

Collection methods $266 million, or 67 percent, was received though income withholding, where employers withhold child support from a non-custodial parent's pay check.

Federal and state tax refunds were intercepted to collect $16 million.

Other collection methods include intercepting reemployment insurance and workers' compensation and voluntary payments.

Child Support Case Data

For state fiscal year 1998, child support cases totaled 223,500, a 6 percent increase from 1997. Nonpublic assistance cases totaled 151,000, an 11 percent increase from 1997. MFIP and foster care cases (including arrears only cases) totaled 72,500, a 5 percent decrease from 1997. 4,600 MFIP cases were closed for which child support was collected. 13,600 paternities were established—9,000 in the hospital through the recognition of parentage and 4,600 by county child support offices.

Average 1998 yearly collections per case were $1,817 per open case; average yearly collection per cases with a court order were $2,546.

Child Support Arrears

The cumulative amount of arrears, or back support, owed as of Sept. 30, 1998 was $827 million. $100 million was paid on arrears in state fiscal year 1998, a 42 percent increase over 1997 payments. The average arrears owed per case with a court order were approximately $5,346, based on preliminary data.

Program Costs

The child support program is largely funded and directed by the federal government. Total federal, state and county funding for state fiscal year 1998 totaled $100.6 million. Federal funding was $77.8; state funding totaled $12.7 million; county spending was $10.2 million.

Enforcement Tools

Withholding child support payments from parents' paychecks and intercepting federal and state income tax returns, and intercepting state lottery winnings of more than $600 to pay child support arrears has been used.

Requiring employers to report newly hired employees to the Department of Human Services to match employee data with child support obligations. Also, suspending driver's and occupational licenses of parents delinquent with child support.

Reporting parents who owe more than $1,000 to credit bureaus.

Reviewing and modifying child support orders periodically and adjusting orders for cost of living increases every two years.

Using the Uniform Interstate Family Support Act to enforce child support across state lines.

Using PRISM, a statewide child support system to automatically handle many child support case activities.

Operating a statewide payment center to process child support payments.

Conclusion

It is too early to determine the long-term effectiveness of welfare reform in reaching the goals of reducing dependency and poverty, but early indications show us that Minnesota is making positive steps toward those goals.

Chapter 14

Arts and Entertainment

Minnesota is tops in the nation in the way state government joins hands with the private sector to support the arts. This was the message of a formal letter of commendation from President Ronald Reagan presented to Governor Rudy Perpich in July of 1984.

In his letter, the president spoke of "the unique and model partnership that exists in Minnesota between the Minnesota State Arts Board and the private sector corporations and foundation funders who have a commitment to the arts."

That commitment to the arts goes back to the days when Minnesota was still a territory and Indians and voyageurs roamed the land.

Painting and Sculpture

Adventuring artists were drawn to Minnesota territory by the beauty of the landscape and interest in the lives of Native Americans. Solder-artists stationed at Fort Snelling, whose job was to record important military information, also contributed to views of the fort and surrounding scenes.

One of the earliest sketches of what would become Minnesota was done by Jonathan Carver who sketched the Falls of St. Anthony in 1776.

In the early 19th century scenes were recorded by Samuel Seymour who was part of the Stephen Long map-making expedition of 1823 and sketched Maiden Rock on Lake Pepin; Peter Rindisbacher who is believed to have worked along the North Dakota-Minnesota border in the 1820s and was the first to paint the daily lives of Indians, and George Catlin of Pennsylvania who visited Fort Snelling and the Plains Indians as well as the sacred quarry at Pipestone.

Seth Eastman's name is synonymous with Minnesota. He was assigned to Fort Crawford (near Prairie du Chien) after graduating from West Point and sketched several Indian tribes in the vicinity. Between 1848 and 1854, Eastman illustrated five books on Indian themes written by his wife, Mary Eastman. The first, *Dahcotah: or, Life and Legends of the Sioux Around Fort Snelling* was the inspiration for Henry Longfellow's poem "Hiawatha."

Eastman spent five years illustrating Henry W. Schoolcraft's six-volume work on Indian tribes of the United States. Forty-six of the watercolors used as a basis for these illustrations were purchased by railroad tycoon James J. Hill and are owned by the Hill Reference Library of St. Paul.

Other early artists who painted in the Upper Mississippi Valley include James Otto Leis, the official government representative commissioned to paint portraits at the Treaty of Prairie du Chien; Charles Deas of Philadelphia who painted Fort Snelling; John Casper Wild, whose 1844 "View of Fort Snelling Seen from Mendota" is owned by the Minnesota Historical Society, and John M. Stanley of New York State and Detroit who visited the fort in 1835 and 1853 and made drawings of St. Paul, Minnehaha Falls and White Bear Lake.

By the time Minnesota became a state in 1858, fewer itinerant artists were visiting the area. But settlers in the more cosmopolitan cities of St. Paul, Stillwater, Winona, and Red Wing were beginning to appreciate art—although "art" could mean anything from ladies' collars to drawings and paintings.

By the 1870s, some citizens were considered patrons of the arts, including Henry M. Rice, E.S. Goodrich, J.C. Burbank, and James J. Hill, whose collection became so extensive, he had to add a gallery onto his house.

Among St. Paul's resident painters in the 1880s were J.D. Larpenteur, Mrs. G.B. Grant, W.H. Frisbie, Vincent de Gornon, and Nicholas R. Brewer and Charles Noel Flagg.

In the 1890s, a group of women started classes that evolved into the St. Paul School of Fine Arts. The school became the St. Paul Gallery and School of Art.

In Minneapolis at about this time, a Dane named Peter Clausen executed frescoes in the Church of the Redeemer (Universalist), the first work in fresco done in Minneapolis.

The Minneapolis Society of Fine Arts was formed in January of 1883, a group which started with no endowment and no quarters of its own. Today, the society supports and governs the Minneapolis Institute of Arts and the Minneapolis College of Art and Design.

The society's first president was William Watts Folwell, then president of the University of Minnesota. The other important man on the Minneapolis arts scene at t time was Thomas Barlow Walker, a civic-minded businessman and collector who established the Walker Foundation, deeding his 6,000 art objects to it, as well as property on which to build a museum. Walker Gallery opened in 1927 and has become an important midwest repository for modern art as the Walker Art Center.

Among the turn-of-the-century artists was Stephen A. Douglas Volk, first director of the Minneapolis School of Art; Alexis Fournier, identified with the French Barbizon school and Robert Koehler, a German whose prize-winning painting, "The Strike," was presented to the city of Minneapolis by the Society of Fine Arts.

Koehler, director of the Minneapolis School of Art until 1914, saw a number of students enrolled at the school who made their mark on the national art scene, including Adolf Dehn who specialized in watercolors; Arnold Blanch, born in Mantorville; Elizabeth Olds of Minneapolis; Wanda Gag, New Ulm children's book author and illustrator; Dewey Albinson who used northern Minnesota scenes or subjects and Cameron Booth, the man who brought Minnesota a national reputation.

In the early 1920s, Booth painted farmlands, the Iron Range and streets of Minnesota but after World War II he worked in the abstract vein. Booth was director from 1929 to 1942 of the St. Paul School of Art, now the Minnesota Museum of Art.

The museum was founded in 1924 by a group of art students known as the Art Students League of St. Paul. The League operated the St. Paul Gallery and School of Art in an old Summit Avenue mansion until 1964 when the institution moved into the new St. Paul Arts and Science Center; in 1969, the name was changed to Minnesota Museum of American Art. In 1972, the museum purchased the old Women's City Club in downtown St. Paul and now operates two facilities.

With a budget of just $1 million, the museum mounts 15 to 18 exhibitions a year and runs an extensive education program as well as museum school.

Other Minnesotans with wide reputations are Josephine Lutz Rollins, Jerome Kamrowski, Eddy May and LeRoy Neiman.

The gallery scene today in Minnesota is active; a survey by the Resource Center For the Arts showed 157 non-profit and for-profit galleries in the state in 1999. Young artists have been especially active in St. Paul's Lowertown area, and there are women's art collectives in both St. Paul and Minneapolis.

Jakob H.F. Fjelde was the first trained sculptor known to have been a resident of the state. Born in Norway, he came to the U.S. in 1887 and lived in Minneapolis until his death in 1896. Fjelde was responsible for the bust of dramatist Ibsen in Como Park and the statue of "Hiawatha and Minnehaha" in Minnehaha Park.

Sculptors who had Minnesota connections and gained national renown are Paul Manship, John B. Flannagan, John Rood, Alonzo Hauser, and Paul T. Granlund.

Manship was born in St. Paul in 1885 and studied at the St. Paul School of Fine Arts before leaving the state for further schooling. His best-known work is the "Prometheus" sculpture in New York's Rockefeller Center. His "Europa and the Bull" is owned by Walker Art Center.

Rood worked in wood, stone and welded metals and his commissions are at St. Mark's Cathedral in Minneapolis and Hamline University in St. Paul.

Hauser was head of the Macalester College art department until 1949. His most visible works is a bronze figure of a young girl seated amidst petals of a large flower. The piece is on the Capital Approach in St. Paul.

Granlund's bronzes characteristically contain falling human forms, human forms in negative spaces, and geometric shapes. He was born in Minneapolis in 1925 and served on the faculty at the Minneapolis College of Art and Design and Gustavus Adolphus College in St. Peter where he remains as sculptor-in-residence. His over 125 works are around the world.

Music

The earliest known music what was to become Minnesota was created by the Sioux and Chippewa Indians who used chants as part of their religious ceremonies.

The late Frances Densmore of Red Wing is responsible for collecting some 3,600 Indian songs, using wax cylinder available in the early part of the century.

The first white men's music was brought into the territory by voyageurs, French-Canadian canoemen and guides. They sang of love and sunny climates, home and adventures, often using a rhythm set by paddle strokes.

By mid-19th century immigrants were arriving, bringing with them music from all parts of Europe, especially Scandinavia and Germany.

As settlements grew into villages instruments began arriving in St. Paul—pianos, harpsichords and melodeons. Violins, cornets and flutes began to be heard and churches began putting together choirs.

By 1863 St. Paul had a Musical Society, a small orchestra which lasted a quarter of a century, often playing in the newly-created city of Minneapolis.

In Minneapolis one of the first instrumental groups was the Quintette Club of the 1850s. In the 60s, the Germans formed the Harmonia Society and, in 1868, the Musical Union, both choral groups.

Two men responsible for bringing music to the Twin Cities were George Seibert, who directed the St. Paul Musical Society, and his brother-in-law, a Fort Snelling bandleader name Frank Danz. Seibert organized the Great Western Band and Orchestra in St. Paul and Danz organized a similar group in Minneapolis.

One of the most important organizations fostering musical excellence is the Schubert Club of St. Paul. The Schubert Club, established in 1882 by Marion Ramsey Furness, Gov. Alexander Ramsey's daughter, is a non-profit arts organization that presents eight concert series annually, operates a Museum of Musical Instruments, runs an annual scholarship competition for music students, provides after-school music lessons at the Martin Luther King Center in Saint Paul and the Sabathani Center in Minneapolis, presents master classes, commissions new musical works by American composers, and produces recordings and books. Through the years the club has sponsored programs by some of the world's greatest musicians, including Isaac Stern, Beverly Sills and the Juilliard String Quartet. The Schubert Club is one of the tenants of the Ordway Music Center in St. Paul.

By the last two decades of the 19th century some 30 opera companies were traveling through Minnesota. The Boston Symphony Orchestra visited in 1890 and the Metropolitan Orchestra in 1893.

The most important organization of the 1890s was the Philharmonic Club, a mixed choral group which sprang out of a Minneapolis organization called the Filharmonix.

By 1902, the Philharmonic Club had become so successful it was organized into the Minneapolis Symphony—now the Minnesota Orchestra.

The orchestra eventually became the first major civic orchestra associated with a university, giving regular concerts in Northrop Auditorium. In 1968, the orchestra became the Minnesota Orchestra, and in 1974 it moved into the new Orchestra Hall in Minneapolis, a building praised for its acoustic perfection and a fitting home for an orchestra that had built a world-wide reputation.

Musicians of exceptional skills have led the Minnesota Orchestra (612-371-5656; www.mnorch.org), including Eugene Ormandy, Dimitri Mitropolous, Antal Dorati, Stanislaw Skrowaczewski, Sir Neville Merriner, Edo de Waart, and Eiji Oue (pronounced AY-gee OH-way).

Offering more than 200 concerts each year, the Minnesota Orchestra presents 24 weeks of classical subscription concerts featuring internationally acclaimed guest artists, as well as Weekender Pops, Adventures in Music for Families, Casual Classics, and Young People's Concerts. During the summer months, the Orchestra presents Cabaret Pops in June and the festive Viennese Sommerfest during July. Through frequent national and international tours, the Orchestra serves as a cultural ambassador for the state.

The Minnesota Orchestra can also be heard across the nation through its live weekly radio broadcasts produced by Minnesota Public Radio or through its extensive discography that dates back to the 1920's.

Although there was a fully professional St. Paul Symphony Orchestra between 1906 and 1914, it was the atmosphere of the 1930s and 40s that led to establishment of St. Paul's current most renown group—The St. Paul Chamber Orchestra.

In the 30s and 40s John J. Becker, a pioneer in the 12-tone technique, conducted a professional group of free-lance musicians in programs featuring American contemporary composers. When Becker moved to California in 1959, Leopold Sipe became director of the St. Paul Philharmonic Society. Becoming a professional group in 1968, the Society became the Chamber Orchestra.

Sipe was replaced by Dennis Russel Davies in 1972, and the orchestra developed a reputation for its 20th century repertoire. Later, the orchestra's artistic director was Pinchas Zukerman and present SPCO conductor is Hugh Wolff.

Creative Chair, Bobby McFerrin, began dabbling in classical music in the early 1990s and adds his voice and baton to the performances of the Orchestra. Christopher Hogwood is principal guest conductor, and Aaron Jay Kernis is composer-in-residence.

With 32 members, the St. Paul Chamber Orchestra has commissioned 50 new works and presented 100 world premieres since its debut in 1959. It is the only full-time professional chamber orchestra in the United States, and has recorded 60 recordings.

The SPCO makes its home in the $45 million Ordway Theater, built without a dime of city taxpayer dollars – thanks to Sally Ordway Irvine, daughter of a 3M founder –opened its doors Jan. 1, 1985. The Ordway is a principal performance venue for The Saint Paul Chamber Orchestra, Minnesota Opera, Schubert Club and Minnesota Orchestra.

The Duluth-Superior Symphony Orchestra dates from 1932; the Fargo-Moorhead Symphony celebrated its 60th anniversary in 1991 and the Rochester Symphony began in the 1920s.

Verna (Mrs. Carlyle) Scott organized the University Artists Course in 1919 and thereafter brought to town scores of the world's finest and most popular artists.

From 1939 to 1971 the St. Paul Women's Institute sponsored big-name entertainers ranging from Victor Borge to Yehudi Menuhin,. In those pre-television days the institute, sponsored by the St. Paul Dispatch and Pioneer Press, would draw as many as 5,000 women to the old St. Paul Auditorium.
Source: SPCO website.
Minnesota Orchestra Media Relations.

Choral Music

Many people maintain that Minnesota is one of the leading states in choral singing. Much credit for that attitude must go to the Apollo Club, a male chorus started in Minneapolis in the 1890s.

In the early 20th century F. Melius Christiansen, a 32-year old Norwegian violinist and teacher, turned the St. Olaf Choir of St. Olaf College, Northfield, into a world class choral group. Succeeding directors were his son, Olaf Christiansen, Kenneth Jennings, and presently Anton Armstrong.

The high St. Olaf standards have permeated the state and nation through hundreds of choral directors that have been influenced by the Christiansen style. At Concordia College in Moorhead, Paul J. Christiansen,

Melius' son, proved that a cappella singing could be nurtured in a small town and his choirs won world-wide acclaim. After a 49 year career, Christiansen was succeeded by noted composer-director René Clausen. Augsburg College, Gustavus Adolphus, Bemidji State University, St. John's University-College of St. Benedict, Hamline University, the University of Minnesota Morris, the University of Minnesota Duluth, and the University of Minnesota Twin Cities have also been important in the choral music field.

The Bach Society originated in 1932 with a group of University of Minnesota music students who loved and wanted to sing the works of Johann Sebastian Bach and other masters of contrapuntal composition—particularly those from the baroque and classical periods. They were under the leadership of Donald Ferguson from 1933 to 1950. The group ceased functioning, then was reorganized in 1959 by Dr. David Le Berge. The Society has from 80 to 90 members and was under the musical directorship of Henry Charles Smith and Paul E. Oakley. The Society's present Music Director is Roderick Kettlewell who began in 1997. They perform 3-5 concerts throughout the year. The Bach Society of Minnesota, Inc.   313 Landmark Center   (651) 225-8101

The 1999-2000 season marks founder Dale Warland's twenty-eighth season as Music Director of the Dale Warland Singers. Through musicianship and attention to detail, he has built one of the finest choral ensembles in the United States, thrilling choral music enthusiasts throughout North America and Europe. The group began in 1970 as the Opera Chorale and the name was changed to the Dale Warland Singers in 1972. The 40 voice a cappella ensemble has earned an international reputation for its commitment to commissioning and performing new choral music. The ensemble is featured on 20-plus recordings and consistently sells out concerts in the Twin Cities. 612-339-9707 or 1-800-CHORAL-7   www.dalewarlandsingers.org

Founded in 1969, the Plymouth Music Series is recognized internationally for its innovative exploration of music for voices and instruments. Each year, artistic director and founder Philip Brunelle leads an engaging series of concerts featuring the 100-voice Chorus, the 24-voice professional Ensemble Singers, and soloists in music ranging from a cappella to symphonic. Concerts are held in venues selected to complement the music, including Orchestra Hall, Ted Mann Concert Hall, Benson Great Hall, and area churches. The Series is respected for commissioning new choral music and re-discovering lost treasures. For more information on the Plymouth Music Series: 612/547-1451 or website   www.plymouthmusic.org.

Founded and directed by Larry L. Fleming, The National Lutheran Choir is comprised of professional choral musicians who perform literature from the entire spectrum of sacred choral works. They have sought excellence in the model of F. Melius Christiansen and the Lutheran College choir tradition. (612) 722-2301   RixWare@aol.com

Opera

Minnesotans' taste for opera was satisfied by touring companies from the 1870s to the 1890s. From the early 1880s on stars and casts of New York's Metropolitan Opera House traveled under various company names. They continued to appear during the first part of the 20th century, then did not return until 1944 when a statewide sponsors' group was set up to arrange a yearly season at Northrop Auditorium. The Met's spring season ran for a week, and, although touring became increasingly expensive, patrons and sponsors of the Metropolitan Opera of the Upper Midwest gave enough money to allow the company to continue its appearances here until the Met quit touring in 1986.

Another anchor tenant of the Ordway, the Minnesota Opera Company was started in 1963 as a performing wing of the Walker Art Center called Center Opera. Seeking to avoid alienating audiences, they avoided the "O" word in the early seasons instead calling their productions "musical theater." The company has established a national reputation for excellence of its productions and dedication to new American music. In 1979, Minnesota Opera received a national award for service to American opera from the National Opera Institute. Of course, the Minnesota Opera Company benefited when the Met quit touring. General director, Kevin Smith and Dale Johnson, artistic director are credited with its growing popularity and present financial success. And, yes, it is now proudly called "opera."

The Minnesota Opera 620 N. First St. Minneapolis, MN 55401 (612) 333-2700

When the Arts Resource Information Center did a survey of Minnesota arts in 1979, they found 122 music organizations. There's no doubt—Minnesotans love to make music.

Theatre

The first theater performances in Minnesota territory may have been put on by bored soldiers stationed at Fort Snelling.

The earliest troupes came to St. Paul in the 1850s, usually in summer when the steamboats were operating. By 1885, when railroads made outlying towns accessible, there were 47 towns housing plays and variety shows.

In the 1860s St. Paul built an Opera House and a wide variety of shows played the Twin Cities, including Shakespearean productions, horse operas and minstrel shows.

In the late 19th century the Twin Cities hosted some of the nation's finest performing artists and the pick of plays from New York.

It was 1878 when John Murray founded a stock company in Minneapolis, the Murray-Carland Company, which lasted until 1883. People's Stock Company of St. Paul lasted about the same length of time.

Through the 1890s there were numerous theaters in the Twin Cities, several owned by L.N. Scott.

The first part of the 20th century is dominated by "Buzz" Bainbridge, Minnesota's most enterprising manager-producer of time. He founded the longest-live stock company in the history of the state, the Bainbridge Players, which lasted from 1912 to 1933.

By the 1920s the heyday of great touring companies was over as movies became popular; old theaters became movie houses or were razed.

The Duluth Playhouse, founded in 1914, is oldest amateur community theater in the United States. The state's oldest "straw hat" theater is the Old Log Cabin in Excelsior, an Equity house (which pays actors full professional wages).

Another Equity phenomenon is the Chanhassen Dinner Theater, a four-stage complex that offers a wide variety of plays.

The 600-seat Main Dinner Theatre opened on October 11, 1968 with *How To Succeed In Business Without Really Trying*. They have served nearly six million guests and is the largest professional dinner theatre in the nation! 147 productions have played on all four stages.

The oldest (Jan. 15, 1953) and one of the most applauded volunteer theaters is Theater in the Round of Minneapolis. In 1973, Theater in the Round Players (TRP) represented the U.S. at the international theater festival in Monaco and in 1983 the troupe took first place in biannual competition for the state of Minnesota. Its 259 seats are at most an intimate 30 feet from the stage. (612) 333-3010

Credit for current interest in theater and the wide variety of vibrant, small groups must go to the Guthrie Theater, giant of the Midwest entertainment scene.

Founded in 1963 by the late Sir Tyrone Guthrie, the theater opened with support from arts patrons and the business community. Guthrie directed *Hamlet*. The Guthrie began as a repertory company, but through the years it has changed to a format of bringing in stars and—occasionally—entire productions. His vision was to nurture both actor and audience and to contribute to society by promoting "the feeling of intimate companionship between audience and stage." A professional company composed of stage veterans Hume Cronyn, Jessica Tandy and Zoe Caldwell and young actors such as George Grizzard and Joan van Ark performed in the inaugural season.

Under the leadership of Rumanian director Liviu Ciulei the theater has tended toward what many is "director's theater," Ciulei's style was highly contemporary and international. He invited distinguished directors including Andrei Serban, Lucian Pintilie and Richard Foreman to reinterpret the classics. Joe Dowling is the Guthrie's seventh and present artistic director. www.guthrietheater.org, box office (612) 377-2224 1-800-44-STAGE

Another theater with a national reputation is the Children's Theater Company (CTC) of Minneapolis. The theater began in the 1960s as the

Moppet Players committed to the idea that theater for young people should and could be artistically excellent. In 1965, artistic director John Clark Donahue took the newly-named Children's Theater Company to the Minneapolis Institute of Arts and in 1974 the company and its school moved to a new building adjoining the institute. It is recognized as the flagship of North American children's theater as well as a major cultural and artistic resource in Minnesota.

CTC produces more than 350 mainstage performances annually and a touring production that performs in nearly 50 Midwest cities. Together they play to over 300,000 theater goers per year. 612-874-0500

Dance

Roy Close, dance writer and critic for the St. Paul Pioneer Press and Dispatch, said in the summer of 1984 that dance is the fastest growing art form in the Twin Cities.

A 1983 survey of arts in the metropolitan area by the St. Paul-Ramsey United Arts Council showed 19 dance companies in the cities, ranging from small, specialized groups through jazz and folk groups.

Among the most prominent was Loyce Houlton's Minnesota Dance Theater and School.   The theater, which had been praised for innovations, has had its ups and downs through financial difficulties but entertained

Despite his cheerfulness, Chuda (Mark Povinelli) is outcast from his village in
A Village Fable at The Children's Theatre Company.
Photo by Sal Skog.

thousands with its yearly performances of the "Nutcracker Fantasy" presented in cooperation with the Minnesota Orchestra.

Since the late 80's dance in Minnesota has seen three major changes:

- The core of the dance community has shifted from about a dozen companies and many "independent choreographers" to over forty companies and few independents.
- The diversity of dance has broadened. Companies have relocated here from all over the country and there is a new consciousness of racial and aesthetic diversity.
- No million-dollar-plus flagship company has arisen since the demise of Minnesota Dance Theater ten years ago, despite tenacious regrowth on MDT's part in the past few years.
- The Minnesota Dance Alliance continues to serve as a focal point for professional dance in Minnesota.

Source: John Munger, Director of Information Services, Dance/USA. Dance/USA is the national service organization for not-for-profit professional dance in America.

Literature

The first written description of what would become Minnesota appeared in Paris in 1683. *Description of Louisiana*, written by Father Louis Hennepin, told of a journey to the Upper Mississippi in 1680.

Other works by early writers about Minnesota territory include Pierre Esprit Radisson's *Voyages of Peter Esprit Radisson*, written in 1688-89; Pierre Margray's six-volume work about travels in Minnesota courtry between 1650 and 1763 and the Englishman Capt. Jonathan Carver's *Travels through the Interior Parts of North American in the Years 1766, 1767 and 1768* which was an instant success in London in 1778.

Lt. Zebulon Montgomery Pike wrote one of the first important American accounts of travel through Minnesota country. He journeyed to Leech Lake in 1806 and his personal diary was published in 1807.

The Mississippi began to attract adventurers from America and Europe in the early 1800s, many with names familiar to today's Minnesotans. Lewis Cass, Stephen H. Long, Giacomo Beltrami, Henry R. Schoolcraft, and Joseph M. Nicollet all left travel narratives.

By the 1830s missionaries had begun to record their observations for eastern and European magazines. Some of them put the Chippewa and Sioux languages in writing.

At the same time Mary Henderson Eastman, wife of artist Seth Eastman, published her work on the legends of the Sioux around Fort Snelling, Henry Hastings Sibley, fur trader and future governor of the state, wrote sports stories for sports journals and sketches for the St. Paul Pioneer newspaper.

Joseph Snelling, son of Col. Josia Snelling, first commandant of Fort Snelling, roamed the countryside as a youth and wrote *Tales of the Northwest*, published in 1830, describing the colorful traders, voyageurs and Indians he knew. He also published many magazine articles and juvenile books.

In 1846 and 1848 a French scientist, Auguste Lamare-Picquot visited Minnesota territory and wrote about his adventures and scientific investigations. The plant "picquotinae" is named for him.

William Whipple Warren, part-Chippewa son of a fur trader, wrote a history of his tribe and its culture in the 1840s which was published in 1853 by the Minnesota Historical Society.

In St. Cloud Jane Grey Swisshelm was protesting slavery and advocating women's rights in her newspaper, *Visitor*, and in Sauk Rapids newspaper editor and author Julia Sargent Wood was turning out novels, articles, poems and short stories.

One of Minnesota's first novelists was Edward Eggleston, whose *The Mystery of Metropolisville* depicts the land speculation craze of the 1850s. By 1894 he was a well known short story writer.

In the history of Minnesota journalism a name that blazes is James Madison Goodhue, owner and editor of Minnesota's first newspaper, the *Minnesota Pioneer*, now the *St. Paul Pioneer Press and Dispatch*. He wrote fierce editorials and was known beyond the boundaries of the state during his career in the 1850s.

That era also brought national attention to writer Ignatius Donnelley. Orator and advocate of third-party movements, he was also the author of a wide variety of books, including *Atlantis, the Antediluvian World*; *Ragnarok, the Age of Fire and Gravel*, and *The Great Cryptogram, Francis Bacon's Cipher in the So-Called Shakespeare Plays*.

Presbyterian minister Edward Duffield Neill, founder and first president of Macalester College in St. Paul, was a respected historian and published his *History of Minnesota* in 1858.

Norwegian Thorstein Veblen spent much of his boyhood in Minnesota and graduated in 1880 from Carleton College, Northfield. In 1899 he published his most famous book, *The Theory of the Leisure Class*. Although Veblen was an economist, he is thought of today as a sociologist and his theory of "conspicuous consumption" is still discussed.

Hamlin Garland became the voice of disenchanted midwest farmers at the turn of the century. He lived much of the time on the Minnesota-Wisconsin border and his best-known work, *A Son of the Middle Border*, was published in 1914.

In 1927 Ole E. Rolvaag's famous *Giants in the Earth* was published, having been translated from its original Norwegian. Rolvaag, born in Norway in 1876, taught in the Norwegian department at St. Olaf College, Northfield.

Peder Victorius, published in 1929, and *Their Father's Gods*, completed the trilogy about a Norwegian immigrant family.

The 1920s brought forward two more of Minnesota's greatest writers. Sinclair Lewis' sixth novel, *Main Street*, published in 1920 and based on Sauk Centre, was a portrait of what he saw as the smug, complacent views of small-town America. His novel *Babbitt* (1922) brought a new word to the language in a story about a man who had no standards. He also wrote *Elmer Gantry* and other novels. Lewis declined the Pulitzer Prize in 1926 but accepted the Nobel Prize for Literature in 1930 "for his vigorous and graphic art of description and his ability, with wit and humor, [to create] new types of characters..."

F. Scott Fitzgerald still fascinates biographers and in the past years there have been at least three works written about the tortured author who documented life among St. Paul's society people in the 1920s. Fitzgerald's legacy includes *The Great Gatsby*, about wealth and youth; *Tender is the Night*, which he wrote while living on St. Paul's Summit Ave. and *The Last Tycoon*.

In the 1940's Frederick Manfred achieved recognition. His novels, mostly set in the midwest, include the still popular *Lord Grizzly*, published in 1954. He was described as "a natural force, related to hurricanes..."

Allen Tate and Robert Penn Warren, both of whom have been on the University of Minnesota faculty, are well known contemporary poets. Tate has written literacy criticism as well as poetry. Warren is critic, novelist, short story writer and poet. Among his most famous works is *All the King's Men*, which won a Pulitzer Prize in 1947.

Another poet of distinction, John Berryman, inspired students at the University of Minnesota until he committed suicide in 1972.

Several nationally known journalists began their careers in Minnesota, including Harrison Salisbury, who covered Russia for *The New York Times*; Eric Sevareid, author and radio and television commentator who was a Minneapolis newspaperman, and television's Harry Reasoner.

Twentieth century fiction writers include Margaret Culkin Banning, Gervert Krause, Max Schulman, Kay Boyle, and Meridel LeSueur, who is also a short story writer and poet.

Writers for juveniles include Carol Brink, Wanda Gag, Laura Ingalls Wilder, and Maud Hart Lovelace.

Writers who are creating national names today are Garrison Keillor, John Hassler, Carol Bly and Robert Bly, Susan Allen Toth, Patricia Hampl, Judith Guest, and Tim O'Brien.

Source; Grace Lee Nute, *A History of Minnesota Books and Authors*, Minneapolis, MN, U of M Press, 1958.

Barbara Stuhler and Gretchen Kreuter, *Women of Minnesota: Selected Biographical Essays*. St. Paul: Minnesota Historical Society Press, St. Paul, 1997; revised edition 1998.

Small Presses and Journals

Since the mid-1980s, Minnesota has been developing a national reputation as a home for non-profit small presses devoted to publishing prose and poetry with an emphasis on quality, rather than marketability. A partial list would include:

New Rivers Press, founded in 1968 by C.W. (Bill) Truesdale in a cold shed in Massachusetts, is the oldest continuously-publishing small press in the nation. He moved to St. Paul in 1978 and to Minneapolis in 1988 where he now publishes about 9 books per year. In 1980 he began the Minnesota Voices competition for new and emerging writers with 6 prizes of $500 and publication of the author's book (three each in poetry and literature).

Graywolf Press in St. Paul began in 1974 in Port Townsend, WA. Fiona McCrae replaced founder Scott Walker in 1994 and "continues the Graywolf reputation for publishing provocative books."

Milkweed Editions head, Emile Buchwald, seeks to publish books that make"a humane impact on society."

Coffee House Press led by Allan Kornblum seeks to publish books that "represent under-represented people." They began in 1984 and publish about 12 books per year.

Holy Cow! Press in Duluth. Publisher Jim Perlman focuses on works by midwestern authors for a regional and national audience. Also, Holy Cow! is committed to publishing works by Native Americans from the entire country. Holy Cow! publishes 6-8 books annually and is about 10 years old.

Spinsters Ink, a for-profit press began in California, moved to The Twin Cities, then moved on to Duluth. It was the project of Joan Drury and Kelly Kager, a mother-daughter team.

The Fifties was the brainchild of poets Robert Bly and William Duffy, who founded it in 1958 with $500 of their own money. Their journal "sought to offer a middle course between the rigid formalism of academia and the rejection of poetic form and subject matter by the Beats." Even with low circulation and size, *The Fifties* played a key role in sparking a free-verse movement in America.

The Minnesota Women's Press celebrated its 15th anniversary in 1999 and, to the great surprise of skeptics, has proved to be a resounding success.

The Hungry Mind Review has a national reputation as a reviewer of Midwest books through the 40,000 issues they distribute to bookstores. Great River Review, founded in 1978 by Winona State University professor and author Emilio DeGrazia, is the oldest continuously published literary journal in Minnesota. Its new home since 1997 is in Red Wing at the Anderson Center (for Interdisciplinary Studies) edited by Richard Broderick.

For 25 years *Minnesota Literature* has been informing Minnesota writers and readers about literary events, opportunities, and publications. The monthly newsletter includes writing news and notices of readings, workshops, conferences, classes, grants, awards, contests, and writing markets. *Minnesota Literature* also publishes a biennial bibliography of Minnesota presses and publications that publish creative writing. A year's subscription is $10: 1 Nord Circle, St. Paul, MN 55127; 651-483-3904.

Minnesota Book Awards began in 1988 as a way to publicize worthy works by Minnesota writers. For the first 10 years the award process was shepherded by Roger Sween. The awards are now "under the auspices of the Minnesota Center for the Book and the annual ceremony has a permanent home at the Minnesota History Center."
Source: Mary Ann Grossmann, St. Paul Pioneer Press

Metronet/Minnesota Center for the Book is the recipient of a federal Library Services and Technology Act grant to publicize electronic reviews of Minnesota publications. The online service picks up where a print publication left off in the early 90's when publication and distribution costs became prohibitive.

Minnesota Reviews Online is available on the Minnesota Center for the Book web site (http://www.mnbooks.org/cfb/mnrev/). Users of the web site are encouraged to download and duplicate the reviews for local and national distribution, either print or online.

Reviewers for Minnesota Reviews Online include librarians, booksellers, and avid readers who keep abreast of the wealth of publications pouring forth from Minnesota writers and publishers. The Minnesota Center for the Book is an affiliate of the Center for the Book at the Library of Congress. The Center operates in Minnesota as an ongoing program and priority of Metronet, the multitype library cooperation system serving the Twin Cities metropolitan area.

Arts Service Organizations

Arts Service organizations, which encourage and support arts producers, have been an important force in the growth and success of artist and arts organizations in the metro area and the state.

The Minnesota Alliance for Arts in Education (MAAE) (the Alliance) was established as an advisory committee to the Minnesota Department of Education in 1974, and has been incorporated as a non-profit organization since August, 1975. In 1985, the Alliance and others were instrumental in the establishment of the Minnesota Center for Arts Education, a state agency that includes a state arts high school and resources and training programs for arts educators. The role of the MAAE has since changed from an arts advisor to the Minnesota Department of Education to a statewide membership organization with a wider mission, to focus on grassroots advocacy with parents, educators, artists, community members and education decision makers to impact and ensure quality of learning in the arts as an essential part of the K-12 education of every child. As a member through the MAAE, the **American Composers Forum** (formerly Minnesota Composers Forum) has begun to serve as both a state and national resource to member alliances around the nation. MAAE offices are located in St. Paul, MN. www.internet.com/~maae/

Minnesota Citizens for the Arts (MCA) is a statewide, grassroots non-profit arts organization of over 1000 individuals and arts organizations. They work to establish common ground for arts supporters, promote unity within the arts community, and lobby on behalf of the non-profit arts at the Legislature and in Congress. MCA publishes a quarterly newsletter with information on arts issues, holds Advocacy Days at the capital, provides advocacy seminars, and works on legislation affecting the arts. Since it was formed in 1975, MCA's mission has been devoted to ensuring opportunities for all people to experience and participate in the arts.   708 N. First St. #235D,   Minneapolis,   MN   55401,   612-338-2970,   mca@mtn.org, www.mtn.org/mca

Resources and Counseling for the Arts (RCA) is a nonprofit service organization whose mission is to providing affordable management infor-mation, consulting and training services designed to improve the business competence and confidence of independent artists and cultural organiza-tions in the Upper Midwest.

RCA was incorporated as an independent corporation in 1991 but has provided management and consulting services to the arts community for more than 20 years. In this time RCA has become recognized as a national model for professional development services to independent artists, small to midsize cultural organizations, nonprofit arts managers, and job seekers in arts administration.

Resources and Counseling for the Arts (651) 292-4381 (651) 292-3218 tty (651) 292-4315 fax, www.rc4arts.org

ArtsConnectEd is the product of a partnership between The Minneapolis Institute of Arts, the Walker Art Center, and MCI. Using the power of the Internet to stimulate new approaches to learning, the goal of ArtsConnectEd is to make arts education timely, engaging, interactive, and pertinent for both teachers and students of all ages. The Minnesota Department of Children, Families & Learning through an appropriation by the Minnesota State Legislature is a major funder for many of the resources that have been developed for ArtsConnectEd. www.artsconnected.org

ArtsNet Minnesota

This website contains more than 50 art works from the Walker Art Center, The Minneapolis Institute of Arts, the Frederick R. Weisman Art Museum, and the Minnesota Museum of American Art.

Each group of art works was thematically selected to encourage student understanding of the art and artists from the collections of these Minnesota

Museums and Art Center. The themes, Environment, Inner Worlds, Identity, What is Art?, and Designing Spaces and Places, include artists' biographies, style characteristics, discussion questions, vocabulary, student activities, and, in some cases, teacher lessons and local student artwork.

The ArtsNet Minnesotas project is sponsored by a grant from the Blandin Foundation. www.artsnetmn.org

Minnesota Center for Arts Education

The Minnesota Center for Arts Education is a state agency combining the Arts High School and the Professional Development Institute.

The Arts High School is a statewide, tuition-free, public high school for 11th and 12th grades. Students accepted to the high school have demonstrated talent or show potential and a desire to grow. Students balance academic programs with one of six arts areas: visual, literary, media, theater, music or dance.

The Professional Development Institute provides Minnesota students, teachers, and artists rigorous, innovative, and comprehensive teaching and learning skills, centered in the arts. Some of the programs include CAPP (Comprehensive Arts Planning Program), MAX (MN Arts eXperience), and DEI (Dance Education Initiative).

The Center is also home to the Learning Resource Center, providing an arts-rich collection to students, teachers and artists throughout Minnesota.

Lola and Rudy Perpich Minnesota Center for Arts Education
Phone: (612)591-4700, 800-657-3515 TDD: (612)591-4770 FAX: (612)591-4747

The Regional Arts Councils provide grants and technical assistance to artists, arts organizations, schools, community groups and the public in their geographic region. Funding is supplied by the Minnesota Legislature and the McKnight Foundation. Contact the Regional Arts Council in your area to find out about current programs.

Region 1
Mara Wittman
Northwest Regional Arts Council
115 South Main Avenue
Warren, MN 56762
Phone: (218) 745-6733, (800) 646-2240
FAX: (218) 745-6438
e-mail: mlunde@nwrdc.org

Region 7E
Mary Minnick-Daniels
East Central Arts Council
100 South Park Street
Mora, MN 55051
Phone: (320) 679-4065
FAX: (320) 679-4120
e-mail: ecac@ncis.com

Region 2
Mary Anne Wilimek
Region 2 Arts Council
426 Bemidji Avenue
Bemidji, MN 56601
Phone: (218) 751-5447, (800) 275-5447
FAX: (218) 751-2777
e-mail: r2arts@northernnet.com

internet:
www.northernnet.com/region2arts

Region 7W
Chuck Gilliam
Central Minnesota Arts Board
P.O. Box 1442
St. Cloud, MN 56302
Phone: (320) 253-9517
FAX: (320) 253-9688
e-mail: cmartsbd@cloudnet.com
internet: www.cloudnet.com/
~cmartsbd

Region 3
Bob DeArmond
Arrowhead Regional Arts Council
101 West 2nd Street, Suite 204
Duluth, MN 55802
Phone: (218) 722-0952, (800) 569-
8134
FAX: (218) 722-4459
e-mail: ARACouncil@aol.com
internet: http://members.aol.com/
aracouncil

Region 9
Brenda Flintrop
Prairie Lakes Regional Arts Council
109 South State Street
Waseca, MN 56093-3042
Phone: (507) 835-8721, (800) 298-
1254
FAX: (507) 835-8799
e-mail: plrac@platec.net
internet: www.platec.net/non-prof-
it/plrac

Region 4
Sonja Peterson
Lake Region Arts Council
133 South Mill Road
Fergus Falls, MN 56537

Phone: (218) 739-5780, (800) 262-
2787
FAX: (218) 739-0296
e-mail: lrac@prairietech.net
internet: www.means.net/~arts

Region 10
Pat Alcott
Southeast Minnesota Arts Council
1610 14th Street Northwest, Suite
306
Rochester, MN 55901
Phone: (507) 281-4848
FAX: (507) 281-8373
e-mail: semac@infonet.isl.net
internet: www2.isl.net/semac

Region 5
Mark Turner
Five Wings Arts Council
611 Iowa Avenue
Staples, MN 56479
Phone: (218) 894-3233
FAX: (218) 894-1328
e-mail: region5@brainerd.net
internet: www.fwac.org

Region 11
Carolyn Bye (CB direct: 523-6390)
Metropolitan Regional Arts Council
2324 University Avenue West
Saint Paul, MN 55114
Phone: (651) 645-0402
FAX: (651) 523-6382
e-mail: mrac@mrac.org / mrac-
bye@mtn.org
internet: www.mrac.org

Regions 6E/6W/8
Greta Murray
Southwest Minnesota Arts &
Humanities Council
FA-221 Southwest State University

Marshall, MN 56258
Phone: (507) 537-1471, (800) 622-5284
FAX: (507) 537-0040?call first
e-mail: smahc@starpoint.net
internet:
www.starpoint.net/~smahc

RAC Forum Office
708 North 1st Street, Suite 235-D
Minneapolis, MN 55401-1145
Phone: (612) 338-3075 FAX: (612) 338-2907
e-mail: mca@mtn.org

Festivals

Minnesotans love festivals. We have over 300 annually from May through September. The Minnesota State Fair, the largest festival of all, celebrated its 138th birthday in 1997 at the State Fairgrounds in Falcon Heights.

Minnesota State Fair Yearly Attendance Totals (Vehicles Excluded)
Period of Fair — 12 Days

1987	1,612,178	1994	1,561,930
1988	1,621,279	1995	1,673,312
1989	1,551,631	1996	1,673,976
1990	1,528,688	1997	1,683,445
1991	1,488,810	1998	1,689,034
1992	1,550,603	1999	1,674,450
1993	1,601,325		

The Minnesota State Fair has a long history, pre-dated by the Minnesota Territorial Fair beginning in 1855. The first fair after statehood was in 1859. Until 1885 the State Agricultural Society, governing body of the fair, held expositions at a variety of locations. Public sentiment called for a permanent fair site and, after some intense maneuvering, the Ramsey County Board of Commissioners donated the 210-acre poor farm northwest of St. Paul for a fair site.

The State Fair has been cancelled only five times in its history; twice for the Civil War, for the Chicago exposition, World War II, and a polio epidemic. The fair was 10 days long until 1972 when it went to 11 days, and in 1975 it went to 12 days.

The Minnesota State Fair is one of the nation's largest and best-attended agricultural and educational entertainment events, in recent years attracting over 1.6 million people annually from across Minnesota, the U.S. and Canada. This 12-day exposition is held each year on a 360-acre permanent fairgrounds situated midway between the downtown areas of St. Paul and Minneapolis.

The fair's agricultural and creative competitions draw over 35,000 entries each year, with competitors vying for a share of more than $600,000 in prize money. Included are categories for livestock, fine arts, school projects, baked goods, fruit, vegetables, crafts, bee and honey products, flowers, butter and cheese.

One of the highlights of fair-going for many people is seeing Grandstand shows by some of the biggest names in the entertainment world. Some recent Grandstand performers include the BoDeans, John Michael Montgomery, Z.Z. Topp, Wynonna Judd, Boston, Vince Gill, Reba McEntire, Brooks & Dunn, Steve Miller Band, Jonny Lang, and Alabama (who has appeared at the Fair 16 times before a total of 256,819 fans).

State Fair Trivia

- On the average, fair visitors consume 500,000 corn dogs each year.
- The State Fair's fine arts exhibition is the largest juried art show in the state.
- Typically, the total weight of all draft horses competing in the 8-horse hitch competition is 90 tons.
- The American Dairy Association's all-you-can-drink concession serves 20,000 gallons of milk per year.
- Teddy Roosevelt delivered his "walk softly and carry a big stick" speech in 1901.
- The Princess Kay of the Milky Way statue is carved from 85 pounds of butter.
- Prize money paid to winning exhibitors totals $500,000.
- All-time Labor Day record attendance of 143,624   1994
- There are 25 different varieties of food-on-a-stick.
- The total economic impact of the State Fair is more than $120 million annually in the Twin Cities area.

Source: MN State Fair Public Relations Office and Website. 651-642-2200

Other major festivals include Shakopee's Renaissance Faire, the St. Paul Winter Carnival, the Minneapolis Aquatennial, WE Fest in Detroit Lakes, A Taste of Minnesota, RiverFest, and Wheels, Wings and Water in St. Cloud.

Film

The Minnesota Film Board was created to promote the state as a viable filming place, as have the other 49 states. Among the 50 states, Minnesota has the only state film commission that raises private funds to match its state legislature allocation. The Film Board's mandate is to bring new spending, tax dollars, jobs, hotel room nights to Minnesota, and to promote the state's public image.

Commercial television spot production, corporate video, and television broadcast account for more than $200 million per year in annual billings (1995 Economic Impact Study of the MN Film/Video Production Industry).

Some of the feature length films shot all or part in Minnesota in the 90's include Grumpy Old Men and Grumpier Old Men; Mighty Ducks I, II, and

III; Feeling Minnesota; Beautiful Girls; Mystery Science Theater 3000; Mall Rats; Fargo; Iron Will; The Good Son; With Honors; Drop Dead Fred; Untamed Heart; Drop Dead Gorgeous; Herman, USA; Cut Glass; Jingle All the Way; Overnight Delivery; Snow; Acid Snow; A Chance of Snow; A Simple Plan; Major League 3; Welcome to Alaska; With or Without You; and Cafe Donna.

Minnesota State Arts Board Information

Established in 1903, the Minnesota State Arts Board promotes the quality of life in Minnesota by making the arts accessible to all citizens, nurturing creative activities, encouraging the development of innovative forms of artistic expression, and preserving the diverse artistic heritage of the people.

Administers a biennial budget of more than $26 million, obtained primarily from the State of Minnesota, with supplemental grants from the National Endowment for the Arts and the private sector.

Through a series of grant programs administered by a professional staff, provides aid for a variety of arts activities in the performing, visual, and literary arts. The board also offers consultant services, mailing lists, workshops, conferences, and publications to individuals, organizations, and schools throughout the state. Main telephone number (651) 215-1600 Toll-free telephone number (800) 8MN-ARTS. TTY number (for the deaf and hard of hearing) (651) 215-6235.   www.arts.state.mn.us

Frequently Asked Questions

How many people attend nonprofit arts events in Minnesota?

No one measures nonprofit arts attendance exactly, but 1991-1997 figures are approximately 7 million to approximately 12 million a year.

How much funding does Minnesota receive from the National Endowment for the Arts?

Since 1988 the NEA has invested more than $55 million around the state. In fiscal year 1998, the NEA reported a total of $2,767,200 to 35 Minnesota artists and organizations.

What's the economic impact of the nonprofit arts industry in Minnesota?

The last economic impact study of the arts in Minnesota was a report entitled Here + Now: A Report on the Arts in Minnesota, published by The McKnight Foundation in 1996. The report estimated the following, based on 1994 figures:

Number of nonprofit arts organizations in Minnesota: 1,767
Estimated direct spending by MN arts organizations: $244 million
Estimated economic impact of MN arts organizations: $900 million

Where can I get a list of arts and craft fairs in Minnesota?

The best single source of art and craft fair information is probably *The Minnesota Arts Directory*, which lists more than 1,200 art fairs & craft fairs in the upper Midwest, with in-depth information about each event: entry fees, deadline dates, and how to contact the promoters.
http://www.mtn.org/mncraft/schiller/schiller.htm
PO Box 580320   Minneapolis, MN 55458   Telephone:(612)871-0813

Minnesota Arts Facts

Arts and the Economy. The arts account for more than $1 billion a year in Minnesota. The arts industry comprises more than 600 nonprofit small businesses, employing more than 8,000 people. Figures from the 1990 census show that Minnesota is home to more than 30,000 artists.

Resources. Minnesota has not one, but two world-class orchestras; not one, but two internationally-recognized museums; the original flagship of American regional theater; one of the world's leading theaters for children; and literally hundreds of small and mid-sized arts organizations that make cultural activity a vibrant and essential part of life here.

Foundation Support. Since 1982, the Arts Board has worked with philanthropic leaders from the Blandin Foundation, Dayton Hudson Foundation, the Jerome Foundation, The McKnight Foundation, the Northwest Area Foundation, and IDS/American Express to serve the needs of Minnesota artists, arts groups, and audiences.

U of M alumni Prominent in the Arts and Literature

Eddie Albert, actor
Loni Anderson, actress
Bob Dylan, singer/songwriter (attended for a short time)
Roger Erickson, WCCO Radio
Peter Graves, actor
Endesha Mae Holland, playwright/author
Greg Howard, cartoonist (Sally Forth)
Garrison Keillor, writer/humorist/radio host
Linda Kelsey, actress (Lou Grant, Murder She Wrote)
Libby Larsen, composer
Jon Pankake, 1997 Grammy winner
Robert Pirsig, author (Zen and the Art of Motorcycle Maintenance)
Robert Thanes, cartoonist (Frank and Ernest)
Yanni, New Age musician
David Zinman, Baltimore Symphony conductor

Chapter 15

Business/Industry

The people of Minnesota, through their farms, mines, industries, and trade and service organizations, produce approximately 1.9 percent of the American gross national product. Minnesota's share of national production has a distinctive composition because of the state's unique location on the maps of America's natural resources and settlement. One finds great economic variety within the state boundaries. But the dominant theme has been vigorous adaptation to a continuing barrage of technological, social, and economic changes that have repeatedly altered both the meaning of the natural resource base and the relative location of state production within the world's markets.

Early settlers discovered a rich environment for enterprise with the standing timber, rich farmland, iron ore, and rivers for transportation and power. Since the transportation way, the Mississippi, froze annually, the territory was isolated. Eastern financiers were reluctant to invest in such a place so entrepreneurial Minnesotans started their own banks and insurance companies. to underwrite the growing commercial economy. Construction of the railway system, the Great Northern, by James J. Hill, allowed a free flow of goods and people both into and out of the state. The trickle of settlers in and goods out turned into a torrent, especially with the leveling of the virgin White Pine forests who's lumber built many Eastern homes and businesses.

In the northeast, the world's largest iron mining district shifted from small, underground mines in pioneer days to the vast, open pits that fed American industrial growth during the automotive age and that ultimately exhausted the easily recovered, high-grade ores. Since the 1950s the same region has been converted again, this time to the world's foremost producer of taconite pellets.

In the southern and western two-thirds of the state, farmers have performed in a remarkable drama. They created a large part of the agricultural Midwest in the pioneer period. They created the nation's first major hard spring wheat region and from that crop earned the first surge of agricultural income to start the upward spiral of farm mechanization and improvement. They created a major part of the nation's commercial dairy region during the heyday of butter and milk consumption in American society and thus laid the foundation for a continuously evolving system of dairy farms, milk processing plants, farm-to-market roads, and financial institutions.

In the twentieth century in the southern half of the state, farmers have thrust the traditional corn-hog system farther north than it has ever been before. Through changes in farm organization and development of specialized sub-regions, farmers have subsequently adapted the Minnesota corn belt to hybrid seeds, shifts in the national diet, introduction of new crops, fluctuations in world-wide demands, and revolutionary changes in machinery, fertilizer, pest-control, tillage, labor costs, lifestyle, and environmental awareness.

In the northwest the bonanza farms of the Red River Valley have been converted to family-operated enterprises with the flexibility to shift enormous acreages dramatically within a wide range of cash crop options in quick response to changes in world-wide needs.

Now the whole productive system has entered a new era, as the age of cheap fossil fuel is drawing to a close. Revolutionary changes are occurring in the technology and the organization of communication, agriculture, transportation, building construction, manufacturing, and basic energy supply. The historic adaptive abilities that have characterized the Minnesota productive system will be needed more than ever. To meet that need, the vital resources of diversified, technologically advanced industries and capital are large and in place.

As one measure of economic vitality, Minnesota has the 12th highest per capita concentration of Fortune 500 companies in the nation. In addition to the 13 listed below that have headquarters in our state, "more than 90% of

---

U of M Alumni Prominent in Minnesota Business

Sidney Applebaum, founder, Rainbow Foods

Curt Carlson (deceased), founder, Carlson Companies (parent of
    Radisson Hotels)

Seymour Cray (deceased), founder, Cray Research and co-founder,
    Control Data Corp.

Bruce Hendry, chair, Minnesota Brewing Company (Pigs Eye, Grain Belt, etc.)

Irwin Goodman, founder, Goodman Jewelers

Stanley Hubbard, CEO, Hubbard Broadcasting (KSTP)

David E. Johnson (B.S. 1959), president of Cenex Land O'Lakes

Harvey Mackay, owner, Mackay Envelope; best-selling author

Harvey Ratner, former co-owner, Minnesota Timberwolves; co-owner,
    Northwest Racquet Club

Roger Schelper, co-founder, Davanni's Pizza

Michael Wright, CEO, SuperValu

the primary U.S. industries are represented in Minnesota--including major concentrations of companies engaged in manufacturing medical products, producing scientific and technical instruments, advertising, legal and accounting services, health care, forest products, computers, printing, publishing, and food processing."ß

Sources: The Making of Money$ota, MN Economic Trends, March, 1999. ßPositively Minnesota, MN Dept. of Trade and Economic Development.

Fortune 500 Companies Headquartered in Minnesota
Dayton Hudson Corporation
  Retail, discount and department store.
Supervalu Inc.
  Wholesale foods; operating of supermarkets.
3M Company
  Diversified industrial and consumer products.
United HealthCare Corporation
  Management of health care delivery systems and HMOs.
Northwest Airlines Corporation
  Passenger airline; international cargo carrier.
Best Buy Company Inc.
  Consumer electronics; major appliances; factory warranty services.
The St. Paul Companies Inc.
  Insurance and risk management; property/liability underwriting.
General Mills Inc.
  Consumer foods.
U.S. Bank
  Bank holding company; diversified financial services.
Nash Finch Company
  Wholesale and retail foods and general merchandise distribution.
Hormel Foods Corporation
  Processed and packaged meats and food products.
Lutheran Brotherhood
  Insurance.
Northern States Power Company
  Gas and electric utilities; energy services; communications.

Source: Fortune, April 27, 1998. [Update-since the article was written, Honeywell was purchased by Allied Signal headquartered in New York, and Norwest Corporation merged with Wells Fargo and now headquarters in San Francisco. Both remain invested in the Twin Cities-Ed.]

State Quality of Life

Our environment, climate, and mix of cultures have combined to create a vital place to live. The four seasons provide us changes of scenery. With their accompanying temperature extremes, the growth of nuisance insects, bacteria, and molds is inhibited which contributes to a healthy climate.

•In addition to large companies, Compare Minnesota reports that Entrepreneur magazine and Dunn and Bradstreet named the Twin Cities "the seventh best U.S. city for small businesses in 1997."

•According to Reliastar Financial Corporation's 1997 State Health Rankings, Minnesota is the nation's healthiest state. In addition, we have the nation's second longest life expectancy: 77.8 yrs (if born between 1979 & 1981)

•The Twin Cities Metro area had the highest 1997 standard of living among the 5 large Midwest metro areas and second highest of 20 large metro areas in the U.S. American Chamber of Commerce, Cost of Living Index.

•We had the nation's highest rate of home ownership in 1997: 75.4%

•Minnesota has 66 state parks and 57 state forests covering more than 3.4 million acres used for hiking, biking, camping, snowmobiling, cross-country skiing, and fishing.

Source: Compare Minnesota

Gross State Product

The sectors of our economy are led almost equally by services; manufacturing; finance, insurance and real estate (FIRE); and wholesale and retail trade, each sector claiming just under 20 percent share. Other sectors in declining order are government at 11%; transportation, communications, and public utilities (TCPU) at 8%; Construction at 4%; and farms at 1%.

The service sector is expected to sustain the highest growth curve with business services leading the way. Health services to care for an aging population will follow while educational services and social service jobs will

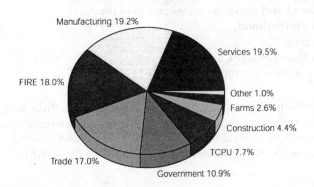

Manufacturing 19.2%

Services 19.5%

FIRE 18.0%

Other 1.0%
Farms 2.6%

Construction 4.4%

TCPU 7.7%

Trade 17.0%

Government 10.9%

round out the top expanding opportunities.

Manufacturing growth industries in the last decade are textile fabricators, makers of equipment for communications, transportation, and medical uses, and food product companies.

Financial companies (FIRE) are strong with Minnesota ranked third behind Illinois and Texas in the total number of bank holding companies, and 540 chartered banks in the state. Employment is projected to rise over 10 percent from 1996-2006. More insurance business will track the aging population providing health and medical products.

Exports

Despite the Asian financial turmoil that dampened Minnesota shipments of products to southeast Asia in 1998, exports remain an important part of our economy. Significant increases to markets in the European Union, Canada, Africa, and the Middle East eased the Asian downturn. Japan remained in Minnesota's top two markets in 1998 for several Minnesota products, in spite of declines from the previous year.

Minnesota Manufactured Exports, by Region 1998

Region	1998 (in millions)
Asia & Oceania	$3,064,000,000
European Union (EU)	2,800,000,000
North America	2,465,000,000
Latin America	355,000,000
Africa & Middle East	199,000,000
Europe, excluding EU	194,000,000
Total	$9,076,000,000

Source: Annual Export Statistics, May, 1999, MN Dept. of Economic Development.

Minnesota ranked 7th in farm exports for 1997. The value of the state's exports came to $2.61 billion versus $3.06 billion in 1996. Feed grains, soybeans, wheat, and their products made up the lion's share of our exports.

Tourism

Lakes, woods, fishing, resorts, wilderness canoeing, sports, shopping and culture are some of the reasons that almost 26 million people trips were made to and through Minnesota in 1997. And four out of five of those were people on pleasure trips. When you consider that travel and tourism inject $25 million per day into our economy, it pays to be "Minnesota nice."

Minnesota's 11,000 plus lakes have been a vacationer's lure ever since early St. Paul residents made the trek out to White Bear Lake to vacation on its shores. The Department of Natural Resources estimates that $1.9 billion is spent in the state on sport fishing each year. They support the cause with a very large stocking and lake testing program.

Mall of America

A more recent attraction in our state both local, national, and international, is Bloomington's Mall of America. It is located 5 minutes from the International Airport and hosts 600,00-900,000 visitors per week. There have been over 250 million visitors to date, as much as the total U.S. population.

This $650 million, 4.2 million square foot complex was opened August 11, 1992. It houses over 520 stores, Knott's Camp Snoopy Theme Park, and UnderWater World a 1.2 million gallon aquarium. Mall officials estimate the economic impact on the state is in excess of $15 billion, the majority of it spent outside the Mall.

Agriculture

With 3.1 percent of the farmable land in the U.S., Minnesota ranks high in the production of many products. For more detailed information see Chapter 12.

Minnesota 1996 Cash Receipts

	Receipts (millions)	Percentage	U.S. Rank
Corn	$1,704	19.3%	5
Soybeans	1,618	18.4	3
Dairy Products	1,362	15.5	5
Hogs	1,116	12.7	3
Cattle and Calves	925	10.5	9
Turkeys	427	4.8	2
Vegetables, Fruits and Other Crops	413	4.7	NA
Wheat	413	4.7	7
Sugar Beets	303	3.4	1
Other Poultry and Eggs	244	2.8	NA
Other Grain and Oil Crops	190	2.2	NA
Other Livestock and Livestock Prod.	93	1.1	NA
TOTAL	$8,809	100.0%	

In 1996, there were 87,000 farms and 29.8 million acres of farmland in Minnesota.

Source: The Minnesota Economy At a Glance, MN Dept. of Trade and Economic Development and Minnesota Agricultural Statistics 1998, MN Dept. of Agriculture

Iron Ore

Production has increased incrementally each year in the last decade with Minnesota supplying over 75 percent of our nations ore. Nearly 47.5 million metric tons were produced in that year.

Minnesota State Lottery

Although it is not technically a private business, the Minnesota Lottery has caused a major economic impact on the state since its inception on April 17, 1990. Over $3.1 billion in sales have netted the state nearly $8 million in contribution to the General Fund and the Environmental Trust Fund.

Minnesota Lottery From Inception Through Fiscal Year 1999

Sales	$3,190,153,000	
Other Income	18,511,099	
Total	3,208,664,099	
General Fund		
Sales Tax	205,413,454	
Net Proceeds	285,629,111	
Unclaimed Prizes	11,107,586	
Total General Fund	502,150,151	15.6%
Environmental Trust Fund		
Net Proceeds	214,817,427	
Unclaimed Prizes	7,405,057	
Total Trust Fund	222,222,484	6.9%
Prizes	1,887,162,541	58.8%
Retailers	182,470,071	5.7%
Lottery Administration	381,019,627	11.3%
Compulsive Gambling	8,745,000	0.3%
Other Payments to State	45,065,223	1.4%
		100.0%

Total Contributions to State. Source: MN State Lottery Public Relations.

FY1990	13,455,354	FY1996	88,835,020
FY1991	86,469,515	FY1997	89,137,950
FY1992	74,444,913	FY1998	87,482,229
FY1993	78,969,123	FY1999	85,891,678
FY1994	81,600,133	Total	771,085,667
FY1995	84,799,752		

Top Minnesota Attractions

1. Mall of America	42,500,000
2. Mystic Lake Casino	5,200,000
3. Grand Casino Hinkley	3,900,000
4. Grand Casino Mille Lacs	2,900,000
5. Metrodome	2,750,520
6. State Fair	1,683,454
7. Target Center	1,300,000
8. Valley Fair	1,300,000
9. Minnesota Zoo	1,115,290
10. Science Museum of Minnesota	1,100,000
11. Walker Art Center	867,210
12. Minnesota History Center	600,000
13. Gooseberry Falls State Park	570,198
14. Fort Snelling State Park	529,417
15. Itasca State Park	503,253
16. Ordway Music Theatre	500,000
17. Orpheum & State Theatres	500,000
18. Whitewater State Park	447,316
19. Orchestra Hall	433,316
20. St. Croix National Scenic River	423,622
21. Canal Park Marine Museum	422,933
22. Minneapolis Institute of Arts	393,620
23. Interstate State Park	344,534
24. Renaissance Festival	340,000
25. Sibley State Park	335,673
26.Children's Theatre	290,000
27. Children's Museum	289,386
28. Guthrie Theater	277,448
29. Tettegouche State Park	266,198
30. Brainerd International Raceway	251,000

Source: MN Office of Tourism. Ranked by estimatedvisitors (measurable admissions) for 1997, which includes local visitors and tourists.

"All business sagacity reduces itself in the last analysis to a judicious use of sabotage." - Thorstein Veblen, economist

"If the Twins and Vikings leave the Twin Cities, we're on our way to becoming a cold Omaha." - Harvey Mackay, businessman

Minnesotans Say the Darnedest Things...

Chapter 16

Communications

Minnesota's first newspaper was James M. Goodhue's "Minnesota Pioneer," founded in St. Paul in 1849. In the early years of the 20th century there were approximately 700 newspapers in Minnesota with an impressive number of them giving European news to the early immigrants in their native languages.

Today, the Minnesota Newspaper Association lists 335 weekly, semi-weekly, and suburban papers in the state, and 29 dailies.

The state's communication network also includes miles of fiber optic cable, some 33 television stations, 298 radio stations and a growing number of cable television and cellular phone companies. It's all about NOW!

Media Ethics and the Law

A center for the study of media ethics and the law was created to aid in the understanding of the role of media in a democratic society. It began August, 1984, at the University of Minnesota, School of Journalism and Communication thanks to a gift of $350,000 from Otto A. Silha, retired chairman of the board of Cowles Media Co., and his wife Helen. Silha's contribution was augmented by a $100,000 grant from The Minneapolis Star and Tribune Foundation. Silha, who graduated in 1940 from the University's school of journalism and mass communications, said of media ethics and the law, "They go to the heart and core of both the profession of journalism and the business."

Cable Television in Minnesota

Cable television companies in Minnesota are now serving over 60% of the homes passed by cable. This amounts to over 870,000 homes in almost every city in the state with a population of 300 or more residents. There is 20,000 miles of cable serving Minnesota communities. Cable technology has also grown tremendously. Over half the houses subscribing to cable are served by an addressable system using fiber optics and advanced computer technology. Today, the average subscriber has more than forty channels of service from which to choose.

Cable today is crossing the threshold of the digital era. Through the

Telecommunications Act of 1996, Congress has opened up the telecommunications market to new competitors and state of the art technology. Your local cable company is part of this revolution and will be offering new services in the years ahead.

In 1999, Seren Innovations (a subsidiary of NSP) was the first company to bundle cable, internet access, and telephone service by one company in Minnesota. The first installation was in the St. Cloud/Waite Park area.

1999 Minnesota Cable Facts
650 communities
415 systems
1.4 million homes passed
878,000 subscribers
20,000 plant miles
1200 schools wired
15 competitive franchises
37% of subscribers served by high-speed data/Internet access
Source: Minnesota Cable Communications Association

Internet

The ubiquitous internet that is firing many imaginations and is steamrolling into mainstream America had its beginning in 1969 with funding by the Department of Defense and its Advanced Research Projects Agency (ARPA). The basic premise was that computers in research centers around the country could be connected to share information in order to implement and reduce costs of developing military products. A series of computer networks were subsequently developed, both for military and research use. Access to these networks has been sold to commercial providers who, in turn, sell access to businesses and individuals. "The Web" and Web Pages" refer to a portion of the internet where the format is graphical as opposed to much of the rest of the internet that relies heavily on the transfer of text between computers. The World Wide Web was developed by the Swiss company, CERN.

People use the internet for accessing databases, sending electronic mail (e-mail), joining newsgroups for discussing shared interests, and obtaining software, shareware and freeware.

According to the Internet Starter Kit book by Adam C. Engst, "in 1980 there were 200 machines on the internet—that number is now [1995] about 4.9 million."

To get on the net you need a computer (although internet access is now being provided with a device attached to television sets); a phone line; a modem; an account through a "provider" such as America Online,

CompuServe, Cloudnet, Astound, etc.; and software that is usually supplied by the provider. Account fees usually range from $5-50 per month for individuals.

December, 1998 Estimate of Current Adult Online Users

	Online Population	User %	Home%	Work%
United States	61.5 million	31%	23%	13%
Minnesota	1.193 million	35%	26%	14%

Source: Cyberdialogue, NY, NY. 12/98 American Internet User's Survey

Minnesota Public Radio

Minnesota Public Radio is a Minnesota-based, independent, nonprofit, member-supported organization which seeks to enrich the mind and nourish the spirit through radio, related technology, and services. Also to enhance the lives and expand the perspectives of their audiences, and thereby assist them in strengthening their communities.

MPR began in1967 at St. John's University, Collegeville, MN, as KSJR, a non-commercial fine arts station for central Minnesota. In 1969 KSJN was established in St. Paul under the sponsorship of the St. Paul Ramsey Arts and Science Council. At the same time a new community corporation Minnesota Public Radio, was formed to extend broadcast coverage to the rest of the state. In 1971 a news and information component was added and by 1999 a network of 30 stations reaching 98% of the population of Minnesota had been built.

MPR's National Programs

A Prairie Home Companion (for information go to the internet site http://phc.mpr.org), Sound Money, Future Tense, Saint Paul Sunday, The Splendid Table.

Classical Music Information

To find out the recording information about a piece of music you heard, view the listings on the music section of mpr.org, call, or email us. Just make note of the date and time you heard it. To order a recording, call the Public Radio Music Source at 800-756-8742.

Source: MPR website www.mpr.org, mail@mpr.org
651-290-1212 or 800-228-7123

"I told a fellow that I had been kicked in the head by a horse. He said, that must have hurt. You bet, I said. That horse limped for days." - Roger Erickson, WCCO announcer

Minnesotans Say the Darnedest Things...

Minnesota Broadcast Highlights

•Minnesota's first commercial radio station was started by Dr. George W. Young, an eye doctor, in 1923 at 909 West Broadway, Minneapolis; hence the call letters WDGY.

•In 1923, the first radio broadcast of a symphony concert in the state, and possibly the nation, was aired by WLAG, the precursor of WCCO, with Walter Damrosch of Boston as the guest conductor. A prominent Minneapolis businessman, E.L. Carpenter, offered a $25 prize for the best critique of the performance. It was won by a 12-year-old boy, Stephen B. Humphrey, later a prominent teacher of English at the University of Minnesota and St. John's University.

•In 1973, WCCO was the first commercial station in the U.S. to receive the Peabody Award.

•Before becoming mayor of Minneapolis, Hubert Horatio Humphrey did a stint as a newscaster on station WTCN.

•The first broadcast from an airplane to the ground for dissemination to public listeners was done by KSTP radio.

•First live coverage of a baseball game, the Minneapolis Millers baseball team from Old Nicollet Park. This was in fact KSTP's first TV broadcast, a remote on April 27th, 1948.

•In May, 1950 unemployed Dave Moore stopped in to use the mens' room at 50 South 9th Street, Minneapolis, while his wife went to see a movie at Radio City next door. Minutes later, he was drafted to read a news broadcast (regular staffers had gone to the Korean police action) and was hired on the spot. Hastening to the theater to give his frau the news, he was shocked to hear Shirley say, "I know, I heard it on the loudspeaker." (The broadcasts were piped into the film house as added feature.) Thus began an illustrious career on WCCO - TV.

•KSTP purchased one of the first RCA commercial cameras manufactured and remote equipment for the purpose of experimenting with closed circuit, and to assist in training personnel for TV work. 1938.

•Governor Jesse Ventura was host of "Talk Radio" on KSTP and a mid-day show at KSAN. He has been a member of the American Federation of Television and Radio Announcers for about 10 years.

The Pavek Museum of Broadcasting houses one of the world's finest collections of antique radio, television, and broadcast equipment. It contains hundreds of examples of radios, televisions, recording devices, phonographs, and literature.

Pavek Museum of Broadcasting
3515 Raleigh Av S
St. Louis Park MN 55416
612-926-8198 www.pavekmuseum.org

Minnesota Radio and Television Stations

City	Call letters	Format	Frequency
Ada	KRJB FM	Country/ Divers.	106.3
Aitkin	KKIN AM	MOR	930
Aitkin	KKIN FM	Country	94.3
Albany	KASM AM	Country	1150
Albany	KASM FM	Oldies 50s-80s RnR	105.5
Albert Lea	KATE AM	News/Full Service	1450
Albert Lea	KCPI FM	Hot/AC (Adult Contemp.)	94.9
Albert Lea	KQPR FM		96.1
Alexandria	KIKV FM	Country	100.7
Alexandria	KSTQ FM	AC/Soft Hits	99.3
Alexandria	KXRA AM	New/Talk/M.O.R.	1490
Alexandria	KXRA FM	Top 40	92.3
Appleton	KRSU FM*	Classical & News	91.3
Atwater	KYRS FM	Country	94.1
Austin	KAUS AM	News/Country	1480
Austin	KAUS FM	News/Country	99.9
Austin	KMSK FM	Public	91.3
Bemidji	KBSB FM		89.7
Bemidji	KBUN AM	Sports/Country	1450
Bemidji	KBHP FM	Sports/Country	101.1
Bemidji	KCRB FM*	Classical	88.5
Bemidji	KNBJ FM*	News/Info.	91.3
Bemidji	KKBJ AM	Country/Talk	1360
Bemidji	KKBJ FM	Contemporary	103.7
Bemidji	KLLZ FM	Classic Hit	99.1
Bemidji	WBJI FM	Oldies	98.3
Benson	KSCR AM	Contemporary	1290
Benson	KSCR FM	Contemporary	93.5
Blue Earth	KBEW AM	Oldies/News	1560
Blue Earth	KBEW FM	Country	98.1
Blue Earth	KJLY FM	Christian/Inspirational	****
Brainerd	KBPR FM*	Classics/Music	90.7
Brainerd	KLIZ AM	AC	1380
Brainerd	KLIZ FM	Classic Hit	107.5
Brianerd	KTCF FM	Country	101.5
Brainerd	KVBR AM	Hot Country	1340
Brainerd	KFGI FM	Hot Country	103.5
Brainerd	WJJY FM	Adult Contemporary	106.7
Brainerd	WWWI AM	News/Talk/Oldies	1270
Breckenridge	KBMW	Country	1450
Breckenridge/			

Wahpeton	KGHB	Oldies	107.1
Breezy Point	KLKS FM	MOR 40+	104.3
Browerville/			
Long Prairie	KXDL FM	Hot A/C	99.7
Buffalo	KRWC AM	Full-Service	1360
Caledonia	KSOF FM	Adult Contemporary	94.7
Cambridge	WREV FM	Modern/Alternative Rock	105.3
Cloquet	WKLK AM		1230
Cloquet	WKLK FM	Oldies	96.5
Collegeville	KJNB FM	New Music	99.9
Collegeville	KSJR FM*	Classical Music	90.1
Collegeville	KNSR FM*	News& Information	88.9
Crookston,MN/			
Grand Forks,ND	KQHT FM	Soft Hits	96.1
Crookston,MN/			
Grand Forks,ND	KROX AM	Soft Adult Contemporary	1260
Detroit Lakes	KDLM AM	Full Service	1340
Detroit Lakes	KRCQ FM	Traditional Country	102.3
Duluth	KDAL AM		610
Duluth	KDAL FM		95.7
Duluth	KDNW FM	Religious	97.3
Duluth	KDNI FM	Religious	90.5
Duluth	KQDS AM	Classic A.O.R.	1490
Duluth	KQDS FM	Classic A.O.R.	94.9
Duluth	KUMD FM		103.3
Duluth	KXTP AM	Adult Standard	970
Duluth	KTCO FM	Hot Country	98.9
Duluth	WDSM AM	Sports	710
Duluth	KRBR FM	Modern Rock	102.5
Duluth	WEBC AM	News, Talk Radio	560
Duluth	KKCB FM	Country	105.1
Duluth	KLDJ FM	Oldies	101.7
Duluth	WIRR FM	Classical/News	90.9
Duluth	WSCN FM*	News & Information	100.5
Duluth	WSCD FM*	Classical	92.9
Duluth	WNCB FM	CHR Christian	89.3
Duluth	WRSR FM	NAC	104.3
Duluth	WWAX FM	Adult Modern Rock	92.1
Duluth	WWJC AM		850
E. Grand Forks	KCNN AM	News/Talk/Sports	1590
E. Grand Forks	KZLT FM	Adult Contemporary	104.3
E. Grand Forks	KYCK FM	Country	97.1
Ely	WELY AM	Eclectic	1450

Ely	WELY FM	Eclectic	92.1
Eveleth	WEVE AM	Contemporary	1340
Eveleth	WEVE FM	Contemporary	97.9
Fairmont	KSUM AM	Country/AC	1370
Fairmont	KFMC FM	Country/AC	106.5
Fargo	KLTA FM	Contemporary	105.1
Faribault	KDHL AM	Country/Rock	920
Faribault	KQCL FM	Country/Rock	95.9
Fergus Falls	KBRF AM	Country/Information	1250
Fergus Falls	KZCR FM	Classic Rock	103.3
Fergus Falls	KJJK AM	Oldies/Country	1020
Fergus Falls	KJJK FM	Oldies/Country	96.5
Forest Lake	WLKX FM	A.C. Christian	95.9
Fosston	KKCQ AM	Country	1480
Fosston	KKEZ FM	A.C. Christian	107.1
Glencoe/			
Hutchinson	KARP FM	Variety (Hit Radio)	96.3
Glenwood	KMGK FM	Soft Hits/Adult	107.1
Grand Rapids	KAXE FM		91.7
Grand Rapids	KAXE FM		94.7
Grand Rapids	KAXE FM		89.5
Grand Rapids	KGPZ FM	Real Country	96.1
Grand Rapids	KOZY AM	Classic Hits/AC	1320
Grand Rapids	KMFY FM	Classic Hits/AC	96.9
Granite Falls	KKRC FM		93.9
Hastings	KDWA AM	Oldies	1460
Hibbing	KADU FM		90.1
Hibbing	WKKQ AM	Country/CHR	650
Hibbing	WTBX FM	Country/CHR	93.9
Hibbing	WMFG AM	Sports Talk	1240
Hibbing	WMFG FM	Oldies	106.3
Hutchinson	KDUZ AM	Full Service/Country	1260
Hutchinson	KKJR FM	Full Service/Country	107.1
Int'l Falls	KBHW FM	Inspirational/CHR	99.5
Int'l Falls	KGHS AM	Classic Hits/Country	1230
Int'l Falls	KSDM FM	Classic Hits/Country	104.1
Jackson	KKOJ AM	CD Country	1190
Jackson	KRAQ FM	Oldies	
LaCrescent	KQEG FM	Oldies	102.7
Lake City	KMFX FM	Country	102.5
Litchfield	KLFD AM	Oldies/Country/AC	1410
Little Field	KLTF AM	News & Information	960
Little Field	KFML FM	Contemporary	94.1

Little Field	WYRQ FM	Modern Country	92.1
Long Prairie	KEYL AM	Country	1400
Luverne	KQAD AM	M.O.R./Country	800
Luverne	KLQL FM	M.O.R./Country	101.1
Madison	KLQP FM	Country	92.1
Mankato	KEEZ FM	Contemporary	99.1
Mankato	KMSU FM		89.7
Mankato	KTOE AM	News/Information	1420
Mankato	KDOG FM	News/Information	96.7
Mankato	KXLP FM	Classic Rock	93.1
Mankato	KYSM AM	Memory Music/Talk	1230
Mankato	KYSM FM	Hot Country	103.5
Marshall	KBJJ FM	Classic Hits	107.5
Marshall	KMHL AM	Rock 40/Country	1400
Marshall	KKCK AM	Rock 40/Country	99.7
Marshall	KARL FM	Rock 40/Country	105.1
Mpls./St. Paul	KBEM FM	Jazz/Traffic Information	88.5
Mpls./St. Paul	KCFE FM	Modern/Alt. Rock	105.1
Mpls./St. Paul	KDWB FM	CHR	101.3
Mpls./St. Paul	KDXL FM	Modern Rock	106.7
Mpls./St. Paul	KDXL AM	Business Radio	****
Mpls./St. Paul	KEGE FM	Modern Rock	93.7
Mpls./St. Paul	KFAI FM	24 HOUR	90.3
Mpls./St. Paul	KFAI FM	24 HOUR	106.7
Mpls./St. Paul	KFAN AM	Sports Radio	1130
Mpls./St. Paul	KEEY FM	Contemporary Country	102.1
Mpls./St. Paul	KKMS AM		980
Mpls./St. Paul	KLBB AM	Adult Standards	1400
Mpls./St. Paul	KMOJ FM	Urban Contemporary	89.9
Mpls./St. Paul	KNOF FM	Gospel/Religious	95.3
Mpls./St. Paul	KNOW FM*	News/Information	91.1
Mpls./St. Paul	KSJN FM*	News/Information	99.5
Mpls./St. Paul	KQQL FM	Oldies	107.9
Mpls./St. Paul	KQRS AM	Rock/100% Simulcast	1440
Mpls./St. Paul	KQRS FM	Rock/100% Simulcast	92.5
Mpls./St. Paul	KREV FM	Modern/Alt. Rock	105.1
Mpls./St. Paul	KSGS AM	Urban Gold	950
Mpls./St. Paul	KMJZ FM	New AC	104.1
Mpls./St. Paul	KSTP AM	Talk	1500
Mpls./St. Paul	KSTP FM	Adult Contemporary	94.5
Mpls./St. Paul	KTCJ AM	Adult Album Rock	690
Mpls./St. Paul	KTCZ FM	Adult Album Rock	97.1
Mpls./St. Paul	KTIS AM	Inspirational	900

Mpls./St. Paul	KTIS FM	Inspirational	98.5
Mpls./St. Paul	KUOM AM	Alternative Rock	770
Mpls./St. Paul	KYCR AM	Contemp. Christian/Teach.	1570
Mpls./St. Paul	WBOB FM	New Country	100.3
Mpls./St. Paul	WCCO AM	Full Service	830
Mpls./St. Paul	WCTS AM	Religious	1030
Mpls./St. Paul	WDGY AM	60s & 70s	630
Mpls./St. Paul	WLOL AM	Adult Standards	1470
Mpls./St. Paul	WLTE FM	Soft Adult Contemp.	102.9
Mpls./St. Paul	WMCN FM	(Macalester College)	91.7
Mpls./St. Paul	WMIN AM	Music of Your Life	740
Mpls./St. Paul	WMNN AM	All news	1330
Mpls./St. Paul	WWTC AM	Children's	1280
Montevideo	KDMA AM		1460
Montevideo	KMGM FM		105
Moorhead/Fargo	KCCM FM*	Classical	91.1
Moorhead/Fargo	KCCD FM*	News	90.3
Moorhead	KVOX AM	MOR	1280
Moorhead	KVOX FM	Country	99.9
Mora	KBEK FM	Oldies & Soft Rock	95.5
Morris	KMRS AM	News/Farm/Sports/MOR	1230
Morris	KKOK FM	Contemporary Country	95.7
Morris	KUMM FM	(U of M, Morris)	89.7
New Prague	KCHK AM	Pure Gold	1350
New Prague	KCHK FM	Pure Gold	95.5
New Ulm	KNUJ AM	Country/Full Service	860
New Ulm	KNUJ FM	Country/Full Service	107.3
New Ulm	KNSG FM	Country/Full Service	94.7
Northfield	KRLX FM	(Carleton College)	88.1
Northfield	KYMN AM	Adult Contemp/Talk	1080
Northfield	WCAL FM	(St. Olaf College)	89.3
Olivia	KOLV FM	Country/ Classics	100.1
Ortonville	KCGN FM	Family/Farm	101.5
Ortonville	KDIO AM	AC	1350
Ortonville	KAHF FM	AC	***
Osakis	KBHL FM	Christian	103.9
Owatonna	KOWZ FM	AC	100.9
Owatonna	KRFO AM	Oldies	1390
Owatonna	KRFO FM	Country	104.9
Park Rapids	KPRM AM	Branson Country	870
Park Rapids	KDKK FM	Stardust	97.5
Pelican Rapids	KBOT FM	Hot Country	104.1
Pequot Lakes	KTIG FM	Religious	102.7

Perham	KPRW FM	Hot AC	95.5
Pine City	WCMP AM	News/Info	1350
Pine City	WCMP FM	Country	92.1
Pipestone	KLOH AM	Country	1050
Pipestone	KISD FM	Super Gold	98.7
Preston	KFIL AM	Farm/News/Talk	1060
Preston	KFIL FM	Country	103.1
Princeton	WQPM AM	Country	1300
Princeton	WQPM FM	Country	106.1
Red Wing	KCUE AM	News/Talk	1250
Red Wing	KWNG FM	Classic Hits	105.9
Redwood Falls	KLGR AM	Country	1490
Redwood Falls	KLGR FM	Pure Gold Oldies	97.7
Rochester	KFSI FM		92.9
Rochester	KLSE FM*	Classical	91.7
Rochester	KZSE FM*	News	90.7
Rochester	KNXR FM	Full Service	97.5
Rochester	KOLM AM	Oldies	1520
Rochester	KWWK FM	Country	96.5
Rochester	KROC AM	Full Ser./News/Talk	1340
Rochester	KROC FM	CHR	106.9
Rochester	KWEB AM	Sports	1270
Rochester	KRCH FM	Classic Rock	101.7
Roseau	KCAJ FM	Country/Mix	102.1
Roseau	KRWB AM		1410
St. Cloud	KCFB FM	Christian/Inspirational	91.5
St. Cloud	KKSR FM	Oldies Based AC	96.7
St. Cloud	KNSI AM	News/Talk	1450
St. Cloud	KCLD FM	CHR	104.7
St. Cloud	KVSC FM	Altern./Progressive	88.1
St. Cloud	KXSS AM		1390
St. Cloud	KLZZ FM		103.7
St. Cloud	WJON AM	News/Sports/Information	1240
St. Cloud	WWJO FM	Country	98.1
St. Cloud	KMXK FM	Oldies	94.9
St. James	KXAC FM	Lite AC	100.5
St. James	KXAX FM	Country	101.5
St. Joseph	KKJM FM	A C Christian	92.9
St. Peter	KGAC FM*	Classical/Arts/News	90.5
St. Peter	KNGA FM*	Classical/Arts/News	91.5
St. Peter	KRBI AM	NWS/Soft AC	1310
St. Peter	KRBI FM	NWS/Soft AC	105.5
Sauk Centre	KMSR FM	Soft Hit AC	94.3

Sauk Rapids	WVAL AM	Rock	660
Sauk Rapids	WHMH FM	Rock	101.7
Shakopee	KKCM AM	Christian/News	1530
Slayton	KJOE FM	Country	106.1
Sleepy Eye	KNUJ FM	AC/Information	107.3
Springfield	KNSG FM	Country	94.7
Spring Grove	KQYB FM	Hot Country	98.3
Spring Valley	KVGO FM	Golden Oldies	104.3
Staples	KNSP AM	Country/Full Service	1430
Stewartville	KYBA FM	Lite AC	105.3
Stillwater	WIMN AM	Nostalgia	1220
Thief River Falls	KKAQ AM	News/Country	1460
Thief River Falls	KKDQ FM	News/Country	99.3
Thief River Falls	KKDQ FM	News/Country	99.3
Thief River Falls	KSRQ FM	Variety Ed./Music	90.1
Thief River Falls	KTRF AM	News/Sports/Oldies	1230
Thief River Falls	KSNR FM	News/Sports/Oldies	100.3
Thief River Falls	KQMN FM*	Classical	91.5
Thief River Falls	KNTN FM*	News	102.7
Virginia	WHLB AM	Nostalgia	1400
Virginia	WIRR FM*	Classical & News	90.9
Virginia	WUSZ FM	Country	99.9
Wabasha	KMFX AM	Country	1190
Wadena	KSKK FM	Adult Contemporary	94.7
Wadena	KWAD AM		920
Wadena	KKWS FM		105.9
Walker	KLLZ AM	Classic Rock	1600
Warroad	KKWQ FM	Country	92.5
Waseca	KOWO AM	Country/Info.	1170
Waseca	KRUE FM	Adult Contemporary	92.1
Watertown	KWOM AM	Variety	1600
Willmar	KDJS AM	Oldies	1590
Willmar	KDJS FM	Country	95.3
Willmar	KWLM AM	Full Service	1340
Willmar	KQIC FM	Hot AC	102.5
Windom	KDOM AM	Country/Oldies	1580
Windom	KDOM FM	Country/Oldies	94.3
Winona	KAGE AM	Country/Full Service	1380
Winona	KAGE FM	Country/Full Service	95.3
Winona	KWNO AM	Country/Full Service	1230
Winona	KWNO FM	Country/Full Service	99.3
Winona	KHME FM	Lite AC	101.1
Winona	KQAL FM	Varied	89.5

Winona	KSMR FM	Album Oriented Rock	92.5
Worthington	KITN FM	Hit Country/Oldies/AC	93.5
Worthington	KRSW FM*	Classical	89.3
Worthington	KWOA AM	News/Talk/Info	730
Worthington	KWOA FM	AC	95.1
Worthington	KNSW FM*	News	91.7

*Minnesota Public Radio Station

Minnesota Television Stations

City	Call letters	Station	Channel
Alexandria	KCCO/KCCW	CBS	7/12
Alexandria	KSAX/KRWF	ABC	42/43
Appleton	KWCM/KSMN	PBS	10/20
Austin	KAAL	ABC	6
Austin	KSMQ	PBS	15
Bemidji	KAWE/KAWB	PBS	9/22
Duluth	KBJR	NBC	6
Duluth	KDLH NEWS	CBS	3
Duluth	KNLD	Fant Broadcasting	21
Duluth	WDIO/WIRT	ABC	10
Duluth	WDSE	PBS	8
Fargo	KBRR/KVRR	Fox	***
Mankato	KEYC	CBS	12
Mpls./St. Paul	KARE	NBC	11
Mpls./St. Paul	KMWB	Warner Brothers	23
Mpls./St. Paul	KMSP	UPN	9
Mpls./St. Paul	KSTP	ABC	5
Mpls./St. Paul	KTCA/KTCI	PBS	2/17
Mpls./St. Paul	KVBM	HSN	45
Mpls./St. Paul	WCCO	CBS	4
Mpls./St. Paul	WFTC	Fox	29
Plymouth	KPXM	***	***
Rochester	KTTC	NBC	10
Rochester	KXLT	America One	47
St. Cloud	WCMN	***	13

Source: Minnesota Broadcasters Association 1997,
3517 Raleigh Av S   POBox 16030, St Louis Park MN 55416-0030
612-926-8123   1-800-245-5838

"The chief cause of problems is solutions." - Eric Sevareid
"One man's excess is another man's minimum." - Robert T. Smith
Source: Minnesotans Say the Darnedest Things...

TACIP Telecommunications Access for Communication Impaired Persons
The TACIP unit is responsible for improving accessibility to the Minnesota telephone network for communication impaired persons. Communications-impaired persons, as defined by the State Legislature, are persons who are certified as deaf, severely hearing impaired, hard-of-hearing, speech impaired, deaf and blind, or mobility impaired, if the impairment significantly impedes the ability to use standard telephone equipment.
Anyone can access the Minnesota Relay Service if the call originates or terminates in Minnesota and if the call involves a voice user and a TTY/TDD user. (A TTY/TDD is a teletypewriter or Telecommunications Device for the Deaf used by a deaf or speech-impared caller.)

Minnesota Relay Service (MRS)
TACIP unit staff are responsible for ensuring the provision of the Minnesota Relay Service, which allows persons who use a teletypewriter / telecommunications device for the deaf to communicate with users of standard telephones. Operators called "Communication Assistants" relay, or translate, 85,000 calls each month.
Individuals who have difficulty using the telephone due to a communication impairment may be eligible to receive specialized telecommunications equipment. For information call: 651-296-0412 (Voice), 651-296-9863 (TTY/TDD),1-800-657-3599 (Voice), 1-800-657-3603 (TTY/TDD)
To contact a deaf, hard-of-hearing, or speech impaired person through the Minnesota Relay Service (MRS) make sure you have the number you wish to call ready, then dial: 1-800-627-3529 Voice, TTY, ASCII
When your call is answered, a Communications Assistant (CA), the person relaying your call, will give you their identification number. Tell the CA the number you wish to call. The CA will place your call while you are on hold.

Important Information
•All conversations are 100% confidential.
•For quality control purposes, always write down the CA's identi fication number.
•The relay operates 24 hours a day, 365 days a year.
•There is no charge to use the MRS except for long distance calls.

Billing of Calls
Several long distance billing options are available: calling card, third party billing, etc. If you are not placing a long distance call, there is no charge to use the relay.
To schedule a free-of-charge MRS presentation for employees, groups or organizations, please call our customer service office: 651-602-9005 Voice, TTY (Metro Area), 1-800-657-3775 Voice, TTY (In-State Only)
Source: Jim Alan, TACIP Administrator, Minnesota Department of Public Service (651)-297-4565 (Voice), (651)-296-1642 (TTY/TDD)

244   The Minnesota Almanac

The Office of Technology was created by an executive order of Governor Carlson in 1996 and authorized by statute in 1997. It is charged with providing leadership and direction for information and communications technology policy in Minnesota. Executive director, JoAnn S. Hanson, was appointed on January 2, 1998.

The office also coordinates the state's strategic investments in information and communications technology as a means of encouraging the development of a technically literate society and ensuring sufficient access to and efficient delivery of government services. As part of these efforts, the office maintains and develops the state's Internet site, North Star at http://www.state.mn.us.

Since 1991, the Carlson Administration has appropriated more than $2 billion for information and communication technology. The Carlson Administration funded $216 million in 1997 with the Office of Technology's assistance. At least $67.6 million of this appropriation was designed to enhance the use of technology in education.

Contact the Minnesota Office of Technology, 332 Minnesota St., E1100, St. Paul, MN 55101, 651.215.3878, or e-mail: keith.pearson@state.mn.us. The North Star site can be reached at www.state.mn.us and the Office of Technology site is at www.ot.state.mn.us. TTY 651.282.2228

Connecting Minnesota

Connecting Minnesota is a public/private partnership initiated by the departments of Transportation and Administration to bring fiber-optic communications to significant portions of Greater Minnesota and increase telecommunications capacity in the Twin Cities metro area.

A private contractor will spend about $195 million to install fiber-optic cable along 2,000 miles of interstate and trunk highways. The project creatively provides the quality and quantity of telecommunications capacity needed by Minnesota at little or no cost to the taxpayer. Work began in the fall of 1998 and scheduled completion is mid-2001.

The State will receive telecommunications capacity for use by public entities—K-12 schools, libraries, higher education and state and local government agencies. The vast majority of the capacity will be available for private use—as a "carrier's carrier," ICS/UCN, the cable installer based in Denver, will market the capacity statewide to providers of communications services on a competitively neutral, nondiscriminatory basis.

Connecting Minnesota will reach to within 10 miles of about 80 percent of the state's population. Connecting Minnesota makes Minnesota an undisputed leader in communications technology.

Office of Alternative Transportation Financing, Minnesota Department of Transportation (651)282-6148

New Metro Area Codes In 2000

The western Metro suburbs will get new area codes according to the Public Utilities Commission (PUC). Starting in February 2000, only Minneapolis, Richfield, Fort Snelling, and St. Anthony will retain the 612 area code. Communities roughly north of I-394 and highway 12 will use the 763 area code. Others south of the line will use the 952 area code. Callers will have an 11 month grace period to use both area codes, but after January 2001, they will have to use the new numbers. The PUC estimates that Minneapolis will run out of numbers in 5 years, the suburbs in 13 years.

763 communities: Brooklyn Center, Fridley, Mounds View, Blaine, Coon Rapids, Circle Pines, Lexington, St. Francis, Isanti, Cambridge, Princeton, Elk River, Becker, Monticello, Buffalo, Waverly, Delano, Medina, Plymouth, and Golden Valley.

952 Communities: Bloomington, Burnsville, Apple Valley, Lakeville, Elko, New Prague, Belle Plaine, Hamburg, Norwood, Mayer, Watertown, Mound, Orono, Wayzata, Minnetonka, Hopkins, Edina, and St. Louis Park. Source: USWest

Minnesota Daily Newspapers

Key:
Town and Zip Code
Newspaper Name
Publisher(s)
Circulation/Publica-
tion Day
Phone

Albert Lea 56007-0060
Albert Lea Tribune
Curtis Williams
7265 Su-F Daily
507-373-1411

Austin 55912
Austin Daily Herald
Neal Ronquist
6798 Su-F
507-433-8851

Bemidji 56619-0455
The Pioneer
Omar Forberg

9203 A / Sun. 9901 A
218-751-3740

Brainerd 56401
Brainerd DailyDispatch
Terry McCollough
13,290 A /Sun. 17,289 A
218-829-4705

Breckenridge 58074-0970
Daily News
Newell C. Grant
4431 T-F, Su
701-642-8585

Crookston 56716-0615
Crookston Daily Times
Randal L. Hultrgren
3995 M-F
218-281-2730

Duluth 55816
The Duluth News-

Tribune
Mary Jacobus
50,616 A /Sun. 77,907 A
218-723-5281

Fairmont 56031-0681
Sentinel
Gary Andersen
9143 A M-Sa
507-235-3303

Fargo /Moorhead
58102-4826
The Forum
William C. Marcil
53,584 A/Sun. 67,853
A701-235-7311

Fairbault 55021
Fairbault Daily News
David Balcom
7433 Tu-Su
507-334-1853

Fergus Falls 56537-0506
Fergus Falls Daily Journal
Dave Churchill
9942 M-Sa
218-736-7511

Hibbing 55746
Hibbing Daily Tribune
Terese Almquist
8006 Su-Sa
218-262-1011

International Falls
56649   Int'l Falls
Daily Journal
Wayne Kasich
4336 M-F
218-285-7411

Mankato 56002-3287
The Free Press
Samuel R. Gett, Jr.
25,585 A M-Sa
507-625-4451

Marshall 56258-0411
Marshall Independent
Russ Labat
8151 A M-Sa
507-537-1551

Minneapolis 55415
Finance and Commerce
Debra Nelson
1122 T-Sa
612-333-4244

Minneapolis 55488
Star Tribune
John Schueler
387,109 A/Su 667,748 A
612-673-4000

New Ulm 56073-0487
New Ulm Journal
Bruce Fenske
9807 A /Sun. 10,228 A
507-359-2911

Owatonna 55060-0346
Owatonna People's
Press
Ron Ensley
7531 A /Sun. 7730 A
507-451-2840

Red Wing 55066-0082
Red Wing Republican
Eagle
Arlin Albrecht
7951 A M-Sa
651-388-8235

Rochester 55903-6118
Post-Bulletin
William C. Boyne
41,154 A /Sat. 45,364 A
507-285-7600

St. Cloud 56302-0768
St. Cloud Times
Sonja Sorenson Craig
28,286 A /Sun. 38,052
A320-255-8700

St. Paul 55101-1309
St. Paul Legal Ledger
Patrick Boulay
547   T-Sa

651-222-0059

St. Paul 55101-1057
Saint Paul Pioneer Press
Rick Sadowski
202,444A/Sun.
262,308A
651-222-5011

Stillwater 55082
Stillwater Evening
Gazette
Michael Mahoney
3870 M-F
651-439-3130

Virginia 55792
Mesabi Daily News
John Murphy
12,515 Su-Sa
218-741-5544

Willmar 56201-0839
West Central Tribune
Steven McLister
17,106 M-Sa/Su 27,599 A
320-235-1150

Winona 55987-5147
Winona Daily News
George Althoff
12,165 A S-Sa /Sun.
13,002 A
507-453-3500

Worthington 56187-2451
Worthington Daily Globe
Dennis Hall
12,517 A M-Sa
507-376-9711

Minnesota Weekly, Semi-Weekly, and Suburban Newspapers

Ada 56510-0148
Norman County Index
John R. Pfund
2157 Tu
218-784-2541

Adams 55909-0283
The Monitor Review
Kim Edward Adams &
John Adams
1316 Th
507-582-3542

Adrian 56110-0160
Nobles County Review
Jerry Johnson
1247 W
507-483-2213

Aitkin 56431-0259
Aitkin Independent
Age
Richard Norlander
5976 W
218-927-3761

Albany 56307-0310
Stearns-Morrison
Enterprise
Don & Carole Larson
2166 Tu
320-845-2700

Albert Lea 56007-0060
Albert Lea Tribune
Curtis Williams
7265 Su-F/DAILY
507-373-1411

Alden 56009-0485
Alden Advance

David Gehrke
968 Th
507-874-3440

Alexandria 56308-0549
The Echo Press
Jody Hanson
9426/10,159 W/F
320-763-3133

Annandale 55302
Annandale Advocate
Steven Prinsen
2562W
320-274-3052

Anoka 55433
Anoka County Union
Julian Andersen
4883 F
612-421-4444

Apple Valley 55439
(Bloomington)
Apple
Valley/Rosemount/
Eagan Sun Current
Frank Chilinski
31,352 W
612-869-4700 and 612-392-6400

Appleton 56208
Appleton Press
Loren Johnson
2055 W
320-289-1323

Arlington 55307-0388
Arlington Enterprise
Gail Kill

1373 Th
507-964-5547

Askov 55704
Askov American
David & Cynthia
Heiller
2087 W
320-838-3151

Atwater/Cosmos/
 Grove City 56288-0910
Tri-City News
Rose Hettig
476 M
320-796-2945

Aurora 55705
Aurora-Hoyt Lakes
Range Facts
Gary Albertson
1960 Th
218-865-6265

Austin 55912
Austin Daily Herald
Neal Ronquist
6798 Su-F/DAILY
507-433-8851

Babbitt 55706-0267
Babbitt Weekly News
William Proznik, Jr.
1271 F
218-827-2363

Bagley 56621-0130
Farmers Independent
Tom Burford
2470 W
218-694-6265

Balaton 56115-0310
Press Tribune
Seth Schmidt
698 W
507-734-5421

Barnesville 56514-0070
Barnsville Record-
Review
Eugene A. Prim
1780 M
218-354-2606

Battle Lake 56515-0098
Battle Lake Review
Jon A. Tamke
2300 W
218-864-5952

Baudette 56623-0240
The Baudette Region
John C. Oren
2205 W
218-634-1722

Becker 55038
Sherburne County
Citizen
Jake Jacobson
10,862 Sa
612-261-5880

Belgrade 56312-0279
The Observer
James R. Lemmer
1218 W
320-254-8250

Belle Plaine 56011
Belle Plaine Herald
C. Edward Townsend
3580 W
612-873-2261

Bemidji 56619-0455
The Pioneer
Omar Forberg
9203/9901 Tu-Sa/Su
218-751-3740

Benson 56215-0227
Swift County Monitor-
News
Reed Anfinson
2909 W
320-843-4111

Big Lake 55309
West Sherburne Tribune
Gary W. Meyer
12,579 A Sa
612-263-3602

Bird Island 55310-0160
Bird Island Union
John & Ken Hubin
899 W
320-365-3266

Biwabik 55708
Biwabik Times
Kathleen Anderson /
Gary Albertson
1530 Th
218-865-6265

Blackduck 56620
The American
Omar Forberg
1122 Su
218-835-4211

Blaine 55449-4923
Blaine Banner
Marilyn Hamm
10,000 Monthly/1st W
845-755-3832

Blaine 55433
Blaine-Spring Lake
Park Life
Julian Andersen
1174 F
512-421-4444

Blooming Prairie 55917
Blooming Prairie Times
Elsie Slinger
1173 T
507-583-4431

Bloomington 55439
Bloomington Sun-
Current
Frank Chilinski
28,322 A W
612-896-4700 and 612-
392-6400

Blue Earth 56013-0100
Fairbault County
Register
Ogden Newspapers
3114 M
507-526-7324

Bovey 55709-0070
Scenic Range News
Douglas D. Deal
1873 W
218-245-1422

Brainerd 56401
Brainerd Daily
Dispatch
Terry McCollough
13,290/17,289 M-F/Su
218-829-4705

Breckenridge 58074-
0970
Daily News
Newell C. Grant
4431 Tu-F, Su/DAILY
701-64-8585

Brooklyn Center 55439
Brooklyn Center /
Brooklyn Park Sun Post
Frank Chilinski
25,309 A W
612-896-4700 and 612-
392-6400

Brooten 56316
Bonanza Valley Voice
Howard & Kayla
Johnson
1124 W
320-5346-2400

Browerville 56438-0245
Browerville Blade
Peter Quirt
1646 Th
320-594-2911

Browns Valley 56219
Valley News
Eugene & Betti Labs
1033 T
320-695-2570

Brownton / Stewart
The Bulletin
William C. Ramige
978 W
320-328-4444

Buffalo 55313-0159
Wright County Journal-
Press

James P. McDonnell Jr.
5844 Th
612-682-1221

Burnsville 55337
Dakota County Tribune
Daniel & Joseph Clay
554 Th
612-894-1111

Burnsville / Savage
/Lakeville 55439
Burnsville Sun Current
Frank Chilinski
29,726 A W
612-896-4700

Byron 55920-0039
Byron Review
Susan Borgen / Garry
Borgen
1045 W
507-775-6180

Caledonia-Houston
555921-0227
The Caledonia Argus
ECM Publishers, Inc.
3256 T
507-724-3475

Cambridge 55008
Cambridge Star
Jim Schmitz
13,499 A W
612-689-1181

Cambridge 55008-0352
County News
Julian Andersen
9766 W
612-689-1981

Canby 56220-0129
Canby News
Don & Ellie Berman
2316 W
507-223-5303

Cannon Falls 55009-
0366
Cannon Falls Beacon
Richard Dalton
4304 Th
507-263-3991

Cass Lake 56633-0398
Cass Lake Times
Victor W. Olson
1230 Th
218-335-2290

Champlin 55369
Champlin-Dayton Press
Don Larson
1873 T
612-425-3323

Chanhassen 55317
Chanhassen Villager
Mark Weber
5135 Th
612-934-5045

Chaska 55318
Chaska Herald
Stan Rolfsrud
4532 Th
612-488-2650

Chatfield 55923
Chatfield News
Michael S. Grieve
1488 W
507-867-3870

Chisholm 55719
The Chisholm Tribune-
Press
Eric Erickson
2470 Th
218-254-4432

Chokio 56221-0096
Chokio Review
Nick and Anne
Ripperger
990 Th
320-324-2405

Clara City 56222-0458
Clara City Herald
T. J. Almen
1415 W
320-847-3130

Claremont 55924-000B
Claremont News
Virginia Sendle
511 W
507-527-2492

Clarissa / Eagle Bend /
Bertha 56440-0188
Independent News
Herald
Ernie & Diane
Silbernagel
2515 T
218-756-2131

Clinton / Graceville
56225-0368
The Northern Star
Jim Kaercher
1905 Th
320-325-5152

Cloquet 55720
Cloquet Journal
Eric Erickson
4835 F
218-879-1950

Cloquet 55720
The Pine Knot
Scott Elwood
3885 Sa/W
218-879-6761

Cokato (& Dassel)
55321
Enterprise & Dispatch
Carolyn Holje
3058 W
320-286-2118

Cold Spring 55720
Cold Spring Record
Mike Austreng
3440 T
320-685-8621

Comfrey 56019-0218
Comfrey Times
Gary Richter
875 Th
507-877-2281

Cook 55723
Cook News-Herald
Gary Albertson
3305 Th
218-666-5944

Coon Rapids 55433
Coon Rapids Herald
Julian Andersen
3783 F
612-421-444

Cottage Grove 55016
South Washington
County Bulletin
Steve Messick
10,520 W
612-459-3434

Cottonwood 56229-0076
Cottonwood Tri-
County News
Jeff & Julie Meyer
1775 W
507-423-6239

Crookston 56716-0615
Crookston Daily Times
Randal L. Hultgren
3995 M-F/DAILY
218-281-2730

Crosby 56441-0067
Crosby-Ironton Courier
Thomas M. Swensen
3988 W
218-546-5029

Dawson 56232-1015
Dawson Sentinel
RBM Publications
1923 W
320-769-2497

Deer River 56636
Western Itasca Review
Bob Barnacle
1635 Th
218-246-8533

Delano 55328
Delano Eagle
Don Larson
1251 M

612-972-6171

Detroit Lakes 56501-0826
Becker County Record
Dennis Winskowski
14,142 W
218-847-3151

Detroit Lakes 56501-0826
Detroit Lakes Tribune
Dennis Winskowski
5784 Su
218-847-3151

Dodge Center 55927
Dodge Center Star Record
Tony & Jacky Pierskalla
1004 Tu
507-374-6531

Duluth 55807-7003
Duluth Budgeteer Press, Inc.
Jeff Swor
49,653 Su/W
218-624-3665

East Grand Forks 56721
The Exponent
Rollin Bergmen & Julie Nordine
1818 W
218-773-2808

Eden Prairie 55344
Eden Prairie News
Mark Weber
10,749 Th
612-934-5045

Eden Prairie 55439
Eden Prairie Sun Current
Frank Chilinski
13,791 W
612-896-4700

Eden Valley / Watkins 55329
Eden Valley Journal Patriot
Steve Swenson
1955 W
320-453-2460

Edgerton 56128-0397
Edgerton Enterprise
Melvin DeBoer
1951 W
507-442-6161

Edina 55439
Edina Sun Current
Frank Chilinski
12,652 W
612-896-4700

Elbow Lake 56531-2019
Grant County Herald
Dave Simpkins
2223 W
218-685-5326

Elk River 55330
Elk River Star News
Julian Andersen
14,020 W
612-441-3500

Ellendale 56026-0037
The Ellendale Eagle
Wayne Schimek
1103 Th

507-684-2315

Ely 55731-1298
Ely Echo
Anne Swenson
4629 M
218-365-3141

Elysian 56028-0119
Elysian Enterprise
E. Charles Wann
465 Th
507-267-4323

Erskine 56535-0016
Erskine Echo
Robert M. Hole
968 Th
218-687-3775

Evansville 56326-0055
West Douglas County Record
Dave and Cathy Bedore
955 Th
320-834-4999

Eveleth 55734
The Eveleth Scene
James Krause
2695 F
218-744-2931

Excelsior 55439
Excelsior / Shorewood /Chanhassen / Sun Sailor
Frank Chilinski
5820 A W
612-896-4700 and 612-392-6400

Fairfax 55332-0589
Fairfax Standard
Charles Warner
1245 W
507-426-7235

Farmington 55024-0192
Farmington
Independent
Todd Heikkila
2170 Th
651-460-6606

Fertile 56540-0128
Fertile Journal
Michael D. Moore
1513 W
218-945-6120

Floodwood 55736-0286
The Forum
Broadaxe Publishing
1479 F
218-476-2232

Foley 56329-0187
Benton County News
Ronald Youso
2162 Tu
320-968-7220

Forest Lake 55025-1381
The Times
Julian Andersen
12,152 A Th
651-464-4601

Fosston 56542-0505
The Thirteen Towns
David Carr
3100 M
218-435-1313

Frazee 56544-0187
Frazee Forum
Delair & Gale Kaas
1628 Th
218-334-3566

Fridley 55113
Fridley / Columbia
Heights Focus
Richard & Collette
Roberts
18,519 A Th
612-633-3434

Fulda 56131-0439
Fulda Free Press
Gerald D. Johnson
1297 W
507-425-2303

Gaylord 55334-0208
The Gaylord Hub
James E. Deis
2131 Th
507-237-2476

Gibbon 55335-0456
The Gibbon Gazette
Charles (Chuck)
Warner
855 Th
507-834-6966

Gilbert 55741
Gilbert Herald
James Krause
1019 F
218-741-4445

Glencoe 55336
Glencoe Enterprise
Annamarie Tudhope

1525 Th
320-864-4715

Glencoe 55336
McLeod County
Chronicle
William Ramige
3181 W
320-864-5518

Glenwood 56334-0157
Pope County Tribune
John R. Stone
3952 M
320-634-4571

Glenwood 56334
Senior Perspective
Jeanne A. Olson
8200 Monthly
320-634-3720

Gonvick 56644-0159
The Leader-Record
Richard D. Richards
1815 Tu
218-487-5225

Grand Marais 55604-
0757
Cook County News-
Herald
Steve & Becky
Fernlund
4934 M
218-387-1025

Grand Meadow 55936
Meadow Area News
Marceil Skifter
W
507-754-5486

Grand Rapids 55744-0220
Grand Rapids Herald
Review
Ron Oleheiser
8356/8474 W/Su
218-326-6623

Granite Falls /
Clarkfield 56241-0099
Advocate-Tribune
Tim Douglass
3155 Th
320-564-2126

Greenbush 56726
The Tribune
Rollin Bergman & Julie
Nordine
1335 Tu
218-782-2275

Grygla 56727-0017
Grygla Eagle
Richard D. Richards
710 Th
218-294-6220

Hallock 56728-0730
Kittson County
Enterprise
Keith O. Axvig
1822 W
218-843-2868

Hancock 562444-0425
Hancock Record
James Morrison
845 W
320-392-5527

Hanska 56041-0045
Hanska Herald
Norman L. Becken

792 Th
507-439-6214

Hastings 55033-0277
Hastings Star Gazette
Steve Messick
5987 Th
651-437-6153

Hawley 56549-0709
Hawley Herald
Eugene Prim
2026 M
218-483-3306

Hayfield 55940-0085
Hayfield Herald
Tony & Jacky Pierskalla
1433 W
507-477-2232

Hector / Buffalo Lake
55342-0278
News*Mirror
John & Ken Hubin
2316 W
320-848-2248

Henderson 56044-0008
Henderson
Independent
Paul Malchow
1035 Th
507-248-3223

Hendricks 56136-0005
Hendricks Pioneer
Charles Hunt
620 W
507-275-3197

Henning 56551-0035
Henning Advocate
Andrew & Debra Barr
1504 W
218-583-2935

Herman 56248-0304
Herman Review
Nick and Ane
Ripperger
1143 Th
320-677-2229

Hermantown 55811
Hermantown Star
Cindy Alexander
1488 Th
218-727-0419

Heron Lake 56137-0227
The Tri County News
Gerald D. Johnson
942 W
507-793-2327

Hills 56138-0457
Hills Crescent
Roger Tollefson
577 Th
507-962-3230

Hinckley 55037-0310
Hinckley News
Patrick O'Donovan
2034 Th
320-384-6188

Hoffman 56339-0247
Hoffman Tribune
K.L. and J.M. Beuckens
1224 W
320-9866-2851

Hopkins 55439
Hopkins / East
Minnetonka
Sun Sailor
Frank Chilinski
13,835 W
612-896-4700

Howard Lake 55349-
0190
Howard Lake Herald
Dale Kovar
1229 M
320-654-2131

Hutchinson 55350-2440
Hutchinson Leader
Matt McMillan
5369 Tu, Th
320-587-5000

Isle 56342-0026
Mille Lacs Messenger
Richard Norlander
5470 W
320-676-3123

Ivanhoe 56142-0100
Ivanhoe Times
Brent & Ellen Beck
1100 Th
507-694-1246

Jackson 56143-0208
Jackson County Pilot
James Keul
2241 Th
507-847-3771

Janesville 56048-0220
Janesville Argus
Judy Winter

1249 W
507-234-6651

Jasper 56144-0188
Jasper Journal
Charles L. Draper
848 M
507-348-4176

Jordan 55352
Jordan Independent
Stan Rolfsrud
1613 Th
612-492-2224

Karlstad 56732-0158
North Star News
Rollin Bergman & Julie
Nordine   2268 Th
218-436-2157

Kasson 55944-2367
Dodge County
Independent
Randy Carlsen
2084 W
507-634-7503

Kenyon 559446
Kenyon Leader
Robert D. Noah
2014 W
507-789-6161

Kerkhoven 56252-0148
Kerkhoven Banner
Theodore J. Almen
1425 Th
320-264-3071

Kiester 56051
Courier-Sentinel

Cynthia A. Matson
1778 Th
507-294-3400

Kimball 55353-0220
Tri-County News
Steve Prinsen
1327 Th
320-398-5000

La Crescent 55947
Houston County News
Tom van der Linden &
Jean Silberman
2005 Th
507-895-2940

Lafayette 56054-0212
Lafayette-Nicollet
Ledger
Douglas W. Hanson
1092 Th
507-228-8985

Lake Benton 56149-0218
Lincoln County Valley
Journal
Charles R. Hunt
736 W
507-368-4275

Lake City 55041-1640
Lake City Graphic
Dennis Schumacher
3148 Th
651-345-3316

Lake Crystal 56055-0240
Lake Crystal Tribune
Don R. Marben
1850 W
507-726-2133

Lake Park 56549-0709
Lake Park Journal
Eugene Prim
2203 M
218-238-6872

Lakefield 56150-0249
Lakefield Standard
Jim Keul
1556 Th
507-662-5555

Lakeville 55044-0549
Lakeville Life & Times
Richard M. Sherman
19,961 A Sa
612-469-2181

Lamberton 56152-0308
Lamberton News
Joseph G. Dietl
1702 W
507-752-7181

Le Center 560557-1502
Le Center Leader
Teresa Emmers-
McMillen
1672 W
507-357-2233

Le Roy 55951-0089
Le Roy Independent
Daniel Ev ans
1153 Th
507-324-5325

Le Sueur 56058
Le Sueur News-Herald
Jim Hensley
1791 W
507-665-3332

Lester Prairie 55354
Prairie Ad News
Lew & Marceil Buss
4602 A M
320-395-2932

Lewiston 55952-0608
Lewiston Journal
Michael, Daniel and
Gary Stumpf
1268 Th
507-523-2119

Lindstrom 55045-0748
Chisago County Press
John A. Silver
3839 Th
651-257-5115

Litchfield 55355-0921
Litchfield Independent
Review
Vern Madson & Stan
Roeser
3819 Th
320-693-3266

Little Falls 56345
Morrison County
Record
Carolyn Holeisel
17,382 A Su
320-632-2345

Long Lake 55364-0082
The Pioneer
Jim Berreth
6846 Sa
612-472-1140

Long Prairie 56347
Long Prairie Leader
Gary Brown

3215 Tu
320-732-2151

Longville 56655-0401
Pine Cone Press-Citizen
Bill and Pat DeLost
6628 A Tu
218-363-2002

Luverne 56156-0837
Rock County Star
Herald
Roger S. Tollefson
2998 Th
507-283-2333

Mabel / Harmony
55954
Mabel / Harmony
News Record
David Phillips
1511 Th
507-493-5204

Madelia 56062-0159
Madelia Times-
Messenger
Michael Whalen
1545 Tu
507-642-3636

Madison 56256
The Western Guard
Richard Gail
2526 W
320-598-7521

Madison Lake 56063-
0128
Lake Region Times
Marie Groebner
987 W
507-263-3031

Mahnomen 56557
Mahnomen Pioneer
Patrick D. Kelly
2775 Th
218-935-5296

Maple Lake 55358-0817
Maple Lake Messenger
Harold Brutlag
1587 W
320-963-3813

Mapleton 56065-0425
Maple River Messenger
Kenneth Warner
1578 W
507-524-3212

McIntosh 56556-0009
McIntosh Times
Richard D. Richards
1312 Tu
218-563-3585

Melrose 56352-0186
Melrose Beacon
Don & Carole Larson
2038 M
320-256-3240

Middle River 56737
The New River Record
Rollin Bergman & Julie
Nordine
954 W
218-222-3514

Milaca 56353-0009
Mille Lacs County
Times
Julian Andersen
3030 W
320-983-6111

Milan 56262
Milan Standard-Watson
Journal
Leslie Ehrenberg
545 W
320-734-4458

Minneapolis 55402-1302
City Business
Stuart Chamblin, III
11,534 A F
612-288-2100

Minneapolis 55401-1387
City Pages
Mark Bartel
115,398 A W
612-375-1015

Minneapolis 55411
Insight News
Al McFarlane
35,000 A M, Tu, W
612-588-1313

Minneapolis 55409-0558
MinneapolisSpokesman
L. Q. Newman
6762 Th
612-827-4021

Minneapolis 55418-3710
Northeaster
Kerry & Margo
Ashmore
33,000 M (bi-weekly)
612-788-9003

Minneapolis 55418-3710
North News
Kerry & Margo
Ashmore
30,000 M (monthly)

612-788-9003

Minneapolis 55418
Pro Family News
MN Family Council
Monthly
612-789-8811

Mpls / St. Paul 55402
Skyway News
Rick Christensen
45,873 A Th
612-375-9222

Minneapolis 55410
The Southwest Journal
Janis Hall
40,000 M (bi-weekly)
612-922-6263

Mpls / St. Paul 55402
Twin Cities Reader
87,855 AW
612-321-7300

Minneota 56264-0008
Minneota Mascot
Jon Guttormsson
1390 W
507-872-6492

Minnesota 55420
Minnesota Real Estate
Journal
Michael B. Kramer
3579 M/bi-wk
612-885-0815

Minnesota 55427-2092
Outdoor News
Glenn Meyer
36,270 F
612-546-4251

Minnesota 55155-2069
Minnesota Legionnaire
Robert D. Skallerud
121,000 monthly
651-291-1800

Minnesota Lake 56068
Minnesota Lake
Tribune
Ken & Marlys Hiscock
990 Th
507-462-3575

Montevideo 56265-0736
Montevideo American-
News
Louie Seesz
4466 Th
320-269-2156

Montgomery 56069-
0049
Montgomery
Messenger
E. Charles Wann
2105 Th
507-364-8601

Monticello 55362-0548
Monticello Times
Donald Q. Smith
2866 Th
612-295-3131

Moose Lake 55767-0506
Arrowhead Leader
Robert Hanson
2320 M
218-485-8420

Moose Lake 55767-0449
Star-Gazette
Jerry DeRungs

2750 Th
218-685-4406

Mora 55051
Kanabec County Times
Wade Weber
2970 Th
320-679-2661

Morgan 56266-0038
Morgan Messenger
Walter M. Olson
1127 W
507-249-3130

Morris 56267-0470
Morris Sun/ Tribune
Jim Morrison
3648 Tu/ 3567 Th
320-589-2525

Mound 55364-0082
The Laker
Jim Berreth
9300 Sa
612-472-1140

Mounds View 55113
Mounds View / St.
Anthony / New
Brighton Focus
Richard & Collette
Roberts
15,252 Th
651-633-3434

Mountain Lake 56159-
0429
Observer / Advocate
Kim Anderson
1856 W
507-427-2725

Nashwauk 55769-1132
Eastern Itascan
Jon and Leanne Stanley
1491 Th
218-885-2100

Nevis 56467-0028
Northwoods Press
Victor W. Olson
1539 Th
218-652-3475

New Brighton 55109
New Brighton Bulletin
N. T. Lillie & R. J.
Enright
26,923 A W
651-777-8800

New Prague 56071-0025
The New Prague Times
E. Charles Wann
4405 Th
612-758-4435

New Richland 56072
New Richland Star
Margaret A. Engesser
2007 W
507-465-8112

New York Mills 56567
New York Mills Herald
Mike & Janet Parta
1825 Th
218-385-2275

North Branch 55056-
0366
ECM Post-Review
Julian Andersen
2250 W
612-674-7025

North Minneapolis 55439
North Minneapolis Sun Post
Frank Chilinski
9201 A W
612-896-4700

North St. Paul 55109
Ramsey County Review
N. T. Lillie & R. J. Enright
26,193 A W
651-777-8800

Northfield 55157-0058
Northfield News
Robert L. Bradford II
5350 W, F
507-645-5615

Northome 56661-0025
Northome Record
J. Reed Anderson/
Karla L. Patch-Anderson
972 Tu
218-897-5278

Norwood / Young America 55368-0067
Norwood-Young America Times
Jim Berreth
2333 Th
612-467-2271

Oakdale 55128
Oakdale Clarion
Lisa Heikkila
1921 F
651-730-9116

Oklee 56742-0009
Oklee Herald
Richard D. Richards
1009 Tu
218-796-5181

Olivia 56277
Olivia Times-Jounral
Rose Hettig
1606 M
320-523-2032

Orr / Tower / Cook 55790
The Timberjay
Marshall Helmberger
2904 Sa
218-753-2950

Ortonville 56278-0336
Ortonville Independent
Jeanette Kaercher
3226 Tu
320-839-6163

Osakis 56360-0220
The Osakis Review
John J. Olson
1316 Tu
320-869-2143

Osseo 55369
Osseo-Maple Grove Press
Don R. Larson
4512 W
612-425-3323

Park Rapids 56470
Park Rapids Enterprise
Dennis Winskowski
5670 W/Sa
218-732-3364

Parkers Prairie 56361
The Independent
Thomas D. & Sheryl K. Myers
1530 Th
218-338-2741

Paynesville 56352-0054
The Paynesville Press
Peter J. Jacobson
2770 W
320-243-3772

Pelican Rapids 56572
Pelican Rapids Press
Gary&Richard Peterson
3365 W
218-863-1421

Pequot Lakes 56472
Lake Country Echo
Peter Anderson
4420 Th
218-568-8521

Perham 56573-0288
Perham Enterprise Bulletin
Michael & Janet Parta
3148 Th
218-346-5900

Pine City 55063
Pine City Pioneer
Wade Weber
3420 Th
320-629-6771

Pine River 56474-0370
Pine River Journal
Peter Anderson
1991 Th
218-587-2360

Pipestone 56164-0277
Pipestone County Star
Charles L. Draper
37524 W
507-825-3333

Plainview 56474-0370
Plainview News
Michael, Daniel and
Gary Stumpf
2726 Tu
507-534-3121

Preston 55965-0496
Fillmore County
Journal
John Torgrimson
9625 A M
507-765-2151

Preston / Lanesboro
Republican-Leader
David Phillips
1257 Th
507-765-2752

Princeton 55371-0278
Princeton Union-Eagle
Julian Andersen
3276 Th
612-389-1222

Prior Lake 55372
Prior Lake American
Laurie Hartmann
7260 Sa
612-447-6669

Proctor 55810-3344
Proctor Journal
Jake P. Benson
1862 Th
218-624-3344

Raymond / Prinsburg
56282-0157
The News
Ted and Kari Jo Almen
948 W
320-967-4244

Red Lake Falls 56750
The Gazette
Keith O. Axvig
1397 W
218-253-2594

Redwood Falls 56283
Redwood Gazette
Rick Peterson
4141 M, Th
507-637-2929

Renville 56284-0468
Renville Co. Star
Farmer News
Rose Hettig
1767 W
320-329-3324

Richfield 55439
Richfield Sun Current
Frank Chilinski
9615 A W
612-896-4700

Robbinsdale 55439
Robbinsdale / Crystal /
Hew Hope / Golden
Valley Sun Post
Frank Chilinski
22,187 A W
612-896-4700

Rochester 55903-6118
Agri News
William C. Boyne

20,522 Th
507-285-7657

Rockford 55373
Rockford Area
Newsleader
Don R. Larson
1230 M
612-477-5771

Roseau 56751-0220
Roseau Times-Region
Jodi Wiskow
3665 M
218-463-1521

Roseville 55113
Roseville / Arden Hills
/ Falcon Heights Focus
Richard & Collette
Roberts
15,933 A Th
651-633-3434

Roseville 55109
Roseville Review
N. T. Lillie & R. J.
Enright
15,997 A Tu
651-777-8800

Rushford 55971-0429
Tri-County Record
Myron J. & Darlene J.
Schober
1680 Th
507-864-7700

Ruthton 56170-0070
Buffalo Ridge Gazette
Charles R. Hunt
278 W
507-658-3919

St. Charles 55972-0617
St. Charles Press
Daniel, Gary and
Michael Stumpf
1765 Tu
507-932-3663

St. James 56081-0067
St. James Plaindealer
Lisa Wolle
2644 Th
507-375-3161

St. Joseph 56374
St. Joseph Newsleader
Janelle Von Pinnon
2330 1st & 3rd F/
280 2nd & 4th F
320-363-7741

St. Louis Park 55439
St. Louis Park SunSailor
Frank Chilinski
11,488 AW
612-896-4700

St. Michael 55376
North Crow River
News
Don R. Larson
2652 M
612-497-3225

St. Paul 55111-0932
Asian Pages
C. Ting Insixiengmay
25,000 1st&15th
651-884-3265

St. Paul 55102-1892
The Catholic Spirit
Archbishop Harry J.
Flynn

85840 Th
651-291-4444

St. Paul 55104-1849
Good Age
Amherst H. Wilder
Foundation
52,000 Monthy
651-917-1210

St. Paul 55116-2296
Grand Gazette
Michael Mischke
22,100 Monthly
651-699-1462

St. Paul/Minneapolis
55106
Korean Quarterly
Stephen Wunrow
4500 Sept., Dec., Mar.,
June
651-771-8164

St. Paul 55103
La Prensa de Minnesota
Mario Duarte
10,000 Th
651-224-0404

St. Paul 55114
Minnesota Women's
Press
Mollie Hoben / Glenda
Martin
40,000 W
651-646-3968

St. Paul 55108
Park Bugle
Winton Pitcoff
11,000 Monthly
651-646-5369

St. Paul 55109
Review East
N. T. Lillie & R. J.
Enright
23,658 A M
651-777-8800

St. Paul 55104
St. Paul Recorder
Launa Newman
10,100 Tu
651-224-4886

St. Paul 55118-3903
The St. Paul Voice
Tim Spitzak
16,000 Monthy
651-457-1177

St. Paul 55116-2296
Villager
Michael Mischke
45,400 W
651-699-1462

St. Peter 56082-0446
St. Peter Herald
Margaret Palmer
2242 Th
507-931-4520

Sanborn 56083-0038
Sanborn Sentinel
Walter M. Olson
565 Th
507-648-3288

Sandstone 55072-0230
Pine County Courier
Richard Coffey
1871 Th
320-245-2368

Sartell 56374
Sartell Newsleader
Janelle Von Pinnon
3336 1st & 3rd F/239
2nd & 4th F
320-363-7741

Sauk Centre 56378
Sauk Centre Herald
Dave Simpkins
2803 Tu
320-352-6577

Sauk Rapids 56379-1407
Sauk Rapids Herald
Roland Doroff
1239 W
320-251-1971

Sauk Rapids 56374
Sauk Rapids-Rice
Newsleader
Janelle Von Pinnon
F
320-363-7741

Savage 55378
Savage Pacer
Laurie Hartmann
5241 Sa
612-440-1234

Scandia
55073-9400
Country Messenger
Kay Hempel
1611 W
651-433-3845

Sebeka / Menahga
56477-0309
The Review Messenger
Timothy M. Bloomquist

3474 W
218-837-5558

Shakopee 55379-0008
Shakopee Valley News
Stan Rolfsrud
4593 Th
612-445-3333

Sherburn 56171-0820
West Martin Weekly
News
Harwood & Polly
Schaffer
1554 W
507-764-6681

Silver Lake 55381
Silver Lake Leader
Kenneth B. Merrill
1294 Th
320-327-2216

Slayton 56172-0288
Murray County News
Gerald D. Johnson
1270 W
507-836-8929

Slayton 56172-0263
Murray County Wheel-
Herald
Willard Beers
7041 A M
507-836-8726

Sleepy Eye 56085-0499
Sleepy Eye Herald-
Dispatch
James C. Hensley
3323 Th
507-794-6511

South St. Paul 55469
So. & W. St. Paul /
Inver Grove Hgts. /
Mendota Hgts. Sun
Current
Frank Chilinski
25,294 A W
612-896-4700 and 612-
392-6400

South St. Paul 55109
South-West Review
N. T. Lillie & R. J.
Enright
24,207 A Su
651-777-8800

Spicer / New London
56288-0910
Times Free Press
Rose Hettig
1701 M
320-796-2945

Spring Grove 55974
Spring Grove Herald
Fred Onsgard
1325 Tu
507-498-3868

Spring Valley 55975-
0112
Spring Valley Tribune
David A. Phillips
1755 W
507-346-7365

Springfield 56087-0078
Springfield Advance-
Press
Peter C. Hedstrom
2102 W
507-723-4400

Staples 56479-0100
Staples World
Russell W. Devlin
2553 Th
218-894-1112

Starbuck 56381-0457
Starbuck Times
Ron Lindquist
1836 Tu
320-239-2244

Stephen 56757-0048
Stephen Messenger
Earl L. Anderson
1879 Th
218-478-2210

Stewartville 55976-0035
Stewartville Star
Sandy Forstner
2213 Tu
507-533-4271

Stillwater 55082-5132
Courier News
Robert P. Liberty
2190 Th
651-430-3037

Storden / Jeffers 56174
Storden-Jeffers Times /
Review
George Parrish
577 Th
507-445-3400

Thief River Falls 56701
Northern Watch
John P. Mattson
21,600 Sa
218-681-4450

Thief River Falls 56701
The Times
John P. Mattson
5500 W
218-681-4450

Tower 55790-0447
Tower News
Anthony Sikora
2188 Th
218-753-3170

Tracy 56175-0188
Tracy Headlight-Herald
Seth Schmidt
2087 W
507-629-4300

Truman 56088-0098
Truman Tribune
Vickie Greiner
964 W
507-776-2751

Twin Valley 56584-0478
Twin Valley Times
Rod Thoreson
1420 Tu
218-584-5195

Two Harbors 55616
Lake County News-
Chronicle
Randi Smith
3875 Th
218-834-2141

Tyler 56178-0466
The Tyler Tribute
Charles R. Hunt
1499 W
507-247-5502

Ulen 56585-0248
Ulen Union
David Evans
995 W
218-596-8813

Verndale 56481-0254
Verndale Sun
Peter Quirt
787 Tu
218-445-5779

Victoria 55386
Victoria Gazette
Sue Orsen
3400 Monthly
612-443-2010

Wabasha 55981
Wabasha CountyHerald
Gary D. Stumpf
3294 W
651-565-3366

Wabasso 56293-0070
Wabasso Standard
Jeff & Julie Meyer
1222 Th
507-342-5143

Waconia 55387-0005
Waconia Patriot
James Berreth
3960 Th
612-442-4414

Wadena 56482-0031
Wadena Pioneer
Journal
Randy Mohs
3838 Th
218-631-2561

Walker 56484-0190
Walker Pilot-
Independent
Joe Sherman
3456 W
218-547-1000

Warren 56762-0045
Warren Sheaf
E. N. Mattson
2774 W
218-745-5174

Warroad 56763
Warroad Pioneer
Rollin Bergman & Julie
M. Nordine
1909 Tu
218-386-1594

Waseca 566093-0465
Waseca County News
Paula M. Patton
3657 Tu,Th
507-835-3380

Watertown 55388-0188
Carver County News
James D. Berreth
2164 Th
612-955-1111

Waterville 56096
Lake Region Life
E. Charles Wann
1495 Th
507-362-4495

Wayzata 55391
Lakeshore WeeklyNews
Rick Christiansen
25,412 Th
612-473-08890

Wayzata 55439
Wayzata / Orono /
Plymouth /Long Lake
Sun Sailor
Frank Chilinski
18,353 A W
612-896-4700

Wells 56097-1927
Wells Mirror
Michael Johnson
1849 Th
507-553-3131

West Concord 55985
West Concord
Enterprise
Ginny Sendle
786 W
507-527-2492

West Minnetonka 55439
West Minnetonka /
Deephaven Sun Sailor
Frank Chilinski
7598 A W
612-896-4700

Westbrook 56183-0098
Westbrook Sentinel /
Tribune
Tom Merchant
1413 W
507-274-6136

Wheaton 56296
Wheaton Gazette
William N. Kremer
2405 Tu
320-563-8146

White Bear Lake 55110

White Bear Press
Eugene D. Johnson
18,268 A W
651-407-1200

White Earth 56591
Anishinaabeg Today
Susan Stanick
9988 Monthly
218-983-3285

Williams 56686-0613
The Northern Light
Julie Nordine / Rollin
Bergman
1198 Tu
218-783-6875

Windom 56101-0309
Cottomwood County
Citizen
Kim Anderson
3528 W
507-831-3455

Winona 55987-0027
Winona Post
John Edstrom
24,005 W,Su
507-452-1262

Winsted 55395-0129
Winsted-Lester Prairie
Journal
Dale Kovar
1330 M
320-485-2535

Winthrop 55396-0478
Winthrop News
Douglas Hanson
1192 W
507-647-5357

Wood Lake 56297-0219
Wood Lake News
Sheri Bengston
585 W
507-485-3141

Woodbury 55125-1014
Woodbury News
Eldon Anderson
12,707 Monthly
651-730-0000

Enright
13,818 M
651-777-8800

Woodbury 55125
The Woodbury Bulletin
Steve Messick
9366 W
651-730-4007

Woodbury / S.
Maplewood 55109
Woodbury / S.
Maplewood Review
N. T. Lillie & R. J.

Zumbrota 55992
News-Record
David A. Grimsrud
4330 W
507-732-7617

Charles and William Mayo, sons of medical pioneer William Worrall Mayo began the Rochester, MN, institution that bears their name, basing their practice on group decision making. Photo courtesy Mayo Clinic.

Chapter 17

Science/Health

That part of the earth known as Minnesota contained a foundation for science thousands of years before people from western Europe reached this area and countless ages before the Indians gave the place a name, calling it "Land of the Sky Blue Waters."

Appropriately enough, the scientific foundation was, and to a great extent still is, based on what nature had provided here. Skies are clear, water is plentiful, the soil is rich with the elements of life and minerals underneath. Utilizing the obvious bountifulness, plus many more elements and conditions that are not so easily noticed, Minnesotans have, during the tiny speck of time called modern history, made scientific contributions ranging from A to Z. From the ATOM to the ZIPPER and encompassing discoveries in technology, medicine, agriculture, theoretical pioneering and humanistic research.

Before attempting to put a statistical finger on man-made contributions, however, it should be informative to introduce a concise inventory of those Minnesota resources that have been particularly significant to science.

These must include:

• Extensive and excellent farm land.

• Clear skies that diffuse more than enough sunlight to compensate for a short growing season, influencing numerous activities of scientific nature.

• Water in abundance, nourishing all growing things and providing power. The power potential of Minnesota's running water is exceptional because large rivers flow from and through the state in all directions; north, south, east, and west.

• Minerals, not only in abundance but also in variety. Iron has been the most plentiful, the most accessible, and the most exploited in the past. More recent years have seen substitution of taconite, an iron-bearing rock from which Minnesota scientists have learned to extract and concentrate ferrous material, replacing the higher grade ore that is no longer easily available.

• Timber, for direct utilization and also as a replenishable source of supply for manufacturing and chemical industries.

• Glacial residues destined to become increasingly valuable as present-day earth materials are used toward the point of practical extinction.

•Climate that is invigorating and healthful for human and animal life.

The way or ways in which those resources have been utilized and the people who have played a role in the process constitute the history and the future potential of science in Minnesota. The input of human effort is naturally most vital, spreading the impact of this area's science far beyond the borders of the state or limits that may exist for physical exploitation of natural resources. It has touched technological, educational, medical, social, and economic facets of life around the world and is reaching out in space.

Because science is essentially a function of the present and the future, this almanac tends to emphasize the contemporary in the discussion which follows.

The great contribution to atomic science from Minnesota was a demonstration for a practical method of isolating and separating two isotopes of uranium, known as U-235 and U-238. This was accomplished in 1940 with development and successful use of a mass spectrograph by Dr. Alfred O. C. Nier, a native of the state and a professor of physics at the University of Minnesota.

Nier's work made it possible for scientists, many of whom also were concentrating on atomic investigations, to establish the fissionable or atom-splitting capabilities of U-235, the power-containing isotope. From that knowledge it then became possible to develop the apparatus and control systems that made utilization of atomic energy practical. Initial application of the power of the atom was in bombs at the climax of World War II. Subsequent developments saw utilization of nuclear power for generating electricity for medical uses and for massive earth movement.

The original mass spectrometer that Nier constructed at the University of Minnesota for is U-235 investigation is in the Smithsonian Institution in Washington, D.C. It is one of two Minnesota-made items in the permanent exhibition there.

Nier, who was born in St. Paul in 1911, received bachelor, masters and doctoral degrees in Minnesota and also studied at Harvard. His mass spectrography research has been directed to other scientific investigations, including studies important to geology, chemistry, and medicine as well as nuclear physics.

While Nier's original mass spectrograph was a two-ton mechanical monster, he has since been a principal developer of smaller instruments that are being utilized in industry as well as in academic research. One such compact model, weighing about eight pounds, was included in the instrument package carried to Mars on the historic Viking Project Flight in 1975-1976. Nier himself had been active for several years on the scientific cadre in the Mars program and was assigned to head a five-man group known as the Science Entry Team. The group's responsibility covered research equipment to probe the atmosphere surrounding the famed red planet and its surface material; and a mass spectrometer incorporating some of Nier's principles was linked to function in conjunction with the soil testing apparatus of the Viking.

Scientific equipment aboard the Viking also included an instrument developed under the direction of Professor William Hanson of the University of Texas, who is a graduate of the University of Minnesota and a native of this state.

Following the mass spectrograph from Minnesota to the Smithsonian was a small flying machine called the "tailless airplane." This had its origins at the university of Minnesota in the mid-thirties and was accepted for permanent display in the Nation Air and Space Museum in 1970.

Identified with the official numbers X14880 (one of less than 5,000 recognized "experimental" aircraft) the little machine had been conceived by Prof. John D. Akerman, then director of the university's fledgling program in aeronautical engineering. Final design and construction were the work of students support by the WPA (Works Progress Administration) during the depression years.

The scientific significance of the tailless airplane was in its unique aerodynamic characteristics. The same principles were later to contribute to the delta wing design high speed military jet planes and supersonic aircraft.

The mid-thirties spawned another contribution to the science of high altitude flight and eventual space exploration from the University of Minnesota campus.

At 6:58 a.m. on June 24, 1936, the first of a series of so-called "stratosphere balloons" was sent aloft from the University's Memorial Stadium by Prof. Jean Piccard and a small army of students. Made of very thin plastic strips, that balloon carried simple instruments, later recovered, which indicated that it had risen somewhere between 13 and 16 miles above the land. It was an altitude that few in that time dreamed it possible to attain.

Refinement of the plastic balloon technology, in which general Mills played a part as it began to diversify from flour milling and grain processing, led to construction of successively larger plastic stratosphere balloons in accordance with Piccard's research findings. Those giant balloons when inflated with helium were as tall as a 20-story building, and they carried research instruments to altitudes calculated to be above 99 percent of the earth's oxygen envelope.

Launched from numerous land stations and from decks of aircraft carriers, the balloons and their instruments gathered information of weather and navigational importance in war or peace.

Prof. Piccard's balloon research, in which he was assisted by his scientist wife, Jeannette, contributed to scientific know-how that was later applied in development of windows for high-altitude where the temperature was 50 degrees below zero, Fahrenheit.

The transistor, tiny source of gigantic power for the electronic industry, owes its birth to three physicists, two of them with research backgrounds at the University of Minnesota. John Bardeen and Walter Brattain, who had studied and taught at the university, and William Shockley shared the 1956 Nobel Prize for physics for their invention of the transistor. Bardeen also shared the 1972 Nobel Prize in physics for other work, mainly at the University of Illinois.

The "Iron Century"

It is awesome to realize how short the recorded history of Minnesota's science has been when compared with the age of rocks in this state, estimated to be among the oldest material of Earth. Iron ore, the state's greatest resource for technology, can be used to dramatize the time scale. The age of rocks in northeastern Minnesota, where the iron concentrations exist, has been estimated into the billions of years. The "Iron Age" as a period in the reckoning of human history began little more than three thousand years ago; the iron history of Minnesota has only recently completed a full century.

In the 1860's Newton Horace Winchell came from the East to be Minnesota's first state geologist and professor in the new Geology department at the university. Traversing the state afoot and by canoe, Winchell developed the first Minnesota geological map. This pinpointed the areas that later became the world's most productive iron mines and also forecast the agricultural potential of the prairies to the West.

It was not until 1890, however, that Leonidas Merritt and his six brothers—the fabulous "Seven Iron Men" of history—were granted their first mining leases on the Mesabi range. Mined mostly by the economical open pit method, the Minnesota ore was so rich in iron content that one pit alone became known as "the mine that won two world wars," supplying the hungry steel mills during the booms of World Wars I and II.

Within little more than half a century, however, Minnesota researchers began to realize that the rich Mesabi ore would run out within foreseeable time. Many of the mines were shut down, some abandoned permanently, because they could no longer be worked profitably and efficiently.

Fortunately for Minnesota, scientists and economists were sufficiently aware of the declining supply of rich iron ore and had begun to do something about it. The most effective "something" was accomplished by E.W. Davis, a professor at the University of Minnesota. Knowing that billions of tons of iron-bearing rock, called taconite, existed around the bodies of rich iron, Davis and his associate devised methods and built equipment to mine that rock and extract the iron from it.

A flame-spewing mechanical monster known as the jet piercing drill was developed to begin cutting the taconite rock. The world's biggest trucks and special railroad cars were designed to transport the rock to huge crushing plants where the material was ground down to the fineness of talcum powder. Then the iron was extracted by magnets and processed into balls or pellets for shipping to the steel mills. When it was learned that some of the crushed iron ore was non-magnetic, the Minnesota scientists found ways to magnetize it so it could be recovered for further processing.

Taconite revolutionized America's steel industry as mills were converted to handle the uniformly rich and sized pellets instead of crude ore of varying quality. Taconite also brought great chances to the shipping industry on the Great Lakes, making it possible to move a relatively greater amount of usable ore in fewer ships. They did not have to carry the waste rock; and because the pellets are of standard size, loading and unloading was speeding up with new machinery.

Despite its technical and economic advantages, however, taconite also brought new problems. The non-ferrous (iron) waste material which used to go to the steel plants for disposal there had been deposited in its powder-fine condition in the Minnesota environment. As much as 67,000 tons of this material has been dumped daily into Lake Superior from one taconite plant at Silver Bay; and elsewhere onetime lakes and river beds are being filled with this waste material. Some of the powdery material is discharged into the air, too, and this may be creating a health hazard because it contains asbestos

Nature and Science Merge in Timber

Timber and wood product industries, being both providers and consumer of scientific material and methods, are future-oriented in Minnesota and becoming more so every year. Lumbering used to be characterized in this state by the Paul Bunyan legends, tall stories of a giant lumberjack who could clear a quarter section or so of pine trees with one sweep of his axe. The more modern picture is of scientists and woodsmen working together in laboratories as well as in the field to save and restore woodlands and learn new ways to use the forests and their products. It is a technological shifting of gears from thinking only of ways of cut down the most trees with the least cost in the shortest time to looking at practices that should insure a perpetual supply for timber for construction, for fuel, and for processing through chemistry and mechanical means.

In its earlier days in Minnesota, roughly the last two decades of the 1800's and something less than three decades of this century, lumbering was strictly an extractive industry. Its employment, though large, was seasonal and thus of restricted economic value. The railroad employment offices, which probably maintained the best job records of those times, reported moving as many as 200,000 loggers each season through the Twin Cities. That number was greater than the regular population of either Minneapolis or St. Paul.

Papermaking, which has been a leader in bringing chemistry and other sciences together with lumbering, was itself a transient industry as long as paper mills could move easily from one place to another as timber lands were cleared of their source of pulp. During the same years that Yankee entrepreneurs were following the timber supply from New England through Pennsylvania, New York, Michigan and Wisconsin into Minnesota, machinery for making paper or finishing lumber was becoming too costly and too complicated to be moved easily. At the same time, the paper companies were getting the know-how from scientists from growing trees as a constant crop and learning how to get chemical by-products from trees.

Alcohol, though it can be an important scientific chemical extracted from trees, is reported to have been a factor in early-day lumbering, but from an entirely different aspect. According to many accounts, some more or less scientific, alcohol was the medium of exchange by which lumber barons acquired forest land and again the key to separating the lumberjacks from their money when they came out of the woods at the end of each logging season.

In today's context, alcohol has to be considered just one of the valuable chemical materials available from wood. Sugar is another; and there are other saps or fibers proving their economic worth in the "new lumbering."

The paper industry depends heavily on chemistry to create papers with special qualities and also needs chemists to solve the problems of pollution of rivers where the big mills discharge wastes. But now the woods are literally full of other scientists—botanists, biologists, physicists, and ecologists studying the complex schemes by which nature grow trees and replenishes the earth. The human sciences also are involved in the lumber and paper industries, being concerned with the recreation or social values of this state's abundant forests. And not least of these efforts is the fact that trees are among the growing things through which solar energy can be transmitted to Earth.

Farm and Food Science

Minnesota scientists, responding to the world's need for food, have made distinguished contributions to both better crops and better equipment to process and preserve the products coming off the land. Additionally, economists from this state have played leadership roles in directing the marketing and distribution of food worldwide.

The major discoveries have come from agricultural research at the University of Minnesota, and the rust-resistant strains of wheat and improved crops of many kinds of developed by men like Profs. Alvin Stakman, Clyde Bailey and J.J. Christiansen have to be rated high on the food chain of all mankind. Wendelin Grim is credited with having developed the Wealthy apple for successful production in northern climates.

On the mechanical side of agriculture, Edmon LaCroix, a Frenchman who worked in mills at Faribault and Minneapolis, designed and built the first "midlings purifier," and with that device revolutionized flour milling.

While those contributions have worldwide impact, the most notable recognition of Minnesota agricultural achievement came in 1970 when Norman Borlaug received the Nobel Peace Prize for his contributions to food production when he developed a disease-resistant and highly adaptable dwarf variety of wheat. Borlaug's research had its roots at the University of Minnesota and was continued with global significance after he joined the Rockefeller Institute.

Minnesota Nobel Laureates

John Bardeen, faculty member at the Institute of Technology, 1938-45, and Walter H. Brattain, '29 Ph.D. received the Nobel prize for Physics (1956) for their development of the transistor. Bardeen received another Nobel in Physics (1972).

Paul D. Boyer, Agricultural Biochemistry faculty from 1945-56 and Physiological Chemistry from 1956-1963. Won the Nobel in Chemistry (1997) when he researched the structure and mechanism of adenosine triphosphate, ATP, an energy-storing molecule.

Melvin Calvin a U of M '35 Ph.D. candidate became a laureate for Chemistry (1961). He described the chemical reactions that occur during photosynthesis.

Another Institute of Technology faculty member, 1916-17, Arthur Compton developed and proved a quantum wavelength theory known as the Compton effect. He received the Nobel in Physics (1927).

Two faculty members at the Graduate School of the Mayo Foundation developed cortisone and received the Nobel for Medicine (1950). They were Philip S. Hench and Edward O. Kendall.

Louis Ignarro, U of M alumnus and one of three winners of the Nobel Prize in Physiology or Medicine (1998). He won the award for his contributions to the concept that a simple gas, nitric oxide, could act as a signaling molecule in the body to promote the dilation of blood vessels. This knowledge served as the basis for, among other things, the development of the anti-impotence drug Viagra.

Ernest O. Lawrence, '23 M.A. was the Nobel Physics (1939) winner for inventing and developing the cyclotron, a device that accelerates atomic particles in a spiral path by means of a fixed magnetic field.

Edward B. Lewis received his bachelors from the U of M in '39, and the Nobel in Biometry in 1995. He discovered a class of genes that control embryonic development and discovered that they are the same in all animals.

The Chemistry (1976) laureat was William N. Lipscomb who described the relationship of molecules' geometric and electronic structures to their chemical physical behavior. He was on the faculty of the Institute of Technology from 1946-59.

John H. Van Vleck, Institute of Technology faculty, 1924-28, received the Nobel in Physics (1977). He pioneered modern magnetism theory.

Additional Nobel Laureates Not Related to the Sciences

This state's first Nobel Laureate native was Sinclair Lewis of St. Cloud, who received the coveted prize in 1930 and was the first American so honored.

Frank Billings Kellogg of St. Paul was appointed Secretary of State by Calvin Coolidge, on March 5, 1915. He traveled extensively in America and in Europe to receive many honors, among them the Nobel Peace Prize (1929).

Saul Bellow, faculty, College of Liberal Arts, 1946-59. Literature, 1976. Portrayed modern man as frightened and alienated in his early novels.

George Stigler, faculty, College of Liberal Arts, 1938-46. Economics, 1982. Questioned the wisdom of state intervention in private economy as far back as the Depression and advocated major deregulation of trucking, oil and airline industries during the Carter administration.

Firsts and Foremosts from Minnesota Medicine

Although Hench and Kendall became famous as Nobel winners, other Minnesotans also have made contributions of top impact in the medical world. An outstanding example revolves around the work and influence of Dr. C. Walton Lillehei, who pioneered surgery on the open heart at University Hospitals in 1954. Surrounding Lillehei under the bright lights in the surgical theater or observing from above through the glass dome of the operating room were perhaps a dozen other doctors who later were to make medical history as follow-ons of Minnesota-inspired training.

Included among those trainees, participants, students and colleagues were Christian Barnard, who later performed the first successful heart transplant, Norman Shumway, probably the most prolific of the transplanters, Richard Varco, who remained as led surgeon of the Minnesota teams, Dr. Robert good, Morley Cohen and practically all the other surgeons who were to perform successful heart transplants during the ensuing years or lead in development of the pumps and blood-purifying devices that are essential adjuncts of heart and organ transplants.

Many of those same doctors had been students or associates of Dr. Owen H. Wangensteen, who was not only an outstanding surgery educator but also an inventor, having created, among other devices, the suction unit that bears his name and is a basic tool of gastric surgery. By the end of the 20th century, faculty would regularly disclose an average of 80-90 ideas annually for new health technologies, ranging from vaccines to dental materials. Patents were awarded to about 50 inventions a year, and with more than 40 licensed to biomedical companies. Annual royalty income from products is about $5 million.

For generations, surgical talent and improvisation were central elements of medical practice not only at the University but also at the Mayo Clinic and hospitals in Rochester, Minnesota, which is self-identified in a clinic publication as "an adventure in medicine." Drs. Will J. and Charles H. Mayo, sons of Dr. William Worrall Mayo who established the institution in 1863 on what was then a medical frontier, both exemplified the surgeon tradition. But they also led the Mayo organization through numerous expansions, diversification, and life-serving discoveries in research, diagnosis and non-surgical phases of medicine. What important medical discoveries have been made at Mayo?

Probably the best known is the isolation and first clinical use of cortisone in the treatment of rheumatoid arthritis. Drs. Edward Kendall and Philip Hench received the Nobel Prize for this accomplishment in 1950.

Probably Mayo's most significant contribution has been the pioneering of the concept of the group practice of medicine, the "team" approach to healthcare, which has become the model for hundreds of other groups around the world.

Other Contributions by Mayo Scientists Include:
• A method of analyzing surgical tissue for quick diagnosis;
• A system for grading the severity of cancers;
• The first isolation of the thyroid hormone thyroxine;
• The first accurate test for measuring anemia;
• The nation's first blood bank;
• The first oxygen mask and pressure suit for pilots;
• The first use of anti-tuberculosis drugs;
• Slipped disc surgery;
• A variety of instruments and technology key to the development of open heart surgery, heart catheterization and pulmonary function testing;
• The first use of CT scanning in North America;

- Studies which refuted the effectiveness of laetrile and vitamin C in cancer treatment; and many more.
- "Mayo hip"was developed by Mayo Clinic orthopedists.
- Mayo cardiologists reported unusual valvular heart disease in patients taking weight-loss medications fenfluramine and phentermine(fen-phen).

In 1915, the Mayo Graduate School of Medicine opened with an endowment from the Mayo brothers. Their program became the first in the world to train medical specialists. Today, more than 13,000 alumni practice throughout the United States and around the world.

More than five million people have been treated at Mayo Clinic since its

---

Dr. William J. Mayo: "The best interest of the patient is the only interest to be considered."

Mayo Mayo Clinic phone numbers
Appointment Office 507-284-2111
General Information, Mayo Clinic
507-284-2511 (phone)
507-284-0161 (fax)
507-284-9786 (hearing impaired - TDD)
www.mayo.edu

---

frontier founding. Today it encompasses three clinics and four hospitals in three states, employing more than 25,000 physicians, scientists, nurses and allied health workers.

No recounting of this state's medical-scientific accomplishments can be considered complete without the mention of Sister Elizabeth Kenny. Not particularly welcome to the medical establishment of either the Mayo Clinic or the University, she defiantly pressed ahead with a unique hotpack and mobility treatment of polio myelitis in Minneapolis. Self-trained as an Australian bush nurse, Sister Kenny has nevertheless left her mark on the healing profession and made Minneapolis a key center during the polio epidemics of the 1940's and 1950's.

Minnesotans and Minnesota resources have made their full share of notable and long-lasting scientific contributions.

At the "Z" end of the alphabet among scientific and technical developments with a Minnesota angle, the modern zipper is credited at least in part to Gideon Sundback, a rural Minnesotan who received a patent in 1913 for the meshed-tooth fastener, one of several items based on a similar idea that gave practical and commercial impetus to widespread use of zippers.

Chapter 18

Weather

Minnesota's climate is strong shaped by its location near the center of the North American continent. Because the state is remote from the oceans, it is warm in the summer, cool in the winter, and basically dry as compared with most places, especially those which are populated to any great extent. The climate will likely prevent Minnesota from ever being heavily populated. The climate produces a people who must be prepared to cope with certain vigors and who must cooperate to some degree from time to time to survive. The remoteness from the sea means that drought must occasionally be expected so that individuals and the people of the state as a group must sometimes expect economic adversity. Various physical and mental tasks are thrust upon Minnesotans that most persons need never face. The climate does have its rewards, however, in providing a favorable outdoor recreational environment eleven months of the year.

Most people are not aware that four atmospheric pressure systems have their "boundaries" in Minnesota. To the northwest and southeast are general high pressure regions. The high pressure system to the southeast, over the Atlantic and the low pressure region to the northeast, near Greenland, are year-round strong features, while high pressure to the northwest is especially well developed in the summer.

Good development of the low pressure to the southwest, which is strongest from around June 1 to July 10 and again from August 20, while the presence of the high pressure system over the Atlantic acts year-round to encourage the intermittent northward flow of moisture-bearing wings. The low pressure system to the northeast during the cold half of the year helps provide a steering current for migrating storms bearing snow.

Quirks in pressure systems act to create mini-seasons within the four main seasons. The first favorable mini-season of the year occurs during the last half of February, which is marked by a very great amount of sunshine and a general lack of stormy weather.

This is followed by a general stormy period from about March 1 to April 5, marked by large storms up to March 19, the snowiest time of year. This period is generally unfit for any recreational activity, expect to offer a challenging opportunity for the sport of orienteering (navigating with a map and compass). The only other type of sport that is possible and still plea-surable at the time needs to be weather independent, such as cross-country soccer. Cross-country soccer consists of each player, kicking a ball to a series of predetermined targets (such as trees, large rocks etc.) each about 1/8 of a mile apart, with the player hitting the targets with the fewest kicks beings the winner.

The period from April 5 to May 28 is marked by warmer weather and afternoon showers. The first week of May usually brings widespread storms, however. The last days of May are characterized by fine, warm weather, but from June 1 to about July 10, the establishment of the low pres-sure to the southwest results in large, widespread evening thunderstorms and sometimes tornadoes or other severe weather.

From July 10 to August 20 is a time of sunny skies, warm temperatures and general lack of rain except for occasional thunderstorms heavily prone to occurring during the night. Southwesterly winds prevail at this time. An exception occurs during the first week of August, when north easterlies gen-erally blow for a day or two, and when rain becomes more likely.

From August 20 to mid-September, the second rainy season occurs. Severe weather and tornadoes becomes more likely, with storms likely to develop around sunrise. After Labor Day, thunderstorms actually are most common during the hours soon after dawn.

The last week of September usually brings the first really cool weather. During the first week of October warm stormy weather often arises, while the period between the 5th and the 20th is usually marked by clear cool nights and mild, hazy and sunny days with lots of southwesterly winds.

Around October 20, northwesterly wings begin to prevail along with sharply colder temperatures and and beginnings of large scale storms. Mid-November brings really cool air and storms, or occasionally blizzards, which are interspersed with cloudy days and light winds.

The arrival of December brings an end to blizzards, with storms until about Christmas, nearly always being accompanied by low or moderate winds. Nearly always, a gentle snowstorm occurs within a few days of December 6. When there are no storms, skies are usually overcast with low stratus clouds at this time.

Between Christmas and mid-February, the weather is characterized by alterations between cold continental polar air and warmer air from the Pacific ocean. The battles between these air masses bring snows, with an occasional blizzard. Continental air often means sunny, cold days while the Pacific air brings warm, hazy days. A warm winter is one dominated by Pacific air; a cold one is under the control of continental air.

Climatic Regions in the State

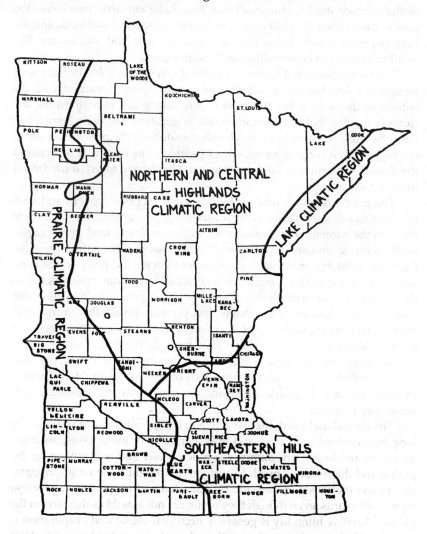

KITTSON · ROSEAU · LAKE OF THE WOODS · KOOCHICHING · ST. LOUIS · COOK · LAKE · MARSHALL · BELTRAMI · POLK · PENNINGTON · RED LAKE · CLEAR WATER · ITASCA · NORMAN · MAHNOMEN · HUBBARD · CASS · CLAY · BECKER · AITKIN · WILKIN · OTTERTAIL · WADENA · CROW WING · CARLTON · TODD · MORRISON · MILLE LACS · KANABEC · PINE · DOUGLAS · STEARNS · BENTON · ISANTI · TRAVERSE · BIG STONE · EVANS · POPE · SWIFT · KANDIYOHI · SHERBURNE · ANOKA · CHISAGO · WRIGHT · MEEKER · LAC QUI PARLE · CHIPPEWA · HENNEPIN · RAMSEY · WASHINGTON · RENVILLE · YELLOW MEDICINE · CARVER · SCOTT · DAKOTA · LINCOLN · LYON · REDWOOD · SIBLEY · NICOLLET · LE SUEUR · RICE · GOODHUE · BROWN · PIPE STONE · MURRAY · COTTONWOOD · WATONWAN · BLUE EARTH · WASECA · STEELE · DODGE · OLMSTED · WINONA · ROCK · NOBLES · JACKSON · MARTIN · FARIBAULT · FREEBORN · MOWER · FILLMORE · HOUSTON

NORTHERN AND CENTRAL HIGHLANDS CLIMATIC REGION

PRAIRIE CLIMATIC REGION

LAKE CLIMATIC REGION

SOUTHEASTERN HILLS CLIMATIC REGION

The general weather prevailing in Minnesota has two major modifiers that cause variations from place to place: one is latitude, and the other is earth surface peculiarity.

Latitude has the well-known effect of making the north colder than the south, especially in the winter. In January, temperatures in southwestern Minnesota are 15 degrees warmer than the northwest, while in July the difference is only five degrees.

However, an even greater modifier of the weather is the nature of the earths' surface itself. Minnesota has four basic climactic provinces: the prairie, the southeastern hill region, the north-and-central highlands and the Lake Superior region. These regions cause the state both storms and fair weather systems to behave differently as they cross.

The southeastern hill region is a place of generally reliable rainfall, with topography and vegetation offering protection against winds. Of all the regions of the state, it has the most evenly distributed rainfall during the summer months, but with definite peaks in mid-June and early September. Partly because this area has a less harsh climate than the prairie and northern highlands, it is the most heavily populated. The climate is reflected in the natural vegetation in the form of general hardwood forest or hardwood trees and savanna.

The prairie region is marked by occasional serious drought and high winds. Over this area, there is great variation in temperature from north to south in the winter, but in the summer, isotherms (these tend to run north-south) indicate similar temperatures. Thus, western Kittson County on the Canadian border is only five degrees cooler than Rock County on the Iowa line. The prairie is also a region of high winds. The countryside is flat so the wind can blow unhindered. Southerly winds generally prevail in this area and are enhanced by a dynamic low pressure trough that forms over the eastern Dakotas in the lee of the mountains to the west. This region of western Minnesota ad the eastern Dakotas is in the "wind alley" of the United States. In winter the prairie winds often cause problems in the form drifting and blowing snow. The hot winds of summer undoubtedly helped to create the ancient prairie by drying the vegetation and spreading fires when they occurred.

The central-and-north highland region is generally an area of rolling or long hills covered with trees and interspersed with many lakes, swamps, meadows and bogs. The summer is much cooler and wetter than on the prairie and the region is much less prone to drought. The rough topography breaks the sweep of the wind so that winter winds produce a pleasant aspect—blizzards, even though they occur, are not as wild as they are on the prairie. Relative humidity is generally high year-round and evaporation is considerably lower than to the south and west. In certain low spots, frost occurs even in July and August and temperatures as low as minus 50 degrees are not uncommon in winter.

The shore region along Lake Superior is the most temperate part of the state, owing to the cool waters which are near 40 degrees out in the lake year-round. This shore area rarely experiences extremes of heat or cold, with average daily temperatures ranging from around 62 degrees in August to about 13 degrees in winter. Precipitation is generous, with rain often occurring along the shore in winter while snow falls inland.   Snows can be heavy,however, when they do occur. The heaviest snow region in the state lies along the high ground about a dozen miles inland from Lake Superior, where upslope motion combines with moisture-laden east winds to produce 100 inches or more in some areas in a season.

Technically, the portion of the state with the least temperature variation is near the point where Minnesota, Wisconsin and Michigan meet in Lake Superior. Here the average monthly temperature runs from 20 degrees in January to about 60 degrees in August. Minnesota waters of Lake Superior provide fogs and storms at times, but tranquil beauty at others.

Micro-Climates

Lurking within each of Minnesota's climactic regions are local micro-climates. These small scale climates, wrought by differences in topography and vegetation often cause strong weather differences within distances on the order of hundreds of feet and sometimes just a few feet.

Wind is very strongly influenced by differences in topography and vegetation. Trees have a strong braking effect on the wind for distances many times their height. In a deep forest there is nearly a calm while the wind around and above blows with gusto Hills offer considerable protection from the full force of wind on the other side. Manmade structures may give good protection, but poor design often results in negative wind effects.

Topography often causes spectacular differences in nighttime temperature in short distances. This happens because the earth's surface cools by radiation to the night sky. Air moving over the surface is cooled by the ground. The chilled air is denser and seeks a lower elevation under the influence of gravity. Pools of cool air build up in low places during the night with even colder air flowing near the surface.

Temperature differences of 20 degrees in an area of several square miles are not uncommon in many parts of the state on clear nights. Even on nights with appreciable cloudiness and wings of 10 miles per hour, differences of 10 degrees appear. Those who live in dells and other low places should not be surprised if their heating bills seems to be higher than their neighbors. In some shadowy low places, the air may chill from a few hours before sunset to well after sunrise.

City dwellers, even in places of 500 inhabitants, generally have lower heating bills than rural people because of heat released by homes and other activities. The "heat island" of Minneapolis-St. Paul warms winter-time temperatures by an average of about 4 degrees, and has even raised the average airport winter temperature by about 2 degrees over the natural.

In rural northern Minnesota there are many places where frost occurs the year round. Weather stations are normally located in areas other than these "frost pockets", so that the cold areas are not highly visible.

Cold areas are places of less atmospheric water vapor; by the same token they are areas where dew concentrates. When the air is chilled by the surface vegetation a considerable amount of atmospheric water vapor is deposited on the surfaces of plants.

The micro-climate features are best developed in the central and northern highland climactic region and most poorly on the flat prairie region. The presence of micro-climactic features make some enormous differences in selecting proper building sites for dwellings and other structures. Those who ignore the micro-climate in planning in Minnesota do so at the peril of their comfort and their pocketbooks.

Sunshine is also much affected by topography and vegetation. Locations on north slopes can be quite miserable, being often in winter's shadows while at the same time suffering from exposure to cold winds from the arctic regions.

Building Sites

Here are some rules for selecting and developing a dwelling site in Minnesota:

1. Pick a spot on the south-facing slope; one which has higher ground immediately to the west is ideal.
2. If there is no high ground to the west or north, plant plant evergreen trees to break the wind and shield against the hot setting of the summer.
3. Plant broadleaf trees to the south and east of the structure. They will provide shading in the summer and interfere little with the sunshine in the cold winter. It is best to plant these trees some distances from the house so that you can take advantage of solar energy. Every south facing window can become a solar collector if you remove any screens and open the drapes when the sun is shining. Fuel savings can be substantial.
4. Choose a neighborhood that is not too densely populated. Concentration of dwellings leads to an insufferable summertime micro-climate. Non-vegetated surfaces store up heat during the day and release it at night, causing miserable conditions for sleeping.
5. Avoid dells, low spots, hilltops, and north slopes.
6. A lake to the southwest is very desirable. During the period from mid-July through about Labor day, lots of hot southwesterly winds blow. The passage of air over the water has the effect of cooling the air and allowing the wind to pick up speed for cooling the body. Strong southwesterly winds are rare in winter, so no problem from them arises.

There are two good places in Minnesota to observe to ideas on site selection. One, Glenwood, is located on south slope along the northeast end of Lake Minnewaska. It is ideally situated from the standpoint of the micro-climate principle. Another is the Windsor Green Townhouses in New Brighton—they are on the south slope to the northeast of Silver Lake.

Storms

Blizzards, tornadoes, and severe thunderstorms rake Minnesota every year, wreaking property damage and often death.

A blizzard generally affects the entire state, a severe thunderstorm several counties, and a tornado one or two counties. Over the years, the severe thunderstorms kill more people than blizzards and tornadoes combined, though the latter two get most of the publicity since they take more lives in one blow.

Without question, the greatest blizzard, in terms of intensity, was that of January, 1975, the "Blizzard of the Century." The greatest tornado of all, in terms of deaths, was the St. Cloud-Sauk Rapids storm of April, 1886. It is impossible to identify clearly the most severe thunderstorm of all time, since the criteria have become difficult to establish. Candidates for such storms where tornado activity was not a significant feature would include that of August 29, 1948, which killed 37 persons and featured some very rare cloud forms, the Black Thursday storm of June 20, 1974, and the Great Hailstorm of July 20, 1903, which laid waste to entire townships in Lincoln, Pipestone, Rock and Nobles counties. The August storm was clearly foremost in deaths, the June storm in terms of wind damage, and the July storm because of hail damage.

Blizzards

The blizzard is a blinding stew of heavy snow, blowing snow, blowing dust, rain, freezing rain, high winds (sometimes of hurricane velocity), sleet, low barometer and stark temperature contrast—to the 60's and even 70's to the front and sub-zero to the rear.

A great blizzard begins with a pickup of northerly winds across the Great Plains and a rush of warm air northward across the Mississippi Valley. The blizzard must take place between November 3 and April 10. Only during that time are the needed ingredients present.

The worst blizzards, that of January1975, took place between the 9th and 12th of the month. The center of the storm passed over the Twin Cities area round 10 p.m. with a measured low pressure of 28.62 inches. The storm center reached the Grand Portage area at dawn on the 11th, with gales and, in some places, hurricane force winds causing zero and near zero visibility from blowing snow and dust on the afternoon of the 11th over most of Minnesota. Gale driven snow was already blowing in western Minnesota. On the morning of the 10th and still on the 12th, high winds were occurring in most parts of the state.

The storm included lightning and thunder near the storm center and there were great temperature variations. While sub-zero readings were being observed in the Dakotas, Wisconsin was reading values in the 50's. Minnesota, in the path of the center had temperatures in the 40's in the southeast, while below-zero values were present in the western portion of the state.

Prior to the 1975 blizzard, the worst in the history of Minnesota was probably that of February 13, 1866. The eight most intense blizzards in the state's history were:

1. The Blizzard of the Centuries, January 9 - 12, 1975
2. The Great Blizzard, February 13 - 15, 1866
3. Blizzard of January 7 - 10, 1873.
4. The Armistice Day Storm, November 11 - 12, 1940
5. The Blizzard of January 13 - 15, 1888
6. The Blizzard of February 23 - 26, 1835
7. The Ides of March Blizzard, March 15 - 16, 1941
8. The Blizzard of January 14 - 15, 1827

Severe Thunderstorms

A ferocious thunderstorm squall line roared through eastern Minnesota and western Wisconsin on the morning of August 29, 1948. The clouds of this system represented the classic profile of a squall line development. The advance edge of the storm cloud was an immense smooth wall approximately 100 miles long that extended from near the ground to about 50,000 feet in the sky. Ahead of the mass was a rotor cloud roughly 200 feet in diameter and scores or miles in length. It rotated at about 35 revolutions per minute as very cold air from its bowels slashed along the ground, sending the old warm August morning air aloft.

As the violence struck Winona County, an unfortunate airliner was caught in the storm's path. Aircraft in those days could not fly above the path of foul weather, and the plane was chewed up in vicious jaws of the wall cloud. All 37 people aboard were killed.

Similar in appearance was the great squall line of July 20, 1903. The wall cloud roared over four southwestern counties of Minnesota. Wind destruction was tempered somewhat by the fact that mostly open prairie was under the storm, but hail damage was the big story. It fell nearly everywhere in the counties, with total damage involving whole townships. Many stones weighed several pounds, and huge holes were torn in the roofs of buildings. The stones in some instances smashed down nearly entire roofs.

Noteworthy for its high winds was the storm of Black Thursday on June 20, 1974. It moved into Minnesota from North Dakota between Fargo and Grand Forks. A pilot described the area under the storm as being "as black as night."

As the disturbance moved over many counties from Fargo to the Iowa line in southeastern Minnesota, it became enlarged and knocked down thousands of trees. Its passage caused farm yard lights activated by automatic switches sensitive to failing light, to glare as the eerie darkness enveloped the land. Short intense hail and rain pelted the region. Winds were clocked at speeds over 100 miles per hour as the storm ground through the state.

On July 23, 1987 the heaviest rain ever fell at the National Weather Service Office in Minneapolis. A total of 10.00 inches was recorded within eight hours from the evening of the 23rd to the early part of the 24th.

A rain of this magnitude can be expected at a given point about once every 10,000 years. However, it should be noted that a rain such as this occurs somewhere in Minnesota every few years. What is unusual is that this storm picked the official airport rain gauge as one of its principal targets.

Tornadoes

Tornadoes make news not according to their size and number in a family, but also according to where they hit. A dozen severe tornadoes slashing through remote forest areas may be little noted, while a single small tornado striking a mobile home park will make headlines because of death and injury.

Very damaging and newsworthy was a family of six or more tornadoes which struck the Twin Cities on May 6, 1965. The western and northern suburbs were hardest hit. A total of 16 persons were killed and 512 were injured, with 325 homes and 278 mobile homes destroyed. In addition, 1197 dwellings and 82 mobile homes were damaged and 241 farms and 65 businesses were demolished.

The Eight Worst Tornadoes in State History, in Terms of Fatalities Were:

Location	Date	Deaths
1. St. Cloud-Sauk Rapids	April 14, 1886	74
2. Fergus Falls	June 21, 1919	57
3. Tyler	August 21, 1918	36
4. Rochester	August 21, 1883	26
5. Twin Cities	May 6, 1965	16
6. Northern Minnesota	August 6, 1969	15
7. Twin Cities	August 20, 1904	15
8. Albert Lea-Wells Waseca-Owatonna	April 30, 1967	12
9. Mankato-Wells	August 17, 1946	11

One of the most unusual tornadoes was the of May 27, 1930. While traveling through Norman County, the famous old train, the Empire Builder, collided with a twister. The cracked train was picked off the tracks and overturned, killing one person.

Other Storms

Climactic disturbances of another nature and less intensity visit Minnesota. Notable in violence but rare in occurrence are "land hurricanes". These are spring and fall phenomena that bring winds of hurricane force (73 miles per hour or over) to the area. The usually originate in the vicinity of New Mexico and move across Minnesota to Canada. Three of these monumental climactic movements occurred on September 16, 1856, October 10, 1949, and May 5, 1950. On at least one such occasion, a well-developed "eye" was observed.

The common "all-day rainstorm" usually appears a few days after a cold front passage when the front stalls to the south. A low pressure zone coming from the west will "pick up" the front, causing it to move northward toward Minnesota as a warm front. The low pressure center moves eastward along the front, with the front to the rear of the storm again moving south as a cold front. When it passes as far as Iowa, Minnesota can receive a lot of heavy rain.

Minnesota Sky and Weather Phenomena

Ice fogs, composed of ice crystals, often present pretty sights on cold winter mornings. They sparkle in the air like millions of diamonds, a delight to natives and a source of amazement to visitors from southern climates. They are caused by freezing of air-born water and begin to appear most often at temperature below minus 20 Fahrenheit. Heavy auto traffic may cause considerable loss of visibility since combustion processes release copious amounts of water into the air.

The aurora borealis, or northern lights, are caused by reactions to the bombardment of the upper atmosphere by solar particles. These fireworks make the air glow, resulting in brilliant displays. They are so common in the state because it is close to the north magnetic pole, just northwest of Hudson Bay. The aurora borealis appears more frequently farther north.

Miscellaneous Minnesota Weather Facts

On a weighted basis, an average of 25.153 inches of rain fell per year in the state between 1901 and 1960. This is 33.37 cubic miles of water per year, enough water to fill a tank 3.2 miles long, 3.2 miles wide and 3.2 miles high. However, it would take 88 years at this rate to equal a volume the size of Lake Superior.

The record highest and lowest temperature are not generally listed correctly. The true high was 114.5° Fahrenheit at Beardsley. Moorhead once had 113.6°. Both round off at 114°, but the Beardsley reading was actually 0.9° higher. The coldest official temperature was minus 59.5° Fahrenheit recorded near Tower on February 2, 1996. Embarass had two unofficial thermometers record minus 60° and 61° for and average of minus 60.5° that day.

Climates, Averages, Extremes

Temperature Degrees Fahrenheit	Duluth	Intl. Falls	Moor.-Fargo	Roch.	St. Cloud	Twin Cities
Yearly Average	38.5	36.8	41.0	43.6	41.5	44.9
January Average	7.0	1.0	5.9	11.5	8.1	11.8
April Average	38.6	39.0	43.0	44.9	43.5	46.4
July Average	66.1	66.7	71.1	70.9	70.1	73.6
October Average	43.7	42.4	45.7	47.9	45.9	48.8
Record High	106.0	103.0	106.0	108.0	107.0	105.0
Record Low	-39.0	-55.0	-48.0	-40.0	-43.0	-41.0
Hottest July	77.1	78.8	80.2	81.8	82.6	81.4
Coldest January	-7.2	-10.4	-7.0	-3.8	-5.7	-6.0
Normal Degree Days	9885	10,471	9254	8313	8903	7981
Precipitation, Inches						
Yearly Average	30.0	24.36	19.45	29.66	27.43	28.32
Wettest Year	43.44	34.35	32.20	43.94	46.01	40.15
Driest Year	19.95	11.63	8.84	11.65	14.64	11.59
January Average	1.22	0.88	0.67	0.78	0.74	0.95
April Average	2.25	1.58	1.82	2.73	2.35	2.42
July Average	3.61	3.59	2.7	4.20	3.11	3.53
October Average	2.49	1.97	1.68	2.32	2.21	2.19
Wettest Month	11.52	11.26	9.90	12.33	12.81	17.90
Driest Month	0.07	0.0	0.01	0.0	0.0	Tr.
Days .01 or More	136.7	133.0	104.0	108.9	109.0	114.7
Most in One Day	3.77	4.82	na	7.47	5.0	10.0
Snowfall						
Average Season	77.3	63.3	40.4	48.1	45.4	49.7
Snowiest Season	168.9	131.8	82.2	89.0	87.9	98.6
Most in One Month	50.1	43.9	30.4	35.1	51.7	46.9
Most in One Day	25.4	17.0	19.2	12.9	14.5	21.0
Days 1" or More	22	18	11	13	13	15
Other						
Fastest Wind, MPH	75	52	115	69	62	110
Average Wind, MPH	11.0	8.9	12.2	12.9	8.2	10.5
Average No. of						
--Clear Days	77	76	88	86	97	95
--Partly Cloudy	102	102	109	97	102	101
--Cloudy	186	187	168	182	166	169
Average Thunderstorm Days	35	30	32	41	35	37

Source: National Climatic Data Center, National Weather Service, MN Climatology Office website http://climate.umn.edu.

Minnesota Weather Safety

It is no secret that thousands of Minnesotans have died from weather related causes. However, for the most part, the deaths have been needless and proper precautions could have averted most of the fatalities. Here are some weather safety hints:

A blizzard can stop your car in its tracks or force it to become stuck in a snowbank. You may face danger from the car being buried in the snow, causing suffocation, by becoming too cold in the metal prison causing frostbite or worse, or making a decision to leave the vehicle and dying by getting lost and freezing.

Generally, it is best you stay in the car and not venture out. Blowing snow can limit visibility to a few feet, and one becomes disoriented. In winter, no trip should begin without blankets, food and drink for a few days and a 3-pound coffee can for body wastes. A portable radio with fresh batteries is an imperative for receiving information about weather and road conditions.

Anyone driving extensively in winter should have a CB radio and an updated road map. Don't forget a flashlight and first aid kit.

When it is raining very hard in warmer weather, pull over, preferably into the driveway of a restaurant or service station. Heavy rain seldom lasts long. Avoid low stream areas where flooding may occur.

Always keep an eye an eye out for squall line clouds, especially if you are in a boat. Learn to recognize them. They bring not only rain, but high winds.

Lightning — The Greatest Killer

The thunderbolt from on high kills more people in the country than hurricanes, floods or tornadoes; but not enough people know how to take basic precautionary steps to protect themselves from lethal electrical strikes.

According to National Oceanic and Atmospheric Administration records, lightning caused the deaths of 7,000 Americans, 55 percent more than were killed by tornadoes and 41 percent more than the combination of floods and hurricanes.

In light of this, statisticians have drawn up some basic safety rules, to wit:

When approaching rumbles of thunder and flashes of light in the sky indicate the onset of a thunderstorm, take these steps for they may save your life:

• DO Watch television and listen to radio alerts
• DO Move to large buildings or house or into an all - metal vehicle (car, truck or the like)
• DO Disconnect appliances, and use the telephone only for emergencies

If Outside:
- DO NOT stay anywhere near metal farm equipment, golf scooters, motorcycles, metal fences, pipes, rails or any other metal objects that could conduct electricity to or near you.
- DO NOT seek shelter in small sheds of isolated buildings in open areas.
- DO drop to your knees and bend forward, putting your hands on your knees - this reduces the chances of a bolt striking near you and using your body as a conductor.
- DO warn members of a group to spread out, not huddle together, to reduce the numbers that might be affected by a strike.

Celsius Scale

Although it has thus far failed to gain acceptance in the United States, the Celsius temperature scale is becoming increasingly familiar to Americans. It is the measuring system used by virtually the entire world beyond U.S.A. boundaries.

There are some clever techniques that can be used to relate Celsius to Fahrenheit. Here are some benchmarks that are easy to remember.
1. Both Celsius and fahrenheit are equal at 40 below zero.
2. At -23° Fahrenheit, turn the numbers around to get approximate degrees Celsius; -32°.
3. Twelve degrees Fahrenheit is minus eleven Celsius, and eleven degrees Fahrenheit is minus twelve degrees Celsius.
4. Freezing, 32° Fahrenheit is minus twelve degrees Celsius.
5. 39° Fahrenheit is 3.9° Celsius.
6. At 61° Fahrenheit, turn the numbers around to get approximate degrees Celsius, 16.
7. At 82° Fahrenheit, turn the numbers around to get approximate degrees Celsius, 28°
8. Some of the easier relationships to remember are:
     95 F is 35 C
     68 F is 20 C
     50 F is 10 C
9. Like 32 Fahrenheit occurs at a memorable O Celsius, 32 Celsius occurs at a memorable 90 Fahrenheit.

If you remember these benchmarks, you can estimate temperatures in the other system recalling that there are almost 2 Fahrenheit degrees (actually 1.8) for 1 Celsius degree. For example, if it is 86 Fahrenheit, remember that 82 Fahrenheit is 28 Celsius. The difference between 86 F and 82 F is 4 F, and half of 4 is 2. Therefore, 28 C + 2 C is 30 C, so 86 F is 30 C.

Calendars

The Twin Cities Weather Calendar has been part of the local Metropolitan scene since 1969. Except for minor alterations, the format is the same now as it was back then.

The long Twin cities weather record, dating continuously back to 1819, is the third longest in the United States, and is the best in the Unites States, and perhaps the world, for so long a time. After such a long time, many climactic fluctuations have occurred. It is likely that the weekly averages on these calendars will remain stable for at least the next several thousand years to a high degree of similarity. Considerable efforts are being made in computer modeling to preclude the possibility that mankind will engage in activities that will alter world climate to a significant extent. These studies, though basic in research, are of great potential applied value, for they could enable America as a nation to change activities or to warn other nations to change their activities so as to not endanger the food supply of the world by ruining the present climate, to which crops are adapted. Argument is strong for the general climate of the past 160 years to prevail for a long time to come. Thus this Weather Calendar should stay valid for many millennia.

The Gregorian Calendar

This calendar, now the world calendar, is known as the Gregorian Calendar, It was proclaimed by Pope Gregory XIII in Rome in 1582 to be in effects as the calendar of the Roman Catholic Church as of October 15th (old October 4th) of the year. The calendar came about after long concern over the fact that the calendar of the Roman Empire as revised by Julius Caesar was losing days by not dropping an extra day every 100 years in 3 centuries out of 4. Caesar had revised and fixed an everchanging calendar, traditionally originated by Romulus, the founder of Rome.

Gregory's calendar became the official calendar in the American Colonies on September 14, 1752 (Gregorian) under our ruler at the time, His Brittanic Majesty, King George II. Despite the fact that an Englishman, the Venerable Bede of Jarrow, pointed out the need for the correction as early as the year 730, England and her subject lands were among the last to adopt the Gregorian calendar.

It is important for many reasons, such as the study of weather and climate, that the calendar stay in synchronization with the seasons. For this purpose, our calendar is fixed on a point in the sky, called the First Point of Aries. This point is related to the moment that spring begins-the moment at which the earth is at the point in its orbit about the sun such that the most vertical "ray" of the sun strikes the earth's equator exactly as the sun appears to proceed northward in the sky as seen from Earth. Our calendar is determined such that this occurs form March 19 to March 21.

The Gregorian calendar makes every year evenly divisible by four a leap year, except for years evenly divisible by 100 but not by 400. Thus, 1800, 1900, 2100, 2200, and 2300 are not leap years, but 2000 and 2400 will be. These adjustments will keep the calendar within 1 day of accuracy until about 5000 if no significant changes occur in the various motions involved in the calculation of time. Around 4800 or 5200, we should need to drop a day-that decision has not yet been made according to sources I contacted. Another day may have to be dropped around the years 10,000, 15,000 and 20,000 etc.

The Gregorian calendar recycles to the same dates and days of the week every 400 years, so that the calendars for 1600, 2000, 2400, and each of the next 399 years thereafter are in synchronization.

One unfortunate change was made in the calendar between the time of Julius Caesar and Pope Gregory. Augustus Caesar took a day out of February and put it into August, the month which he named after himself. One simple calendar reform might be to take a day from January and March and give them to February, so that all those months will have 30 days, a more even distribution. Leap day then could be February 31.

Other Calendars

We use the calendar that evolved from Rome since the dominant cultural heritage of today's world came from or through Rome. This was a result of the spread of civilization by that city's vast empire, and the subsequent world-wide expansion of its former domains such as England, Spain and France. The calendar of Rome became the calendar of the colonies and dominions of these lands and remains such though the colonies and dominions are now free.

Both other calendars were in use at one time by other cultures, with some being superior to the Roman calendar.

Locally, the Ojibwa calendar was reckoned by moons and by days of each moon. The Ojibwa moons were highly related to weather or weather-associated events. They bear such names as the Freezing Moon and Deep Snow Moon. One way to reckon Ojibwa Moons is by the following method: Let the first full moon after the vernal equinox be the Snowshoe Breaking Moon (the moon when snowshoes are no longer needed because the snow melts away during the moon). Let the next 12 months follow in order by the names listed below except when it becomes necessary to drop one moon due to the year. To do this, let the last full moon before the vernal equinox always be the Crust of Snow Moon, with the Sucker Moon dropping out if there is no full moon between February 8th and 18th. The names are according to Duane Chatfield.

Table of Ojibwe Moons

Full Moon Dates		Moon Names	New Moon Dates	
Earliest	Latest		Earliest	Latest
Mar 20	Apr 18	Snowshoe Breaking	Mar 6	Apr 13
Apr 19	May 17	Maple Sugar	Apr 14	May 2
May 19	Jun 16	Budding Plants	May 3	June 1
Jun 17	July 16	Strawberry	June 2	June 30
July 16	Aug 14	Midsummer	July 1	July 29
Aug 15	Sep 12	Harvest	July 30	Aug 28
Sep 13	Oct 12	Wild Rice Harvest	Aug 29	Sep 26
Oct 13	Nov 10	Falling Leaves	Sep 27	Oct 26
Nov 11	Dec 10	Freezing	Oct 27	Nov 25
Dec 11	Jan 8	Descending Cold	Nov 26	Dec 25
Jan 9	Feb 7	Deep Snow	Dec 26	Jan 24
Feb 8	Feb 18	Sucker	Jan 25	Feb 4
Feb 19	Mar 20	Crust of Snow	Feb 5	Mar 6

Year	New Moon	First Quarter	Full Moon	Last Quarter
2000				
Deep Snow	Jan 6 18:14	Jan 14 13:34	Jan 21 04:41 t	Jan 28 07:58
Crust of Snow	Feb 5 13:04 P	Feb 12 23:21	Feb 19 16:27	Feb 27 03:55
Snowshoe Breaking	Mar 6 05:18	Mar 13 06:59	Mar 20 04:44	Mar 28 00:23
Maple Sugar	Apr 4 18:13	Apr 11 13:30	Apr 18 17:41	Apr 26 19:32
Strawberry	May 4 04:13	May 10 20:01	May 18 07:34	May 26 11:56
Midsummer	Jun 2 12:15	Jun 9 03:29	Jun 16 22:27	Jun 25 01:01
Harvest	Jul 1 19:20 P	Jul 8 12:53	Jul 16 13:56 t	Jul 24 11:03
Wild Rice Harvest	Aug 29 10:20	Sep 5 16:28	Sep 13 19:38	Sep 21 01:29
Falling Leaves	Sep 27 19:53	Oct 5 10:59	Oct 13 08:54	Oct 20 08:00
Freezing	Oct 27 07:58	Nov 4 07:26	Nov 11 21:16	Nov 18 15:26
Descending Cold	Nov 25 23:12	Dec 4 03:55	Dec 11 09:04	Dec 18 00:43
2001				
Deep Snow	Dec 25 17:23 P	Jan 2 22:32	Jan 9 20:25t	Jan 16 12:36
Sucker Moon	Jan 24 13:08	Feb 1 14:02	Feb 8 07:12	Feb 15 03:25
Crust of Snow	Feb 23 08:22	Mar 3 02:03	Mar 9 17:23	Mar 16 20:47
Snowshoe Breaking	Mar 25 01:23	Apr 1 10:49	Apr 8 03:22	Apr 15 15:32
Maple Sugar	Apr 23 15:27	Apr 30 17:08	May 7 13:53	May 15 10:12
Budding Plants	May 23 02:47	May 29 22:10	Jun 6 01:40	Jun 14 03:29
Strawberry	Jun 21 11:58 T	Jun 28 03:20	Jul 5 15:04 p	Jul 13 18:47
Midsummer	Jul 20 19:44	Jul 27 10:09	Aug 4 05:56	Aug 12 07:54

Harvest Moon	Aug 19 02:55	Aug 25 19:54	Sep 2 21:44	Sep 10 19:00
Wild Rice				
Harvest	Sep 17 10:27	Sep 24 09:30	Oct 2 13:50	Oct 10 04:20
Falling Leaves	Oct 16 19:23	Oct 24 02:57	Nov 1 05:42	Nov 8 12:22
Freezing	Nov 15 06:40	Nov 22 23:20	Nov 30 20:50	Dec 7 19:53
Descending				
Cold	Dec 14 20:48 A	Dec 22 20:57	Dec 30 10:41 n	

Eclipses

The table above also indicates whether or not an eclipse of the Sun or Moon occurred on the date in question and gives the eclipse type. Note that an eclipse of the Sun can occur only at New Moon, while an eclipse of the Moon can occur only at Full Moon. In any calendar year there are between 2 to 5 eclipses of each kind (solar and lunar, including penumbral). However, there cannot be any more than 7 eclipses in any one year (4 solar and 3 lunar, or 5 solar and 2 lunar).

Solar	Lunar
Eclipses: T - Total	Eclipses: t - Total (Umbral)
A - Annular	p - Partial (Umbral)
H - Hybrid (Annular/Total)	n - Penumbral
P - Partial	

Algorithms used in predicting the phases of the Moon as well as eclipses are based on Jean Meeus' Astronomical Algorithms (Willmann-Bell, Inc., Richmond, 1991). All calculations are by Fred Espenak, and he assumes full responsibility for their accuracy.
Source: NASA Astronomical Ephemeris Data website.

Calendar Trivia

In the year 2000 we will have a February 29th in a year divisible by 100 for the first time since His Majesty, King George II, declared the Gregorian calendar to be that of his realms. We thus get an extra day that our forefathers in this country never had.

In the year 2001, the calendar will be the same as it would have been for the year 1 if the Gregorian calendar had been in use. Christmas Day, December 25, in that year, was on a Tuesday.

Every year, except leap years, begins and ends on the same day of the week.

Ralph W. Samuelson is the credited inventor of waterskiing on Lake Pepin in 1922. The skis are 8 foot by 9 inch pine boards he also used to jump over a greased ramp. Photo by Eugene D. Becker, Minnesota Historical Society.

Chapter 19

Recreation

The Minnesota Department of Natural Resources Division of Parks and Recreation oversees 68 state parks and 57 state forests and recreation areas for nearly seven million visitors annually.

Income from park permits, campground fees, refreshments, and souvenirs exceeds $2 million.

The National Park Service (www.nps.gov) administers three park areas in Minnesota. These include Voyageurs National Park with 218,000 acres of land and water on the Canadian Border, Pipestone National Monument near the southwest corner of the state and the National Wild and Scenic Riverway on the St. Croix.

There are two National Forests in Minnesota's north woods, The Chippewa and Superior.

The Minnesota Office of Tourism promotes Minnesota as a multi-faceted, four-season vacation destination. 651-296-5029, 1-800-657-3700, www.explore.state.mn.us

Lifejacket Requirement

On May 1, 1996, new personal flotation device (PFD) requirements became effective for all waters within and bordering Minnesota. This makes Minnesota's law match federal law and those of the surrounding states.

The new requirements for PFDs are as follows: On all boats (except a sailboard) regardless of length (includes canoes, kayaks, and duck boats), there must be a readily accessible Coast Guard approved Type I, II, or III wearable PFD (life jacket) for each person on board. Type IV throwable devices, such as buoyant cushions, are no longer acceptable primary life-saving devices. Ski belts do not meet state PDF requirements.

In addition, on boats 16 feet or longer (except canoes and kayaks), there must also be at least one Coast Guard approved Type IV throwable device, such as a buoyant cushion or ring buoy immediately available for each boat.

The law does not state that PFDs must be worn, only that they are readily accessible except for personal watercraft where they MUST be

worn (water scooters, Jet Skis, etc.). However... we highly recommend that PFDs always be worn by everyone on board any boat.
Source: Minnesota Boating Guide 1999, MN Department of Natural Resources

All-terrain Vehicles, Off-highway Motorcycles & Off-road Vehicles

In general, ATVs, OHMs, and ORVs may be operated on 1) your own land, 2) private land with the owner's permission, 3) on frozen waters where you have legal access, and 4) on land posted with signs specifically permitting the use of recreational motor vehicles.

These vehicles may not be operated 1) on the median of a four-lane highway, 2) within the right-of-way of any interstate highway, 3) on the right-of-way between opposing lanes of traffic, 4) at airports, 5) in any state park, state recreation area, state historic site, Wildlife Management Area or state Scientific and Natural Area with the exception of posted trails and areas, 6) on any frozen waters located in a restricted area, or frozen waters where you don't have legal access, 7) in any areas restricted by local ordinance or municipalities, 8) in a tree nursery or planting area, or 9) along or on the shoulder or inside bank or slope of a public right-of way.

Minnesota has 624 miles of off-highway vehicle Grant-in-Aid trails (GIA) statewide. This is spread among 17 different clubs and three trail systems. Other opportunities to ride OHV's exist in the State Forests that are presently in an "open unless posted closed" status. This means you can ride on all existing State Forest roads and trails unless they are posted closed. This also applies to the Superior National Forest. The Chippewa National Forest has some opportunities as well, but the OHV status there is "all roads and trails are closed to OHV use unless posted open".
Contact the Department of Natural Resources for complete regulations.
Source: Recreational Motor Vehicles Regulations—1997 & 1999, MN DNR.

Campsites

There are more over 9,400 state and federal campsites in Minnesota, not including county, municipal, and private campsites. More than 4,900 campsites are provided in the state parks and state forests. The north woods provide over 2000 campsites in the two national forests and one national park, plus an additional 2,200 water-access sites in the Boundary Waters Canoe Area Wilderness. The Army Corps of Engineers maintains over 300 campsites on lands near Upper Mississippi River Water Control Areas.

State Parks contain 4,378 campsites, 1,255 miles of trail and 33 fishing piers.

Trails

Trails provide year-round outdoor recreational opportunities. The following figures are from the MN DNR, 7/1/96. They include both public and private trails:

Hiking	4,392.8
Ski	2,826.6
Horse	1,450.2
Bike	950.3
Snowmobile	16,076.5
Total	21,213.2

State Recreation Trails, www.dnr.state.mn.us

SP = state park access, **C** = camping, **F** = fishing, **S** = swimming, **BR** = bike rental nearby.

*Arrowhead State Trail. 135 miles from near Tower to International Falls. The natural surface trail is used primarily for snowmobiling. Parts are suitable for horseback riding, mountain biking and hiking, although a number of areas have standing water in the summer. Mainly forest. (C, F, REST).

Cannon Valley Trail. (Not under DNR jurisdiction) 19.7 miles from Cannon Falls to Red Wing. Paved former Chicago Great Western railroad bed. Hiking, cycling, in-line skating, mountain biking (Wheel Pass required for non-pedestrian and non-wheelchair users ages 18 and over), skiing (Great MN Ski Pass required, ages 16-64. Call 612-296-6157 or 1-800-766-6000 in MN for pass). Trail information 507-263-3954 or 612-258-4141.

Casey Jones. 12 miles in Pipestone County. Undeveloped/unmarked, natural surface. Horseback, snowmobile.

*Douglas State Trail. 12.5 miles from Rochester to Pine Island. Bituminous and natural treadways on an abandoned railroad bed. Hiking, cycling, horseback, in-line skating, skiing, snowmobiling, wheelchair access. (RA) Mainly agricultural.

*Gateway State Trail. 18.3 miles starting in St. Paul. Paved railroad bed with unpaved adjacent section between I-694 and Pine Point Park. Hiking, bicycling, horseback, in-line skating, skiing, wheelchair accessible. (S, F,RA). Urban, parks, lakes, fields.

**Glacial Lakes State Trail. 40 miles from Willmar to Richmond. Willmar to New London 12 miles paved with parallel grass for horseback (wheelchair access) (SP, C, S, F). 6 miles New London to Harwick crushed granite. 22 miles Harwick to Richmond undeveloped with original railroad stones as a surface with some bridges removed. Hiking, cycling, in-line skating, mountain biking, skiing, horseback, snowmobiling (within

Kandyohi County). Mainly agricultural with remnants of virgin prairie, wetlands, and scattered woodlots.

Harmony-Preston Valley State Trail. 19 miles between Harmony and Preston in southeastern MN. Railroad bed to be completely paved in the summer of 1997. Hiking, bicycling, horseback, in-line skating, mountain biking, skiing, wheelchair accessible. Woods and farm land. (BR).

Heartland State Trail. 49 miles from Park Rapids to Cass Lake. Abandoned railroad bed. Park Rapids to Walker paved plus grass (C, F, S, BR). Walker to Cass Lake compacted gravel and railroad ballast (C, S, F). Hiking, cycling, horseback, mountain biking, snowmobiling, wheelchair accessible. Mostly forested.

Luce Line State Trail. 63 miles. 7 miles from Plymouth to Stubbs Bay (BR), 23 miles from Stubbs Bay to Winsted (S, F), limestone surfaced railroad bed with parallel treadway for horseback riding. 33 miles from Winsted to Cosmos (F), natural surface with 3 missing bridges, . Hiking, bicycling, mountain biking, horseback, snowmobiling. Mainly agricultural.

Minnesota Valley Trail. 19 miles from Fort Snelling to Shakopee (SP, C, F, BR), 5 miles from Shakopee to Chaska (C, F, BR), 20 miles from Swing Bridge to Belle Plain. Hiking, bicycling, horseback, in-line skating, mountain biking, skiing, snowmobiling.

Willard Munger State Trail. Three segments. 80 miles "Boundary Segment" from near Pine City to Holyoke through State Park and State Forest land (SP, C, S, F). Hiking, mountain biking, horseback, snowmobile. 16 miles Alex Laveau Memorial Trail from Carlton south to the Wisconsin border (SP, C, F, BR). 63 miles Hinkley-Duluth Fire Segment (SP, C, S, F, BR). Laveau and Hinkley segments: hiking, bicycling, in-line skating, snowmobiling.

North Shore Trail. 146 miles from Duluth to Grand Marais. Hiking, horseback, mountain biking, snowmobiling. Rugged mixed forest, streams. (SP, C, F).

Paul Bunyan State Trail. 100 miles from Brainerd/Baxter to Bemidji. Mostly railroad bed paved from Baxter to Hackensack (C, F, BR), with remaining mostly original railroad ballast from Hackensack to Bemidji (C, F). Hiking, bicycling, in-line skating, mountain biking, snowmobiling, wheelchair accessible. Mostly forest.

Root River State Trail. 35 miles from Fountain to 5 miles east of Rushford in southeastern MN. Paved abandoned railroad bed. Hiking, bicycling, horseback, in-line skating, mountain biking, skiing, wheelchair accessible. Mainly agricultural, riverbank bluffs. (C, BR).

Sakatah Singing Hills State Trail. 39 miles from Mankato to Faribault. Paved railroad bed with several horseback segments between

Lime Valley Road (near Mankato) to Eagle Lake and from Sakatah Lake
State Park to Morristown. Hiking, bicycling, horseback, in-line skating,
skiing, snowmobiling, wheelchair accessible. (SP, C, S, F, BR).

   Taconite State Trail. 165 miles from Grand Rapids to Ely. 6 miles
from Grand Rapids paved, the balance is natural surface. Hiking, bicycling, horseback, in-line skating, skiing, wheelchair accessible, snowmobiling. Some standing water in summer. Mainly forest with areas impacted
by iron ore mining. (SP, C, S, F).

Minnesota State Forest Campgrounds and Trails

   State Forest campgrounds are of the primitive type designed to furnish only the basic needs of individuals who camp for the enjoyment of
the outdoors. Each campsite consists of a parking spur, fire ring, and
table. In addition, vault toilets, garbage containers, and drinking water
from a hand pump are provided. A $9.00 fee per night per campsite is
charged at campgrounds that charge a fee. The honor system is used.
Most fee campgrounds have handicapped accessible campsites and toilet
facilities (call ahead for specifics). Facilities without a use fee require users
to pack out all trash.

   The maximum recreational vehicle length which can be accommodated is 20 feet. For more information concerning other state forest and parks
campgrounds, trails, and recreational facilities contact the DNR
Information Center, 500 Lafayette Road, St. Paul, MN 55155-4040. Twin
Cities Metro Area: 296-6157. MN toll free: 1-800-766-6000. TDD: 296-5484
or 1-800-657-3929. www.dnr.mn.us

Bear Island State Forest near Ely
   Fishing and Putnam Lakes Trail, snowmobile 13.0.
Beltrami Island State Forest near Warroad
   Bemis Hill Campground. No fee. 4 campsites, drinking water, 6 pic-
nic sites, picnic shelter, sledding hill. 218-425-7793
   Blueberry Hill Campground. No fee. 8 campsites, drinking water, 4
picnic sites, blueberry picking, 5.0 ski trail. 218-634-2172.
   Faunce Campground. No fee. 4 campsites, drinking water, 6 picnic
sites, wooded site, hunting camping. 218-634-2172.
   Beltrami Island Snowmobile Trail, 95.0.
   Baudette/Norris Snowmobile Trail, 53.0.

Big Fork State Forest near Big Fork
   Big Fork River Canoe Campsites. No fee. 11 campsites, water access,
fishing, 5 locations along river. 218-278-6651.
   Long Lake Day Use Area. No fee. Drinking water, 2 picnic sites,
water access, fishing, Panfish, Walleye, Bass Lake. 218-743-3694.

Birch Lakes State Forest near Melrose

Birch Lake Campground. Fee. 29 campsites, drinking water, 5 picnic sites, swimming, water access, fishing, walleye lake, group camping, nature trail. 320-255-4276.

Birch Lake Trail, hiking, 3.0; snowmobile, 4.0.

Bowstring State Forest near Grand Rapids

Crazy Jim's. No fee. 2 campsites, 1 picnic site, water access, fishing, on Mississippi, no road access. 218-246-8343.

Cottonwood Lake Campground. Fee. 10 campsites, drinking water, water access, fishing, panfish lake. 218-246-8343.

Buena Vista State Forest near Bemidji

Buena vista Trail, snowmobile, 22.5.

Chengwatana State Forest near Pine City

Snake River Campground. Fee. 26 campsites, drinking water, water access, fishing, boat access 1 mi. on St. Croix River. 320-384-6146.

Chengwatana Trails, snowmobile, 8.4.

Red Horse Trail, hiking, 6.2.

Cloquet Valley State Forest near Two Harbors

Cloquet Valley Canoe Campsites. No fee. 4 campsites, water access, fishing, on Cloquet River canoe route. 218-723-4669.

Indian Lake Campground. Fee. 25 campsites, drinking water, swimming, water access, fishing, on Cloquet River canoe route/Group Camp. 218-834-6602.

Cloquet Valley Trail, hiking, 39.5; snowmobile Grant-in-Aid (GIA— maintained by snowmobile club, not DNR)

Taft Area Trail, hiking, 27.0; snowmobile GIA.

Crow Wing State Forest near Brainerd

Greer Lake Campground. Fee. 33 campsites, drinking water, 2 picnic sites, swimming water access, fishing, panfish lake, nature trail. 218-828-2565.

Harvey Drake Landing. No fee. 1 picnic site, water access, fishing, Pine River near Mississippi. 218-828-2565.

Staircase Landing Day Use Area. No fee. 4 picnic sites, swimming, water access, fishing, Pine River, canoe access only. 218-828-2565.

Pelican Beach Day Use Area. No fee. 2 picnic sites, swimming, Pelican Lake, changing building. 218-568-4566.

Pine Lake Landing. No fee. 1 picnic area, water access, fishing, on Pine Lake. 218-828-2565.

Bass Lake Nature Trail, hiking, 1.8.

Finland State Forest near Silver Bay

Eckbeck Campground. Fee. 30 campsites, drinking water, 4 picnic sites, fishing, Baptism River near North Shore. 218-834-6602.

Finland Campground. Fee. 35 campsites, drinking water, 10 picnic sites, fishing, on Baptism River. 218-834-6602.

Sullivan Lake Campground. Fee. 11 campsites, drinking water, 2 picnic sites, water access, fishing, hiking trail. 218-834-6602.

Sullivan Lake Hiking Trail, 2.5.

Moose Walk Trail, hiking & snowmobile, 22.0.

Fond Du Lac State Forest west of Cloquet

Fond Du Lac Trail, snowmobile GIA.

Fond Du Lac Ski Trail, 12.0.

Foot Hills State Forest north of Staples/Motley

Spider Lake Trail, hiking & ski, 7.3.

General C. C. Andrews State Forest near Moose Lake

Dago Lake Day Use Area. No fee. 4 picnic sites, fishing. 218-485-5400.

Willow River Campground. Fee. 41 campsites, drinking water water access, fishing, Zaleski Lake, Group campground. 218-485-5400.

General C. C. Andrews Trail, snowmobile and OHV, 8.6.

George Washington State Forest north of Grand Rapids

Bear Lake Campground. Fee. 30 campsites, drinking water, 7 picnic sites, swimming, water access, fishing, Walleye-Crappie lake. 218-262-6760.

Button Box Lake Campground. Fee. 12 campsites, drinking water, 3 picnic sites, water access, fishing, Panfish-Bass lake. 218-262-6760.

Larson Lake Campground. Fee. 12 campsites, drinking water, water access, fishing, designated trout lake. 218-743-3694.

Lost Lake Campground. Fee. 15 campsites, drinking water, water access, fishing, Panfish lake. 218-743-3694.

Owen Lake Campground. Fee. 21 campsites, drinking water 3 picnic sites, swimming water access, fishing, Panfish lake. 218-743-3694.

Thistledew Lake Campground. Fee. 20 campsites, drinking water, 2 picnic sites, swimming, water access, fishing, Walleye-Crappie lake. 218-262-6760.

Tim Corey Trail, snowmobile, 17.9.
Bear Lake Trail, snowmobile, 10.0.
Circle L Trail, snowmobile, 24.8.
Circle T Trail, snowmobile, 39.5.
Thistledew Trail, ski, 10.0.

Golden Anniversary State Forest near Grand Rapids
Cowhorn Lake Loop, hike & ski, 4.6.
River Road Loop, hike & ski, 1.7.

Grand Portage State Forest near Grand Marais
Grand Portage Dispersed Campsites. No fee. 7 campsites, picnic sites, water access, fishing, Devilfish, Esther, Chester, McFarland Lakes. 218-387-1075.

Hill River State Forest south of Grand Rapids
Moose-Willow-Washburn Lake Trail, snowmobile, 15.0.

Huntersville State Forest southeast of Park Rapids
Shell City Landing Campground. Fee. 18 campsites, drinking water, water access, fishing, on Crow Wing River Canoe Route. 218-472-3262.
Huntersville Forest Landing Campground. Fee. 21 campsites, drinking water, water access, fishing, on Crow Wing River Canoe Route. 218-472-3262.
Huntersville Trail, horseback, 24.0; snowmobile, 18.0.
Kabetogama State Forest southeast of International Falls
Ash River Campground. Fee. 9 campsites, drinking water, 2 picnic sites, water access, fishing, Ash River near Lake Kabetogama. 218-757-3274.
Hinsdale Island Boat-In Campground. Fee. 11 campsites, drinking water, water access, fishing, boat-in only, island in Lake Vermillion. 218-753-4500.
Wakemup Bay Campground. Fee. 21 campsites, drinking water, 2 picnic sites, swimming, water access, fishing, on L. Vermillion near Cook. 218-753-4500.
Wooden Frog Campground. Fee. 59 campsites, drinking water, 10 picnic sites, swimming, water access, fishing, L. Kabetogama, Voyageurs National Park. 218-757-3274.
Ash River Recreation Trail, hiking, 6.5; ski, 12.5.
Gheen Hills Trail, hiking & ski, 6.5.
Koochiching State Forest south of International Falls
Johnson Landing Campground. No fee. 2 campsites, water access,

fishing, on Big Fork River. 218-276-2237.

    Littlefork River Canoe Access. No fee. Water access, fishing, on Littlefork River. 218-278-6651.

    Moose Lake Day Use Area. No fee. 1 picnic site, water access, fishing, small bog lake. 218-278-6651.

    Tilson Creek Trail, hiking, 1.0; ski, 6.3.

Land O' Lakes State Forest north of Brainerd/Cross Lake

    Baker and White Oak Lake Campsites. No fee. 2 campsites, water access, fishing, off Moose River ATV trail.

    Clint Converse Memorial Campground. Fee. 32 campsites, drinking water, 7 picnic sites, swimming, water access, fishing, on Washburn Lake, a Walleye lake. 218-568-4566.

    Moose River Trail, snowmobile & OHV, 25.0.

    Washburn Lake Solitude Area, hiking and ski, 15.0; horseback, 8.5.

Lost River State Forest near Roseau

    E. D. A. Trail, snowmobile, 20.0.

    Mississippi Headwaters State Forest west of Bemidji

    Mississippi River Canoe Campsites. No fee. 16 campsites, fishing, many locations along river. 218-755-2265.

    Rognlien Beach and Picnic Area. No Fee. 15 picnic sites, swimming, water access, fishing, on Grant Lake. 218-755-2890.

    Bemidji/Itasca Trail, snowmobile, 26.0.

Nemadji State Forest east of Moose Lake

    Gafvert Campground. Fee. 9 campsites, drinking water, 2 picnic sites, water access, fishing, on Pickerel Lake. 218-485-4474.

    Gandy Dancer Trail, horseback, snowmobile & OHV, 14.1.

    Nemadji Trail, hiking, 3.0; snowmobile, 26.9; OHV, 13.6.

Northwest Angle State Forest

    M & O Day Use Area. No fee. 1 picnic site, on road to NW Angle. 218-386-1304.

Pat Bayle State Forest north of Tofte/Grand Marais

    Pat Bayle Dispersed Campsites. No fee. 3 campsites, water access, fishing, on East Twin Lake. 218-387-1075.

Paul Bunyan State Forest north of Akeley

    Mantrap Lake Campground. Fee. 38 campsites, drinking water, 5 picnic sites, swimming, water access, fishing, designated muskie lake/hiking trail. 218-732-3309.

    Gulch Lakes Recreation Area. Fee. 8 campsites, 4 picnic sites, water access, fishing, 6 units different lakes/primitive.

    Paul Bunyan Trail, snowmobile, 75.4.

Pillsbury State Forest near Brainerd

Green Bass Daily Use Area. No fee. Water access.

Rock Lake Campground. Fee. 43 campsites, drinking water, 8 picnic sites, swimming, water access, fishing, Group Camp available. 218-828-82565.

Schafer Lake Daily Use Area. No fee. 4 picnic sites, water access.

Walter E. Stark. Fee. 100 campsites, drinking water, 4 picnic sites, horseback rider, camping. 218-828-2565.

Pillsbury Trail, hiking, horseback & snowmobile, 27.0; ski, 3.0; OHV (motocross only), 12.0.

Rock Lake Trail, hiking, 1.5.

Pine Island State Forest southwest of International Falls

Benn Linn Landing. No fee. 3 campsites, water access, fishing, on Big Fork River. 218-276-2237.

Sturgeon River Landing. No fee. 2 campsites, water access, fishing, on Big Fork River. 218-276-2237.

Red Lake State Forest

Waskish Campground. Fee. 30 campsites, drinking water, 10 picnic sites, swimming, water access, fishing, on Upper Red Lake, a Walleye lake. 218-835-6684.

Richard J. Dorer Memorial Hardwood Forest southeast of Rochester

Hay Creek Management Unit. No fee. Drinking water, 3 picnic sites, fishing, on Hay Creek, a Trout stream-no camping. 612-345-3216.

Kruger Management Unit. Fee. 19 campsites, drinking water 13 picnic sites, water access, fishing, on Zumbro River, hiking trails. 612-345-3216.

Reno Management Unit. No Fee. 12 campsites, drinking water, shelter and horse corral. 507-724-5264.

Snake Creek Management Unit. No fee. Drinking water, fishing, on Snake Creek, a Trout stream. 612-345-3216.

Vinegar Ridge Management Unit. No fee. 7 campsites. 507-742-5264.

Zumbro Bottoms Management Unit. No fee. 20 campsites, drinking water, picnic sites, water access, fishing, Zumbro River, horse camp and trails. 612-345-3216.

Trails

Brightsdale Management Unit, hiking & ski, 5.7.

Bronk Management Unit, hiking & ski, 6.5.

Cannon Falls Management Unit, hiking & mountain biking, 2.0.

Hay Creek Management Unit, hiking & horseback, 20.0; ski, 5.8; snowmobile, 12.5.

Isinour's Demonstration Woodland, hiking, 4.0; ski, 3.2.

Kruger Management Unit, hiking, 8.0 (includes a .75 mile wheelchair trail), ski, 3.0; horseback, 5.0.

Oak Ridge Management Unit, hiking, ski & horseback, 8.8; snowmobile, 2.5.

Reno Management Unit, hiking, 13.9; horseback, 9.5; snowmobile, 14.9.

Snake Creek Management Unit, hiking, 11.9; ski, 3.0; horseback, snowmobile & OHV, 6.7.

Trout Valley Management Unit, hiking, horseback, snowmobile & OHV, 7.4.

Vinegar Ridge Management Unit, hiking & snowmobile, 3.8; horseback, 2.8.

Zumbro Bottoms Management Unit, hiking, 18.0; horseback, 10.0.

Rum River State Forest near Milaca

Kanabec Trail, snowmobile, GIA.

St. Croix State Forest east of Hinckley

Boulder Campground. Fee. 19 campsites, drinking water, 6 picnic sites, water access, fishing, on Rock Lake. 320-384-6146.

Tamarack River Horse Camp. Fee. 12 campsites, horse camp and trails. 320-384-6146.

Gandy Dancer Trail, hiking, horseback, snowmobile & OHV, 5.2.

St Croix Trail, hiking & horseback, 21.0; snowmobile, 19.8; OHV, 14.9.

Sand Dunes State Forest near Elk River

Ann Lake Campground and Day Use Area. Fee. 36 campsites, drinking water, 7 picnic sites swimming, fishing, Panfish lake, Group camping. 612-856-4826.

Ann Lake Trail (No Hunting), hiking, 4.0; ski, 3.0.

Orrock Trail, horseback, 18.0; snowmobile, GIA.

Savanna State Forest west of Cloquet

Hay Lake Campground. Fee. 20 campsites drinking water 5 picnic sites swimming, water access, fishing, Panfish lake, hiking trail, fall color. 218-697-2476.

Hay Lake Trail, hiking, 2.0.

Remote Lake Trail, hiking, 12.0; ski, 13.8.

Smokey Hills State Forest west of Park Rapids
Smokey Hills Trail, snowmobile & OHV, 13.0.

Two Inlets State Forest near Park Rapids
Hungryman Lake Campground. Fee. 14 campsites, drinking water, 3 picnic sites, swimming, water access, fishing, Cedar Lake Picnic Area. 218-732-3309.

Two Inlets Trail, snowmobile 27.5.

White Earth State Forest north of Detroit Lakes
White Earth Trails, snowmobile, 65.0.

Forestry Administered Facilities
Gambler's Point. No fee. 3 campsites, drinking water 1 picnic site, fishing, on Mississippi, no road access. 218-246-8343.

Paul Bunyan Campsites. No fee. 2 campsites, water access, fishing, bike and canoe access. 218-568-4566.

Moose Lake Campground. Fee. 12 campsites, drinking water, water access, fishing, Walleye lake, near Deer River. 218-246-8343.

South Bend Canoe Campsites. No fee. 2 campsites, water access, fishing, on Pine River. 218-568-4566.

Wabana Lake Campsites. No fee. 6 campsites, water access, fishing, Walleye, Bass, Panfish lake, no road access. 218-246-8343.

A Partial List of State Forest Rules
The following activities are permitted on state forest lands:
- Hunting, fishing, and trapping in accordance with state regulations.
- Hiking, both on and off designated trails.
- Picking fruit and mushrooms.
- Use of dead wood for recreational fires.

Activities requiring a permit and/or fee include:
- Cutting of commercial timber on state land.
- Cutting fuel wood for home use on state land.
- Open burning on all lands.
- Camping in designated state forest campgrounds.

It is unlawful while in a designated state forest campground or day-use area to:
- Possess explosives.
- Possess a firearm unless it is unloaded and completely contained in a guncase or trunk of a car.

- Possess a bow and arrow unless either unstrung or completely contained in a case or trunk of a car.
- Build a fire except in a fireplace or a fire ring provided for the purpose.

State Canoe and Boating Routes

All rivers have accesses and a number of campsites and picnic sites depending upon their length and usage. An asterisk (*) shows access to state parks. Many have equipment rental and shuttle service.

Rivers designated Family are generally mild, slow moving rivers giving a person or group with the basic knowledge of canoeing skills a pleasant experience. Rivers designated Experienced require more advanced knowledge of canoeing and rapid water behavior. They will require some navigation of rapids and swift current. Quick decisions are necessary.

Rivers designated Whitewater are for the experienced whitewater paddler only. Dangerous water conditions arise rapidly and require split second decisions and maneuvering.

Big Fork 165 miles from Dora Lake near Big Fork to the Rainy River. Experienced, some stretches of Whitewater. Mostly pine forest, few towns, good fishing. Primitive campsites.

Cannon* 80 miles from Highway 13 bridge west of Sakatah Lake (west of Faribault) to the Mississippi River. Family river. Very scenic wooded valley and bluffs.

Cloquet 101 miles from Indian Lake to the St. Louis River. Experienced upper section to Island Lake Reservoir, remote, forested. Family in southern section, forest and farmland, some towns, good fishing.

Crow, North Fork 130 miles from Lake Koronis near Paynesville to the Mississippi River. Family river, shallow. Few towns, mostly agricultural.

Crow Wing* 115 miles from 10th Crow Wing Lake near Akeley to the Mississippi. Family lakes and river. Scenic, mostly forest, clear water, sandy bottom.

Des Moines* 70 miles from Talcot Lake north of Worthington to Iowa. Family river. Scenic from Windom to Jackson, mostly agricultural.

Kettle* 55 miles from Minnesota 27 near Moose Lake to the St. Croix River. Experienced river to Banning State Park. Whitewater from Banning to St. Croix River. Very scenic, densely forested banks, primitive. Campsites in state forests and parks.

Little Fork 140 miles from Cook to the Rainy River. Experienced to whitewater. Primitive, almost no towns, forest & farmland, good fishing.

Minnesota* 368 miles from Big Stone to the Mississippi River. Family river. Wide, good current in places. Large barges near Twin Cities, mostly agricultural.

Mississippi* 752 miles from Lake Itasca to the Iowa border. Family river going through some lakes. Rapids generally easy, except at Sauk Rapids. Wilderness at headwaters to wide, large, busy at Twin Cities. Caution to be exercised around motorized traffic, especially near locks and dams. Good fishing in some locations.

Pine 52 miles from Backus to the Mississippi River. Family river. Clear water, hardwood and pine forest.

Red Lake 195 miles from Lower Red Lake to East Grand Forks. Family river. Forest, bluffs, agricultural.

Root 111 miles from Highway 75 near Chatfield to the Mississippi River. Family river. Forest, scenic bluffs, Root River Trail.

Rum* 145 miles from Mille Lacs Lake to the Mississippi River. Experienced from Lake Onamia to Princeton. Good fishing, few towns. Family river from Princeton to Anoka. Dense hardwood forest.

St. Croix* 150 miles from the state border east of Sandstone to the Mississippi River. Family through whitewater river. National Scenic Riverway, wilderness-like. Mostly forest and rock bluffs, broad and placid in south. Campsites in state parks.

St. Louis 94 miles from U. S. 53 to Cloquet. Family to experienced. Mostly primitive, forest, good fishing.

Snake 85 miles from County Road 26 west of Sandstone to the St. Croix River. Experienced to whitewater, many rapids. Mostly primitive, dense forest.

Straight 34 miles from U. S. 14 to Faribault. Family river. Narrow and quiet through wooded farmland, good day trip.

Vermillion 39 miles from Lake Vermillion to Crane Lake. Family to whitewater river. Mostly forest. Campsites.

Zumbro 115 miles from Rochester to the Mississippi River. Family river. Scenic, deep valley, high limestone bluffs, dense forest.

Things To Know About Minnesota State Parks

- There are 70 state parks in all regions of the state.
- State Park Permits are required on each vehicle entering Minnesota State Parks. They are available at a park or the DNR Building, St. Paul (see fee schedule below listing).
- Hours are from 8:00 a. m. to 10:00 p. m. 365 days a year.
- Camping and lodging reservations can be made 24 hours a day, seven days a week, by calling The Connection at 612-922-9000 in the Twin Cities, or 1-800-246-CAMP fee charged).
- Handicapped accessibility. All parks are working to make facilities accessible to people of all abilities. Call the specific state park you are planning to visit for up-to-date information on accessibility.

• Pets are welcome in state parks but must be kept on a leash of not more than six feet and must be personally attended at all times. No pets, other than hearing or seeing eye dogs, are allowed in state park buildings or on beaches.
• Not Allowed: Drugs or alcohol; metal detectors, fireworks, hunting with out permission from the DNR, visible weapons.

Minnesota State Park Campgrounds
• All toilets are flush toilets and both showers and toilets are handicapped accessible unless specified.
• Dump stations summer only unless specified.
• Phones means public pay phones.
• All trails lengths listed in miles.
• "Near" means within 10 miles of the park.

Afton (Afton) 612-436-5391 (1,702 acres) 24 backpack sites, 1 canoe in, 2 group camp, picnic shelter, swimming, fishing, volleyball, horseshoes, visitor center, interpretive exhibits, firewood sales, sliding, warming house, phones. Trails: .75 (miles) self-guided trail, 20 hiking, 4 bicycle, 5 horse, 19 ski.

Banning (Tower) 218-245-2668 (6,237 a.) 34 drive-in sites, 11 electric, 50' RV limit, 1 backpack site, 4 canoe in, 2 handicapped, showers/toilets, camping cabin rental, picnic, fishing, boat access, playground, visitor center, summer naturalist, interpretive exhibits, historic site, firewood sales, canoe shuttle near, waterfall, phones. Trails: 1.8 self-guided, 17 hiking, 2 horse, 12 ski, 6 snowmobile.

Bear Head Lake (Tower) 218-365-7229 (4,375 a.) 73 drive-in sites, 53' RV limit, 5 backpack, 1 boat in, 4 handicapped, showers/toilets, year around dump station, 1 group camp, guest house, picnic, shelter, swimming, fishing (handicapped), boat access, no water skiing, boat speed restrictions, boat/canoe rentals, firewood/ice sales, phones. Trails: 17 hiking, 0.4 handicapped, 9 ski, 1 snowmobile.

Beaver Creek Valley (Caledonia) 507-724-2107 (1,214 a.) 42 drive-in sites, 16 electric, 55' RV limit, 6 walk-in, non- handicapped showers, dump station, 1 group camp, picnic, shelter, fishing, volleyball, playground, warming house, interp. exhibits, firewood sales, phones. Trails: 8 hiking, .05 snowmobile.

Big Stone Lake (Ortonville) 320-839-3663 (1,118 a.) 40 drive-in, 10 electric, 50' RV limit, showers/toilets, dump station, 1 group camp, picnic, swimming, fishing, boat access, horseshoes, firewood sales, phones. Trails: 1.5 hiking, 305 snowmobile.

Blue Mounds (Luverne) 507-283-4892 (2,028 a.) 73 drive-in, 40 electric, 50' RV limit, 14 walk-in, showers/toilets, dump station, 1 group camp, picnic, shelter, swimming, fishing, carry in boat access, no motors, volley-ball, horseshoes, playground, visitor center, summer naturalist, interp. exhibits, historic site, canoe rental, firewood/ice sales, observation tower, gift shop, phones.   Trails: 13 hiking, 7 snowmobile.

Buffalo River (Moorhead) 218-498-2124 (1,367 a.) 44 drive-in, 8 electric, 50' RV limit, 44 handicapped, showers/toilets, summer dump station, 1 group camp, picnic, shelter, swimming, fishing, horseshoes, warming house, visitor center, summer naturalist, interp. exhibits, firewood & ice sales, phones.   Trails: 1 self-guided, 12 hiking, 6 ski.

Camden (Marshall) 507-865-4530 (1,745 a.) 80 drive-in (2 drive-through), 29 electric, 45' RV limit, 2 handicapped, 12 horse camp sites (max. 50), showers/toilets, dump station, 1 group camp, picnic, shelter, swimming, fishing (handicapped), boat access, electric motors only, volley-ball, horseshoes, warming house, summer naturalist, historic site, canoe rental, firewood/ice sales, phones.   Trails: 15 hiking, 4.25 mountain bike, 10 horse, 6 ski, 1.3 skate-ski, 8 snowmobile.

Carley (Plainview) 507-534-3400 (204 a.) 20 drive-in, 30' RV limit, 1 group camp, picnic, fishing, playground, firewood sales, phones.   Trails: 1 self-guided, 5 hiking, 6 ski.

Cascade River (Grand Marais) 218-387-1543 (2,813 a.) 40 drive-in (3 drive through), 35' RV limit, 5 backpack, non-handicapped showers/toilets, dump station, 2 group camps, picnic, shelter, fishing, warming house, firewood/ice sales, waterfall, phones. Trails: 18 hiking, 17 ski, 2 snowmobile.

Charles A. Lindbergh (Little Falls) 320-632-9050 (330 a.) 38 drive-in, 15 electric, 50' RV limit, 2 canoe in, showers/toilets, dump station, 1 group camp, picnic, shelter, fishing, boat access, volleyball, horseshoes, playground, warming house visitor center, historic site, snowshoe rental, firewood sales, phones.   Trails: 6 hiking, 5.5 ski.

Crow Wing (Brainerd) 218-829-8022 (2,042 a.) 61 drive-in, 12 electric, 45' RV limit, 1 boat in, 2 handicapped, showers/toilets, dump station, 1 group camp, camping cabin rental, picnic, shelter, fishing, boat access, inquire about boat restrictions, volleyball, horseshoes, playground, summer naturalist, interp. exhibits, historic, boat/canoe rental, firewood/ice sales, phones.   Trails: 0.5 self-guided, 18 hiking, 6 ski, 6 snowmobile.

Cuyuna Country Rec. Area (Brainerd) (5,000 a.) In planning/acquisition stage.

Father Hennepin (Isle) 320-676-8763 (318 a.) 103 drive-in, 41 electric, 60' RV limit, 4 handicapped, showers/toilets, dump station, 1 group camp, picnic, shelter, swimming, fishing (handicapped), boat access, volleyball, playground, firewood/ice sales, phones.   Trails: 4 hiking, 12 bicycle near camp, 0.25 handicapped, 1.5 snowmobile.

Flandrau (New Ulm) 507-354-3519 (805 a.) 90 drive-in (2 drive through), 35 electric, 66' RV limit, showers/toilets, dump station, 1 group center, picnic, shelter, swimming, fishing, carry in boat access, volleyball, horseshoes, playground, warming house, historic site, snowshoe/ski rental, firewood sales, phones. Trails: 1 self-guided, 8 hiking, 8 ski, 1.3 snowmobile.

Forestville/Mystery Cave (Wykoff) 507-3582-5111 (2,691 a.) 73 drive-in, 23 electric, 50' RV limit, 80 horse camp sites (480 max.), showers/toilets, dump station, 2 group camps, picnic, shelter, fishing, warming house, summer naturalist, interp. exhibits, historic site, tours (additional fee), firewood sales, phones. Trails: 1 self-guided, 16 hiking, 14 horse, 10 ski, 5.5 snowmobile.

Ft. Ridgely (Fairfax) 507-426-7840 (584 a.) 39 drive-in (1 drive through), 8 electric, 60' RV limit, 3 walk in, 20 horse camp (80 max.), non-handicapped showers/toilets, dump station nearby, 1 group camp, picnic, shelter, fishing, volleyball, horseshoes, playground, sliding hill, warming house, visitor center, interp. exhibits, historic site, firewood/ice sales, golf course, golf rental, phones. Trails: 1 self-guided, 11 hiking, 7 horse, 3 ski, 7 snowmobile.

Ft. Snelling (St. Paul) 612-725-2390 (3,300 a.) Handicapped flush toilets, picnic, shelter, swimming, fishing (handicapped), boat access, electric motors only, volleyball, playground, visitor center, year around naturalist, interp. exhibits, canoe rental, golf course, phones. Trails: 18 hiking, 5 bicycle, 18 ski, 9 skate-ski.

Franz Jevne (Birchdale) (118 a.) 12 drive-in, 3 walk in, fishing, boat access. Trails: 2 hiking.

Frontenac (Lake City) 612-345-3401 (2,773 a.) 58 drive-in, 19 electric, 46' RV limit, 6 walk in, 40 handicapped, showers/toilets, dump station, 1 group camp, picnic, shelter, fishing, boat access near, playground near, sliding hill, warming house, summer naturalist, interp. exhibits, historic site, firewood sales, canoe shuttle near, excursion boat near, phones. Trails: 2.5 self guided, 15.4 hiking, 6 ski, 6 ski-skate, 8 snowmobile.

George Crosby Manitou (Finland) 218-226-3539 (5,259 a.) 21 backpack, fishing, carry in boat access, electric motors only, no water skiing, waterfall. Trails: 24 hiking.

Glacial Lakes (Starbuck) 320-239-2860 (1,755 a.) 39 drive-in (1 drive through), 14 electric, 45' RV limit, 4 backpack, 3 boat in, 2 handicapped, 3 horse camp (45 max.), showers/toilets, dump station, 3 group camp, picnic, shelter, swimming, fishing, boat access, electric motors only, volleyball, playground, interp. exhibits, boat/canoe/snowshoe rental, firewood sales, phones. Trails: 0.5 self-guided, 16 hiking, 11 horse, 6 ski, 11 snowmobile.

Glendalough (Fergus Falls) 218-864-5403 (1,924 a.) 26 CT sites, handicapped showers/toilets, 4 camper cabins, picnic shelter. Fishing, inquire about boat access and restrictions. Trails: 0.75 self-guided, 0.5 handicapped, 8 hiking, 6 ski.

Gooseberry Falls (Two Harbors) 218-834-3855 (1,662 a.) 70 drive-in (3 drive through), 40' RV limit, 1 kayak, showers/toilets, dump station, 3 group camps, picnic, shelter, fishing, visitor center, summer naturalist, interp. exhibits, historic site, snowshoe/ski rental near, firewood/ice sales, gift shop, waterfall, phones. Trails: 18 hiking, 10 mountain bike, 15 ski, 3 snowmobile.

Grand Portage (Grand Portage) 218-475-2360 (300 a.) Picnic, fishing, year around naturalist, waterfalls, boardwalk. Trails: 0.75 hiking, 0.5 handicapped.

Great River Bluffs (rural Winona) 507-643-6849 (2,835a.) 31 drive-in, 60' RV limit, 5 bike-in, 31 handicapped access., handicap toilets/showers, 1 group camp, picnic, playground, sliding hill, firewood, phones. Trails: 3 self-guided, 6.5 hiking, 9.2 ski, 3 skate-ski.

Hayes Lake (Roseau) 218-425-7504 (2,950 a.) 35 drive-in, 9 electric, 40' RV limit, 2 backpack, 1 handicapped, showers/toilets, dump station, 1 group camp, camping cabin rental, picnic, swimming, fishing (handi-capped), boat access, electric motors only, no water skiing, horseshoes, playground, sliding hill near, interp. exhibits, historic site, firewood sales, gift shop, phones. Trails: 1.5 self-guided, 13 hiking, 5 mt. bike, 3 horse, 6 ski, 6 snowmobile.

Hill Annex Mine (Grand Rapids) 218-247-7215 (635 a.) Handicapped toilets, picnic, shelter, playground, visitor center, summer naturalist, interp. exhibits, historic site, tours (additional fee), gift shop, observation tower.

Interstate (Taylor's Falls) 612-465-5711 (293 a.) 37 drive-in, 22 elec-tric, 34' RV limit, 1 handicapped, showers/toilets, dump station, 1 group camp, picnic, shelter, fishing, boat access, no water skiing, boat speed restrictions, volleyball, visitor center, summer naturalist, interp. exhibits, historic site, firewood/ice sales, canoe shuttle, excursion boat, gift shop, phones. Trails: 1.5 self-guided, 4 hiking, 0.5 handicapped.

Itasca (N. of Park Rapids) 218-266-2114 (32,690 a.) 198 drive-in, 100 electric, 60' RV limit, 11 backpack, 11 cart in, 2 handicapped, showers/toi-lets, dump station, 1 group camp, 1 group center, camping cabin rental, lodge/motel/cabin rental, picnic, shelter, swimming, fishing (handi-capped), boat access, no water skiing, boat speed restrictions, volleyball, warming house, visitor center, year around naturalist, interp. exhibits, his-toric site, boat/ bike/ canoe/snowshoe rental, firewood/ice sales, restau-rant, observation tower, excursion boat, gift shop, phones. Trails: 3.25 self-guiding, 33 hiking, 6.5 bicycle, 31 ski, 10 skate-ski, 31 snowmobile.

Jay Cooke (Duluth) 218-384-4610 (8,818 a.) 80 drive-in (1 drive through), 21 electric, 60' RV limit, 4 backpack, 3 walk in, 10 handicapped, showers/toilets, dump station, 2 group camps, picnic, shelter, fishing, inquire about boat restrictions, volleyball, horseshoes, playground, warming house, visitor center, naturalist, interp. exhibits, historic site, snowshoe rental, firewood/ice sales, gift shop, waterfall, phones. Trails: 50 hiking, 5 bicycle, 8 mt. bike, 8 horse, 32 ski, 8 skate-ski, 12 snowmobile.

John Latsch (Winona) 507-932-3007 (1,534 a.) 10 walk in sites, picnic. Trails: 0.5 hiking.

Judge C. R. Magney (Grand Marais) 218-387-2929 (4,514 a.) 33 drive-in, 45' RV limit, 1 backpack, showers/toilets, picnic, fishing, interp. exhibits, firewood sales, waterfall, phones. Trails: 7 hiking, 5 ski.

Kilen Woods (Jackson) 507-662-6258 (228 a.) 33 drive-in (3 drive through), 11 electric, 50' RV limit, 3 boat in, 4 walk in, showers, dump station, 1 group camp, picnic, shelter, fishing, carry in boat access, inquire about boating restrictions, volleyball, horseshoes, sliding hill, warming house, visitor center, summer naturalist, interp. exhibits, firewood sales, observation tower. Trails: 5 hiking, 1.5 ski, 3.5 snowmobile.

Lac Qui Parle (Montevideo) 320-752-4736 (530 a.) 50 drive-in (1 drive through), 22 electric, 50' RV limit, 5 backpack 11 walk in, 5 horse camp (50 max.), handicapped showers, non-handicapped flush toilets, dump station, 3 group camp, picnic, shelter, swimming, fishing, boat access, warming house, historic site, firewood sales, canoe shuttle near, phones. Trails: 6 hiking, 5 horse, 5 ski.

Lake Bemidji (Bemidji) 218-755-3843 (1,688 a.) 98 drive-in (4 drive through), 43 electric, 50' RV limit, 3 handicapped, showers/toilets, dump station, 2 group camp, 1 group center, picnic, shelter, swimming, fishing, boat access, volleyball, warming house, visitor center, year around naturalist, interp. exhibits, historic site, boat & snowshoe rental, firewood/ice sales, golf near, excursion boat, gift shop, boardwalk, phones. Trails: 1 self-guided, 14 hiking, 1 bicycle, 5 mt. bike, 9 ski, 1 skate-ski, 3 snowmobile.

Lake Bronson (Lake Bronson) 218-754-2200 (2,983 a.) 194 drive-in, 35 electric, 50' RV limit, 1 handicapped, showers/toilets, dump station, 1 group camp, picnic, shelter, swimming, fishing (handicapped), boat access, boat speed restriction (inquire at park), volleyball, playground, summer naturalist, boat/canoe/snowshoe rental, firewood/ice sales, observation tower, phones. Trails: 1 self-guided, 14 hiking, 5 mt. bike, 7 ski, 3 snowmobile.

Lake Carlos (Alexandria) 320-852-7200 (1,395 a.) 126 drive-in, 68 electric, 50' RV limit, 2 walk in, 6 horse camp (30 max.), shower/toilets, dump station, 2 group camps, 1 group center, picnic, shelter, swimming, fishing, boat access, horseshoes, warming house, visitor center, summer naturalist, interp. exhibits, snowshoe rental, firewood sales, gift shop, phones. Trails: 2.8 self-guided, 12.6 hiking, 8 horse, 5 ski, 9 snowmobile.

Lake Louise (LeRoy) 507-324-5249 (1,168 a.) 22 drive-in, 11 electric, 60' RV limit, 6 horse camp (50 max.), non-handicapped showers, dump station, 1 group camp, picnic, shelter, swimming, fishing, carry in boat access, electric motors only, no water skiing, firewood sales, phones. Trails: 1 self-guided, 11.6 hiking, 9.7 horse, 2.2 ski, 9.3 snowmobile.

Lake Maria (Monticello) 612-878-2325 (1,590 a.) 16 backpack, toilets, 2 group camps, camping cabin rental, picnic, shelter, fishing (handi-capped), boat access (inquire about restrictions), volleyball, skating rink, warming house, visitor center, naturalist program, interp. exhibits, boat/canoe rental, firewood sales. Trails: 1 self-guided, 14 hiking, 6 horse, 14 ski, 2 skate-ski.

Lake Shetek (Slayton) 507-763-3256 (1,109 a.) 98 drive-in (1 drive through), 67 electric, 60' RV limit, 10 walk in, 2 handicapped, showers/toilets, dump station, 2 group camps, 1 group center, camping cabin rental, picnic, shelter, swimming, fishing, boat access, volleyball, horseshoes, playground, warming house, visitor center, summer naturalist, interp. exhibits, boat/canoe rental, firewood/ice sales, observation tower, gift shop, phones. Trails: 1 self-guided, 8 hiking, 2.8 ski, 5 snowmobile.

Maplewood (Pelican Rapids) 218-863-8383 (9,250 a.) 60 drive-in, 35' RV limit, 3 backpack, 6 horse camp (300 max.), showers/toilets, year around dump station 1 group camp, guest house rental, picnic, swimming, fishing, boat access (inquire about restrictions), interp. exhibits, boat/canoe rental, firewood sales, phones. Trails: 1.2 self-guided, 25 hiking, 20 horse, 13 ski, 15 snowmobile.

McCarthy Beach (Hibbing) 218-254-2411 (2,311 a.) 86 drive-in, 50' RV limit, 3 walk in, 1 handicapped, showers/toilets, dump station, 1 group camp, picnic, shelter, swimming, fishing, boat access (inquire about restrictions), horseshoes, summer naturalist, interp. exhibits, boat/canoe/motor rental, firewood sales, restaurant near, grocery store near, phones. Trails: 18 hiking, 17 mt. bike, 8 horse, 5 ski, 12 snowmobile.

Mille Lacs Kathio (Onamia) 320-532-3523 (10,585 a.) 70 drive-in, 60' RV limit, 20 horse (80 max.), showers/toilets, dump station, 1 group camp, picnic, swimming, fishing, boat access, playground, sliding hill, warming house, visitor center, year around naturalist, interp. exhibits, historic site, boat/canoe/snowshoe/ski rental, firewood/ice sales, observation tower, phones. Trails: .08 self-guided, 35 hiking, 25 horse, 19.6 ski, 19 snowmobile.

Minneopa (Mankato) 507-625-4388 (1,145 a.) 62 drive-in, 6 electric, 60' RV limit, 2 handicapped, showers/toilets, 1 group camp, picnic, shelter, fishing, carry in boat access, volleyball, horseshoes, visitor center, interp. exhibits, historic site, firewood sales, waterfall, phones. Trails: 4.5 hiking, 4 ski.

MN Valley Rec. Area (Jordan) 612-492-6400 (5,490 a.) 25 drive-in, 50' RV limit, 8 walk in, 1 group camp, picnic, shelter, fishing, boat access, warming house, firewood sales. Trails: 4.5 self-guided, 46.5 hiking, 6.5 bicycle, 35 mt. bike, 35 horse, 5 ski, 35 snowmobile.

Monson Lake (Sunburg) 320-366-3797 (187 a.) 20 drive-in, 60' RV limit, picnic, shelter, fishing, boat access, historic site, firewood sales. Trail: 1 hiking.

Moose Lake (Moose Lake) 218-485-5420 (1,194 a.) 18 drive-in, 60' RV limit, 1 handicapped, showers/toilets, 1 group camp, picnic, swimming, fishing (handicapped), boat access (inquire about restrictions), volleyball, horseshoes, playground, interp. exhibits, boat/canoe rental, firewood sales. Trails. 4 hiking, 7 ski, 2 snowmobile.

Myre-Big Island (Albert Lea) 507-373-5084 (1,648 a.) 99 drive-in, 32 electric, 60' RV limit, 2 canoe in, 2 bike in, 2 handicapped, toilets, dump station, 1 group camp, 1 group center, picnic, shelter, fishing, warming house, interp. exhibits, canoe rental, firewood/ice sales, phones. Trails: 8.25 self-guided, 16 hiking, 7 mt. bike, 8 ski, 7 snowmobile.

Nerstrand-Big Woods (Northfield) 507-334-8848 (2,825 a.) 55 drive-in, 28 electric, 50' RV limit, 13 walk in, 1 handicapped, showers/toilets, dump station, 1 group camp, picnic, shelter, volleyball, horseshoes, playground, warming house, visitor center, year around naturalist, interp. exhibits, firewood sales, canoe shuttle near, waterfall, phones. Trails: 2 self-guided, 14 hiking, 8 ski, 5 skate-ski, 5 snowmobile.

Old Mill (Warren) 218-437-8174 (406 a.) 26 drive-in, 10 electric, 67' RV limit, showers/toilets, 1 group camp, picnic, shelter, swimming, fishing, carry in boat access, volleyball, horseshoes, playground, sliding hill, skating rink, warming house, summer naturalist, interp. exhibits, historic site, snowshoe/ski rental, firewood/ice sales, phones. Trails: 0.7 self-guided, 7 hiking, 6.5 ski, 0.5 snowmobile.

Rice Lake (Owatonna) 507-451-7406 (1,056 a.) 42 drive-in, 16 electric, 42' RV limit, 5 canoe in, 5 walk in, 1 handicapped, showers/toilets, 1 group camp, picnic, shelter, swimming, fishing, boat access (inquire about restrictions), horseshoes, playground, warming house, summer naturalist, interp. exhibits, canoe rentals, firewood/ice sales, phones. Trails: 4.3 hiking, 0.5 handicapped, 4 ski, 2.5 snowmobile.

St. Croix (Hinckley) 612-384-6591 (34,037 a.) 213 drive-in, 42 electric, 60' RV limit, 2 backpack, 13 canoe in, 4 walk in, 6 handicapped, 50 horse camp (100 max.), showers/toilets, dump station, 8 group camps, 3 group centers, guest house rental, picnic, shelter, swimming, fishing, boat access (inquire about restrictions), volleyball, horseshoes, playground, warming house, visitor center, year around naturalist, interp. exhibits, historic site, canoe/bike rental, firewood/ice sales, canoe shuttle, observation tower, gift shop, grocery store, phones. Trails: 1.5 self-guided, 127 hiking, 5.5 bicycle, 24 mt. bike, 75 horse, 1.5 handicapped, 21 ski, 80 snowmobile.

Sakatah Lake (Waterville) 507-362-4438 (842 a.) 63 drive-in, 14 electric, 60′ RV limit, 1 boat in, 4 bike in, showers/toilets, dump station, 2 group camps, picnic, shelter, swimming, fishing, boat access (inquire about restrictions), volleyball, horseshoes, playground, warming house, visitor center, summer naturalist, interp. exhibits, boat/canoe rental, firewood/ice sales, phones. Trails: 5 hiking, 3 bicycle, 5 ski, 3 snowmobile.

Savanna Portage (McGregor) 218-426-3271 (15,818 a.) 64 drive-in (4 drive through), 18 electric, 45′ RV limit, 7 backpack, 1 canoe in, 3 handicapped, showers/toilets, dump station, 1 group camp, camping cabin rental, picnic, shelter, swimming, fishing, boat access (inquire about restrictions), volleyball, horseshoes, playground, warming house, summer naturalist, interp. exhibits, historic site, boat/canoe/motor rental, firewood/ice sales, gift shop, boardwalk, phones. Trails: 1.4 self-guided, 17 hiking, 10 mt. bike, 16 ski, 2 skate-ski, 60 snowmobile.

Scenic (Big Ford) 218-743-3362 (3,560 a.) 117 drive-in (20 drive through), 20 electric, 50′ RV limit, 6 backpack, 4 bike in, 2 handicapped, showers/toilets, dump station, 1 group camp, guest house rental, picnic, shelter, swimming, fishing (handicapped), boat access, no water skiing, speed limit restrictions, warming house, visitor center, summer naturalist, interp. exhibits, boat/canoe/snowshoe rental, firewood/ice sales, canoe shuttle near, observation tower, gift shop, boardwalk, phones. Trails: 1 self-guided, 14 hiking, 2 bicycle, 10 ski, 12 snowmobile.

Schoolcraft (Deer River) 218-566-2383 (295 a.) 30 drive-in, 35′ RV limit, 2 canoe in, 1 group camp, picnic, fishing, boat access, boat/canoe rental, firewood sales, phones. Trails: 0.5 self-guided, 1.5 hiking.

Sibley (New London) 612-354-2055 (2,926 a.) 138 drive-in (9 drive through), 52 electric, 55′ RV limit, 2 handicapped, 5 horse camp (50 max.), showers/toilets, dump station, 1 group camp, 1 group center, picnic, shelter, swimming, fishing (handicapped), boat access, volleyball, horseshoes, sliding hill, warming house, visitor center, year around naturalist, interp. exhibits, historic site, boat/canoe/bike rental, firewood/ice sales, observation tower, gift shop, grocery store, phones.

Soudan Underground Mine (Soudan) 218-753-2245 (1,300 a.) Picnic, fishing, boat access, visitor center, year around naturalist, interp. exhibits, historic site, tour (additional fee), gift shop. Trails: 0.3 self-guided, 5 hiking, 3 snowmobile.

Split Rock Creek (Ihlen) 507-348-7908 (400 a.) 28 drive-in, 19 electric, 52′ RV limit, 6 walk in, 2 handicapped, showers, toilets, year around dump station, 1 group camp, picnic, shelter, swimming, fishing (handicapped), boat access, no water skiing and speed restrictions, volleyball, horseshoes, playground, sliding hill, warming house, visitor center, interp. exhibits, historic site, snowshoe rental, firewood sales, phones. Trails: 4.5 self-guided, 4.5 hiking, 0.5 handicapped, 2 ski, 1.5 snowmobile.

Split Rock Lighthouse (Two Harbors) 218-226-3065 (1,987 a.) 4 backpack, 20 cart in, 2 handicapped, showers/toilets, picnic, shelter, fishing, warming house, visitor center, summer naturalist, interp. exhibits, historic, tours (additional fee), firewood/ice sales, gift shop, waterfall, phones. Trails: 6 self-guided, 12 hiking, 6 mt. bike, 8 ski.

Temperance River (Grand Marais) 218-663-7476 (539 a.) 55 drive-in (4 drive through), 18 electric, 50′ RV limit, 3 cart in, showers/toilets, picnic, fishing, carry in boat access, playground, firewood sales, canoe shuttle near, waterfall, phones. Trails: 1 self-guided, 8 hiking, 15 ski, 8 skate-ski, 5 snowmobile.

Tettegouche (Silver Bay) 218-226-3539 (9,346 a.) 28 drive-in, 60′RV limit, 6 walk in, showers/toilets, cabin rental, picnic, shelter, fishing, carry in boat access, electric motors only, no water skiing, warming house, visitor center, interp. exhibits, historic site, canoe/snowshoe rental, firewood/ice sales, waterfall, phones. Trails: 2 self-guided, 23 hiking, 1.5 mt. bike, 15.5 ski, 4 skate-ski, 12 snowmobile.

Upper Sioux Agency (Granite Falls) 320-564-4777 (1,280 a.) 30 drive-in, 45′ RV limit, 45 horse camp, 1 group camp, picnic, shelter, fishing, boat access (inquire about restrictions), volleyball, horseshoes, playground, sliding hill, warming house, visitor center, interp. exhibits, historic site, firewood sales. Trails: 1 self-guided, 19 hiking, 16.5 horse, 16.5 snowmobile.

Whitewater (St. Charles) 507-932-3007 (2,700 a.) 106 drive-in (5 drive through), 40′ RV limit, 4 walk in, 32 handicapped, showers/toilets, dump station, 1 group camp, 1 group center, picnic, shelter, swimming, fishing (handicapped), volleyball, horseshoes, visitor center, year around naturalist, interp. exhibits, snowshoe rental, firewood/ice sales, gift shop, phones. Trails: 2 self-guided, 10 hiking, 5 ski.

Wild River (Almelund) 612-583-2125 (6,803 a.) 96 drive-in (2 drive through), 17 electric, 60′ RV limit, 8 backpack, 8 canoe in, 2 handicapped, 20 horse camp (120 max.), showers/toilets, dump station, 1 group camp, guest house rental, picnic, shelter, fishing, boat access (inquire about restrictions), playground near, warming house, visitor center, year around naturalist, interp. exhibits, historic site, canoe/ski/snowshoe rental, firewood/ice sales, canoe shuttle, gift shop, grocery store near, phones. Trails: 2.7 self-guided, 35 hiking, 18 horse, 35 ski.

William O'Brien (Marine on St. Croix) 612-433-0500 (1,403 a.) 125 drive-in, 62 electric, 60' RV limit, 2 walk in, 7 handicapped, showers/toilets, dump station, 4 group camps, picnic, shelter, swimming, fishing, boat access, no water skiing and speed restrictions, volleyball, horseshoes, playground, warming house, visitor center, year around naturalist, interp. exhibits, canoe rental, firewood/ice sales, canoe shuttle, phones. Trails: 1.5 self-guided, 12 hiking, 2 bicycle, 11.5 ski, 10 skate-ski, 2 snowmobile.

Zippel Bay (Williams) 218-783-6252 (2,906 a.) 57 drive-in, 30' RV limit, showers, dump station, 1 group camp, picnic, shelter, swimming, fishing (handicapped), boat access, volleyball, historic site, firewood/ice sales, canoe shuttle near, phones. Trails: 6 hiking, 6 horse, 3.5 ski, 5 snowmobile.

Minnesota State Park Fees 2000 (current as of 6/99)

Vehicle Permits

Annual Permit	$ 20
Second Vehicle Permit	$ 15
Minnesota Handicapped Annual Permit (MN handicapped plates or certificate)	$ 12
Daily Permit (Same rate for all vehicles.)	$ 4
Daily Group Permit (10 permit minimum, 24 hour notice. Check at park office for details.)	$ 2

Camping

Semi-Modern Site (with showers)	$ 12
Electric Hookup (where available)	add $ 2.50
Rustic Site (no showers)	$ 8
Backpack or Canoe Site	$ 7

Half-priced camping at semi-modern and rustic sites is available Sunday through Thursday for Minnesota resident seniors or handicapped campers.

Lodging

Fees for lodging vary with the facility to be rented. Camper cabins fees are the same regardless of the park in which the cabin is located.

Camper Cabin	$ 27.50
Camper Cabins (with electricity)	$ 30
Reservations	
2000 Reservation Fee	$ 7

DNR Information Center, 500 Lafayette Road, St. Paul, MN 55155-4040. Twin Cities metro area: 612-296-6157. MN toll free: 1-800-657-3929
Source: Minnesota Department of Natural Resources

In 1998, Minnesota State Parks hosted a record 8,622,965 visitors.

National Forest Campgrounds

The information in this guide was collected in September, 1999. You may want to call in advance to confirm dates and facilities.

Reservation Information

Reservations accepted for all National Forest Service campgrounds in the nation by calling toll free 1-800-280-CAMP, 1-877-444-6777, or TTY 1-800-879-4496 ($8.65 reservation fee charge). Reservations are also accepted for Army Corps of Engineers sites (no reservation fee).

Chippewa National Forest

Cass Lake 56633, 218-335-8600, fax 218-335-8637

Established in 1908, the Chippewa National Forest encompasses 1.6 million acres with about 666,000 acres managed by its 150 employees. There are over 700 lakes, 920 miles of streams, 150,000 acres of wetlands, and over 160 miles of trail. It "boasts of being home to the largest breeding population of bald eagles in the lower 48 states."

Facilities vary from flush toilets and showers to rustic campgrounds with vault toilets and hand pumps. Each campsite has a picnic table, fireplace, tent pad and parking spot. Fees listed are for the summer recreation period when full services are provided, usually early May to October. At other times fees at some sites are reduced or not charged.

There are over 400 dispersed recreation sites which are free of charge with limited facilities. Facilities listed below have a boating site, fishing and drinking water unless stated otherwise.

Cass Lake Loop. Fee $14. 23 camp units (incl. extra long), flush toilets & showers, dump station, picnic, swimming, interp. trail, open year around.

Chippewa Loop (Cass Lake). Fee $16. 46 camp units (incl. extra long), flush toilets & showers, handicapped access, dump station, picnic, swimming, interp. trail, reservations*.

Clubhouse Lake (E of Marcell). Fee $12. 47 camp units, vault toilets, handicapped accessible, swimming, open year around, reservations*.

Cut Foot Sioux Information Center (N of L. Winnibigoshish). Interp. trail, historical site. Cut Foot Horse Camp $10. 23 camp units, vault toilets.

Deer Lake (on L. Winnibigoshish). Fee $12. 48 camp units, swimming, hiking, open year around, reservations*.

East Seelye Bay (on L. Winnibigoshish). Fee $12. 13 camp units, vault toilets, picnic, swimming, hiking.

Knutson Dam (Cass Lake). Fee $12. 14 camp units (incl. extra long), vault toilets, handicapped accessible.

Mable Lake (W of Remer). Fee $12. 22 camp units, picnic, swimming.

Middle Pigeon (N of L. Winnibigoshish). 3 camp units.

Mosomo Point (on L. Winnibigoshish). Fee $12. 23 camp units, vault toilets, hiking, historical site, open year around.

Noma Lake (Wirt). Fee $10. 14 camp units, vault toilets, picnic, open year around.

North Star (Marcell). Fee $12. 21 camp units, vault toilets, handicapped accessible, swimming.

Norway Beach (Cass Lake). Fee $14. 55 camp units (incl. extra long), flush toilets, dump station, picnic, swimming, interp. trail, reservations*.

Nushka Group Site (Cass Lake). Fee $40/50, reservation required, 218-335-8600. 2 camp sites for groups up to 60, vault toilets, picnic, no boat ramp.

O-Ne-Gum-E (N of L. Winnibigoshish). Fee $12. 46 camp units (incl. extra long), vault toilets, handicapped accessible, historical site, hiking, reservations*.

Plug Hat Point (on L. Winnibigoshish). 13 camp units, picnic, historical site.

Richard's Townsite (on L. Winnibigoshish). 7 camp units.

Six Mile Lake (S of L. Winnibigoshish). Fee $10. 11 camp units, vault toilets.

South Pike Bay (Cass Lake). Fee $12. 24 camp units (incl. extra long), vault toilets, handicapped accessible, picnic, swimming.

Star Island (Cass Lake). No fee. 3 camp units, vault toilets, hiking, no boat ramp.

Stony Point (Walker). Fee $16. 44 camp units (incl. extra long), vault toilets & showers, handicapped accessible, dump station, picnic, swimming, open year around, reservations*.

Tamarac Point (on L. Winnibigoshish). Fee $12. 33 camp units (incl. extra long), vault toilets, boat ramp, open year around.

Wanaki Loop (Cass Lake). Fee $14. 46 camp units (incl. extra long), flush toilets & showers, dump station, picnic, swimming, interp. trail.

Webster Lake (S of Blackduck). Fee $10. 24 camp units, handicapped accessible, picnic.

West Seeyle Bay (on L. Winnibigoshish). Fee $10. 22 camp units, hiking.

Williams Narrows (on L. Winnibigoshish). Fee $12. 17 camp units, picnic, swimming.

Winnie. Fee $12. 40 camp units, vault toilets, picnic.

Source: Chippewa National Forest brochures.

Superior National Forest

Duluth 55801, 218-720-5324, TTY 218-720-5433

This 3 million acre forest spans 150 miles of the Canadian border. One third of the Forest is the Boundary Waters Canoe Area Wilderness (BWCAW). 695 square miles of the forest is surface water with 1,300 miles of cold water streams and 950 miles of warm water streams. It is home to the last stronghold of the timber wolf in the lower 48 states (300-400 wolves). It's 27 campgrounds have over 500 campsites plus more than 250 primitive backcountry sites. There are over 2,000 miles of hiking/mountain bike trails.

The BWCAW has 1 million acres, 1500 miles of canoe routes, over 2000 lakes and streams, and nearly 2,200 designated campsites.

All Superior National Forest toilets are the vault type (privvy), electricity is available at only two campgrounds (§). Campsites contain a picnic table, fire grate, and tent pad, and can accommodate trailers. Additional fee for extra vehicles. At least one toilet and campsite is handicapped accessible at campgrounds marked (HA), accessible fishing piers (FP), and drinking water from accessible levers, no pumping, are marked (AL).

North Shore Area, Tofte District 218-663-7981 (Voice & TTY)

Backcountry Sites* No fee. 15 campgrounds with 1-5 sites each, tent pad or room for small camper, picnic table, fire grate, vault toilet, similar looking to BWCAW without reservations (first come, first served), permits, group size limits, can/bottle use, or motorized use. Call for information. Canoeing outside the BWCAW. 13 routes, 1-11 portages, similar looking to BWCAW without reservations (first come, first served), permits, group size limits, can/bottle use, motor use. Backcountry campsites have firegrate, box latrine, tent pads. Call for information.

Baker Lake* No fee. 5 campsites.

Crescent Lake. Fee $9. 32 campsites (1 group site), HA, FP, boat ramp, manager on site, .25 m. hiking.

Divide Lake. Fee $6. 3 campsites, HA, carry down boat access, 2 m. hiking.

Eighteen Lake Hiking Trail* No fee. 3 secluded campsites, no water, 2.5 hiking.

Flathorn Lake. No fee. Picnic, swimming, boat carry down, 2 m. hiking & ski.

Little Isabella River. Fee $6. 11 campsites, HA, picnic, hiking (fishing trail).

Kawishiwi Lake* No fee. 5 campsites, no water.

McDougal Lake. Fee $6. 21 campsites, HA, AL, picnic, boat ramp, swimming, bath house, 1 m. hiking.

Ninemile Lake. Fee $8. 24 campsites, HA, AL, boat ramp, manager on site.

Poplar River* No fee. 4 campsites, no water.

Sawbill Lake. Fee $9. 51 campsites, HA, FP, AL, picnic, boat carry down, interp. trail, BWCAW entry point, manager on site, outfitter (showers).

Temperance River. Fee $9. 9 campsites, mountain bike near.

North Shore Area, Gunflint District 218-387-1750 (Voice & TTY)

Cascade River. No fee. 4 campsites, no water

Devil Track Lake. Fee $8. 15 campsites, HA, AL, boat ramp near, canoe carry down.

East Bearskin Lake. Fee $10. 31 campsites, HA, AL, boat ramp, hiking, mountain bike.

Flour Lake. Fee $10-12. 35 campsites, AL, boat ramp, hiking.

Iron Lake. Fee $10. 7 campsites, canoe carry down, remote campground.

Kimball Lake. Fee $8. 10 campsites, HA, AL, FP and swimming near, picnic, boat ramp,.

Trails End. Fee $10/12. 33 campsites, HA, RV water hook-ups, BWCAW entry points, end of Gunflint Trail.

Two Island Lake. Fee $8. 37 campsites, HA, picnic, boat ramp, near Eagle Mt., highest point in Minnesota.

Ely Area, Kawishiwi District 218-365-7600, TTY 218-365-7692

Birch Lake. Fee $10 lake/9 other. 29 campsites, drinking water, boat ramp, interp. program.

Fall Lake. Fee $8/10/12 § (add $2 for electricity). 65 campsites, HA, boat ramp, picnic, swimming, manager on site, direct access to BWCAW, naturalist, concession.

Fenske Lake. Fee $10. 15 campsites, HA, FP, boat ramp, picnic, swimming, open log pavilion, nature trail, near BWCAW, hiking, mountain bike,

South Kawishiwi River. Fee $10 lake/9 others. 31 campsites, HA, boat ramp, picnic, swimming, manager on site, log pavilion, interp. program, concession, mountain bike.

Crane Lake Area, La Croix District 218-666-5251 (Voice & TTY)

Echo Lake. Fee $8. 24 campsites (1 group), HA, AL, boat ramp, picnic, playground, swimming, interp. program, 1.5 m. hiking, 3 rustic campsites/no fee.

Lake Jeanette. Fee $8. 12 campsites, boat ramp, interp. program.
Iron Range Area, Laurentian District 218-229-3371 (Voice & TTY)
Cadotte Lake. Fee $7/8. 27 campsites, HA, FP, picnic, playground, swimming, boat ramp, manager on site.
Pfeiffer Lake . Fee $7. 15 campsites, HA, FP, picnic, playground, swimming, boat ramp, manager on site, interp. trail & program.
Whiteface Reservoir. Fee $7 § (add $2 for electricity). 52 campsites , HA, FP, AL, picnic, playground, swimming, boat ramp, hiking, manager on site, concession.
Source: Superior National Forest brochures and website.

National Park System

Voyageurs, Minnesota's only national park and the nations premier national park, was established in 1975. It commemorates the French-Canadian Voyageurs who carried trade goods and furs between Montreal and the northwest from 1673 to 1842. Their feats of stamina and endurance in paddling 16-hour days and walking over long portages are still recalled with awe. The 26-foot North Canoe carried a crew of eight. On portage trails between lakes, the men often made many trips carrying loads of 180 pounds or more. Two men carried the 300 pound North Canoe.

The park contains Kabetogama Lake and shares three large border lakes with Canada east of International Falls. An additional 26 smaller lakes and over 500 beaver ponds help cover 84,000 of the park's 218,000 acres. No entrance or camping fees are charged. Winter brings 30,000 snowmobilers to the park, and summer brings mostly motorboaters. There are 60 resorts nearby; 114 campsites for motorboaters, canoers, and tenters; and 65 houseboat sites.

There are 3 Visitor Centers (Rainy Lake, Kabetogama Lake, and Ash River), 5 boat ramps, 45 visitor docks, 8 day use sites, boat tours, 24 historical sites, 10,000 museum artifacts. Trails: 24 hiking, 10 ski, 110 snowmobile, 3 canoe portages. There is no entrance fee or any charge for use of park facilities. Voyageurs National Park, International Falls 56649-8904, 218-283-9821, FAX (218) 285-7407

The St. Croix National Scenic Riverway is a 252 mile long corridor which consists of the St. Croix and Namekagon rivers. The Riverway is one of the initial rivers designated under the Wild and Scenic Rivers act of 1968. The Lower St. Croix was added in 1972. The Riverway is a unique area with a diversity of habitat, which provides many opportunities for viewing wildlife. A variety of recreational activities can be enjoyed in this picturesque setting. St. Croix National Scenic Riverway, P.O. Box 708, St. Croix Falls, Wisconsin 54024, 715-483-3284

Mississippi National River and Recreational Area is a 72-mile river corridor through Minneapolis/St. Paul metropolitan area is characterized by surprising diversity. Shallow and wide at the upper end, by the time the Mississippi reaches its confluence with the St. Croix River it has become a vast and powerful part of the largest inland navigation system on earth. Within the fifty-four thousand acre area, dozens of state and local parks provide outstanding recreational opportunities.

Congress added the Mississippi National River and Recreational Area to the National Park System in 1988 to represent the national significance of the Mississippi River.

175 E. 5th Street,Suite 418, Box 41, St. Paul, MN 55101-2901 (651) 290-4160, FAX: (651) 290-3214

Fees: Some parks within the Mississippi National River and Recreation Area (such as Fort Snelling State Park and Coon Rapids Dam) do require permits or may charge an entrance fee. Other parks and facilities, like St. Anthony Falls Historic District, provide educational and recreational opportunities without charge.

Grand Portage National Monument is a fur trade site of the late 1700's. It is comprised of the reconstructed great hall, kitchen and canoe warehouse, as well as a palisade wall and the eight and one-half mile Grand Portage. The centuries old Grand Portage became a major gateway into the interior of North America for exploration, trade and commerce. It linked Lake Superior with an inland system of lakes and rivers. During the late 18th century, Grand Portage served as the inland headquarters for the North West Company, and was the location for a summer rendezvous involving traders, agents, partners, voyagers and Indians.

P.O. Box 668, 315 South Broadway, Grand Marais, Minnesota, 55604 (218) 387-2788 (TDD) or (218) 387-2790 (FAX)

Monument headquarters is located in the U.S. Coast Guard Building in Grand Marais, Minnesota, approximately 36 miles west of Grand Portage.

The entrance fee is $2.00 per person for those 17 through 61 years of age, with a maximum of $5.00 per family. Federal access passes are sold and accepted (i.e., Golden Age, Golden Access and Golden Eagle). Voluntary donations are accepted.

Pipestone National Monument is located in Pipestone, MN, near the South Dakota border. Within the monument, there are pipestone (Catlinite) quarries, native tallgrass prairie, quartzite bluffs, and a creek with a water- fall. The first act to establish the monument was approved on August 25, 1937 with approximately 116 acres of land. There were two main purposes for the establishment of the monument; (1) to preserve and manage the ethnological, historical, archeological, and geological resources of the area for the betterment and enjoyment of all, and (2) to manage the pipestone quarries to provide American Indians the ability to quarry the pipestone. A second act was passed on June 18, 1956 which authorized the addition of more land. 167 acres were added bringing the total to approximately 283 acres.

Pipestone National Monument, 36 Reservation Avenue, Pipestone, Minnesota 56164, (507) 825-5464 , (507) 825-5466 FAX

Entrance Fee: $2.00 per person with a maximum of $4.00 per family. American Indians, educational groups, and those under 16 years of age are exempt from the fee. All Department of Interior Passports (Golden Eagle, Golden Age, and Golden Access) are applicable to the entrance fee.
Source: National Park Service website   www.nps.gov.

U.S. Army Corps of Engineers

Army Corps of Engineers Centre, 190 Fifth Street East, St. Paul 55101-1638, 612-290-5680 www.ncs.usace.army.mil

The U.S. Army Corps of Engineers was established in the earliest days of our nation as part of the Continental Army. In the early years, Army engineers blazed trails for westward migration and cleared waterways and harbors for commerce. The expertise gained in these early missions enabled the Corps to assume Congressionally authorized duties in the fields of flood control, hydropower production, shore protection and restoration, water supply, disaster assistance, fish and wildlife management, and recreation.

Providing a safe channel for navigation on the Mississippi River was one of the Corps' first civil works missions. Within Minnesota you will find a number of Corps recreation areas.

Big Stone Lake (Ortonville). Fishing, hunting, hiking, x-country skiing, nature watching. 10,700 acre wildlife refuge.

Cross Lake/Pine River Reservoir (near Brainerd). Fee. 218-692-2025. 120 campsites (some electric), handicapped showers, drinking water, dump station, picnic, boat ramp, visitors center, swimming, playground, privies, handicapped fishing, phone.

Duluth Visitor Center & Marine Museum. 218-727-2497. View ship traffic, artifacts, models, reconstructions of ships' quarters. Restrooms, drinking water, phone.

Gull Lake (Brainerd). 218-829-3334. 39 campsites (some electric and handicapped accessible), handicapped showers & restrooms, drinking water, dump station, picnic, boat ramp, visitor center, swimming, playground, fishing, hiking trails, Indian burial grounds, phone.

Lac Qui Parle (Montevideo). Replicas of early Indian life, restrooms, drinking water, picnic.

Leech Lake (Walker). 218-654-3145. 74 campsites (some electric, 2 handicapped accessible), showers, handicapped restrooms, drinking water, dump station, picnic, boat ramp, marina, playground, fishing, game area, phone.

Orwell Lake (Fergus Falls). Restroom, drinking water, picnic.

Pokegama Lake (Grand Rapids). 218-326-6128. 20 campsites (some electric, 1 handicapped accessible), handicapped restrooms, drinking water, dump station, picnic, boat ramp, playground, fishing, phone.

Big Sandy Lake (McGregor). 218-426-3482. 44 campsites (some electric), 3 tent sites, 1 group camp, showers, restrooms, drinking water, dump station, picnic, boat ramp, swimming, playground, privies, fishing, hiking trail, interpretive site, phone.

Lake Traverse (Wheaton). Restrooms, drinking water, picnic, boat ramp.

Lake Winnibigoshish (Deer River). 218-246-8107. 22 campsites (many electric), restrooms, drinking water, dump station, picnic, boat ramp, swimming, playground, fishing, hiking trail, interpretive site, phone.

Locks, Dams, and Recreation Areas on the Mississippi River

All lock & dam areas bordering Minnesota have restroom facilities and drinking water except for Lower St. Anthony Falls.

Upper St. Anthony Falls Lock & Dam (Minneapolis). Visitor center

Lower St. Anthony Falls (Minneapolis). Just downstream of Upper Falls.

Lock & Dam 1 (Minneapolis/St. Paul). Bridge with interpretive signs provides a birds-eye view of the lockages.

Lock & Dam 2 (Hastings).

Lock & Dam 3 (Red Wing).

Lock & Dam 4 (Alma, WI).

Lock & Dam 5 (Minnesota City).

Lock & Dam 5A (Fountain City, WI).

Lock & Dam 6 (Trempealeau. WI).

Lock & Dam 7 (La Crescent).

Lock & Dam 8 (Genoa, WI).

Source: U.S. Army Corps of Engineers brochures (EP 1130-2-423, 8/92)

Minnesota became the second oldest state park system in the country with the establishment of Itasca State Park on April 20, 1891. The next state park added to the system was Interstate State Park on April 25, 1895.

Chapter 20
Fishing, Hunting and Wildlife

Minnesota Fishing

"Where-to-go and how-to-get-'em" is important. But "when" may be even more so for Minnesota anglers.

The "when" is anytime - 24 hours daily, 365 days yearly.

While the general fishing season for the big ones - muskies, northern pike and walleyes - opens on the weekend nearest May 15, crappie, sunfish, white and rock bass, catfish and bullhead fishing never closes.

State fisheries officials believe many more persons fish for crappies and sunfish than for any other species.

The "where" is just as easy.

Fishing starts right in the Twin Cities. Catches of trophy walleyes and sauger are common in the Mississippi River, which also has excellent fishing for bass. So good is the fishing here that the DNR protects the populations of walleyes, sauger, largemouth bass and smallmouth bass with a catch-and-release recommendation.

Minneapolis city lakes, Calhoun, Harriet, and Cedar in particular, are deep and have been benefited by plantings of large game fish seined by state crews from lakes threatened by winter kills. All of the city lakes also furnish hours of pleasant sport for shore casters seeking sunfish and crappies.

West of the Twin Cities, 14,000-acre Lake Minnetonka is one of the top bass lakes in the U.S. It also has had stockings of muskies and provides excellent fishing for northern pike, walleye and panfish.

The St. Croix River, east of the Twin Cities, adds scenery including pine shores, to excellent angling for northern pike, walleyes and smallmouth bass. It has given up sensational catches of silver bass.

The seven-county metropolitan area of Hennepin, Ramsey, Anoka, Carver, Dakota, Scott and Washington holds a total of 230 known game-fish lakes. In addition to Minnetonka, some of the best are White Bear, Waconia, Bald Eagle, Coon, Medicine, Forest, Big Marine and Prior.

1999 Kid's Fishing Ponds

The Minnesota DNR is committed to improving angling opportunities for all anglers. Our kid's fishing pond program is intended to serve primarily the youngest anglers by stocking local ponds, which otherwise would not have any fishing. Last spring the DNR-Metro Fisheries stocked 14 small neighborhood lakes with crappies & bluegills.

There are numerous shore fishing opportunities for young and old alike throughout the seven-county Twin Cities region. Call the DNR Information Center at 651-296-6157 and ask for a free copy of the Metro Shore Fishing map.

Spreading out from the Twin Cities, Mille Lacs, 100 miles north, draws more walleye anglers than any other state water. Walleyes usually are found in the larger lakes. Mille Lacs, at 132,000 acres, usually is a high producer, particularly for early season anglers. Other big waters are Red Lake, at 288,800 acres (the largest entirely within Minnesota); Leech, 111,500 acres; Winnibigoshish, 69,821; Vermilion 37,915; Pepin (a wide spot on the Mississippi) 25,000 and Kabetogama, 19,000.

Trout enthusiasts head principally for southeastern Minnesota limestone streams. Lake Superior, or the portion that washes the Minnesota shore, has make a comeback in lake trout fishing. The recovery of this native species, previously decimated by an invasion of the exotic sea lamprey, is one of the DNR's most notable achievements.

Minnesota has 2 million anglers, each with his or her own ideas for how to catch them. Fishing is always good - whether the catch is or not.

The Resource Minnesota has 11,842 lakes 10 acres or larger, of which 5,483 are fishing lakes. Excluding Lake Superior, the state has 3.8 million acres of fishing water. Minnesota's portion of Lake Superior is 1.4 million acres.

There are 15,000 miles of fishable streams in Minnesota, including 2,600 miles of trout streams. Minnesota waters support 153 species of fish.

Fisheries The DNR Section of Fisheries is responsible for managing the state's diverse fisheries resources. Minnesota has 2.3 million anglers, and sport fishing generates approximately $1 billion direct expenditures, making angling one of the state's largest industries.

The DNR Section of Fisheries has a full-time staff of 300. There are 6 regional and 28 area fisheries offices. The state operates 21 hatcheries: 5 for trout and salmon and 12 for coolwater species.

The annual budget for the Section of Fisheries is approximately $17 million, which is funded primarily by fishing license and stamp fees and by a federal excise tax on fishing and boating equipment.

License Requirements Fishing regulations for 2000 will be available about March 1, 2000 when they become effective.

To qualify as a resident, a person must maintain a legal residence in Minnesota for at least 60 consecutive days before purchasing a license.

All residents age 16 or older must have the appropriate license on their person when fishing. Exceptions: Mothers on Take A Mom Fishing Weekend (May 10-11) and adults accompanying children under age 16 on Take A Kid Fishing Weekend (June 7-8) may fish without a license on those dates.

Residents in the U.S. Military who are stationed outside the state must have leave or furlough papers on their person to fish without a license.

Daily Limits and/or Possession Since 1922

Species	1922	1930	1939	1947	1948	1953	1956	1962	1975	1981	1987	1999
Lake Trout	25	5	5	5	5	5	5	3	3	3	5*	3
Trout	25	15	15	15	15	10	10	10	5	3	10*	-
Black Bass	15	6	6	6	6	6	6	6	6	6	6	6
White Bass	-	-	-	-	-	-	-	-	-	-	-	30
Rock Bass	-	-	-	-	-	-	-	-	-	-	-	30
Muskellunge	5	2	2	2	2	2	1	1	1	1	1+	1^
Northern Pike	No Limit	10	8	6	3	3	3	3	3	3	3	3£
Walleye/ Sauger	15	8	8	8	8	8	6	6	6	6	6	6∞
Sunfish	25	15	15	15	15	30	30	30	30	30	30	30
Crappie	20	15	15	15	15	15	15	15	15	15	15	15

*Trout stamp required. Size limit: not more than 3 over 16."
+Minimum size: 36"   £Not more than 1 per day over 30"
^Minimum size: 40"   ∞Not more than 1 walleye per day over 24"
Source for whole chapter: Minnesota DNR, Division of Fish and Wildlife

General Restrictions
Possessing and Transporting Fish

Daily and possession limits are the same. Possession of more than one limit of each fish species is unlawful. Fish are in an angler's possession whether on hand, in cold storage, in transport, or elsewhere.

Fish must be transported in a way that they can be counted and the species of each fish can be identified. If statewide length limits apply to the species, the head and tail must be intact so the fish can be measured, except for northern pike and walleye.*

For purpose of display in a home aquarium, a person age 16 or under may transport largemouth bass, smallmouth bass, yellow perch, rock bass, black crappie, white crappie, bluegill, pumpkinseed, green sunfish, orange spotted sunfish, and black, yellow, and brown bullhead taken by angling. No more that four of each species may be transported at any one time, and any individual fish can be no longer than 10 inches in total length.

It is illegal for anglers to transport live fish, including in livewells of trailered boats. See 2000 Minnesota Fishing Regulations booklet for details.

Angling Methods, partial list of regulations

Anglers may use only one hook. An artificial lure is considered one hook. A treble hook, when not part of an artificial lure, is considered three hooks and is not legal. The exceptions are: Three artificial flies may be used when angling for trout, crappie, sunfish, and rock bass.

Anglers may use only one line. The exceptions are: a) Two lines may be used through the ice (other than on designated trout lakes and streams); and b) Two lines maybe used on Lake Superior when more than 100 yards from the point where a tributary stream or river enters the lake.

Using whole or parts of game fish, goldfish, or carp for bait is unlawful.

Angling with an unattended line, setline, or trotline is unlawful.

Angling for any species on a designated trout water is unlawful when the trout season is closed.

Anglers must remain within 200 feet of their tip-up.

Possessing or using live minnows on designated stream trout lakes is unlawful.

Using an artificial light to lure or attract fish, or to see fish when spearing, is unlawful.

The use of explosives, firearms, chemicals (not including fish scents), or electricity for taking fish is unlawful.

It is unlawful to intentionally take fish by snagging.

Fishing Ethics

Suggestions to make fishing safe and enjoyable for all anglers:
• Don't litter monofilament fishing line, styrofoam, plastic bags, six-pack holders, and other plastics, which can kill fish and wildlife that eat or get tangled up in these products.
• Prepare your boat and trailer before you are on the ramp so that you can launch quickly.
• Ask for permission before entering private land.
• Keep only the amount of fish you can use.
• Release some medium-sized fish so they can grow larger and be caught in the future.

Catch-and-Release

Improved fishing technology and increasing fishing pressure have caused fishing quality to decline in many waters. Catch-and-release fishing offers anglers a way to enjoy their sport with less harm to the resource. Each year, more anglers discover the satisfaction of watching a fish they've caught swim away. Here are some tips for proper catch-and-release:

• Don't place fish you plan to release on a stringer or in a livewell, because they have less chance of surviving. Make the decision to release a fish when you catch it.

• Play and land the fish quickly. A prolonged struggle places too much stress on a fish and causes a build-up of harmful lactic acids, which can kill the fish after it is released.

• Handle the fish gently and keep it in the water as much as possible. If pos sible, unhook the fish without lifting it from the water.

• Don't drop the fish in the boat. Fish bruise easily, and the damage to their internal organs can be fatal.

• When lifting fish for a photograph or just to admire it, don't hold it by the eye sockets or gills. You can damage the internal organs of fish, especially larger ones, by lifting them from the water. Use both hands to evenly sup port the fish's weight.

• Use a pliers to remove hooks. If a hook is deeply imbedded, cut the line. Fish have strong digestive acids which will dissolve metal. Studies have shown that fish released in this manner have a higher survival rate than do fish that have had hooks torn from their throat or stomach.

• A fish that can be legally kept should not be released if it is bleeding heav- ily, which indicates its chance of survival is poor.

• You cannot intentionally fish for any species during its closed season.

• Fish can be revived by holding them upright in the water and moving them forward slowly to force water through the gills. Don't release a tired fish until you are sure it can swim away on its own.

• In streams, release fish into calm water. A tired fish placed in fast water can die by tumbling downstream into rocks. Gently slide the fish back into the water.

Weigh Your Fish With a Ruler

Fish can be injured when weighed with portable scales. To estimate the weight with a length measurement (in inches), use the following formulas:

• Walleye: Length x Length x Length divided by 2,700. For example: An 18- inch walleye weighs approximately 2.16 pounds [5,832 (18 x 18 x 18) divided by 2,700=2.16].

• Pike: Length x Length x Length divided by 3,500

• Sunfish: Length x Length x Length divided by 1,200

• Bass: Length x Length x Girth (girth is the distance around the body) divided by1,200

• Trout: Length x Girth x Girth divided by 800

State Record Fish

Catching a big fish, no matter what the species, is always a thrill, and it usually requires exception fishing skill. To recognize the achievements of anglers who catch the biggest fish in each species, the DNR annually presents an award of recognition to any angler who breaks a state record.

If you catch a fish that you think could be a record, follow these steps:
• Weight the fish on a state-certified scale (found at most bait shops and butcher shops) witnessed by two observers.
• Take the fish to a DNR fisheries office for positive identification and a state record fish application.
• Complete the application and send it along with a clear, full-length photo of your fish to the address listed on the form.

The following is a complete list of Minnesota's state record fish and where they were caught. Weights given are in pounds and ounces (example: 55-5 is 55 pounds, 5 ounces.) Counties are in parenthesis.

Kind of Fish	Weight	Location Caught
Bass, Largemouth	8—12.75	Tetonka Lake (LeSueur)
Bass, Rock	2—0	Osakis Lake (Todd)
Bass, Smallmouth	8—0	West Battle Lake (Otter Tail)
Bass, White	4—0	St. Croix River (Washington); and
	4—0	Genoa Barge (Houston)
Bluegill	2—13	Alice Lake (Hubbard)
Bowfin	10—15	Mary Lake (Douglas); and
	10—15	French Lake (Rice)
Buffalo, Bigmouth	41—11	Mississippi River (Goodhue)
Buffalo, Black	20—0.5	Minnesota River (Nicollet)
Buffalo, Smallmouth	13—4	Mississippi River (Ramsey)
Bullhead, Black	3—13.12	Reno Lake (Pope)
Bullhead, Brown	7—1	Shallow Lake (Itasca)
Bullhead, Yellow	3—7.5	Osakis Lake (Todd)
Burbot	18—4.8	Lake of the Woods (Lake of the Woods)
Carp	55—5	Clearwater Lake (Wright)
Carpsucker, River	3—15	Mississippi River (Ramsey)
Catfish, Channel	38—0	Mississippi River (Hennepin)
Catfish, Flathead	70—0	St. Croix River (Washington)
Crappie, Black	5—0	Vermillion River (Dakota)
Crappie, White	3—4	Coon Lake (Anoka)
Drum, Freshwater	35—2	Mississippi River (Houston)
Eel, American	6—9	St. Croix River (Washington)
Gar, Longnose	16—12	St. Croix River (Washington)

Gar, Shortnose	4—9.6	Mississippi River (Hennepin)
Goldeye	2—5.76	Root River (Houston)
Hogsucker, Northern	1—15	Sunrise River (Chisago)
Mooneye	1—15	Minnesota River (Redwood)
Muskellunge	54—0	Lake Winnibigoshish (Itasca)
Muskellunge, Tiger	34—12	Lake Elmo (Washington)
Perch, Yellow	3—4	Lake Plantaganette (Hubbard)
Pike, Northern	45—12	Basswood Lake (Lake)
Pumkinseed	1—6	Leech Lake (Cass)
Quillback	6—14.4	Mississippi River (Ramsey)
Redhorse, Golden	2—13.28	Otter Tail River (Otter Tail)
Redhorse, Greater	11—13	Upper South Long Lake (Crow Wing)
Redhorse, River	10—3	Kettle River (Pine)
Redhorse, Shorthead	7—15	Rum River (Anoka)
Redhorse, Silver	7—9.3	Rainy River (Koochiching)
Salmon, Atlantic	12—13	Baptism River (Lake)
Salmon, Chinook	33—4	Poplar River (Cook); and
	33—4	Lake Superior (St. Louis)
Salmon, Coho	10—6.5	Lake Superior (Lake)
Salmon, Kokanee	2—15	Caribou Lake (Itasca)
Salmon, Pink	4—8	Cascade River (Cook)
Sauger	6—2.75	Mississippi River (Goodhue)
Splake	12—4.48	Larson Lake (Itasca)
Sturgeon, Lake	94—4	Kettle River (Pine)
Sturgeon, Shovelnose	5—5	Mississippi River (Goodhue)
Sucker, Blue	14—3	Mississippi River (Wabasha)
Sucker, Longnose	3—2	Rainy River (Koochiching)
Sucker, White	9—1	Big Fish Lake (Stearns)
Sunfish, Green	1—2.7	Scheuble Lake (Carver)
Sunfish, Hybrid	1—12	Zumbro River (Olmsted)
Trout, Brook	6—4.48	High Lake (St. Louis)
Trout, Brown	16—12	Lake Superior (St. Louis)
Trout, Lake	43—8	Lake Superior (Cook)
Trout, Rainbow (Steelhead)	17—6	Knife River (Lake)
Tullibee (Cisco)	4—3	Big Sandy Lake (Aitkin)
Walleye	17—8	Seagull River (Cook)
Walleye-Sauger Hybrid	9—13.4	Mississippi River (Goodhue)
Whitefish, Lake	12—4.5	Leech Lake (Cass)
Whitefish, Menominee	2—7.5	Lake Superior (Cook)

Minnesota Fish Facts

Minnesota is first nationally in the sales of fishing licenses per capita.

Fish species	156
Fishing waters	3,800,000 acres
Fishable lakes	6,000
Fishable streams	15,000
Trout streams	1,900
Trout stream improvements	80 miles
Trout lakes (reclaimed)	134
Number of anglers	2,100,000
Annual fish harvest—commercial	4,500,000 lbs.
Annual fish harvest—anglers	5,000,000 lbs.
Fish hatcheries	5 trout, 12 walleye
Fish raised and stocked	202,600,000
Fish stocked per year:	Walleye 2.3 mil.; Muskie 31,500; Trout 1.5 mil.
Walleye rearing ponds	225
Northern Pike spawning areas	19
Fish trapping and rescue sites	15
Licensed anglers '97:	1,535,039
Amount spent in Minnesota each year on sport fishing—	$1.9 billion
Minnow industry:	1800 businesses-$42 mil.
The most caught fish:	1st Panfish, 2nd Walleye, 3rd Northernpike

Maps

Contour maps of lake bottoms have been prepared by the Department of Natural Resources and cover most of Minnesota's important walleye waters. These maps locate the bottom features, holes, reefs, drop-offs, and deep areas—so important to walleye fishing. They are available from the Minnesota Bookstore, 117 University Ave, St. Paul, MN 55155 (651) 297-3000 or (800) 657-3757.

DNR Public Recreation Information Maps (PRIM) show the boundaries of state and national forests, WPAs, and WMAs. Available at major sports retailers and the DNR gift shop in St. Paul. Suggested retail price: $4.95.

USGS Topo Maps:They don't indicate property boundaries, but they do show practically everything else - including hill contours and even tiny streams. Available in atlas form in some bookstores or individually from the Minnesota Geological Survey in St. Paul. Phone: 651-627-4780. Cost: $2.75 per map.

County Plat Books: These show who owns all parcels of land in each of the state's 87 counties. Available from county courthouses and some land abstracting firms. The cost varies from county to county.

Minnesota Hunting

Believe It or Not!

There was no firearms-related fatality in Minnesota for the entire 1998 hunting season, which ran from mid-September through the end of December, with more than 500,000 hunters in the field. It was the safest hunting season recorded in Minnesota, and it marked the fifth consecutive year that hunting fatalities among Minnesota hunters have declined.

That decline is reflected in the most recent statistics by the National Safety Council, which ranks hunting, in injuries per 100,000 participants (7 injuries), above billiards (20 injuries), bowling (57), and golf (186).

Trespassing

Most of Minnesota is private property. And most hunters hunt on private land. Minnesota's trespass laws have been written to protect human life, livestock, and the rights of landowners. These laws, summarized in the 1997 DNR Hunting Handbook, require hunters to:

- Get permission to hunt agricultural land.

- Hunters can't hunt any posted private land unless they have written permission, and

- They can't hunt land if they've been told to leave. To find out if unmarked land is private, inquire at the county auditor's office.

Hunting in Minnesota: An Overview

Both the hunted and the hunter have fared well in Minnesota. The richness that was—the vast wilderness, sliced with waterways and secluded marshes, the transition line to the prairie land and the prairie lands themselves—gave Minnesota a vast variety of animal and bird life.

It was so vast that a young nation, hell bent to cut and dam and control the land's wild forces somehow could not completely dominate Minnesota nor leave its boundaries irreparably harmed.

Of course there were some casualties—many well known. The **bison** that once roamed much of southern Minnesota was used as a pawn in the Indian Wars. And the big beast was destined to be harnessed within barbed wire, no longer free to roam in gigantic herds.

Elk were prairie animals and once native to our state. After logging, the growing deer herds infected elk with a parasite that killed them off. **Caribou** perhaps traveled the state's northern reaches. **Antelope** shared the prairies.

The **prairie chicken**, a colorful grassland dancer, was abundant. And as parts of the prairie were sliced by the pioneer's plows, the prairie chicken population exploded, enough to darken the sky. But as the plow bit into the earth and more farmers settled in Minnesota, the tide of the prairie chicken was turned. For with little prairie left, the bird was without habitat.

The forests of the north were plundered; the fur bearers were trapped by the carloads; the predators, timber wolves, coyote, fox, etc., were considered enemies and open warfare was declared by the early settlers.

Occasionally reported by pioneers arriving in what is today Minnesota, the **wild turkey** had disappeared from the state by the turn of this century. Wild turkey numbers took off only after years of trial and error. The first successful stockings occurred in 1973, when biologists traded 85 ruffed grouse from Minnesota for 29 wild turkeys from Missouri. The wild turkeys were released in the hilly terrain of Houston County. Wildlife biologists continue to trap wild turkeys in areas of Minnesota where the birds are abundant and then relocate them to suitable new areas. They have spread west to Jackson County and North to Becker County.

Within 25 years the state's wild turkey population has grown from a few birds to more than 30,000. Harvest has followed suit. In the state's first wild turkey season in 1978, hunters bagged 94 birds. In 1998, a record 4,349 wild turkeys were shot during the spring season, up more than 1,000 from 1997.

By the mid-1920s, the **fisher** and the **pine marten**-two relatives of the mink-had practically disappeared from Minnesota. Unregulated trapping and extensive logging had pushed the few remaining animals to the state's northeastern tip. In 1927 the state ended trapping for both species. The legal protection paid off. Helped also by forest regrowth, the furbearers slowly repopulated part of their original range during the next 50 years.

In 1977 the DNR decided to reopen the fisher trapping season. By 1985 the pine marten population had recovered enough for a limited trapping season to begin.

In the 1930s, local **Canada geese** had all but disappeared from Minnesota and most other states. Several thousand migrants still flew through the state each fall and spring, but the combination of egg gathering, unregulated hunting, and prairie marsh drainage had eliminated local flocks.

Not until the 1980s did the **"giant" Canada goose**, a subspecies that makes up the state's local breeding population, take off. The breeding population of giant Canadas has grown from about 5,000 pairs in 1979 to more than 50,000 pairs in 1998. "Today there are resident flocks in Grand Rapids and Grand Marais, and throughout the northern forest region." So successful has been the restoration of locally breeding Canada geese over the past 30 years that today they are a nuisance in some cities and farming communities.

Goose hunting harvests have increased accordingly. Minnesota often tops the nation in annual harvest with more than 100,000 resident and migrant geese killed. Yet resident goose numbers continue to grow.

People used to hate **bears**. From 1945 to 1965, the state paid a $10 bounty to anyone who shot and killed a nuisance bear. Viewed as varmints, bears were shot on sight and often left to rot. As a result, Minnesota's bear population stayed low.

Today Minnesota has 23,000 bears-up nearly threefold from 1980. Once confined to northern forests, bears now live as far south as Little Falls and as far west as Detroit Lakes. In1971 Minnesota held its first hunting season for the black bear. The state's bear population began to rise rapidly after 1982, when the DNR began restricting harvest with a quota system.

In the early 1960s, it was relatively uncommon to see **whitetails** in southwestern Minnesota. People would actually call the DNR to report sightings of deer.

Though the deer herd in the state's northern forest region has grown little over the past 30 years, the farmland region's deer population has increased remarkably. In the 1960s, only 25 percent of the state's deer harvest came from the farmland region. By the 1990s, that share had grown to more than 60 percent.

Because farmland deer have few places to hide, killing too many does is easy. Deer populations and deer hunters both benefited when the DNR began its antlerless permit system in 1976. The system allows biologists to adjust the number of does and fawns to be killed by hunters each year-and thus grow or shrink herds as necessary in each of the state's 120 permit areas. Over the next 20 years, deer numbers went skyward, due to this management flexibility and improvements in deer habitat from a logging boom. The total deer population in the state tripled in size from the 1970s to the 1990s. During this same time, the deer harvest also climbed, breaking records between1986 and 1996. The goal of deer management in Minnesota is a sustained annual harvest of approximately 150,000 whitetails.

Minnesota is to **ruffed grouse** what Montana is to elk and North Dakota is to ducks. Hunters shoot more of these woodland birds in Minnesota than in any other state. Moreover, the past two winters, while tough on deer and pheasants, were excellent for grouse, which hide from predators in deep snow. Another big factor has been extensive logging of mature aspen stands. The young aspen that shoots up after logging provides ideal grouse habitat.

Though nature does the most to hurt or help ruffed grouse populations, the DNR has had a big role in providing as many hunting opportunities as possible. In particular, research on ruffed grouse biology. It wasn't always so. During the first half of the 20th century, wildlife workers poorly understood the rise and fall of animal populations, such as the decade-long cycle of ruffed grouse numbers.

Minnesota's ruffed grouse hunting season lasted just eight days back in 1939, but a hunter in 1997 could pursue ruffed grouse from September 12 through December 31—a total of 111 days. And all this hunting isn't hurting ruffed grouse populations one bit. Minnesota's grouse population today is probably higher than even before European settlement.

Management of wildlife resources replaced senseless eradication. Hunting was controlled; lands for wildlife habitat were preserved and refuges were established. Even duck populations, which plummeted in the 1980s, have rebounded to meet and in some cases beat ambitious goals set by the state and federal conservation agencies and hunting organizations that established the North American Waterfowl Management Plan in 1986.

The **ring-necked pheasant**, despite its hardy nature, cannot cope with a countryside that is becoming uniformly blackened by the plow. Deer need a young forest; the ruffed grouse prefers a forest of mixed-age trees. The **moose**, now plentiful enough to support limited hunting, must also be given forest room to roam. Ducks and muskrat need marshes. Redwings need cattails and rabbits like brush patches.

Ecosystem-based Management

Roger Holmes Director, DNR Division of Fish and Wildlife writes that **ecosystem-based management** is the smartest and most cost-effective way to manage our wildlife. The basic idea of ecosystem-based management is that you manage ecosystems rather than specific species or disciplines. In other words, you don't manage pheasants as much as you manage the ecosystem the pheasants live in. If the ecosystem is improved, it will produce more pheasants naturally.

For example, waterfowl managers and hunters have for years known that they couldn't stem the decline in duck numbers without first protecting the wetland ecosystem, which includes uplands and watersheds. They learned you can't sustain duck populations without first sustaining the wetland ecosystem.

The overriding theme of ecosystem management is sustainability. That means preserving the entire ecosystems over the long haul to provide more recreation, a healthier environment, and stronger economies.

An environmentalist and hunter and the father of modern wildlife management, Aldo Leopold was touting ecosystem-based management 50 years ago. He called it land stewardship, but the principle was the same: The natural world is interconnected and you can't fix one part without looking at the entire system. Let's consider how the whitetail has been managed on a system-wide basis.

The Whitetail's Minnesota History

The whitetail is Minnesota's most common big game animal. It is found in every county of the state. Before the lumberjack period, about 1900, deer were rather uncommon in the northern evergreen forests. However, logging and burning removed the mature timber and encouraged the succulent new growth of vegetation upon which deer feed. By 1920, deer were fairly common over much of the northeastern part of Minnesota.

During settlement of the southern counties of Minnesota, unregulated hunting reduced the herd to the extent that by 1880 deer had almost disappeared. At about the turn of the century, the enactment of more restrictive game laws prepared the way for natural restocking of the farmland country.

By the early 1940's, deer had exceeded the carrying capacity of the range in many northern areas and crop damage complaints were frequent in the south. As the herd increased and the food supply dwindled, winter starvation took a heavy toll in many localities.

Deer Management

Deer management seeks maintenance of the deer population at a level high enough to make common the enjoyment of seeing deer, and high enough to produce a good crop for harvest by hunters annually without undue depredation to landowners. Within the limits of the land to produce such levels, the size of the deer herd must also be a compromise between the maximum desired for sport and enjoyment, and the most that can be supported without undue damage to other interests such as farms and forest crops and automobile safely.

The principal means of maintaining a desired deer population level are (1) by hunting regulations that either increase or decrease the harvest of deer, and (2) by habitat improvements to increase the capacity of an area to support deer.

Winter food is not a problem in the agriculture areas. Here the deer feed primarily at the expense of the farmer. But there is a limit to how much of this can be allowed. Deer, if they are numerous, can be extremely damaging to crops, especially orchards. Therefore, in agricultural areas we must maintain the deer herd at a size compatible with people and agriculture.

Setting Hunting Regulations

Determinations must be made regarding:

1. The extent to which the number of animals currently on hand is above or below the limit that can be supported by the food supply.
2. Whether it is easy or difficult for hunters to take the number that should be harvested.
3. The number of hunters that can be allowed in an area while maintaining safety for people and private property.

In the fall of 1971, the DNR was forced to close Minnesota's entire deer hunting season. The reason? To protect the state's deer herd, which had been ravaged by severe winters in the late 1960s, an overharvest of does, and habitat loss.

Deciding whether it is easy or difficult to take a deer in a particular area enters into setting regulations. Where hunters have an advantage the season must be shorter to avoid over-harvesting.

Maintaining safety for people and property during the hunting season requires regulations that will not create an undue concentration of hunters. The state has been zoned, and some zones have been split into separate seasons to distribute hunting pressure and help to regulate harvest.

Habitat improvement, as well as proper hunting regulations, is necessary to maintain a satisfactory deer population in Minnesota. Large deer herds can be supported only where a large portion of the forest is in a brush, reproduction stage. Wildlife managers work with forestry agencies to create areas of younger forest and grassy "openings" to provide food resources for deer. Spruce-fir, the climax forest of this region, is poor habitat for deer. To restore these areas as good deer habitat, sites must be clear cut to set succession back to the aspen sprout stage which produces fore deer food while still maintaining adequate conifers for deer winter cover.

Minnesota Deer Facts

Estimated Statewide Deer Population: 800,000 (fall, 1997)
Estimated Nationwide White-tailed Deer Population: 29 million
Losses:
>   Estimated Annual Car Kills: 15,000 (4,000 in 7-county metro area)
>   Estimated Deer Killed by Wolves Each Year: 40,000 (fawns and adults)
>   Estimated Deer Taken by Other Predators (coyotes, bears, bobcats,
>   fisher) Each Year: 60,000 (Mostly fawns)

Hunting Facts

Public hunting	11 million acres
Wildlife management	1,260 acres
Game species 110	
Licensed big game hunters '95	548,082
Licensed firearms deer hunters '95	462,440
Licensed small game hunters '95	300,147
Number of waterfowl stamps sold '95	122,261
Number of pheasant stamps sold '95	105,253
Licensed bow hunters '95	72,832
Licensed trappers '95	5,656
Value of fur harvested by trapping '95	$7 million
Bear Lottery Licenses '95	10,287
Spring Turkey Lottery Licenses '95	9,459
Fall Turkey Lottery Licenses '95	2,128
Moose Lottery Licenses '95	379
Deer harvest	160,000
Bear harvest	1,900
Moose harvest	220

Small game harvest:

Waterfowl	1,800,000	Coot	25,000
Ruffed grouse	700,000	Wilson's snipe	5,000
Wild turkey	3,000	Squirrel	270,000
Pheasant	400,000	Rabbit/hare	110,000
Sharp-tailed grouse	10,000	Red fox	90,000
Hungarian partridge	30,000	Coyote	20,000
Woodcock	80,000		

Annual Deer Harvest:

	1991	1992	1993	1994	1995
Firearms	206,275	229,236	188,109	178,283	198,193
Archery	12,964	13,004	13,722	13,818	14,521
Muzzleloader	961	828	1,097	1,725	2,452
Total	220,200	243,068	202,928	193,826	215,166

Estimated Nationwide White-tailed Deer Harvest: 12 million

Hunting Regulations for 2000-2001 for big and small game is released every August. Contact the DNR Division of Fish and Wildlife. 1-888 MINN-DNR

Wildlife–Minnesota's Mammals

Eighty different kinds of mammals have been recorded in the state, either living here now, or in the past. They range in size from the tiny pigmy shrew, weighing just a few ounces, to the mighty moose, over six feet tall and weighing over 1000 lbs. Listed here are the seven orders:

Opossum (Order Marsupialia) They have taken residency here in only recent years, coming northward from southern Minnesota. This is their northernmost range.

Moles and Shrews (Order Insectivora) In addition to the pigmy, the least, the shortest of all mammals, and the water shrew, so small and light-weight it can run on top of water. Occurring also here are the cinerous, Richardson and shorttailed shrews.

Unlike shrews, moles spend most of their time underground. There are two varieties of moles in Minnesota - the star-nose and the common mole.

Bats (Order Chiroptera) Seven of the nation's different kinds of bats are found in Minnesota - the little brown-bat, Ken's little brown bat, the big brown bat, pipistrelle bat, the silver-haired bat, hoary bat and the red bat.

Rabbits and Hares (Order Lagomorphia) The white-tailed jack rabbit is the state's largest rabbit. This highly nocturnal animal lives in prairie country and has been timed for several miles running at speeds up to 25 miles per hour. Snowshoe hares, so called because the soles of their feet are furred, enabling them to get around in soft, deep snow, live the northern evergreen forests. Minnesota's smallest rabbit, the cottontail, and live in the hardwood forests and brush country of southern Minnesota.

Rodents (Order Rodentia) This order has the largest number of varieties. Squirrels and their relatives (Woodchucks, ground squirrels, chipmunks, tree squirrels and flying squirrels). The largest, the woodchuck, is also known as the groundhog. No one in Minnesota seems to observe its activities as a prophet concerning the end of winter.

Richardson's ground squirrel lives mostly on dry prairie.

The Minnesota Gopher is a striped ground squirrel with 13 lines alternating from light to dark. It is found throughout most of the state.

The Franklin's ground squirrel, or pocket gopher, is found in brushy fields and rock piles. The Eastern Chipmunk lives off nuts and berries in the brushlands. Least chipmunks prefer the evergreen forests. The Red Squirrel, the smallest of our tree dwellers, is at its noisy and entertaining best in the northern forest. Bushy-tailed Gray Squirrels are common throughout the state, like the Fox Squirrel which is the largest animal of this kind in the state. Sharp eyed observers may also spot two varieties of flying squirrels.

Minnesota has two kinds of true gophers - the Dakota and the Mississippi Valley pocket gophers. Great diggers, they make burrows along the edges of roads, and have hunted relentlessly by farmers for years.

The beaver is the largest of the rodents. Rare at the turn of the century when trappers had nearly wiped them out, they are now quite numerous.

The porcupine is a fearless animal who survives because of his barbed quills.

The largest group of rodents is mice and rats. These are the harvest mouse, pocket mouse, grasshopper mouse, prairie white-footed mouse, Canadian white-footed mouse, northern white-footed mouse, bog lemming, northern bog lemming, red-backed mouse, common meadow mouse, rock vole, prairie vole, pine mouse, and the muskrat.

Old world rats and mice occur throughout the world, and Minnesota is no exception. We have the Norway or house rat and the house mouse. The meadow jumping mouse and the rare woodland jumping mouse are the only jumping mice native to the state.

Meat-Eaters (Order Carnivora) Minnesota's largest carnivore, the black bear, reaches 250 to 300 pounds, from a mere 12 ounces at birth. They are protected in certain areas but may be hunted during the deer season. Extinct as a wild animal in the state, the grizzly bear once lived in the Red River Valley where they followed herds of buffalo.

The ring-tailed, black-masked racoons' population is directly related to the availability of acorns - the more the merrier. Rarely seen are the tree-climbing pine martens. On the up swing are the fishers, formerly quite abundant in the forest.

Minnesota has the "least weasel," the world's smallest carnivore, the long-tailed weasel, and the sort-tailed weasel. This weasel's brown coat turns to white in winter except for the black-tipped tail in which phase they are known as ermine.

Mink are the state's most valuable fur-bearers, with 50,000 pelts taken annually.

The largest of the weasel clan, the wolverine, is extinct in the state. However, because of occasional sightings, it is not surprising that some will move down from Canada. The playful and frolicsome otter, though trapped to the point of extinction, is making a comeback in the north and is occasionally observed in southern Minnesota. Two versions of the 'pole-cat' or 'woodpussy' are the striped skunk or civet cat. To meet them is to know them. Except for the northeast, the badger digs his den throughout the state. Native to the state are the red fox and the gray fox, both nocturnal, the latter being most common in southeastern Minnesota.

Coyotes, looking like large-eared, medium-sized German Shepherd dogs, are to be found most anywhere in the state.

Timber, or gray, wolves are larger and more heavily bodied than coyotes and prefer the heavy cover of forests. Once found throughout the state, they are limited to the wildest of the north country and their population is estimated to be between 1,200 and 1,500. Their numbers have approximately doubled in the last 20 years.

The Cougar, or mountain lion, the largest member of the cat family, is the only long-tailed cat in Minnesota. Once roaming throughout the state, especially when deer herds were prolific, the cat was officially reported in Becker County in 1897, but recently has not been reported. Though now quite rare, the Canada lynx is still taken in small numbers in the northern part of the state. Bobcats live in wooded areas of southern Minnesota, and have been seen recently in the northlands.

Hooved Animals (Order Artiodactyla)   The white-tailed deer is Minnesota's most abundant big game animal. It is found in all 87 countries. Rare members of this family include the mule deer (rarely seen along the Red River) and the elk (roughly 40 remain).

Before extensive lumbering in the 1800s, thousands of moose roamed northern Minnesota. The largest of our state deer, the herd had dwindled by 1922 to about 2500 animals. •Conservation practices in the 1970s and 1980s brought the population to the point where the state legislature authorized the taking of a limited number of moose on an experimental basis. The state's moose population is estimated now at between 6,000 and 7,000. Moose hunting is allowed every other year.   Now extirpated from Minnesota, the woodland caribou was last seen in the boggy area of Red Lake. In 1967, a herd of four pronghorn antelope was seen in southwestern Minnesota. Conservation experts say they have never been regular visitors.

The mighty buffalo once were common in the southern two-thirds of the state. Indians stampeded them to their deaths over steep cliffs at what is now Blue Mounds State Park in Rock County. Early records tell of 400 killed by LeSueur's party in the 1700s to use as winter food provisions near the present city of Mankato. The last account, in June 1880, reported four buffalo chased over the prairie by Indians in an area which is now the Carlos Avery Wildlife Management Area.

Minnesota's Flora and Fauna

Minnesota is located at a biological crossroads of three great vegetation regions: the western plains and prairies, the northern coniferous forest, and the eastern hardwood forest.

Our North Star State, because of its unique location and climate, even features a touch of the Arctic in our cold northern muskeg, while some plants characteristic of the southern Appalachians are found in our southeastern counties. Then there are countless lakes, streams and wetlands that provide a great variety of aquatic and marsh plants.

All of these habitat types, their developmental stages, environmental niches, and margins where habitat types merge (econtones), are the homes of many different kinds of plants and animals.

Each type of habitat favors certain kinds of plants and animals, and in turn, the habitat is modified by them.

If we add up the kinds (species) of plants and animals that thrive without care in Minnesota, such wildlings total approximately as follows: 69 Ferns and relatives; 13 Pines and relatives; 1,700 Flowering plants (1,500 of which are native to Minnesota); 80 Mammals; 240 Birds ("regular species"); 27 Reptiles; 18 Amphibians; and 156 Fish.

The above list is of "resident" species, in the sense that they reproduce in Minnesota. However, many of the birds that nest here winter elsewhere, and in this sense are "migratory". The American Eel is an exceptional case since it spends most of its adult life in inland waters, but spawns in the sea.

Most, but not all, of the wild plants are natives. About 200 of our wild flowering plants originally came from other places, especially Eurasia, and are accidental introductions or escaped cultivated plants. Many of these plants thrive in disturbed situations and soils. Some examples are the common dandelion, quack grass, catnip, curled pondweed, eurasian watermilfoil, and ox-eye daisy.

A smaller proportion of wild animals are non-natives. Among the mammals are the house mouse and Norway rat; the alien birds include the English sparrow, starling, common pigeon, ring-necked pheasant, Hungarian partridge, and quite recently, the cattle egret and monk parakeet; introduced fish include the German carp, ruffe, round goby, zebra mussel, rainbow trout, and brown trout.

To nurture Minnesota's rich variety is a worthy goal for all of us.

Chapter 21

Sports

From the legends of the Vikings to the present day arm wrestling and soccer, the state of Minnesota has had a rich tradition in the world of sports. No doubt the voyageurs raced their canoes as is done today and we know the early woodsmen had birling and tree climbing contests. Scandinavians were skiing cross country and downhill long before it became fashionable. The first ski club was organized in Red Wing and the first water skis were made in Minnesota. Snowmobiling, curling, ice fishing, skiing and ice boating are just not possible in most states but thousands of Minnesotans eagerly look forward to winter just to participate in these sports.

Football's Pudge Hefflefinger and baseball's Chief Bender were Minnesotans who had attained national fame by the turn of the century. Pudge is generally regarded as one of the eleven best football players of all time (along with Bronko Nagurski). The Chief, a native of Brainerd, is a member of baseball's Hall of Fame.

Other Minnesotans who attained national fame were Bernie Bierman, an outstanding coach (and Bud Grant's mentor); Bronko Nagurski, who became a legend in his own time with the Gophers and the Chicago Bears; Bruce Smith, the only Gopher to win the Heisman trophy, in 1941; Jeannie Arth who won the U.S. National Doubles championship twice and Wimbledon in 1959 (with Darlene Hard); Cindy Nelson of Lutsen won a bronze medal in the 1976 Olympics. Patty Berg, co-founder and first president of the LPGA, won 83 National Womens' Professional Golf Association titles and is a member of Golf's Hall of Fame. Hibbing's Roger Maris hit 61 home runs to break Babe Ruth's record. Though not Minnesotans by birth, future Baseball Hall of Famers Ted Williams (1939), Ray Dandridge (1950), Willie Mays (1951), and Carl Yastrzemski (1960) all played for the Minneapolis Millers.

From 1924 to 1927 Ole Haugsrud's Duluth Eskimos played in the National Football League with the famous Ernie Nevers on the team. When the NFL expanded in 1961, George Halas of Chicago saw that Ole retained his NFL franchise for Minnesota and Ole became an owner of the Vikings. Since the Eskimos a succession of major league teams have come and gone from the Minnesota scene. After WWII, the Minneapolis Lakers came into being and brought national basketball championships to Minneapolis along with George Mikan, Vern Mikkelson and Jim Pollard. When attendance sagged they moved to Los Angles but kept their name. Metropolitan stadium attracted the Washington Senators to Bloomington for the 1961 season as the Minnesota Twins.

Herb Brooks, coached the 1980 Olympic gold medal-winning hockey team. Team member Neal Broten, who became an NHL player, was also U of MN's first Hobey Baker award winner, for the 1980-81 season.

Tom Lehman, 1996 British Open champion, was the 1996 PGA Player of the Year.

Kevin McHale, former Boston Celtic, is part owner, vice president of basketball operations and general manager of the Minnesota Timberwolves. He was inducted into the Basketball Hall of Fame in October 1999.

Minnesota Vikings

Vikings Facts

Name: Minnesota Vikings (name depicts aggressive warriors and has ties to the Nordic and Scandinavian ancestry of many area residents).

Franchise Granted—January, 1960

First Season—1961

Team Colors: Purple and White with Gold trim

Home Field:1961-1981 Metropolitan Stadium, Bloomington capacity (48,446 1982 to present: Hubert H. Humphrey Metrodome, Minneapolis capacity 64,152

Training Camp: Mankato State University, Mankato, Minnesota 56001 (612) 828-6500

Affiliation: National Football League, National Football Conference, Central Division

Championships: Central Division: 1968, 69, 70, 71, 73, 74, 75, 76, 77, 78, 80, 89, 92, 94

NFL Western Division 1969

National Football League 1969

National Football Conference 1973, 74, 76

Club All-time Record through 1998: 313 wins, 244 losses, 9 ties regular season. Post-season record 15wins, 21 losses.

Office: Winter Park, 9520 Viking Drive, Eden Prairie, MN 55344 (612) 828-6500

Ticket Office:500 11th Avenue South, Minneapolis, MN 55415 (612) 333-8828

Owner: Red McCombs

President: Gary Woods

Head Coaches: 1961-66 Norm Van Brocklin; 1967-83 & 85 Bud Grant; 1984 Les Steckel; 1986-91 Jerry Burns;

Dennis Green
Head Coach 1992 to Present

In his seven seasons at the helm of the Minnesota Vikings, Dennis Green has averaged 9.5 wins per year, made the playoffs three times and won two NFC Central division titles while adding young talent to a roster that went five years (1988-92) without a first-round draft choice. At the Metrodome under Green, the Vikings are 21-11 (.656). Overall, Minnesota has posted the division's best record (21-11) against NFC Central teams the past four years.

Green is one of only seven people in league history to lead his team to the playoffs in each of his first three seasons as a head coach in the NFL. He earned NFL Coach of the Year honors from the Washington Touchdown Club and NFC Coach of the Year honors from United Press International and College & Pro Football Newsweekly.

Prior to joining Minnesota, Green head coached at Stanford and helped the San Francisco 49ers to a Super Bowl title by coaching receivers.

Hall of Fame

Fran Tarkenton, inducted in 1986, retired as the National Football League record holder for career passing yards with 47,003, played 13 of his 18 seasons with the Vikings. He was the 1975 NFL MVP. He is the Vikings all-time leader in passing attempts (4,569), completions (2,635), yards (33,098), touchdown passes (239), and rating (80.2). A third-round draft choice in 1961, Tarkenton led the Vikings to Super Bowl appearances in 1973, 74, and 76.

Alan Page, inducted in 1988, made his mark as a member of the famous "Purple People Eaters" defense. The Vikings' first-round draft choice in 1967 out of Notre Dame, Page had 108 career sacks and 16 blocked kicks, third and second, respectively, on the Vikings all-time list. Page was a nine-time Pro Bowler and the league MVP in 1971. He is currently an Associate Justice of the Minnesota Supreme Court.

Bud Grant, inducted in 1994, was head coach of the Vikings from 1967-83 and 85. With the Vikings his teams compiled a regular-season record of 158-96-5, made the playoffs 12 times, and won 15 championships. Prior to coming to Minnesota, Grant coached the Winnipeg Blue Bombers from 1957-66. He is also a member of the Canadian Football League Hall of Fame.

Jim Finks, inducted in 1995, was the Vikings General Manager from 1964-1973. Credited with hiring Bud Grant and overseeing the Vikings as they played in Superbowls IV and VIII.

Paul Krause, inducted in 1998, played safety from 1968-79. Holds the NFL interception record with 81 and ranks third all-time interception return with 1,185 yards. His 10 interceptions in 1975 remain a club record. He was an 8-time Pro Bowler, started in 4 Superbowls, voted All-NFL four times and All-NFC five times.

Other Hall of Famers who spent time with the Vikings include Hugh McElhenny, HB, 1961-62; Norm Van Brocklin, head coach, 1961-66; Jim Langer, C, 1980-81; and Jan Stenerud, K, 1984-85.

Viking All-Time Leaders

RUSHING

Player	Att.	Yards	Avg.	Long	TD
1. Foreman, Chuck (1973-79)	1,529	5,879	3.8	51	52
2. Brown, Bill (1962-74)	1,627	5,757	3.5	48	52
3. Brown, Ted (1979-86)	1,117	4,546	4.1	60	40
4. Osborn, Dave (1965-75)	1,172	4,320	3.7	73	29
5. Nelson, Darrin (1982-89, 1991-92)	981	4,231	4.3	72	18
6. Mason, Tommy (1961-66)	761	3,252	4.3	71	28
7. Smith, Robert (1993-97)	**646**	**3,095**	**4.8**	**78t**	**17**
8. Allen, Terry (1990-94)	641	2,795	4.4	55t	23
9. Tarkenton, Fran (1961-66, 1972-78)	453	2,543	5.6	52t	22
10. Anderson, Alfred (1984-91)	626	2,374	3.8	29	22

RECEIVING

Player	No.	Yards	Avg.	Long	TD
1. Carter, Cris (1990-97)	**667**	**7,986**	**12.0**	**78t**	**70**
2. Jordan, Steve (1982-94)	498	6,307	12.7	68t	29
3. Carter, Anthony (1985-93)	478	7,636	16.0	73t	52
4. Rashad, Ahmad (1976-82)	400	5,489	13.7	76t	34
5. White, Sammy (1976-86)	393	6,400	16.3	69t	50
6. Brown, Ted (1979-86)	339	2,850	8.4	67t	13
7. Foreman, Chuck (1973-79)	336	3,057	9.1	66t	23
8. Reed, Jake (1991-97)	**308**	**5,007**	**16.3**	**82t**	**26**
9. Young, Rickey (1978-83)	292	2,255	7.6	48	14
10. Brown, Bill (1962-74)	284	3,177	11.2	76t	23

RUSHING-RECEIVING

Player	Rushing	Receiving	Total
1. Foreman, Chuck (1973-79)	5,879	3,057	8,936
2. Brown, Bill (1962-74)	5,757	3,177	8,934
3. Carter, Cris (1990-97)	**21**	**7,986**	**8,007**
4. Carter, Anthony (1985-93)	290	7,636	7,926
5. Brown, Ted (1979-86)	4,546	2,850	7,396

PASSING *(Min. 1,500 Att.)*

Player	Att.	Comp.	Pct.	Yards	TD	Long	Int	Rating
1. Tarkenton, Fran (1961-66, 72-78)	4,569	2,635	57.7	33,098	239	89t	194	80.2
2. Wilson, Wade (1981-91)	1,665	929	55.8	12,135	66	75t	75	73.3

SCORING

Player	TD	2 pt.	PAT	FG	Total
1. Cox, Fred (1963-77)	—	—	519	282	1,365
2. Reveiz, Fuad (1990-95) ·	—	—	199	133	598
3. Brown, Bill (1962-74)	76	—	—	—	456
4. Foreman, Chuck (1973-79)	75	—	—	—	450
5. Carter, Cris (1990-97)	**70**	**5**	**—**	**—**	**430**
6. Danmeier, Rick (1978-83)	—	—	154	70	364
7. Carter, Anthony (1985-93)	54	—	—	—	324
8. Brown, Ted (1979-86)	53	—	—	—	318
9. White, Sammy (1976-86)	50	—	—	—	300
10. Nelson, Chuck (1986-88)	—	—	128	55	293

TACKLES

Year	Player	Solo	Assists	Total
1961	*Hawkins, Rip	106	28	134
1962	Hawkins, Rip	74	16	90
1963	Hawkins, Rip	94	20	114
1964	Hawkins, Rip	61	38	99
1965	Vargo, Larry	78	10	88
1966	Warwick, Lonnie	66	26	92
1967	Warwick, Lonnie	90	23	113
1968	Page, Alan	66	30	96
1969	Warwick, Lonnie	70	6	76
1970	Warwick, Lonnie	60	11	71
1971	Hilgenberg, Wally	87	23	110
1972	Page, Alan	99	33	132
1973	Siemon, Jeff	112	43	155
1974	Siemon, Jeff	107	46	153
1975	Siemon, Jeff	85	40	125
1976	Siemon, Jeff	120	41	161
1977	McNeill, Fred	92	44	136
1978	Siemon, Jeff	170	59	229
1979	Hannon, Tommy	127	47	174
1980	Studwell, Scott	153	54	207
1981	Studwell, Scott	156	74	230
1982	Studwell, Scott	85	37	122
1983	Studwell, Scott	133	83	216
1984	Studwell, Scott	143	72	215
1985	Studwell, Scott	109	97	206
1986	Browner, Joey	107	52	159
1987	Solomon, Jesse	92	29	121
	Browner, Joey	87	34	121
1988	Studwell, Scott	81	45	126
1989	Studwell, Scott	102	71	173
1990	Merriweather, Mike	99	54	153
1991	Merriweather, Mike	101	88	189
1992	Del Rio, Jack	113	40	153
1993	Del Rio, Jack	108	61	169
1994	Del Rio, Jack	118	67	185
1995	McDaniel, Ed	96	40	136
1996	Brady, Jeff	89	57	146
1997	McDaniel, Ed	77	58	135

* Rookie

Minnesota Vikings Single Game Playoff Records

Category	Player	Performance	
Rushing Yards	Chuck Foreman	(12/26/76)	118
Passing Yards	Randall Cunningham	(1/3/98)	331
Passing Touchdowns	Fran Tarkenton	(12/18/76)	3
" "	Randall Cunningham	(1/3/98)	3
Receiving Yards	Anthony Carter	(1/9/88)	227
Receptions	Amp Lee	(1/1/95)	11
Interceptions	Bobby Bryant	(12/30/73, 12/26/76)	2
"	John Turner	(1/9/83)	2
"	Joey Browner	(12/26/88)	2
Field Goals	Chuck Nelson	(1/9/88)	5
Touchdowns Eight times - last by Cris Carter		(1/3/98)	2
Points	Chuck Nelson	(1/9/88)	18

Source: Courtesy Minnesota Vikings Media Relations

Minnesota Twins

Twins Facts

Name: Minnesota Twins (former Washington Senators, named after the sister cities of Minneapolis and St. Paul)

Franchise Granted: January, 1960   First Season: 1961

Home Field: 1961-1981: Metropolitan Stadium, Bloomington (capacity 48,446)

1982 to present: Hubert H. Humphrey Metrodome, Minneapolis (capacity 48,678). Twins signed a lease here through the 2000 season.

Affiliation: American League, Central Division

Division Championships: 1969, 70, 87, 91

American League Pennants: 1965, 87, 91

World Series Champions: 1987, 91

Club All-time Record: Oct. 1999--3052 wins, 3126 losses, 8 ties in 39 seasons.

Office—The Metrodome, 34 Kirby Puckett Place, Minneapolis, MN 55415

(612) 375-1366   Ticket info—(612) 33-TWINS or 1-800-33-TWINS

www.mntwins.com

Owner: Carl R. Pohlad   President: T. Geron (Jerry) Bell

Tom Kelly

Manager 1986-Present

A native of Minnesota, born in Graceville, Tom (T. K.) Kelly joined the Twins as a third base coach in 1983 and replaced Ray Miller as manager in September, 1986, with 23 games left to go in the season. After a 6th place finish in the Western Division the previous year, Kelly led the team to the first of two World Series Championships in his first full year as manager in 1987. The Twins defeated the St. Louis Cardinals in seven games, with all victories in the Metrodome. He was the youngest manager (37) to lead a club into the American League Championship Series, became the 18th rookie manager to guide a team to a World Series, and the 5th to win it. He was named UPI's AL Manager of the Year. The Twins were also the come-back kids four years later when they went from 7th place in the Division to defeating the Atlanta Braves in the next year's World Series in 1991. T. K. guided the AL All-Stars to a win in 1992. He recorded his 700th career win in September, 1995. This manager's style is characterized by teamwork and utilizing his player's strengths to their fullest.

Kelly's baseball career began as a Seattle Pilot's fifth round pick in June, 1968 free agent draft. The Twins signed him as a free agent, April 1971, and he played minor league ball until adding managing in 1977 with Tacoma of the Pacific Coast League. He played with the Twins during the 1975 season. Kelly has the most tenure of any other manager or head coach in all of professional sports.

TWINS' YEARLY STANDINGS

Year	Won	Lost	Tied	Pct.	Pos.	GA/GB	Manager	Attendance
1961	25	41	0	.318	9	-17.5	Lavagetto	
	45	49	1	.479			Mele	
	70	90	1	.438	7	-38.0		1,256,723
1962	91	71	1	.562	2	-5.0	Mele	1,433,116
1963	91	70	0	.565	3	-13.0	Mele	1,406,652
1964	79	83	1	.488	6*	-20.0	Mele	1,207,514
1965	102	60	0	.630	1	+7.0	Mele	1,463,258
1966	89	73	0	.549	2	-9.0	Mele	1,259,374
1967	25	25	0	.500	6	-6.0	Mele	
	66	46	2	.589			Ermer	
	91	71	2	.562	2*	-1.0		1,483,547
1968	79	83	0	.488	7	-24.0	Ermer	1,143,257
1969	97	65	0	.599	1	+9.0	Martin	1,349,328
1970	98	64	0	.605	1	+9.0	Rigney	1,261,887
1971	74	86	0	.463	5	-26.5	Rigney	940,858
1972	36	34	0	.514	3	-9.5	Rigney	
	41	43	0	.488			Quilici	
	77	77	0	.500	3	-15.5		797,901
1973	81	81	0	.500	3	-13.0	Quilici	907,499
1974	82	80	1	.506	3	-8.0	Quilici	662,401
1975	76	83	0	.478	4	-20.5	Quilici	737,156
1976	85	77	0	.525	3	-5.0	Mauch	715,394
1977	84	77	0	.522	4	-17.5	Mauch	1,162,727
1978	73	89	0	.451	4	-19.0	Mauch	787,878
1979	82	80	0	.506	4	-6.0	Mauch	1,070,521
1980	54	71	0	.432	4	-26.5	Mauch	
	23	13	0	.639			Goryl	
	77	84	0	.478	3	-19.5		769,206
1981 (1)	11	25	1	.306	6	-11.5	Goryl	
	6	14	0	.300			Gardner	
	17	39	1	.304	7	-18.0		
1981 (2)	24	29	0	.453	4	-6.0	Gardner	469,090
1982	60	102	0	.370	7	-33.0	Gardner	921,186
1983	70	92	0	.432	5*	-29.0	Gardner	858,939
1984	81	81	0	.500	2*	-3.0	Gardner	1,598,692
1985	27	35	0	.436	6	-7.5	Gardner	
	50	50	0	.500			Miller	
	77	85	0	.475	4*	-14.0		1,651,814
1986	59	80	0	.425	7	-21.5	Miller	
	12	11	0	.522			Kelly	
	71	91	0	.438	6	-21.0		1,255,453
1987	85	77	0	.525	1	+2.0	Kelly	2,081,976
1988	91	71	0	.562	2	-13.0	Kelly	3,030,672
1989	80	82	0	.494	5	-19.0	Kelly	2,277,438
1990	74	88	0	.457	7	-29.0	Kelly	1,751,584
1991	95	67	0	.586	1	+8.0	Kelly	2,293,842
1992	90	72	0	.555	2	-6.0	Kelly	2,482,428
1993	71	91	0	.438	5*	-23.0	Kelly	2,048,673
1994	53	60	0	.469	4	-14.0	Kelly	1,398,565
1995	56	88	0	.389	5	-44.0	Kelly	1,057,667
1996	78	84	0	.481	4	-21.5	Kelly	1,437,352
1997	68	94	0	.420	4	-18.5	Kelly	1,411,064
1998	70	92	0	.432	4	-19.0	Kelly	1,165,980
Totals	2,989	3,029	7	.497				51,008,612

(* — Denotes tie.)

Finishes (full-season): First-5; Second-6; Third-6; Fourth-8; Fifth-5; Sixth-2; Seventh-5.

(Note: Two divisional play began in 1969; Three divisional play began in 1994; Split-season in 1981.)

All-Stars

AGUILERA, Rick, p 1991, 92, 93
ALLISON, Bob, of, 1b 1963, 64
BATTEY, Earl, c 1962, 62, 63, 65, 66
BLYLEVEN, Bert, p 1973
BRUNANSKY, Tom, of 1985
CARDENAS, Leo, ss 1971
CAREW, Rod, 2b, 1b1967, 68, 69, 70,
    71, 72, 73, 74, 75, 76, 77, 78
CHANCE, Dean, p 1967
CORBETT, Doug, p 1981
ENGLE, Dave, c 1984
GAETTI, Gary, 3b 1988, 89
GRANT, Jim, p 1965
HALL, Jimmie, of 1964, 65
HISLE, Larry, of 1977
HRBEK, Kent, 1b1982
KAAT, Jim, p 1962, 66
KILLEBREW,Harmon,3b,1b, of
    1961, 62, 63, 64, 65, 66, 67, 68, 69,
    70, 71
KNOBLAUCH, Chuck, 2b1992, 94,
    96, 97
LANDREAUX, Ken, of 1980
LAUDNER, Tim, c1988
MORRIS, Jack, p 1991
OLIVA, Tony, of 1964, 65, 66, 67, 68,
    69, 70, 71
PASCUAL, Camilo, p1961, 62, 62, 64
PERRY, Jim, p1970, 71
PUCKETT, Kirby, of1986, 87, 88,
    89, 90, 91, 92, 93, 94, 95
RADKE, Brad, p1998
REARDON, Jeff, p1988
ROLLINS, Rich, 3b1962, 62
ROSEBORO, John, c1969
SMALLEY, Roy, ss1979
VERSALLES, Zoilo, ss1963, 65
VIOLA, Frank, p1988
WARD, Gary, of1983
WYNEGAR, Butch, c1976, 77

Minnesota Natives

Player	Position	Seasons
Fred Bruckbauer	rhp	1961
Tom Burgmeier,	lhp	1974-77
Jim Eisenreich,	cf	1982-84
Bob Gebhard,	rhp	1971-72
Paul Giel,	rhp	1961
Dave Goltz,	rhp	1972-79
Kent Hrbek,	1b	1981-94
Tom Johnson,	rhp	1974-78
Tom Kelly,	1b	1975
Jerry Kindall,	2b	1964-65
Jerry Koosman,	lhp	1979-81
Mike Mason,	lhp	1988
Paul Molitor,	dh-1b	1996-98
Jack Morris,	rhp	1991
Greg Olson,	c	1989
Mike Poepping,	rf	1975
Tom Quinlan,	3b	1996
Brian Raabe,	2b	1995-96
Terry Steinbach,	c	1997-
Dick Stigman,	lhp	1962-65
Jerry Terrell,	ss	1973-77
George Thomas,	lf	1971
Charley Walters,	rhp	1969
Dave Winfield,	of	1993-94

Single Season Batting Average

In 1977, Rod Carew chased .400, but finished with .388 and an AL MVP.

1) Rod Carew	.388*	1977
2) Rod Carew	.364*	1974
3) Rod Carew	.359*	1975
4) Kirby Puckett	.356	1988
5) Rod Carew	.350*	1973
6) Chuck Knoblauch	.341	1996
6) Paul Molitor	.341	1996
8) Kirby Puckett	.339*	1989
9) Tony Oliva	.337*	1971
10) Lyman Bostock	.336	1977

* = Led League

No-Hitters				
Pitcher	Date	Opponent	On Base	Score
Jack Kralick	8-26-62	KC	1	1-0
Dean Chance	8-6-67 (5 inn.)	Boston	0	2-0
Dean Chance	8-25-67	at Cleveland	6	2-1
Scott Erickson	4-27-94	Milwaukee	5	6-0
Eric Milton	9-11-99	Anaheim	2	7-0

Single Season Runs Batted In

Harmon Killebrew had over 100 RBIs in 8 of his 14 years with the Twins.

1) Harmon Killebrew 140* 1969
2) Harmon Killebrew 126* 1962
3) Harmon Killebrew 122 1961
4) Kirby Puckett 121 1988
5) Harmon Killebrew 119* 1971
5) Larry Hisle 119* 1977
7) Harmon Killebrew 113 1967
7) Harmon Killebrew 113 1970
7) Paul Molitor 113 1996
10) Kirby Puckett 112 1994
* = Led League

Single Season Homeruns

Killebrew hit 573 HRs in his career. He is fifth on the all-time list and second only to Babe Ruth in the AL.

1) Harmon Killebrew 49* 1964
1) Harmon Killebrew 49* 1969
3) Harmon Killebrew 48* 1962
4) Harmon Killebrew 46 1961
5) Harmon Killebrew 45* 1963
6) Harmon Killebrew 44** 1967
7) Harmon Killebrew 41 1970
8) Harmon Killebrew 39 1966
9) Bob Allison 35 1963
10) two players tied 34
* = Led League
** = Tied for League Lead

Retired Numbers

Harmon Killebrew	No. 3
Rod Carew	No. 29
Tony Oliva	No. 6
Kent Hrbek	No. 14
Kirby Puckett	No. 34.

Source: Courtesy Minnesota Twins Media Relations

Minnesota Timberwolves

Wolves Facts

Name: Minnesota Timberwolves
Franchise Granted—April, 1987   First Season—1989-90
Team Colors—Blue and White
Home Field—Target Center, opened October 16, 1990 (capacity 19,006)
First season played in the Metrodome.
Affiliation—National Basketball Association, Western Conference, Midwest Division
Club All-time Record—The Timberwolves were 25-25 in 1998-99. Overall, the Wolves are 263-529, including post-season play, in 10 seasons.

Office—600 First Avenue North, Minneapolis, MN 55403 612-673-1600
Ticket Office—Timberwolves Ticket Office, Target Center, 600 First Avenue
North, Minneapolis, MN 55403 or call Ticketmaster ticket centers. Group
orders: call 612-337-DUNK
Owner—Glen Taylor   President—Rob Moor
Head Coaches—1989-91 Bill Musselman; 1991-93, Jimmy Rodgers; 1993-94 ,
Sidney Lowe; 1994-95, Bill Blair; 1995-present, Phil "Flip" Saunders.

Flip Saunders
Head Coach/General Manager

Saunders was named general manager of the Timberwolves May, 1995,
and in addition, was named head coach in December of the same year. As
head coach, he has earned a 156-174 record including a best ever 45-37
record for 1997-98. He led Minnesota to its first playoff series in 1997 against
the Houston Rockets. During this series, the Timberwolves tied an NBA
playoff record with the fewest turnovers in a three-game series (28).

Before coming to the Timberwolves, Saunders spent seven seasons as a
coach in the Continental Basketball Association where he ranks second all-
time with 253 victories. He established a reputation in the CBA for turning
around losing teams and producing winning records the next season.

The First Wolves All-Stars In the 1997 All-Star game, Tom Gugliotta finished with nine points, eight rebounds, and three assists and Kevin Garnett
added six points, nine rebounds, and one assist. Garnett returned to the All-
Star game in 1998 where he scored 12 points and grabbed 4 rebounds.

TOTAL POINTS

97-98	Kevin Garnett	1518
96-97	Tom Gugliotta	1672
95-96	Isaiah Rider	1470
94-95	Isaiah Rider	1532
93-94	Isaiah Rider	1313
92-93	Doug West	1543
91-92	Pooh Richardson	1350
90-91	Tony Campbell	1678
89-90	Tony Campbell	1903

FIELD GOALS ATTEMPTED

97-98	Kevin Garnett	1293
96-97	Tom Gugliotta	1339
95-96	Isaiah Rider	1206
94-95	Isaiah Rider	1249
93-94	Isaiah Rider	1115
92-93	Doug West	1249
91-92	Pooh Richardson	1261
90-91	Tony Campbell	1502
89-90	Tony Campbell	1581

SCORING AVERAGE

97-98	Kevin Garnett	18.5
96-97	Tom Gugliotta	20.6
95-96	Isaiah Rider	19.6
94-95	Isaiah Rider	20.4
93-94	Christian Laettner	16.8
92-93	Doug West	19.3
91-92	Tony Campbell	16.8
90-91	Tony Campbell	21.8
89-90	Tony Campbell	23.2

FIELD-GOAL PERCENTAGE

97-98	Tom Gugliotta	(319-635)	.502
96-97	Dean Garrett	(223-389)	.573
95-96	Kevin Garnett	(361-735)	.491
94-95	Christian Laettner	(450-920)	.489
93-94	Thurl Bailey	(232-455)	.510
92-93	Doug West	(646-1249)	.517
91-92	Doug West	(463-894)	.518
90-91	Felton Spencer	(195-381)	.512
89-90	Tyrone Corbin	(521-1083)	.481

MOST POINTS

Career:	6216	Doug West	1989-98
Season:	1903	Tony Campbell	1989-90
Game:	44	Tony Campbell	vs. Boston, 2/2/90
Half:	30	Tony Campbell	vs. Boston (2nd), 2/2/90
Period:	23	James Robinson	@ Cleveland (4th), 12/30/96
Overtime:	9	Stephon Marbury	vs. Dallas, 2/15/98

MOST FIELD GOALS MADE

Career:	2530	Doug West	1989-98
Season:	723	Tony Campbell	1989-90
Game:	16	Pooh Richardson	vs. Golden State, 1/19/91;
		Doug West	@ Golden State, 12/19/92 (OT);
		Tom Gugliotta	@ Houston, 1/16/98 (OT)
Half:	11	Most recently: Kevin Garnett	@ Portland (1st), 1/25/97
Period:	9	Most recently: Tom Gugliotta	@ Vancouver (1st), 1/23/97
Overtime:	4	Stephon Marbury	vs. Dallas, 2/15/98

MOST CONSECUTIVE FIELD GOALS MADE

13	Felton Spencer	11/7/90 to 11/13/90;
	Kevin Garnett	12/3/97 to 12/5/97

MOST FIELD GOALS ATTEMPTED

Career:	5225	Doug West	1989-98
Season:	1581	Tony Campbell	1989-90
Game:	31	Tony Campbell	vs. Orlando, 2/22/91;
		Tony Campbell	vs. Houston, 3/19/91
Half:	20	Tony Campbell	@ Golden State (2nd), 2/12/91;
		Tom Gugliotta	vs. L.A. Clippers (2nd), 1/11/97

HIGHEST FIELD-GOAL PERCENTAGE

Career:	.502	(327-651) Cherokee Parks	1996-98
Season:	.573	(223-389) Dean Garrett	1996-97
Game:	.917	(11-12) Tom Gugliotta	@ San Antonio, 2/26/97
Half:	1.000	(8-8) Christian Laettner	vs. Sacramento (2nd), 11/19/93;
		(8-8) Isaiah Rider	vs. Portland (1st), 4/22/94;
		(8-8) Kevin Garnett	vs. Indiana (2nd), 12/3/97
Period:	1.000	(7-7) Randy Breuer	@ Utah (1st), 2/13/90;
		(7-7) Doug West	@ Houston (3rd), 2/5/93

MOST THREE-POINT FIELD GOALS MADE

Career:	295	Isaiah Rider	1993-96
Season:	139	Isaiah Rider	1994-95
Game:	8	Stephon Marbury	@ Seattle, 12/23/97
Half:	6	James Robinson	@ Cleveland (2nd), 12/30/96
Period:	6	James Robinson	@ Cleveland (4th), 12/30/96
Overtime:	2	Tony Campbell	@ Cleveland, 2/2/91

MOST CONSECUTIVE THREE-POINT FIELD GOALS MADE

7	Stephon Marbury	@ Seattle, 12/23/97

Source: Courtesy Minnesota Timberwolves Media Relations

Minnesota Lynx

Lynx Facts

Name: Minnesota Lynx

Franchise Granted—April, 1998   First Season—1999

Home Field—Target Center (capacity 19,006)

Affiliation—Womens National Basketball Association, Western Conference.

Club All-time Record—The Lynx were 15-17 in 1999.

Office—600 First Avenue North, Minneapolis, MN 55403 612-673-1600 fax

612-673-1699   www.wnba.com

Operating Owner—Glen Taylor   President—Rob Moor

Head Coach—Brian Agler.

Brian Agler
Head Coach/General Manager

Agler was named head coach and general manager for the Minnesota Lynx on November 17, 1998. He led the team to a 15-17 first season.

He joined Minnesota in their inaugural season after serving as head coach of the American Basketball League (ABL) Columbus Quest. He led the Quest to back-to-back Eastern Conference regular-season titles and back-to-back ABL World championships in 1997 and 1998.

In April, 1998, Timberwolves owner, Glen Taylor was awarded an expansion WNBA team to be operated by the Timberwolves. Under the expansion plan, Minnesota was added to the six-team Western Conference, including the Houston Comets, Los Angeles Sparks, Phoenix Mercury, Sacramento Monarchs, and Utah Starzz. The Orlando Miracle, the second expansion team for 1999 played in the six-team Eastern Conference with the Charlotte Sting, Cleveland Rockers, Detroit Shock, New York Liberty, and Washington Mystics. The Lynx played a 32 game schedule in 1999 from June through August.

Tonya Edwards, represent the team in the **All-Star** game played July 14th at Madison Square Garden.

The WNBA is owned collectively by the 29 NBA teams .

•Ball size is 28.5" same as high school and NCAA women's.

•3-point line is 19'9" same as NCAA

•Games are two 20 minute halves and there is a 30 second shot clock.

1999 Regular Season WNBA Records Set or Tied

Individual Records

Most games, season - 32 — (tied) Tonya Edwards, Kristin Folkl, Andrea Lloyd-Curry, Angie Potthoff, Sonja Tate, 1999

Most three-point field goals, none missed, game - 5 — Andrea Lloyd-Curry, Minnesota at Sacramento, June 22, 1999

Team Records
Most three-point field goals per game, season - 6.3 — Minnesota, 1999 (200/32)
Most three-point field goals, game -14 — Minnesota at Utah, June 26, 1999
Source: Courtesy Minnesota Lynx Media Relations

Minnesota Wild Hockey

NHL hockey is scheduled to return to Minnesota as the expansion team, Minnesota Wild, opens its inaugural season at the new St. Paul arena in October, 2000.
Franchise granted—June 25, 1997
Lead investor & Chairman—Bob Naegele, Jr
Minnesota Wild ticket information:
Mail: Minnesota Wild ,Piper Jaffray Tower, 444 Cedar Street, Suite 900, St. Paul, MN 55101   Fax: (651) 222-1055   Telephone: Call (651) 222-WILD (9453) or Ticketmaster at (612) 989-5151 in the Twin Cities metro area. Or call your local Ticketmaster number.
You can request a printed brochure by e-mailing them at NHL2000@wild.com   website: www.wild.com/
Source: Minnesota Wild Media Relations

University of Minnesota

The University of Minnesota Athletic program has been dominated over the years by football, basketball, hockey and baseball. On the following pages is a statistical representation of the history of some of these and other sports at the University.
Further information about any of the men's or women's 22 inter-collegiate athletic programs can be obtained by contacting the University of Minnesota Sports Information Office, Room #208, 516 15th Avenue, South East, University of Minnesota, Minneapolis, Minnesota   55455.   Men's Athletics 612-625-4838. Ms. Athletics 612-624-8000.

The Big Ten Conference
The Big Ten Conference was born on January 11, 1895 when President James H. Smart of Purdue University called a meeting of the presidents of seven midwestern universities at Chicago for the purpose of considering regulation and control of intercollegiate athletics.
Just over a year later, representatives from the University of Chicago, the University of Illinois, the University of Michigan, the University of Minnesota, Northwestern University, Purdue University, and the University of Wisconsin met at the Palmer House in Chicago to establish standards and machinery for the regulation and administration of intercollegiate athletics.

All-Time Minnesota Football Coaching Records

Coach	Seasons	Years	Won	Lost	Tied	Pct.
Murray Warmath	18	1954-71	86	78	7	.528
Cal Stoll	7	1972-78	39	39	0	.500
Joe Salem	5	1979-83	19	35	1	.352
Lou Holtz	2	1984-85	10	12	0	.455
John Gutekunst	6+	1986-91	29	37	2	.441
Jim Wacker	5	1992-96	16	39	0	.291
Glen Mason	2	1997-	8	15	0	.348

Top 10 Career Total Offense

Name	Years	Rush	Pass	Total
Rickey Foggie	1984-87	2,150	5,162	7,312
Cory Sauter	1994-97	226	6,834	6,608
Marquel Fleetwood	1989-92	875	5,279	6,154
Mike Hohensee	1981-82	63	4,792	4,855
Tony Dungy	1973-76	1,165	3,515	4,680
Darrell Thompson	1986-89	4,654	22	4,676
Paul Giel	1951-53	2,188	1,922	4,110
Tim Schade	1993-94	31	3,986	4,017
Craig Curry	1969-71	734	3,060	3,79
Scott Schaffner	1987-91	174	3,472	3,646

Top 10 Career Tackles

Name	Years	Assist	Solo	Total
Pete Najarian	1982-85	245	237	482
Tyrone Carter	1996-present	92	321	413
Bill Light	1969-71	192	203	395
Steve Stewart	1974-77	146	179	355
Parc Williams	1994-98	117	234	351
Russ Heath	1990-93	159	170	329
Bruce Holmes	1983-86	153	170	323
Joel Staats	1988-91	141	177	319
Justin Conzemius	1992-95	199	118	317
Glenn Howard	1978-81	144	164	308

Minnesota Mentions in the Guinness Book of World Records
Shortest Fight There is a distinction between the quickest knock-out and the shortest fight. The shortest fight on record appears to be one in a Golden Gloves tournament at Minneapolis on November 4, 1947, when Mike Collins floored Pat Brownson with the first punch and the contest was stopped, without a count, four seconds after the bell.

U of M Men's Basketball All-Time Records

Season	Conf. W	L	Overall W	L	%	Conf. Finish
Clem Haskins						
1998-1999	8	8	17	11	.607	6th-tie
1997-1998	6	10	20	15	.571	18th
1996-1997	16	2	31	4	.886	1st
1995-1996	10	8	20	12	.594	5th-tie
1994-1995	10	8	20	11	.613	5th-tie
1993-1994	10	8	21	12	.636	4th
1992-1993	9	9	22	10	.688	5th
1991-1992	8	10	16	16	.500	6th
1990-1991	5	13	12	16	.429	9th
1989-1990	11	7	23	9	.719	4th
1988-1989	9	9	19	12	.613	5th
1987-1988	4	14	10	18	.357	9th
1986-1987	2	16	9	19	.321	9th
Coach: Jimmy Williams (2-9 Big Ten, 2-9 overall)						
1986	2	9	2	9	.182	8th
Coach: Jim Dutcher (98-89 Big Ten, 190-113 overall)						
1985-1986	3	4	13	7	.650	8th
1984-1985	6	12	13	15	.464	8th
1983-1984	6	12	15	13	.536	8th
1982-1983	9	9	18	11	.621	6th
1981-1982	14	4	23	6	.793	1st
1980-1981	9	9	19	11	.633	5th
1979-1980	10	8	21	11	.656	4th
1978-1979	6	12	11	16	.407	8th
1977-1978	12	6	17	10	.630	2nd
1976-1977	15	3	24	3	.889	- *
1975-1976	8	10	16	10	.615	6th

Coach: Bill Musselman (38-22 Big Ten, 69-32 overall)
*NCAA declared season forfeited to 0-27

New Sports Stadium Fund...

In 1999 Gov. Ventura proposed that citizens whosupported the building of a new professional sports stadium donate their tax rebate checks to a fund. The Metropolitan Sports Facilities Commission will accept checks through June 2000. At that time if there is no stadium plan, money will be returned. Make checks payable to: Metropolitan Sports Facilities Commission, 900 South 5th Street, Minneapolis, MN 55415 and write "New Stadium Fund" on the memo line.

U of M Men's Hockey

Year	G	W	L	T	Fin.	%
John Mariucci						
1956-57	29	12	15	2	3	.448
1957-58	26	15	11	0	4	.577
1958-59	22	11	9	2	#	.545
1959-60	24	8	15	1	6	.354
1960-61	24	16	7	1	2	.688
1961-62	20	9	10	1	6	.475
1962-63	27	16	7	4	4	.667
1963-64	24	14	10	0	3	.583
1964-65	27	14	12	1	3	.537
1965-66	27	16	11	0	2	.593
Glen Sonmor						
1966-67	29	9	19	1	8	.328
1967-68	30	19	11	0	5	.633
1968-69	30	14	13	3	5	.517
1969-70	32	20	12	0	1	.625
1970-71	29	13	15	1	5	.466
Glen Sonmor/Ken Yackel						
1971-72	32	8	24	0	10	.250
Herb Brooks						
1972-73	34	15	16	3	6	.485
1973-74	39	22	11	6	2	.641
1974-75	42	31	10	1	1	.779
1975-76	42	27	13	2	3	.667
1976-77	40	16	21	3	7	.438
1977-78	38	22	14	2	4	.605
1978-79	44	32	11	1	2	.739
Brad Buetow						
1979-80	41	26	15	0	2	.634
1980-81	45	33	12	0	1	.733
1981-82	36	22	12	2	3	.639
1982-83	46	33	12	1	1	.728
1983-84	40	27	11	2	3	.700
1984-85	47	31	13	3	2	.691
Doug Woog						
1985-86	48	*35	13	0	2	.729
1986-87	49	34	14	1	2	.704
1987-88	44	34	10	0	1	.773
1988-89	48	34	11	3	1	.74
1989-90	40	28	16	2	2	.630
1990-91	45	30	10	5	2	.722
1991-92	44	33	11	0	1	.750
1992-93	42	22	12*	8	2	.619
1993-94	42	25	13	4	2	.619
1994-95	44	25	14	5	4	.625
1995-96	12	30	10	2	2	.733
1996-97	42	28	13	1	1	.679
1997-98	39	17	22	0	6	.436
1998-99	43	15	19	9	5	.453

All-Time Record • 77 Seasons
2,143 games • 1,305-734-104 (.633)
* = UM Best
# = No League Play

University of Minnesota Women's Athletics (Ms.)

Ms. Soccer

• The Ms. Soccer Team claimed Big Ten Championships in 1995 and 1997.

• Head coach Sue Montagne was named the Big Ten Coach of the Year in both 1995 and 1997.

• Jennifer McElmury was given All-American second team honors in 1995 and 1996, and earned first-team All-American honors in 1997.

• Big Ten Player of the Year honors were given to Jennifer Walek in 1995 and Jennifer McElmury in 1996 and 1997. In addition, McElmury earned the Big Ten Medal of Honor and was named an Academic All-American 1997.

U of M Wrestling

Year	Duals	BigTen	NCAA
Wally Johnson			
1969-70	12-14-1	6th	15th
1970-71	9-10-1	6th	23rd
1971-72	10-6-1	4th	12th
1972-73	14-3-0	4th	19th
1973-74	16-4-0	5th	16th
1974-75	7-5-0	7th	18th
1975-76	15-5-0	2nd	7th
1976-77	15-7-0	2nd	4th
1977-78	14-7-0	4th	36th
1978-79	15-4-0	3rd	7th
1979-80	12-4-0	3rd	19th
1980-81	11-6-0	2nd	18th
1981-82	16-2-0	2nd	16th
1982-83	9-8-0	3rd	27th
1983-84	10-5-2	3rd	31st
1984-85	8-11-0	8th	40th
1985-86	16-7-0	4th	22nd
J Robinson			
1986-87	7-14-0	6th	T19th
1987-88	15-6-0	6th	16th
1988-89	14-9-0	2nd	7th
1989-90	10-6-0	T3rd	10th
1990-91	11-4-0	7th	8th
1991-92	8-14-0	4th	T21st
1992-93	21-3-1	4th	9th
1993-94	20-2-0	2nd	11th
1994-95	15-5-1	3rd	12th
1995-96	10-8-1	6th	19th
1996-97	16-4-0	2nd	3rd
1997-98	19-2-0	3rd	2nd
1998-99	18-2-0	1st	2nd

Ms. Softball Coaching History

Coach	Years	Record	pct	Big Ten Titles	NCAA
Linda Wells	1974-75& 77-89	365-273-1	.572	1986, 1988	1988
Jenny Johnson	1976	16-4	.800		
Teresa Wilson	1990-91	79-59	.572	1991	
Lisa Bernstein	1992-99*	288-202-1	.586	1996,1998, 1999	
Julie Standering	1999*	48-20	.705	1999	

* Julie Standering and Lisa Bernstein became co-head coaches in 1999

U of M Womens Ms. Basketball Records

Career Scoring

Name	Years	Pts
Carol Ann Shudlick	1990-94	2097
Laura Coenen	1981-85	2044
Linda Roberts	1944-81	1856
Molly Tadich	1973-87	1706
Carol Peterka	1982-86	1441
Ellen Kramer	1987-91	1371
Debbie Hunter	1979-83	1361
Marty Dahlen	1978-82	1345
Angie Iverson	1994-98	1162
Shannon Loeblein	1991-95	1030

Career Rebounds

Name	Years	Reb
Linda Roberts	1944-81	1413
Molly Tadich	1973-87	1135
Laura Coenen	1981-85	1029
Angie Iverson	1994-98	848
Carol Peterka	1982-86	744
Ellen Kramer	1987-91	728
Carol Ann Shudlick	1990-94	727
Marty Dahlen	1978-82	703
Denise Erstad	1974-77	677
Elsie Ohm	1976-77	670
Diane Kinney	1984-88	638
Dana Joubert	1989-92	638

Ms. Team Big Ten Champions

Sport	Year(s)
Golf	1989
Gymnastics	1988, 1989, 1991, 1998
Soccer	1995, 1997
Softball	1986 (tie), 1988, 1991
Swimming/Diving	1999

Source: Courtesy U of M Women's Athletics Media Relations and Men's Athletics Media Relations. U of M sports website.

Jenny Walek, U of M Soccer Big Ten Player of the Year 1995
Photo: Gerry Vuchetich

The Minnesota Amateur Sports Commission (MASC) was created in 1987 by the Minnesota State Legislature to promote the economic
and social benefits of sports. In the 13 years since the inception of the
MASC, Minnesota has become a role model state for its proactive methods
of creating benefits from amateur sports. The MASC has been at the forefront of this effort. The agency has become best known for two things:
•Creating amateur sports events which attract out-of-state attendance,
    generating economic impact for the state.
•Fostering public/private and state/local partnerships. Many MASC
    programs have utilized this model, including facility construction and
    the Mighty Ducks and Mighty Kids grant programs.

Facility Specifications
•Currently 250 acres, expanding to
    602 acres in 2001.
•55 soccer fields
•12,000 seat outdoor stadium
•250-meter cycling velodrome
•58,000 square foot indoor sports
    hall
•Cafeteria and Residence Hall
•Schwan's Super Rink, 4-sheet ice
    arena
•Columbia Arena (Fridley), 2-sheet
    ice arena

•National Youth Golf Center (opening in 2001)
•Estimated Users (1990-1998)
1990-1992: 1,158,000
    (annual average: 386,000)
1993-1994: 875,000
    (annual average: 435,000)
1995-1996: 1,493,445
    (annual average: 746,722)
1997-1998: 1,551,236
    (annual average: 775,618)
Total users since opening (1990):
    5,077,681

Major Events Hosted In 1997 & 1998
Minnesota Thunder pro soccer games
Minnesota State HS Track & Field Championships
Schwan's USA CUP Youth Soccer Tournament
All-American Girls Hockey Tournament
All-American Girls Soccer Tournament
Minnesota Youth Soccer Association State Tournament
U.S. Soccer Festival (1997)
Big Ten Women's Soccer Tournament (1997)
Twin Cities Vulcans hockey games
USCF Regional Cup cycling event
NSC Cup soccer tournament
Minnesota True Team Track & Field Championships
Northern Lights Volleyball Tournament
USA International Hockey Cup
World Ultimate Disc Championship (1998)
Source: Paul Erickson, Executive Director; MASC website.

Sports and Activities Served	
Archery	Public Ice Skating
Basketball	Rugby
Broomball	Soccer
Cycling	Track and Field
Figure Skating	Ultimate Disc
Ice Hockey	Volleyball
Jazzercise/Precision Dance	Weightlifting

High School Athletics

The Minnesota State High School League

The Minnesota State High School League was first organized in 1916 as the State High School Athletic Association. Its primary purposes were (1) to promote amateur sports, and (2) to establish uniform eligibility rules for interscholastic athletic contests.

In 1929, it broadened its scope by including all interscholastic activities and added speech and debate. At that time the name was changed to the Minnesota State High School League. Music was added in 1965 and Girls' Athletics in 1969.

The opportunities provided through League-sponsored activities has grown from the original program of football, basketball, track of baseball to include 13 athletic activities for boys; 10 athletic activities for girls.

The League has existed as a non-profit, voluntary association of the public high schools since its inception. In 1960 it was officially incorporated under the laws of the State of Minnesota as a non-profit corporation.

Four hundred and eighty-one (481) public and non-public schools in Minnesota belong to the Minnesota State High School League.

Reorganization and reassignment of schools

On April 17, 1975 the member schools of the Minnesota State High School League approved amendments that provided the changes necessary to implement reorganization for two class competition.

The new plan provided that district, region and state competition be conducted in two classes, "A" and "AA", in each of those activities that have more than 50% of the member schools participating in that activity. The largest 128 schools by enrollment will be in the large school or "AA" classification. All other member schools would be in the "A" class. The "AA" schools were organized into eight regions of sixteen schools each. The "A" schools membership was reassigned into eight regions, each containing four districts, or a total of 32 districts.

Source: All information on high school athletics is from the Minnesota State High School League Yearbook, 1998-99 and the League's monthly Bulletin.

State Football Playoff Championship Games 1982 - 1998

Class	Champions	Runners-up	Score
1982			
AA	Stillwater	Owatonna	34-27
A	Brooklyn Center	East Grand Forks	30-8
B	LeCenter	Mahnomen	12-6
C	Truman	Belgrade	16-14
9-Man	Westbrook	Hillcrest Lutheran Academy, Fergus	34-12
1983			
AA	Coon Rapids	Bloomington Jefferson	34-31
A	Hutchinson	Park Rapids	36-14
B	Jordan	Breckenridge	27-0
C	Southland, Adams	Bird Island-Lake Lillian	28-0
9-Man	Silver Lake	Norman County West/Climax	
1984			
AA	Stillwater	Burnsville	36-33
A	Hutchinson	Centennial, Circle Pines	32-7
B	Granite Falls	Breckenridge	13-7
C	Harmony	Glyndon-Felton	20-14
9-Man	Norman County West	Silver Lake	37-20
1985			
AA	Burnsville	Apple Valley	27-21
A	New Prague	Mora	16-12
B	Jackson	Mahnomen	26-20
C	Glyndon-Felton	Zumbrota	38-14
9-Man	Westbrook	Norman County West	45-18
1986			
AA	Apple Valley	Osseo	35-6
A	Cambridge	Stewartville	24-0
B	Watertown-Mayer	Granite Falls	29-6
C	Minneota	Sherburn-Dunnell	52-19
9-Man	Argyle	Silver Lake	32-7
1987			
AA	Moorhead	Winona	13-7
A	Cambridge	Lakeville	28-14
B	Granite Falls	Ely	43-20
C	Minneota	Grand Meadow	27-7
9-Man	Silver Lake	Verndale	30-14
1988			
AA	Blaine	Cretin-Durham Hall	25-24
A	Lakeville	Staples-Motley	35-28
B	Breckenridge	Morris	21-7
C	Minneota	Rushford	42-28

9-Man	Hallock	Stewart	35-24
1989			
AA	Burnsville	Stillwater	21-7
A	Albany	Totino Grace, Fridley	41-32
B	Gibbon-Fairfax-Winthrop	Perham	27-15
C	Waterville-Elysian	Mahnomen	14-7
9-Man	St. Clair	Albrook	47-12
1990			
AA	Anoka	Elk River	19-14
A	Fridley	Sartell	34-12
B	BOLD, Olivia	DeLaSalle, Minneapolis	15-14
C	Mahnomen	Becker	27-7
9-Man	Hills-Beaver Creek	Argyle	28-21
1991			
AA	Burnsville	Lakeville	10-7
A	Spring Lake Park	Rocori, Cold Spring	20-0
B	BOLD, Olivia	Deer River	14-0
C	Mahnomen	Mankato Loyola	42-0
9-Man	Chokio-Alberta	Grygla/Goodridge	7-6
1992			
AA	Lakeville	Cretin-Durham Hall	19-7
A	Detroit Lakes	Farmington	21-0
B	Saint Cloud Cathedral	BOLD, Olivia	7-6
C	Mahnomen	Mankato Loyola	20-13 (OT)
9-Man	Stephen	Cromwell	36-20
1993			
AA	Apple Valley	Rochester John Marshall	29-7
A	Detroit Lakes	Northfield	21-14
B	St Cloud Cathedral	Zumbrota-Mazeppa	28-6
C	Mahnomen	Minneota	43-23
9-Man	Chokio-Alberta	LeRoy-Ostrander	35-0
1994			
AA	Anoka	Alexandria	34-7
A	Sartell	Northfield	24-21
B	Triton, Dodge Center	Becker	40-21
C	Chatfield	Red Lake Falls	34-14
9-Man	Kittson Central, Hallock	Verndale	36-16
1995			
AA	Stillwater Area	Rochester Mayo	31-7
A	Detroit Lakes	Saint Peter	30-15
B	Kingsland, Spring Valley	Breckenridge	22-3
C	Chatfield	Hawley	12-6
9-Man	Cromwell	LeRoy-Ostrander	26-18

1996

AA	Eden Prairie	Blaine	23-22
A	Mora	Northfield	7-3
B	Breck School-Golden Valley	Windom Area	24-7
C	Chatfield	Hawley	12-7
9-Man	Cromwell	Verndale	46-44

1997

AAAAA	Eden Prairie	Blaine	32-28
AAAA	Northfield	Detroit Lakes	28-0
AAA	Albany	Jackson County Central	55-7
AA	Pelican Rapids	Waterville-Elysian-Morristown	34-32
A	Cook County-Grand Marais	Adrian	13-12
9-Man	Verndale	Cromwell	18-12

1998

AAAAA	Woodbury	Champlin Park	28-7
AAAA	Hutchinson	Owatonna	21-20
AAA	Foley	Jackson County Central	21-7
AA	Mahnomen	BOLD, Olivia	27-26
A	Cook County-Grand Marais	Adrian	15-8
9-Man	Cromwell	Hillcrest Lutheran Academy	40-22

Prep Bowl -- Individual Records

Most Yards Rushing: 299, Brent Miller, Mahnomen-1993

Most Rushing Attempts: 34, Matt Hammond, Lakeville-1992; Nathan Maker, Chatfield-1994

Best Rushing Average (15+ att.): 10.2, Chris SanAgustin, Apple Valley-1985

Most Touchdowns Rushing: 4, Jason Miller, Mahnomen-1991

Longest Run From Scrimmage: 80 yds., Brent Miller, Mahnomen-1993

Most Yards Passing: 309, Kirk Midthun, Triton, Dodge Center-1994

Most Passes Attempted: 41, Chris Meidt, Minneota-1987

Most Passes Completed: 26, Chris Meidt, Minneota-1987

Best Pass Completion PCT. (10+ att.): .778 (14-18), George Rosburg, Truman-1983

Longest Pass Completion: 90 Yards, Charlie Nelson, Perham-1989

Longest Pass Reception: 90 Yards, Jon Toedter, Perham-1989

Most Passes Caught: 11, Eric Hennen, Minneota-1987

Most Yards Pass Receptions: 171, (X passes) Judge Gisslen, Triton, Dodge Center-1994

Most Touchdowns Passing: 6, Kirk Midthun, Triton, Dodge Center-1994

Most Touchdown Receptions: 4, Judge Gisslen, Triton, Dodge Center-1994

Most Touchdowns (Rushing/Receiving/Passing): 4 (2/2/0) Kermit Klefsaas, Brooklyn Center-1982

Most Offensive Yards (Passing/Rushing): 311 (309/2), Kirk Midthun, Triton, Dodge Center-1994

Most Passes Intercepted: 3, Pete Roback, Anoka-1990; Mark Olsonawski, Kittson Central, Hallock-1994; Mason Hansen, Cromwell-1998.

Most Pass Interception Yards:66, Chris Brown, Watertown-Mayer-1986

Longest Kick-Off Return: 93 Yards, Craig Fredrickson, Detroit Lakes-1995

Total Yards Kick-Off Returns: 146, Aaron Oden, Stillwater-1984

Longest Punt Return: 74 Yards, Brad Biehn, New Prague-1985

Total Yards Punt Returns: 76 (2 returns), Brad Biehn, New Prague-1985

Total Yards All Returns: 146, Aaron Oden, Stillwater-1984

Longest Punt: 68 Yards, Guy Osterfeld, BOLD, Olivia-1991

Best Punting Average (4 or more kicks): 44.25, Brad Defauw, Apple Valley-1993

Longest Field Goal: 42 Yards, Brian Smiddle, Blaine-1996

Most Unassisted Tackles: 18, Matt Jarland, Harmony-1984

Most Unassisted, Assisted Tackles: 21, Joel Staats, Winona-1987

Prep Bowl -- Team Records

Most Points (One Team): 55, Albany-1997

Most Points (Two Teams): 90, Cromwell (46) vs. Verndale (44)—9-man-1996

Fewest Points (Two Teams) in a title game: 10, Mora (7) vs. Northfield (3), Class A-1996

Most First Downs: 25, Minneota-1988

Most Rushing First Downs: 21, Mahnomen-1993

Most Passing First Downs: 15, Minneota-1986; Minneota-1987

Most Yards Rushing: 412, Mahnomen-1993

Most Rushing Attempts: 67, Cromwell-1998

Most Passes Completed: 27, Minneota-1986

Most Passes Attempted: 42, Minneota-1987

Most Yards Passing: 309, Triton, Dodge Center-1994

Best Pass Completion PCT.: .737 (14-199 for 197 Yds.), Truman-1982

Most Passes Intercepted: 6, Breck School, Golden Valley-1996

Most Offensive Plays: 78, Minneota-1986

Most Total Offensive Net Yards: 510, Albany-1989

Best Average Yards Per Play: 9.6, Stillwater-1982

Most Fumbles: 8, Silver Lake-1987

Most Fumbles Lost: 5, Jackson-1985

Longest Game (time): 3:09, Cook County, Grand Marais vs. Adrian-1998

Longest Scoring Drive (elapsed time): 9:36, Stillwater (68 yards)-1984

Longest Drive for Score (distance): 97 Yards (14 plays), Mahnomen-1982

State Boys Basketball Tournament, All-Time Records
Team Records--Tournament—3 Games
Most Points: 274, Wabasso-1997
Most Field Goals Made: 109, Wabasso-1997
Best Field Goal Percentage: .600 (66 of 110), Hawley-1987
Most Free Throws Made: 75, Hibbing-1957
Best Free Throw Percentage: .846, (55-65), Stillwater, 1976
Most Rebounds: 131, Glencoe-1977
Most Players Fouled Out: 7, Minneapolis South-1969
Most Three-Point Field Goals: 25, Wabasso-1997
Single Game:
Most Points: 117, Wabasso (vs. Red Lake)-1997
Most Field Goals Made: 48, Red Lake (vs. Wabasso)-1997
Best Field Goal Percentage: .758, (25-33), Staples-Motley (vs. Crosby-Ironton)-1997
Most Free Throws Made: 37, Hibbing (vs. St. James)-1954
Best Free Throw Percentage: 1.000 (10 of 10), St. Cloud Tech. (vs. Chaska)-March 24, 1990
Most Rebounds: 65, Glencoe (vs. Twin Valley)-1977
Most Players Fouled Out: 6, East Grand Forks (vs. Brainerd)-1951
Most Three-Point Field Goals: 11, Delano (vs. Storden-Jeffers)-1993; and 11, Wabasso (vs. Red Lake)-1997

Individual Records, Tournament-3 Games:
Most Points: 113, Randy Breuer, (Lake City)-1979
Most Field Goals Made: 50, Randy Breuer, (Lake City)-1979
Best Field Goal Percentage: .794, (27-34), Kevin McHale, (Hibbing)-1976
Most Free Throws Made: 37, Martin Norton, (Minneapolis Central)-1921
Best Free Throw Percentage: 1.000 min. 20 attempts (20-20) Mark Nelson, (Stillwater)-1976
Most Rebounds: 69, Bob Laney, (Proctor)-1964
Most Three-Point Field Goals: 13, Justin Hegna, Becker-1991
Single Game:
Most Points: 50, Jimmy Jensen, Bemidji (vs. Woodbury)-1978
Most Field Goals Made: 20, Jimmy Jensen, Bemidji (vs. Woodbury)-1978
Best Field Goal Percentage: 1.000 (10-10), John Wilson, St. Anthony Village (vs. Winona Cotter)-1984
Most Free Throws Made: 19, Tom Norland, Minneapolis Roosevelt-1957
Best Free Throw Percentage: 1.000, min. 12 attempts (13-13), Tom Bock, North St. Paul-1971
Most Rebounds: 32, Bob Laney, (Proctor)-1964
Most Three-Point Field Goals: 9, Khalid El-Amin, Minneapolis North (vs. St. Thomas Academy)-1996

State Girls Basketball Tournament All-Time Records
Team Records--Tournament—3 Games:
Most Points: 241, Rochester Mayo-1997   Most Rebounds: 146, Albany-1980
Most Field Goals Made: 90, New York Mills-1978
Best Field Goal Percentage: .539 (68-126), Staples-1985
Most Free Throws Made: 61, St. Louis Park-1986
Best Free Throw Percentage: .868 (46-53), New Prague-1992
Most Players Fouled Out: 3, Rochester Lourdes, Bloomington Jefferson-1976
and 3, Coon Rapids-1979
Most Three-Point Field Goals: 18, Esko-1989
Single Game:
Most Points: 88, Eden Valley-Watkins (vs. Cass Lake)-1984
Most Field Goals Made: 39, New York Mills (vs. Fertile-Beltrami)-1978
Best Field Goal Percentage: .638 (30-47), New York Mills (vs. Buhl)-1977
Most Free Throws Made: 27, Burnsville, (vs. Woodbury)-1989
Best Free Throw Percentage: .923 (12-13) Win-E-Mac (vs. Tracy/Milroy
/Walnut Grove)-1989
Most Rebounds: 67, Archbishop Brady (vs. Redwood Falls)-1979
Most Players Fouled Out: 4, Moose Lake-1980
Most Three-Point Field Goals: 10, Esko (vs. Kenyon)-1988
Individual Records--Tournament—3 Games:
Most Points: 102, Kelly Skalicky, Albany-1981
Most Field Goals Made: 47, Kelly Skalicky, Albany-1981
Best Field Goal Percentage: .750 (18-24) Kristi Wolhowe, Staples-1985
Most Free Throws Made: 23, Jackie Reese, New London-Spicer-1988; Kristi
Duncan, Duluth East-1991; Mary Froelich, New Prague-1992
Best Free Throw Percentage and Most consecutive Free Throws Made (22):
1.000 (22-22), Laura Gardner, Bloomington Jefferson-1978
Most Rebounds: 64, Janice Streit, Eden Valley-Watkins-1983
Most Consecutive Field Goals Made: 9, Heather Gillis, Storden-Jeffers-1989
Most Three-Point Field Goals: 13, Sara Schoenrock, Christ's Household of
Faith, St. Paul-1997
Single Game:
Most Points: 45, Kelly Skalicky, Albany (vs. Bagley)-1981
Most Field Goals Made: 21, Kelly Skalicky, Albany-1981
Best Field Goal Percentage: .900 (9-10), Melanie Moore, Marshall-University
(vs. Esko)-1976
Most Free Throws Made: 15, Carol Thelen, Albany-1983
Best Free Throw Percentage: 1.000 (10-10), Laura Gardner, Bloomington
Jefferson-1978 and Tess Rizzardi, Hill-Murray-1978
Most Rebounds: 27, Janica Streit, Eden Valley-Watkins-1983
Most 3-Point Field Goals: 7, Angela Gryssendorf, Esko (vs. Kenyon)-1988

State Hockey Tournament Place Winners 1970-1999

Year	Champion	Runner-up	Score
1970	Minneapolis Southwest(24-0-1)	Edina	1-0*
1971	Edina (22-2-3)	Roseau	1-0
1972	International Falls (22-3-1)	Grand Rapids	3-2
1973	Hibbing (22-4-2)	Alexander Ramsey	6-3
1974	Edina East (24-0)	Bemidji	6-0
1975	Grand Rapids (23-4)	Minneapolis Southwest	6-1
1976	Grand Rapids (22-5)	Richfield	4-3
1977	Rochester John Marshall (25-2)	Edina East	4-2
1978	Edina East (25-1)	Grand Rapids	5-4**
1979	Edina East (22-4)	Rochester John Marshall	4-3*
1980	Grand Rapids (21-5)	Hill-Murray	2-1
1981	Bloomington Jefferson (17-8-1)	Irondale	3-2
1982	Edina (22-4)	White Bear Mariner	6-0
1983	Hill-Murray (28-0)	Burnsville	4-3
1984	Edina (21-4-1)	Bloomington Kennedy	4-2
1985	Burnsville (24-1-1)	Hill-Murray	4-3
1986	Burnsville (20-5-1)	Hill-Murray	4-1
1987	Bloomington Kennedy (25-1)	Burnsville	4-1
1988	Edina (21-5-1)	Hill-Murray	5-3
1989	Bloomington Jefferson (25-3)	Rochester John Marshall	5-4*
1990	Roseau (26-2)	Grand Rapids	3-1
1991	Hill-Murray (22-6)	Duluth East	5-3
1992-I	Bloomington Jefferson (25-2-2)	Moorhead	6-3
-II	#Greenway,Coleraine/Nashwauk-Keewatin(16-12)	Rosemount	6-1
1993-I	Bloomington Jefferson (28-0)	Hill-Murray	4-0
-II	Eveleth-Gilbert (14-14)	#Lake of the Woods, Baudette MN/Rainy River, Ontario	3-2**
1994-AA	Bloomington Jefferson (26-1-1)	Moorhead	3-1
-A	Warroad (24-4)	Hibbing	5-3
1995-AA	Duluth East (25-3)	Moorhead	5-3
-A	#International Falls (20-7-1)	Totino Grace, Fridley	3-2
1996-AA	Apple Valley (27-1)	Edina	3-2
-A	Warroad (24-4)	Red Wing	10-3
1997-AA	Edina (25-3-0)	Duluth East	1-0
-A	Red Wing (28-0-0)	Warroad	4-3
1998-AA	Duluth East (25-3-0)	Anoka	3-1
-A	Eveleth-Gilbert (22-6-0)	Hermantown	2-1
1999-AA	Roseau (27-1-0)	Hastings	4-0
-A	Benilde-St. Margaret's (26-2-0)	East Grand Forks	4-2

*Overtime Game   **Double Overtime Game
#Denotes cooperative program: International Falls/Littlefork-Big Falls

State Wrestling Team Champions 1980-1999

Year	School	Region/Section
1980	Bloomington Kennedy (AA)	6AA
	Goodhue (A)	1A
	and Staples (A)	6A
1981	Albert Lea (AA)	1AA
	Staples (A)	6A
1982	Brainerd (AA)	8AA
	Staples (A)	6A
1983	Apple Valley (AA)	1AA
	Staples (A)	6A
1984	Bloomington Kennedy (AA)	6AA
	Staples (A)	6A
1985	Apple VAlley (AA)	1AA
	Staples (A)	6A
1986	Apple Valley (AA)	1AA
	Canby (A)	3A
1987	Simley (AA)	3AA
	Paynesville (A)	5A
1988	Simley (AA)	3AA
	Canby (A)	3A
1989	Simley (AA)	3AA
	St. James (A) (tie)	2A
	and Foley (A) (tie)	7A
1990	Anoka (AA)	4AA
	Paynesville (A)	5A
1991	Apple Valley (AA)	1AA
	Paynesville (A)	5A
1992	Simley (AA)	3AA
	Frazee (A)	8A
1993	Forest Lake (AA)	7AA
	Foley (A)	7A
1994	Apple Valley (AA)	6AA
	Canby (A) (tie)	3A
	and Foley (A) (tie)	7A
1995	Apple Valley (AA)	6AA
	Canby (A)	3A
1996	Hastings (AA)	3AA
	*St. Michael-Albertville (A)	4A
	*Wheaton/Herman-Norcross (B)	6B
1997	Apple Valley (AAA)	6AAA
	*St. Michael-Albertville (AA)	4AA
	Hayfield (A)	2A

1998	Owatonna (AAA)	1AAA
	Dassel-Cokato (AA)	5AA
	St. James (A)	2A
1999	Apple Valley (AAA)	6AAA
	*Jackson county Central (AA)	3AA
	Frazee (A)	8A

Four-time State Wrestling Champions
Jim Van Gorden, Minneapolis Marshall (1937-40)
Steve Carr, Battle Lake (1976-78) & Moorhead (1979)
John Miller, Renville-Sacred Heart (1982-85)
Ty Friederichs, Osseo (1992-95)
Chad Erickson, Apple Valley (1994-97)

Three-time State Wrestling Champions
Dick Pierson, Robbinsdale (1943-45)
Chas Ofsthun, Robbinsdale (1948-50)
Dick Mueller, Anoka (1949-51)
Kermit Zelke, Winona (1950, 1952-53)
Al DeLeon, Blue Earth (1955, 1957-58)
Stan Christ, Mankato (1957-59)
Gary Erdman, Mound (1958-60)
Ron Ankeny, Blue Earth (1961-63)
Howard Leopold, Redwood Falls (1961-63)
Tom Jean, Albert Lea (1970-72)
Rick Goeb, Monticello (1981) & Anoka (1982-83)
Mark Krier, Plainview (1983-85)
Matt Demaray, Apple Valley (1984-86)
Corey Olson, Hayfield (1986-88)
Chad Nelson, Stewartville (1989-91)
Brandon Paulson, Anoka (1990-92)
Chad Kraft, Heron Lake-Okabena-Lakefield (1992-94)
Jon Fitzgerald, Martin County West, Sherburn (1993-95)
Pat McNamara, Scott West (1994-96)
Brad Pike, Hayfield (1994-96)
Luke Becker, Cambridge-Isanti (1996-98)
Darin Bertram, Wheaton/Herman-Norcross (1996-98)
Dana Gostomczik, Janesville-Waldorf-Pemberton (1996-98)
Mark Carlson, Staples-Motley (1997-99)
Luke Eustice, Blue Earth Area (1996, 1998-99)
Matt Nagel, Frazee (1997-99)
Jacob Volkman, *Battle Lake/Underwood/Henning (1997-99)

All-Time Boys State Track and Field Records

Event	Record	Record Holder	School	Year
100 Meter Dash	:10.61	Tim Whitney	St. Paul Arlington	1998
200 Meter Dash	:21.4	Mark Lutz	Rochester Mayo	1970
400 Meter Dash	:47.59	Randy Melbourne	Minneapolis Washburn	1993
800 Meter Run	1:50.56	Steve Holman	Richfield	1988
1600 Meter Run	4:05.1	Garry Bjorklund	Proctor	1969
3200 Meter Run	9:02.7	Dennis Fee	White Bear Lake	1972
110 Meter High Hurdles	:14.	Mike Siskin	Wayzata	1977
300 Meter Intermediate Hurdles	:36.97	Dan Banister	Mpls.North	1987

4 X 100 Meter Relay :42.10 Dan Carlson,
Pat Schottel, Paul Simbi, Tim Whitney   Roseville Area   1999

4 X 200 Meter Relay 1:28.87 Mike Morgan,
Jon Gibbs, Spencer Wiggins, Ryan Noree   Bloomington Jefferson   1999

4 X 400 Meter Relay 3:17.39 Adam Runk,
Sancer Lumby, Neil Langer, Trevor Mitchel   Stillwater Area   1997

4 X 800 Relay   7:49.35 Pete Prince,
Greg Wilkelius, Kevin Doe, Chris Boldt   Stillwater Area   1998

*Sprint Medley Relay (200-200-400-800)   3:28.7   Art   Horecki,   Mike
Goblirsch, Andy Overman, Ben Porter   Edina East   1974

Event	Record	Record Holder	School	Year
Long Jump	24'9 1/4"	Von Shepard	St. Paul Central	1982
Triple Jump	48'9 3/4"	Leonard Jones	MinneapolisPatrick Henry	1989
High Jump	7'1"	Rod Raver	Rochester John Marshall	1973
Pole Vault	15'7"	Tim Koupal	Anoka	1997
Discus	192'7"	Mike Yonkey	Wells-Easton	1987
Shot Put	62'8"	Tim Senjem	Hayfield	1996
*100 Yard Dash	:9.9	James McClearie	Brainerd	1933
		Norman Anderson	St. James	1954
		Blaine Chatham	Minneapolis Center	1964
		Edward Wade	Minneapolis North	1955
		Greg Lokken	Moorhead	1957
		Mark Lutz	Rochester Mayo	1969, 1970
		Greg Geiger	Richfield	1971
		Terry Lewis	Minneapolis North	1974
		Jeff Byrd	Minneapolis Central	1978

*4 X 220 Yard Relay 1:28.4 Roby Anderson,
Jim Gravalin, Todd Watson, Terry Swanson Moorhead   1972
*Event is no longer held.

Minnesota Mentions in the Guinness Book of World Records
The right biceps of Denis Sester of Bloomington, MN measure 30 1/2
inches cold.

All-Time Girls State Track and Field Records

Event	Record	Record Holder	School	Year
100 Meter Dash	:12.06	Toni Lawshea	St. Paul Arlington	1998
200 Meter Dash	:24.58	Heather Van Norman	Windom	1987
400 Meter Dash	:55.4	Christy Vitse	Rochester Mayo	1977
800 Meter Run	2:08.77	Jeanne Kruckeberg	Blooming Prairie	1986
1600 Meter Run	4:48.79	Jeanne Kruckeberg	Blooming Prairie	1986
3200 Meter Run	10:30.28	Carrie Tollefson	Dawson-Boyd/LacquiParle Valley	1994
100 Meter High Hurdles	:14.54	Anna Ratzloff	Little Falls	1990
300 Meter Hurdles	:42.62	Liesa Brateng	Roseau	1987
4 X 100 Meter Relay	:48.8	Georgia Ulmar, Kim Watts, Dana Watts, Delene Hawkins	Saint Paul Central	1978
4 X 200 Meter Relay	1:41.86	Maggie Stolp, Katherine McQuin, Naomi Sutton, Jessica Mittelstadt	Mankato West	1998
4 X 400 Meter Relay	3:52.13	Katie Curran, Shani Marks, Maggie Curran, Tracy Frerk	Apple Valley	1997
4 X 800 Meter Relay	9:20.12	Tracy Dahl, Nancy Uzelac, Tanya Cornelius, Cara Daniels	Anoka	1986
Long Jump	19'	Charlene Butler	Bertha-Hewitt/Verndale	1997
Triple Jump	38'1"	Heidi Lundervold	Woodbury	1994
High Jump	5'10"	Linda Barsness	Rochester John Marshall	1986
Pole Vault	11'3"	Jody Tarasweicz	Park, Cottage Grove	1999
Discus	156'0"	Sandy Fuchs	Rocori, Cold Spring	1993
Shot Put	47'4 1/4"	Jamie McKibbon	Hibbing	1993
*100 Yard Dash	:11.0	Lynne Vos	Holdingford	1975
		Erin Donalley	Red Wing	1978
*100 Meter Low Hurdles	:14.0	Kathy Borgwarth	Brainerd	1978
*200 Meter Low Hurdles	:28.49	Beth Lindblad	St. Louis Park	1984

*Events no longer held.

Minnesota Mentions in the Guinness Book of World Records

Jeff Brennan of LaCrescent, MN is the only person known to have squeezed his entire body through the frame of an unstrung tennis racket. Brennan, known as the Rubber Man, performed the feat on the set of *Guinness World Records: Primetime* on July 10, 1998. From top to bottom the feat took him only one minute 17.85 seconds.

The lowest live birth weight accurately recorded for a calf is 9 pounds for a Friesian heifer called Christmas born on December 25, 1993 on the farm of Mark and Wendy Theuringer in Hutchinson. Sadly she died of scours at five weeks.

Minnesota Mentions in the Guinness Book of World Records

The largest balloon ever made had an inflatable volume of 70 million square feet and was 1000 feet in height. The unmanned balloon, manufactured by Winzen Research, Inc. (now Winzen Engineering, Inc.) of South St. Paul, did not get off the ground and was destroyed at launch on July 8, 1975.

The largest dog biscuit at 7 feet 9 3/8 inches long by 1 foot 11 5/16 inches wide by 1/38 inches thick was produced by the People's Company Bakery in Minneapolis on August 11, 1999. The 88.5-pound biscuit contained 20 pounds of white flour, 20 pounds of whole wheat flour, 12 pounds of eggs and 15 pounds of water. The biscuit was unveiled at the Phalen Pork pavilion in St. Paul for the annual Walk and Talk for Homeless Animals event on August 20, 1999.

The largest ice palace completed in January 1992, used 18,000 blocks of ice, at St. Paul during the Winter Carnival. Built by TMK Construction Specialties Inc. It was 166 feet 8 inches high and contained 10.8 million pounds of ice.

The most people kissed in eight hours was by Alfred A.E. Wolfram of N. St. Paul who kissed 11,030 people at the Minnesota Renaissance Festival in Shakopee on September 12, 1998.

The highest paid author is Deborah Schneider of Minneapolis who in 1958 wrote 25 words to complete a sentence in a competition for the best blurb for Plymouth cars. She beat about 1.4 million entrants to claim a prize of $500 every month for life. On normal life expectations she should collect $12,000 per word. The winning phrase is in a deed box at her bank "Only to be opened after death". She passed $9,000 a word in 1995.

The largest collection of chewing gum belongs to Valerie Boettcher of Stillwater. She has collected 2,646 packs of chewing gum beginning in 1976. Over the years she has collected packs from countries around the world including Egypt, Sri Lanka, and Zimbabwe. The collection also includes several rare unopened packs of gum dating back to the early 1920s.

Source: Guinness Media, Inc. used with permission

Chapter 22

Myth, Humor and Comedy

Two firm-jawed women stare from the cover of John Louis Anderson's book, "Scandinavian Humor & Other Myths."

That the women are not smiling—in fact, they look positively grim—is the point of the joke. Minnesotans know very well the women may be guffawing inside, but they're certainly not going to let it show.

Anderson, a Minneapolis free-lance writer and photographer, has sold more than 100,000 copies of his self-published book. In it, he's caught the spirit of this state's humor with his pictures of Convolu, the God of Sullen Depression; Lefse, the Goddess of Unseasoned Food, and Comatose, God of Fishing. He warns non-Minnesotans never to confuse hot dish which is the thing you eat, with casserole—the thing in which you put the hot dish.

Howard Mohr, a free-lance writer from southwestern Minnesota, explains the rituals of the state's social life in his book, "How to Talk Minnesotan."

He gravely takes the reader through "The Long Goodbye," in which a couple takes several hours to depart after a visit, and offers the uninitiated a way to respond to the invitation to have "a little lunch." His list of the 15 opening gambits in Minnesota conversation begins with "The heat's not bad if you don't move around."

Mohr honed his craft as a writer from Garrison Keillor's A Prairie Home Companion, the public radio show for which the Anoka-born Keillor invented Lake Wobegon, the mythical little Minnesota town "that time forgot."

Keillor ended the show in the summer of 1987, but for more than 10 years, PHC had entertained some three million Americans with nostalgic tales of life in Lake Wobegon sponsored by Bertha's Kitty Boutique and the Fearmonger's Shoppe. Keillor's book, "Lake Wobegon Days," was a national best-seller.

Keillor, Mohr, and Anderson illustrate the elements of Minnesota's unique sense of humor. It is low key, going for grins rather than guffaws. It pokes gentle fun at the state's inhabitants. It focuses on the little pleasures of life, like nice weather and potluck suppers; it shows its immigrant roots by celebrating family, friends, and church doings. And it is clean.

Whether or not Minnesotans have a sense of humor, and what makes them laugh, was probably a matter of supreme indifference to the rest of the country until Walter Mondale, who is Norwegian, ran for President of the United States in 1984.

Mondale's campaign was covered by political reporters from other states who just didn't understand the Minnesota psyche. One nationally-syndicated scribe allowed as how he couldn't always tell when Fritz was awake, much less when he was enjoying himself.

Molly Ivins, who was a journalist for the Twin Cities for three years, tried to explain Minnesotans to readers of her column in the Dallas Times Herald newspaper.

"Like other Midwestern tribes," Ivins wrote, "Minnesotans are almost terminally sensible; another deep cultural trait of the Minnesotans is reticence. They do not believe in putting themselves forward; they consider it unseemly."

Ivins ended her affectionate essay by saying, "It's utterly hopeless to criticize Mondale for being dull: in Minnesota, excitement is frowned upon."

Not that famous Minnesotans haven't been chided before for lacking a sense of humor. Charles A. Lindbergh, the state's most celebrated aviator, was noted for having almost never said anything funny. Someone is supposed to have explained that by saying: "Well, did you ever try to tell a joke in Minneapolis?"

When the first white settlers began building towns in Minnesota in about the 1840s, there wasn't much to joke about. These immigrants from Scandinavian countries, Germany and, later, from Ireland, were fleeing harsh social and political times in their homelands and faced a difficult and untamed land when they arrived. These pioneers liked strong words. They liked action even better.

James M. Goodhue, editor of the Minnesota Pioneer , typified the kind of journalism the settlers approved. When Territorial Secretary Charles K. Smith was hounded from office in 1851, Goodhue recalled with satisfaction his prediction two years earlier that "Secretary Smith had stolen into the Territory, and stolen in the Territory and would in the end steal out of the Territory, with whatever plunder he could abstract from it."

Goodhue was a wit, too. In a notice concerning a well-known local vagrant, he even anticipated a line that would later be used to good effect by Mark Twain, who was still a small boy in Hannibal, Missouri at the time: "Bog Hughes, who it was feared was drowned, requests us to say that the report of his death is undoubtedly premature and greatly exaggerated."

History, folklore and humor come together in Minnesota's most famous character—Paul Bunyan.

It's been assumed that Paul is a true American myth, a character spun out of whole cloth by lumberjacks telling tall tales around the stove during

Northwoods icons Paul Bunyan and Babe the Blue Ox in Bemidji
Photo: Minnesota Almanac

long winter nights.

It's not that simple. Paul Bunyan himself was very likely a genuine folk character, with French-Canadian roots. The first published Paul Bunyan story appeared in 1910 in a Detroit newspaper. It concerned the Round River drive, a long drive which took place on a river that seemed to go on forever until the loggers realized that it was a circular stream; they were passing the same point over and over.

In 1914, the American Lumberman , a journal published by Minnesota's Red River Company, printed a Paul Bunyan poem. The company also issued a booklet that same year, entitled "Introducing Mr. Paul Bunyan of Westwood, California."

Why Westwood, California? Because Red River had just opened a new mill there, and wanted to expand its market for California pine.

The author of these works was William B. Laughead (yes, that was his real name), who insisted that he had heard Paul Bunyan stories in the lumber camps well before 1910. Laughead, however, took sole credit for creating Babe the Blue Ox, Johnny Inkslinger, and the rest of Paul's supporting cast.

Laughead wrote Paul Bunyan stories for the company until its sale in the 1940's. Scholars think that most of the tales we know today were Laugheads' creations and not real lumberjack yarns at all.

Minnesota has authentic lumberjack heroes. One was Otto Walta, whom the Finns of St. Louis county in northern Minnesota speak of with pride. Walta was born in Finland in 1875 and died in 1959. He came to America in 1898, but never learned to speak English. Even in his old age, they say, he could rip trees from the ground, carry boulders, and bend a three-inch steel bar into a fishhook shape. He was alleged to have once ripped up an 800-pound piece of the railroad to use for prying up stumps on his farm.

Minnesota's Swedes also have a lumberjack hero, the trickster Ola Varmlanning, who achieved immortality when he moved to the Twin Cities during the 1880's and became a regular at various bars, singing and playing the accordion for drinks.

They tell how Ola once took offense at a rookie Irish policeman who was trying to arrest him. So Ola took away the young man's badge, club and revolver, locked him to a call box (from which policemen phoned in reports to the station) and proceeded to the nearest station house. There he turned in the hardware and asked to be arrested in a more courteous manner. He was, and "sentenced to 90 days" became a Swedish-American saying.

Today, Scandinavian humor still provides a bedrock for many of the jokes that make Minnesotans smile. (Or at least twitch their mouths.) Scandinavian jokes, which have now spread into the general population, can be roughly divided into three groups. But anyone reading humor about immigrants should remember that the immigrants themselves may never told some of these jokes; rather, the jokes were told to ridicule newcomers. A staff member at St. Paul's Irish American Institute said this is especially true of "Pat and Mike" jokes that were told about the Irish but are offensive to them.

The first kind of Scandinavian-derived joke is all-purpose, in that it can be told on any ethnic group:

Ole and Yon were shingling a roof. Yon noticed that Ole was studying his nails carefully and discarding many of them. He asked why. Ole said, "Dose are no gude—da heads are on da wrong end."

"Ya lunkhead, Ole," Yon replied. "Dose nails are left-handed nails vich ve use ven ve are vorking on de odder side of dis roof."

Second, there's the dialect joke, as in, "Ya know, ven ay kom to America saz years ago, ay couldn't even speak 'Enyinear'—an now, by golly, ay are vun."

Some Scandinavian humor revolved around rivalries and antagonisms among the immigrants from various nations.

The Danes tell this one: A Swede came home drunk one night and collapsed in a pigsty. He woke the next morning and felt a warm body next to

him. He asked the obvious question, "Er de Svensk? (Are you Swedish?)"
The pig replied, grunting, "Norsk, norsk."

The third kind of Scandinavian humor is a little harder to describe. It
reflects the stern, uncompromising conditions the immigrants left in
Scandinavia, conditions which produced a humor that scorned petty considerations like a punch line.

A good example is the comic strip, "Han Ola og Han Per," which
appeared in the Norwegian-American newspaper, Decorah Posten, from
1918 to 1942.

Dr. Johan Buckley, professor of English at Concordia College,
Moorhead, has researched and co-edited a book about Ola and Per. Buckley
says the comic strip is significant today because it "illustrates the traditional primary values of humor: as entertainment; as literary and graphic
artistry; and as history, with predominant folklore elements that mainly
reflect an immigrant society's pains and difficulties of adapting to mainstream American with its rapidly changing customs and attitudes."

Created by Peter Julius Rosendahl, a farmer-artist from Spring Grove,
Minnesota, who died in 1942, the Ola and Per strips were in Norwegian.
Buckley explains that the main humorous theme is the tension between the
dream world and the real world of the immigrants.

In one strip, Per complains he never has a chance with the young girls.
Ola advises him that the problem is simply that he cannot speak "Yeinki."
Following Ola's advice, the next time Per meets a young girl, he lifts his hat
and greets her, "Hello, Pie Faes." Per lands in the gutter, where he comforts
himself with the favorite sentimental song of Norwegians in America, "Kan
de glemme Norge?" (Can you Forget Old Norway?)

"The comic strip is a unique document of the times that span the coming of not only immigrant but also the machine age to the American farm,"
Buckley says. "As the human being struggled to bridge the Old and New
worlds, the comic strip gives ample humorous evidence that the individual
endures."

"Up on Irish Ridge, all the farmers were Irish but one. He was a
Norwegian. Finally he went into the woods and hanged himself."
- Oscar Olson, retired Lanesboro farmer.

In response to a question about microwaving lutefisk... "There's no reason
why you can't. Of course, you'll have to throw away the microwave
when you finish." - Warren Berg, Ingebretsen's Market.

"Chaos is a friend of mine." - Bob Dylan
Minnesotans Say the Darnedest Things...

In the 1920's and 30's Minnesota, somewhat surprisingly, became a sort of "blue humor" capitol of the nation, because it was from Robbinsdale that Wilford Fawcett published a magazine called Captain Billy's Whiz-Bang , which filled the niche in its time that National Lampoon fills in ours, with just a touch of the National Enquirer thrown in.

One veteran of Captain Billy's Whiz-Bang was Cedric Adams. As a news reporter for WCCO radio and columnist for the Minneapolis Star and Sunday Tribune , Adams dispensed folksy, friendly information and advice from the 20's through the 50's.

His typically Minnesota humor was subtle, producing good feelings more than guffaws.

Another Minnesota humorist who gained wide respect was Clelland Card, best known for his Scandinavian-dialect character, Axel Torgerson, whom he portrayed on radio and television in the late 40's and 50's.

The tradition of radio humor started by Adams and Card continued in the 60's and 70's with WCCO's Charlie Boone and Roger Erickson, the irreverent pair who have made the Worst Jokes a kind of institution. The pair celebrated their 25th year on the air in August, 1984, and Steve Cannon, host of WCCO's drive-time shows, invented a whole cast of bizarre characters, including the folksy Ma Linger, Morgan Mundane and Backlash LaRue.

Charles Schulz, whose Peanuts cartoon strip runs in hundreds of newspapers, started drawing Charlie Brown and his friends while he worked at the St. Paul Pioneer Press. Unfortunately, Schulz was told by an editor that nobody wanted to look at pictures of "a round-headed little kid." Said editor kept a Schulz drawing in his office for years, as a constant humbling reminder of his ability to make mistakes.

More quirky (some say indefinable) humor enlivened the Twin Cities when cartoonist Dick Guindon worked for the Minneapolis Tribune.

Guindon, who has moved to Detroit, was tuned into every nuance of Minnesota living. From his drawing board leaped well-dressed, upwardly mobile little kids from Wayzata, ice fisherman wearing flap-eared caps sitting motionless by their holes in the ice, and the two ladies in what had to be polyester dresses commenting on the world at large. Guindon's cartoons about carp could only by appreciated in Minnesota. In fact, there are now Guindon-inspired carp T-shirts and there are even carp festivals in the state.

In the late 1970's and early 80's, a new source of laughter came onto the scene as Minnesota began to produce stand-up comedians who made names for themselves nationally. One of the earliest producers of comedy was Dudley Riggs with his Comedy All Stars.

Jeff Gerbino, Louis Anderson, Joel Hodgson, Joe Madison, and Jeff Cesario are all young comics who started in Minneapolis clubs and moved to Los Angeles. In addition to performing, they have often done writing and producing for other entertainers. Hodgson worked with Mystery Science Theater 3000 in Hopkins, appeared on Saturday Night live and the David Letterman television shows. Madison became a producer on the sitcom "Malcolm and Eddie." Louis Anderson appeared in a feature film. Cesario appeared is several cable comedy specials and was the last executive producer of the "Larry Shandling Show."

Both Anderson and Hodgson have said they are glad they began their careers in the Twin Cities, where they could experiment with various styles. Minnesota audiences, Anderson said, made him work hard and forced him to keep his act clean. "They force you to use material rather than just swearing," he said.

Louie Anderson

"Don't you love do-it-yourselfers? They spend a hundred thousand on tools, then when you go over to their house they say, "See this wall--built that sucker for 40 bucks."

On fatness... "I was voted the first kid on my block most likely to become a group."

"Minnesota is the only place where people have an extra room in the house for their parkas. It's the state garment."

The mid-1980's found the Twin Cities and Chicago to be a developing place for up and coming comics. Clubs opened by Scott Hansen brought in soon-to-be-famous comics like Jay Leno, Jerry Seinfeld, and Roseann Barr. Barr, incidentally, met her husband, Tom Arnold, while working together at the Comedy Gallery. At its height the Cities comedy clubs numbered six full time. In the early 90's the comedy market shrank so that in 1999 there are two fulltime clubs, Acme and Knuckleheads.

Hansen said, "The Twin Cities is a good area for comedy because they are so many clubs and colleges to play."   He takes his own act to Los Angeles and New York, and is in a good position to talk about contemporary Minnesota humor.

"Minnesota audiences will give the benefit of the doubt," he said. "They're polite, they'll take political humor during elections; otherwise, forget it. They like to be lampooned."

Hansen does joke about deer hunting, ice fishing and the weather—traditional sources of Minnesota humor, as well as jokes about the St. Paul-Minneapolis rivalry.

But Hansen does not do ethnic jokes, nor do any of the other comics he knows.

Then he pauses and admits, "Well, sometimes I add a Norwegian accent when I'm doing ice fishing jokes."

But what, a non-Minnesotan might ask, could be funny about ice fishing in the first place? Why does it, and other code words, automatically draw smiles?

Ice fishing is funny because so many people love it even though it's a form of slow torture in cold weather.

Lutefisk is funny because, even though it smells awful and doesn't even taste very good, kids are still being subjected to it during the holidays by their Scandinavian grandmothers.

"Uff dah" is funny because, even though the immigrants may never have said it, it now means anything from rage to embarrassment.

Even Minnesotans who leave the state cling to their roots, as show in a Minneapolis Tribune letter to the editor from a woman who now lives in Casper, Wyoming.

She wrote, "My 5-year-old son came home from kindergarten and reported an extremely amusing incident. "It was so funny I almost laughed," she explained gravely. "I was a proud mother that day. The Norwegian taboo against ever looking like you're having fun had been thoroughly internalized."

"Henny Youngman headlined at my club in the 1950's. Every time I introduced him on the show, he would thank me and say, "Sit down, Jimmy, you make the place look shabby." - Jimmy Hegg

Reflections on greatness... "Your first reaction when you become a public figure is, "Aren't I important." "Who's going to call next?" But you can't let it turn your head, or you'll mess yourself up forever. You have to take your job seriously, but you can't take yourself seriously. This could pass so quickly." - Brent Musberger

"I'm so happy, there ought to be a law against it." - Mike Todd

"God has a terrific sense of humor. Just study the world and all its creatures, and you'll laugh forever and ever." -
"A bishop is a man who has not been able to find honest work."
 - Father Bill Anderson, Pastor, Ss. Peter and Paul Mazeppa

"It's really hard to sing in Mr. McMusic's class...you have to be so tall."
Why is that?
"He keeps saying, 'Higher! Higher!'" - Brian Aschenbrenner, 1st grade.

Minnesotans Say the Darnedest Things...

Index

Act, Old Age Assistance, 4
  Taft-Hartley, 177
  Technology, 215
  Telecommunications, 232
  Violent Sex Offender Registr., 9
  Volstead, 136
Adams, Cedric, 380
Adams, John, 247
AFDC, 193-194
AFL-CIO, 166, 177, 179
Agassiz, Glacial Lake, 32
Agler, Brian, 354
Agriculture, 5, 53, 78-79, 81, 94, 122,
126, 135, 151, 180, 185-187, 189, 191,
224, 228, 265, 271, 337
Air Force, 23-24
Airlines, Northwest, 9-10, 225
Airport, International, 24, 53, 228
Alaskans, Native, 61
Albertson, Gary, 247-248, 250
Alien Registration Card, 75
Allison, Bob, 350-351
Ambassadors, United States, 62
Amendment, Equal Right, 164
America Online, 232
American Express, 222
Americans, African, 61
Americans, Native, 201, 214
Anderson, Elmer, 92, 127, 131
Anderson, John Louis, 375
Anderson, Louie, 381
Anderson, Paul H., 108, 111
Anderson, Russell A., 108, 112
Anderson, Wendell R., 5, 92, 132
Angle, Northwest, 31, 301
Angling, 325-328

Antarctica, 8
Apprenticeship Program, 183
Armed Forces, 4, 26, 134
Armstrong, Anton, 206
Army, 6, 16-18, 20, 23-24, 28-29, 64,
123, 176, 267, 294, 317, 323-324
Arnold, Tom, 381
Art, Minnesota Museum of American,
203, 216
Arts, Minneapolis Institute of, 202,
210, 216, 230
Asian-Pacific Islanders, 63
Asians, Southeast, 64, 71
Asp, Robert, 184
Assistance, Medical, 140, 197, 199
Association,
    American Dairy, 220
    MN Broadcasters, 242
    MN Cable Communications, 232
    MN Education, 150, 162, 179
    MN Newspaper, 123, 231
Athletics, High School, 362
Average, Dow Jones Industrial, 11
Avery, Carlos, 130, 342
Award, Peabody, 234
Awards, Minnesota Book, 215
Baby Boom, 147, 170
Bach, Johann Sebastian, 207
Bacon, Francis, 212
Bancroft, Anne, 8
Bank, U. S., 225
Banning, Margaret Culkin, 168, 213
Baraga, Anthony R., 152
Bardeen, John, 268, 271
Barnard, Christian, 272
Barr, Roseann, 381

Baseball Hall of Famers, 343
Beets, Sugar, 228
Bellow, Saul, 272
Beltrami, Giacomo, 211
Benson, Elmer A., 92, 131
Benson, Joanne E., 167
Big Ten, 151, 355, 357-361
Bill, GI, 147
Birth, Certificate of, 74
Bishop, Harriet, 145, 162
Black Thursday, 281-282
Blackmun, Harry, 10, 194
Blair, Bill, 352
Blatz, Kathleen A., 108, 111
Blizzards, 5, 9, 276, 278, 281-282
Blueberries, 52
Bly, Carol, 169, 213
Bly, Robert, 213-214
Board, Minnesota Crime Victims Reparations, 116
Board, Minnesota Film, 220
Board, MN State Arts, 201, 221
Board, Pardons, 91
Boise Cascade, 8, 178
Bonaparte, Napoleon, 1
Boone, Charlie, 380
Borlaug, Norman, 271
Boschwitz, Rudy, 136
Bostock, Lyman, 350
Boundary Waters Canoe Area Wilderness, 13, 294, 319
Brattain, Walter H., 271
Breuer, Randy, 367
Brewery, Stroh, 12
Brooks, Herb, 6, 344, 358
Broten, Neal, 344
Brown, Charlie, 380
Brown, Hallie Q., 163, 169
Browner, Joey, 347
Brownson, Pat, 356
Bruckbauer, Fred, 350
Brule, Etienne, 34
Brunelle, Philip, 207
Bryan, William Jennings, 124
Bryant, Bobby, 347
Buchanan, James, 2

Buchwald, Emilie, 169, 214
Buckley, Dr. Johan, 379
Buetow, Brad, 358
Building Sites, Ideal, 280
Bull Run, 21
Bunyan, Paul, 269, 296, 301, 304, 376-377
Burger, Warren, 11, 135
Burnquist, J. A. A., 92, 130
Burns, Jerry, 9, 344
Business, 9, 11-13, 60, 66, 77, 81, 87-88, 90, 95, 106, 112, 121, 138, 148, 159, 161, 166, 179, 209, 216, 223-227, 229-231, 238, 256
Caesar, Augustus, Julius, 288-289
Calendars, 288-289
Calves, 186-187, 228
Calvin, Melvin, 271
Cambodians, 64
Camp Release, 21
Camp Ripley, 24
Camping, 75, 226, 295, 297-298, 302-304, 306-308, 310, 312, 314, 316, 321
Campsites, 294, 297-306, 319-321, 323-324
Campuses, 151-153, 155, 162
Canada, 3, 11, 15, 29-32, 34, 45, 74-76, 219, 227, 284, 321, 334, 341
Canada, Entering, 75-76
Cannon, Steve, 380
Canoeing, 227, 305, 319
Canterbury Downs, 8
Capita, Tax Collections Per, 137
Carew, Rod, 12, 350-351
Carlson, Arne H., 71, 167
Carlson, Curt, 224
Carter, Anthony, 347
Carter, Cris, 347
Carter, Jimmy, 5, 127
Carter, Tyrone, 356
Carver, Jonathan, 201, 211
Cass, Lewis, 211
Catch-and-Release, 325, 328-329
Catholic, 162, 260, 288
Caucuses, 134
Census, 2, 61-62, 64

Center,
  Cut Foot Sioux Information, 317
  Hjemkomst Interpretive, 184
  Landmark, 207
  Learning Resource, 217
  Martin Luther King, 204
  National Youth Golf, 361
  Ordway Music, 205
  Target, 230, 351-352, 354
  Walker Art, 202-3, 208, 216, 230
CERN, 232
Cesario, Jeff, 380
Chance, Dean, 350-351
Chief Two Gun Whitecalf, 82
Child Support, 114, 198-200
Chilinski, Frank, 247-249, 251, 254, 258-261, 263
Choir, National Lutheran, 207
Chosa, Heart Warrior, 132
Christiansen, F. Melius, 206-207
Christiansen, J. J., 206, 271
Christiansen, Olaf, 206
Christiansen, Paul J., 206
Christianson, Theodore, 92, 130-1
Church, 8, 11, 60, 146, 163, 165, 185, 202, 288, 375
Church, Evangelical Lutheran, 8
Church, Roman Catholic, 288
Cities, Minnesota Index, 41
Citizenship, Certificate of, 74
Ciulei, Liviu, 209
Civil Rights, Office of, 168
Clausen, René, 207
Climate, 58, 76, 81, 226, 266, 275, 278, 285, 288, 342
Clinic, Mayo, 264, 273-274
Clinton, Bill, 127
Club, Apollo, 206
Club, Schubert, 163, 204-206
Coen, Ethan & Joel, 12
Coleman, Norm, 12-13, 127, 133
Colleges, Minnesota State, 153-155
Colleges, Private, 158-159
Colonies, American, 288
Comedy All Stars, 380
Comedy Gallery, 381

Commerce, 33, 80-81, 91, 93, 177, 226, 246, 322-323
Commission,
  Metropolitan Airports, 80
  Metropolitan Sports Facilities, 357
  MN Amateur Sports, 361
  Public Safety, 176
  Public Utilities, 245
Communication, 136, 224, 231, 243-244
Communication Impaired Persons, 243
Communities, 24-25, 61, 64-66, 71, 150-153, 162-163, 231-233, 245, 334
Companies,
  Best Buy Company, 225
  Carlson, 224
  Control Data, 224
  Dayton Hudson, 225
  General Mills, 225
  Honeywell, 13
  Hormel, 176
  Minnesota Sugar, 62
  Nash Finch, 225
  Norwest, 13
  North West, 1, 322
  Northern States Power, 225
  Pillsbury, 111
  Red River, 377
  Supervalu, 225
  United HealthCare, 225
Composers Forum, American, 216
Congress, 2, 10, 15, 20-21, 26, 28, 58, 71-72, 107, 121, 123, 136, 215-216, 232, 322
Constitution Provides, 77-78, 85-88, 90-91, 93, 106, 108-110, 113
Construction, 6, 14-15, 62, 93, 178, 183-184, 223-224, 226, 267, 269, 361, 374
Coolidge, Calvin, 127, 272
Council,
  Chicano Latino Affairs, 62-63
  Minnesota Indian Affairs, 60
  National Safety, 333
  Spanish Speaking Affairs, 62

Court,
Conciliation, 107, 110
Probate, 110
Supreme, 10-12, 20, 95, 105-110, 113-114, 135, 167, 194, 198, 345
Tax, 107, 109, 115
Appeals,105, 107, 111-114, 167
Courthouse, Stillwater, 105
Courts, 36, 79, 91, 105-111, 113-115, 117, 119, 167
Cowles Media Co., 231
Cows, Milk, 187
Cray, Seymour, 224
Cray Research, 12, 224
Credit, Tax Hope Scholarship, 160
Credit, Tax Lifetime Learning, 160
Crime, 54, 59, 69, 81, 90, 94, 105, 107, 109, 111, 113, 115-117, 119, 135
Crimes Against Children, Jacob Wetterling, 9
Criminal Apprehension, Bureau, 115
Crops, 4, 10, 13, 20, 186, 224, 228, 270-271, 288, 337
Cunningham, Randall, 347
Customs Regulations, 76
Cuyuna Range, 44, 308
Cyberdialogue, 233
Dairy, 52, 187-188, 220, 223-224, 228
Dance Alliance, Minnesota, 211
Dates, Full Moon, 290
Davies, Dennis Russel, 206
Davis, Cushman K., 22, 92, 128
Day, Christmas, 52, 291
Days, Normal Degree, 285
Deer, 44, 250, 304, 314, 317, 324, 333, 335-341, 364, 381
Department, Minnesota State
Highway, 176
Children, Families and Learning Minnesota, 150, 216
Corrections, 115
Economic Security, 180-181
Education, 111, 163, 215
Health, 73
Human Services, 193-194, 197, 200
Labor, 179, 183-184
Natural Resources, 35, 198, 228, 293-294, 316, 332
Public Safety, 111, 115-116
Public Service, 115, 243
Revenue, 142
Trade, 181
Transportation, 244
Veterans Affairs, 25
Depression, 4, 6, 8, 66, 163, 173, 176, 185, 267, 272, 375
Development, Economic, 95, 181, 225, 227-228
Dewey, Tom, 125
District, Congressional, 78-82, 109
Districts, Minnesota Legislative, 104
Diversity, 63, 161, 165, 168, 179, 184, 211, 321-322
Doctors, 54, 153, 162, 165, 272-273
Donnelly, Ignatius, 3, 122-123, 129, 212
Dorati, Antal, 205
Douglas, Stephen, 58
Drinking, 8, 146, 297-304, 317, 319-320, 323-324
Dulhut, Daniel Greysolon, 1
Duluth Playhouse, 209
Durenburger, Dave, 11
Dutcher, Jim, 357
Dutcher, Judith H., 88-89, 167
Dylan, Bob, 222, 379
Eberhart, Adolph O., 92, 130
Economic Trends, MN, 180, 225
Economy, 5, 34, 66, 69, 122, 141-142, 148, 153, 176, 178-180, 222-223, 226-228, 272
Education, 11, 13, 54, 59, 63, 65-66, 68, 71, 77, 86, 93, 95, 111, 138, 142, 144-151, 153, 155, 157, 159-160, 162-163, 165-166, 178-180, 182-183, 203, 215-217, 244
Education, Higher, 142, 144, 165, 244
Education Statistics, 150
Educators, Early, 145
Eisenhower, Dwight D., 125
Eisenreich, Jim, 350
Election, 4, 80, 88, 93, 95, 109-110, 114, 125, 127, 133-135, 152, 162, 167
Empire Builder, 283

Engineers, Army Corps of, 294, 317, 323-324

Entertainment, 201, 203, 205, 207, 209, 211, 213, 215, 217, 219-221, 379

Environment, 36, 69, 95, 165, 179, 217, 223, 226, 269, 275, 336

Episcopalian, 163

Erickson, Roger, 222, 233, 380

Ethics, Media, 231

Expenditures, Per Capita, 141-142

Exports, Agricultural, 187-188

Exports, Minnesota, 188

Facts, Minnesota Arts, 222

Minnesota Deer, 338

Minnesota Fish, 332

Minnesota Weather, 284

Minnesota Workforce, 181, 196

Fair, Minnesota State, 219

Fair, Valley, 230

Falls, St. Anthony, 1-2, 17-18, 29, 33, 49, 58, 201, 322, 324

Farm Crisis, 185-186

Farming, 60, 67, 182, 185, 334

Festivals, 60, 219-220, 380

Filipino, 24, 64

First Shotters, 23

Fish, State Record, 330

Fishing Daily Limits, 327

Fitzgerald, F. Scott, 213

Fleming, Larry L., 207

Flight, Freedom, 30

Flight, Viking Project, 266

Floods, Red River Valley, 115

Foggie, Rickey, 356

Folkl, Kristin, 354

Football, 8-9, 135, 168, 343-345, 355-356, 362-363

Forests, National, 293-294, 332

Fort Beauharnois, 1

Fort, Bois, 71

Fort Crawford, 201

Fort Ridgely, 21

Fort Ripley, 44

Fort Snelling, 1-3, 15-18, 20-21, 27, 49, 58, 201-202, 204, 208, 211-212, 230, 245, 296, 322

Fort St. Anthony, 1, 16

Fort St. Antoine, 1

Foundation,
Amherst H. Wilder, 260

Blandin, 217, 222

Jerome, 222

Mayo, 271

McKnight, 217, 221-222

Freeman, Orville L., 92, 131-132

Fund, Environmental Trust, 9, 229

Gag, Wanda, 203, 213

Gallows, Largest Hanging One, 144

Gambling, Compulsive, 229

Gambling, Lawful, 143

Garnett, Kevin, 12, 352

Geography, 31, 33, 35, 37, 39, 41, 43, 45, 47, 60, 149, 154

Geology, 266, 268

Gerbino, Jeff, 380

Giel, Paul, 350, 356

Gilbert, James H., 108, 112

Goodhue, James M., 231, 376

Gopher State, 52

Gophers, 8, 340, 343

Government, Comparative, 82

Government, Local, 89, 137-138, 141, 244

Governor, MN Vote For, 128

Governors Since Statehood, 92

Grammy, 222

Grams, Rod, 78, 135

Grange, 121, 162

Grant, Bud, 8, 343-345

Grant-in-Aid, 294, 298

Graves, Peter, 222

Green, Dennis, 345

Griffith, Calvin, 7

Grossmann, Mary Ann, 215

Growe, Joan Anderson, 167

Growth, Projected Employment, 181

Growth, Rank Occupation, 181

Grunseth, Jon, 9, 127, 132

Guard, MN National, 23-25, 123

Guards, Minnesota Pioneer, 20

Guest, Judith, 169, 213

Gugliotta, Tom, 352

Guidelines, Current Poverty, 196
Guindon, Dick, 380
Guthrie, Sir Tyrone, 209
Gutknecht, Gil, 78
Haaf, Jerry, 10
Habitat, 321, 334-338, 342
Hailstorm of July, Great, 281
Hall, Orchestra, 205, 207, 230
Hall, Ted Mann Concert, 153, 207
Hansen, Scott, 381
Hanson, Douglas W., 254, 263
Harvest, 66, 290-291, 332, 334-335, 337-340
Harvest, Annual Deer, 339
Haskins, Clem, 357
Hasselmo, Nils, 8
Hassler, John, 213
Hatch, Mike, 91
Health Rankings, State, 226
Hegg, Jimmy, 382
Hench, Philip S., 271
Hennepin, Father Louis, 1, 211
Hernandez, Mario A., 63
Hettig, Rose, 247, 258-259, 261
Hiawatha, 33, 201, 203
Highlights, Broadcast, 234
Highlights, Political, 127
Hill, James J., 175, 202, 223
Hmong, 64, 71
Hockey, 6, 8-9, 12, 344, 355, 358, 361-362, 369
Hogan II, William E., 152
Hogs, 186-187, 228
Hogwood, Christopher, 206
Holtz, Lou, 8, 356
Honor, Congressional Medal , 28
Hospital, Fairview, 11
Hottest July, 285
Houlton, Loyce, 169, 210
Hrbek, Kent, 350-351
Hubbard, Lucius F., 92, 129
Hubbard, Stanley, 224
Humor, 125, 213, 375-382
    Scandinavian, 375, 378-379
Humphrey, Hubert H., 5, 7, 123, 126, 344, 348
Humphrey, Skip, 13, 127, 133

Humphrey, Stephen B., 234
Hungarian, 60, 339, 342
Hunting, 11, 297, 303-304, 307, 323, 325, 327, 329, 331, 333-339, 341, 381
Hunting Regulations, Setting, 337
Husbandry, Patrons of, 162
Ignarro, Louis, 271
Illegal Sports Bookmaking, 143
Immigration, 2, 4, 59-60, 64-65, 71, 74-75
Income, Farm, 189
Index, Cost of Living, 226
Indian Affairs, Bureau of, 61
Indians, American, 59-61, 71, 323
    Chippewa, 72, 204
    Displacement of, 66
    Sioux, 144, 201
Industries, Minnesota, 181
Industry, Video Production, 220
Information, Classical Music, 233
    Narcotic Arrest, 119
    Traffic, 238
Inkslinger, Johnny, 377
Institute, Melpomene, 169
Institution, Smithsonian, 266
Internet, 11, 216, 218-219, 232-233, 244
Internet User, American, 233
Ireland, Archbishop, 22
Iron, 3, 5-7, 40, 45-46, 50, 59-60, 66, 143, 176, 178, 203, 221, 223, 229, 265, 268-269, 297, 320-321
Irvine, Sally Ordway, 206
January, Coldest, 285
Jefferson, Thomas, 1, 15
Jennings, Kenneth, 206
Johnson, Carol C., 90
Johnson, John A., 92, 122-124, 130
Johnson, Lyndon B., 5
Johnson, Wally, 359
Jones, Casey, 295
Judicial System, 105-107
Kay, Princess, 220
Keillor, Garrison, 8, 213, 222, 375
Keller, Kenneth, 8
Kellogg, Frank Billings, 127, 272
Kelly, Tom, 348, 350
Kennedy, John F., 126

Kenny, Sister Elizabeth, 274
Kiffmeyer, Mary, 87, 167
Killebrew, Harmon, 7, 350-351
King, Jr., Martin Luther, 52
King, Reatha Clark, 169
King George II, 288, 291
Knoblauch, Chuck, 350
Knuckleheads, 381
Knutson, Coya, 167
Korea, 23-24
Kosovo, 23-24
Krause, Paul, 345
Kreuter, Gretchen, 170, 213
Kvamme, Joel, 194
Labor, Organized, 173-175, 177, 179, 181, 183
LaCroix, Edmund N., 3, 271
Lake Names, Most Popular, 34
Lake Superior, 31-33, 50, 53, 156, 269, 278-279, 284, 322, 326, 328, 331
Lake Wobegon, 8, 375
Lakers, Minneapolis, 12, 343
Lakes, Number of, 34, 52-53
Lang, Jonny, 220
Langer, Jim, 346
Larry Shandling Show, 381
Larsen, Libby, 222
Laughead, William B., 377
Laux, John, 11
Law School, U of M, 89, 111-2, 114
Laws, Passage of, 96
Lawyers, 106-107, 113-114
Le Berge, Dr. David, 207
League, American, 9, 348
Lee, Amp, 347
Lefse, 375
Legislators, 4, 8, 93-94, 96-97, 107, 145, 166, 197
Legislature, Minnesota, 93, 95, 107, 146, 149, 164, 169, 217
LeMond, Greg, 9
Leno, Jay, 381
Leopold, Aldo, 336
LeSueur, Meridel, 12, 213
LeVander, Harold, 92, 132
Lewis, Sinclair, 4, 213, 272

Lewis, Terry, 62, 372
License, Marriage, 73
Life Expectancy, 59, 69, 172, 226
Lifejacket Requirement, 293
Lighthouse, Split Rock, 315
Lightning, 281, 286
Lillehei, Dr. C. Walton, 272
Lincoln, Abraham, 3, 21, 151
Lindbergh, Charles A., 5, 28, 123, 308, 376
Liquor, 16, 76, 140, 143
Literature, Minnesota, 214-215
Little Crow, 3, 21
Livestock, 122, 186-187, 219, 228, 333
Long, Stephen H., 1, 211
Longfellow, Henry, 201
Lottery, Minnesota State, 229
Louisiana Purchase, 1, 15
Lovelace, Maud Hart, 168, 213
Lumbering, 269-270, 341
Lutefisk, 379, 382
Luther, William P., 81
Lutheran Brotherhood, 225
Mackay, Harvey, 224, 230
Magrath, C. Peter, 7
Mall of America, 228, 230
Management, Deer, 335, 337
    Ecosystem-based, 336
Manufacturing, 55, 174, 178-180, 224-227, 265
Maps, USGS Topo, 332
Maris, Roger, 343
Mariucci, John, 358
Mayo, Charles H., 273
Mayo, Dr. William J., 274
Mayo, Dr. William Worrall, 273
Mays, Willie, 343
McCarthy, Eugene J., 123
McCombs, Red, 13, 344
McCrae, Fiona, 169, 214
McDormand, Francis, 12
McFerrin, Bobby, 206
McHale, Kevin, 344, 367
McKinley, William, 22, 122
McMusic, Mr., 382
Measures That Matter, 69, 71

Medicine, 38, 46, 58, 66, 159, 165, 265-266, 271-274, 325
Merriner, Sir Neville, 205
Metrodome, Hubert H. Humphrey, 7, 344, 348
Metronet, 215
MFIP Cases, Number of, 194
Migrant, 63, 334
Milestones, Minnesota, 69, 71
Militia, Early, 20
Millers, Minneapolis, 234, 343
Minge, David, 10, 79
Mining, 35, 66, 176, 178, 223, 268, 297
Mink, 186-187, 341
Minnehaha Falls, 33, 36, 202
Minnesota,
    Apprenticeship Program, 183
    Bach Society of, 207
    Bookstore, 332
    Compare, 181, 226
    Connecting, 244
    Historical Society, 18, 63, 170, 202, 212-213, 292
    History, 124, 215, 230, 336
    In Profile, 52
    League of Women Voters, 167
    Lynx, 354-355
    Minerals of, 39
    Planning, 68-69
    Reviews Online, 215
    Science Museum of, 230
    State High School League, 362
    Thunder, 361
    Timberwolves, 10, 224, 344, 351, 353
    Twins, 7, 12, 344, 348, 351
    Vikings, 8, 13, 344-345, 347
    Wild Hockey, 355
    Women of, 161, 165, 167-170, 172, 182, 213, 358
    Workers, 179
MinnesotaCare, 140, 197
Minnesotan, How to Talk, 375
Minorities, Racial, 60
Mississippi Headwaters, 301
Mitropolous, Dimitri, 205
MnSCU, 153, 155

MNWorkForceCenter, 181
Mohr, Howard, 375
Molitor, Paul, 350-351
Mondale, Walter F., 5, 123, 127
Month, Driest, 285
Month, Wettest, 285
Monument, Pipestone National, 4, 293, 322-323
Moons, Table of Ojibwe, 290
Moor, Rob, 352, 354
Moore, Dave, 12, 234
Morris, Jack, 350
Motorcycles, Off-highway, 294
Musberger, Brent, 382
Museum
    Broadcasting, Pavek, 234
    Canal Park Marine, 230
    Weisman Art, 153, 216
Museums, 217, 222
Music, 8, 62, 204-208, 217, 230, 233, 235-236, 238-239, 241, 362
Music, Choral, 206-207
Music Source, Public Radio, 233
Musselman, Bill, 352, 357
NAACP, 135
NAFTA, 179
Nagurski, Bronko, 343
Najarian, John, 10
Naturalization, Certificate of, 74
Navy, 28-29, 82, 85, 112, 125
NCAA, 8, 10, 168, 354, 357, 359
Neel III, H. Bryan, 152
Neiman, LeRoy, 203
Nelson, Knute, 92, 129
Newspapers, 65, 173, 175, 231, 245, 247-248, 380
Nicollet, Joseph N., 2
Nixon, Richard M., 126
North Shore, 32-33, 296, 299, 319-320
Northrop Auditorium, 153, 205, 208
Norwegians, 60, 379
Nursing, 87, 140
Nute, Grace Lee, 168, 213
Oakley, Paul E., 207
Oberstar, James L., 82
Occupations, Fastest Growing, 181
Ojibway, 10, 12, 60-61, 66, 71-72, 169

Mille Lacs Band of, 10, 12, 169
Oliva, Tony, 350-351
Olson, Floyd B., 4, 92, 123, 125, 130-131, 176
Olympics, 6, 10, 343
Olympics, International Special, 10
Opera, 205-208
Opera Company, Minnesota, 208
Orchestra, 11, 62, 204-207, 211, 230
Orchestra, Minnesota, 11, 205-206, 211
Orchestra, St. Paul Chamber, 205-206
Ordinance, Northwest, 71
Organizations, Arts Service, 215
Organizations, Veterans, 25
Oue, Eiji, 11, 205
Page, Alan, 10, 345
Pardons, Board of, 113
Park, Camp Snoopy Theme, 228
Park System, National, 321-322
Parks, Minnesota State, 306, 316
Party, Democratic-Farmer-Labor, 122
Party, Reform, 13, 85, 127, 167
Passports, 74-75, 323
Patents, 273
Patrol, State, 115
Pattern, Development of Rail, 66
Peanuts, 380
Pearl Harbor, 22
Perpich, Rudy, 5, 7, 11, 92, 132, 167, 201, 217
Peterson, Collin C., 81
Philippines, 24, 29
Pigs Eye, 224
Pike, Lt. Zebulon Montgomery, 211
Pillsbury, John S., 92, 129
Pintilie, Lucian, 209
Pirsig, Robert, 222
Plan, MN Family Investment, 196
    Payment, Ave. MFIP, 194-195
Poet, 65, 213
Pohlad, Carl R., 348
Pole, North, 8, 169
    South, 169
Police, 10-11, 16, 23, 72, 81, 89-90, 116, 126, 141-142, 234
Polish, 60
Politics, 7-8, 10, 12, 64, 121, 123-127,

129, 131, 133, 135, 161, 164, 166, 169, 177, 185
Pope Gregory XIII, 288
Pope Leo XII, 22
Population, 2-4, 21, 26, 53-56, 58-71, 107, 115, 138, 141, 147, 149, 180, 198, 226-228, 231, 233, 244, 270, 317, 333-338, 340-341, 378
Poverty, 55, 64, 68, 149, 193-200
POW-MIA, 30
Prairie Home Companion, A, 8, 233, 375
Prairie Island, 10, 72
Precipitation, 58, 278, 285
PreK-12 Enrollment, 150
Prep Bowl, 365-366
Presbyterian, 212
Presses, Small, 214
Private Colleges, 158-159
Prize,
    Nobel, 153, 213, 268, 271, 273
    Pulitzer, 213
Procedure, Juvenile Court, 118
Process, Felony Case, 117
Process, Settlement, 65
Product, Gross State, 142, 226
Prohibition, 122, 128
Projections,
    County Population, 56
    Employment, 181
    MN Population, 65
Prosperity, 64, 174
Puckett, Kirby, 12, 348, 350-351
Quality of Life, State, 69, 226
Quie, Al, 6, 92, 127, 132
Raceway, Brainerd International, 230
Racism, 11, 165
Radio, Minnesota, 233, 235
Radio, Public, 8, 205, 233, 242
Radisson, Pierre Esprit, 211
Railroad, Burlington Northern, 11
Rainbow Division, 22, 24
Ramsey, Alexander, 3, 58, 92, 128, 204, 369
Ramstad, Jim, 79, 135
Range, Mesabi, 3, 32, 66, 156, 158, 177, 268

Reagan, Ronald, 201
Reasoner, Harry, 213
Rebate, Sales Tax, 141-142
Reciprocity, 143, 154
Records, Death, 72-73
Records, Guinness Book of World, 356, 372-374
Records, Team, 355, 367-368
Recreation, 95, 270, 293-295, 297, 299-301, 303, 305, 307, 309, 311, 313, 315, 317, 319, 321-324, 332, 336
Red Bull, 23-24
Red River Valley, 5, 12, 60, 115, 186, 224, 340
Refining, Koch, 13
Representatives, 2, 4, 78, 80-81, 96, 100, 111, 123, 127, 135, 142, 167, 184, 355
Representatives, U. S. House, 127
Reservation,
    Red Lake Chippewa, 72
    Shakopee Mdewakanton
        Sioux, 72
    Indian, 70-71
Revenues, 6, 116, 138, 140-143, 166
Rice, Cultivated Wild, 186-189
Riggs, Dudley, 380
River, Red, 1, 5, 12, 31-33, 53, 59-60, 115, 186, 224, 340-341, 377
Riverway, National Scenic, 306, 321
Rolvaag, Karl F., 5, 92, 132
Roosevelt, Theodore, 4
Rubber Man, 373
Ruth, Babe, 343, 351
Sabo, Martin Olav, 80
Saint Paul Sunday, 233
Samuelson, Ralph W., 292
SAT, 20, 149, 154, 246
Saunders, Flip, 352
Sayles-Belton, Sharon, 12
Scandinavia, 76, 185, 204, 379
Scandinavian, 123, 344, 375-376, 378-379, 382
School, Arts High, 215, 217
Schoolcraft, Henry Rowe, 33
Schools, K-12, 150, 244
Schools, Number of Public, 150

Schubert Club, 163, 204-206
Schulz, Charles, 380
Schunk, Mae A., 86
Scott, Dred, 20
Scottish, 59
Scouts, Philippine, 28
Sculptors, 32, 203
SEAL, Navy, 85
Seaway, St. Lawrence, 5, 33-34
Seinfeld, Jerry, 381
Senate, Minnesota, 79, 81, 98
Senators, Washington, 344, 348
Serbian, 60
Seren Innovations, 232
Service, Internal Revenue, 107
    Minnesota Relay, 243
    National Weather, 58, 283, 285
Service, Naturalization, 74
Service, U. S. Customs, 74
Sessions, Regular, 95
Sessions, Special, 6, 94
Settlement, 4, 13, 16, 58-60, 65-66, 71, 74, 106, 143, 176, 197, 223, 336-337
Settlement, Tobacco, 143, 197
Sevareid, Eric, 213, 242
Sibley, Henry Hastings, 2, 211
Signal, Allied, 13, 225
Silha, Otto A., 231
Sioux, Dakota, 1, 61
Sioux Uprising, 3
Skrowaczewski, Stanislaw, 205
Sky Blue Waters, 265
Slovakian, 60
Smith, Charles K., 376
Smith, Robert T., 242
Snelling, Colonel Josiah, 16
Snowiest Season, 285
Snowmobiling, 226, 295-297, 343
Soccer Tournament, USA CUP Youth, 361
Somalia, 27
Somalis, 71
Sommerfest, Viennese, 205
Soo-Line, 11
Sound Money, 233
Sounds of Blackness, 62
Spencer, LaVyrle, 169

Spiess, Gerry, 7
Splendid Table, The, 233
Sputnik, 147
St. Paul, Chapel of, 2
St. Paul, Hill Reference Lib., 202
St. Paul Companies Inc, 225
Stadium, Memorial, 267
Stadium, Metropolitan, 7, 344, 348
Stadium Fund, New Sports, 357
Stanley Cup, 9
STARBASE, 25
Stassen, Harold E., 92, 125, 131
State
    Bird, 51
    Capitol, 2-4, 85-86, 91, 113
    Constitutional Officers, 85
    Flag, 49
    Flower, 50
    Gemstone, 50
    Grain, 51, 189
    History, 5-6, 178, 283
    Mottoes, 52
    Planning Agency, 53
    Seal, 49
    Song, 51
    Symbols, 52
    Tree, 50
State Universities, 153-154, 159
Statehood, Early, 3
States, Rank Among, 186
Stations, Television, 231, 235, 242
Statistics, Annual Export, 227
    Bureau of Labor, 182
    MN Agricultural, 189, 228
    Occupational Employment, 181
    Personal, 72
    State Board of Labor, 175
    Vital, 49, 51, 53-55, 57, 59, 61, 63,
65, 67, 69, 71, 73, 75
Statutes, Revisor of, 96
Steele, Franklin, 2, 21
Storms, 275-276, 278-279, 281, 284
Stuhler, Barbara, 170, 213
Sugar, American Crystal, 62
SummerSlam, 13
Superbowls, 345
Swedish-American, 378

Swiss, 60, 232
Taconite, 7, 33, 48, 66, 143, 223, 265,
268-269, 297
Tandy, Jessica, 209
Tarkenton, Fran, 345, 347
Tax, Controlled Substance, 143
    Property, 36, 137-141, 144
    Benefits, 160
Taxes, 72, 76, 124, 137-141, 143
Taylor, Glen, 10, 352, 354
Teachers, 6, 54, 146-150, 162-163, 177-
179, 216-217
Teamsters, 176
Technology, Office of, 244
Telephone, New Metro Area Codes In
2000, 245
Television, Cable, 231
Testing, 149, 228, 267, 273
Theater, Chanhassen Dinner, 209
    Guthrie, 209, 230
    Old Log Cabin Theater, 209
    State and Orpheum Theatres, 230
    World, 8
    In the Round, 209
Thursday Musicale, 163
Tibetans, 71
Tim, Tiny, 12
Timber, 66, 175, 223, 265, 269-270, 304,
319, 334, 336, 341
Top Minnesota Attractions By
Numbers of Visitors, 230
Tornadoes, 12, 276, 281, 283, 286
Tornadoes, Eight Worst, 283
Tour de France, 9
Tourism, 53, 75, 82, 227, 230, 293
Trades, 174, 177-178, 183-184
Trails, State Recreation, 295
Trials, 7, 107, 114, 193
Trophy, Heisman, 343
Truesdale, C.W. (Bill), 214
TTY/TDD, 243
Twin Cities Gospel Sounds, 62
U of M Board of Regents, 152
U of M Sports, 357, 359-360
UnderWater World, 228
Unemployment, 7, 59, 71, 95, 142, 177,
179

Unions, 125, 149, 166, 173-174, 176, 179, 184

United Nations, 125, 168

USWest, 245

Van Brocklin, Norm, 344, 346

VanSant, Samuel R., 92, 129

Veblen, Thorstein, 212, 230

Vehicles, All-terrain, 294

Vento, Bruce F., 80

Ventura, Jesse, 13, 85, 92, 127, 133, 167, 234

    Janos, James George, 85

Veterans, 23-27, 77, 81, 95, 126, 209

Veterans, Jewish War, 26

Viagra, 271

Vietnam, 23-24, 26-27, 64

Volstead, Andrew, 136

Volunteers, First Minnesota Infantry, 21

Volunteers, Thirteenth Minnesota, 24

Voyageurs, 34, 201, 204, 212, 293, 300, 321, 343

Waart, Edo de, 205

Wacker, Jim, 356

Wahl, Rosalie, 167

Walker, Scott, 214

Wangensteen, Dr. Owen H., 273

War, Civil, 3, 16, 20-21, 24, 26, 61, 219

    French-Indian, 1

    Indian, 3, 333

    Persian Gulf, 9, 23-24, 27

    Revolutionary, 1, 15, 26-27

    Sioux, 20-21, 24

    Spanish American, 21, 24

Warland, Dale, 207

Warmath, Murray, 356

Washington, George, 15, 25, 27, 79, 112, 299

Weather, 7, 10, 58, 186, 267, 275-279, 281-289, 291, 375, 381-382

Weber, Vin, 10

Weekend, Take A Kid/Mom Fishing, 327

Welfare, 59, 73, 122, 126, 142, 164, 166, 169, 193-200

Welfare Reform, 193-195, 199-200

Wells Fargo, 13, 225

Wellstone, Paul David, 77

Wetlands, 34, 296, 317, 342

Wetterling, Jacob, 9

Whitney, Wheelock, 7, 132

Wilder, Laura Ingalls, 213

Wilson, Paul A., 142

Wilson, Woodrow, 123

Wind, Fastest, 285

Winfield, Dave, 350

Winter, Max, 12

Wolff, Hugh, 206

Women,

    Economic Status, 169-170, 172, 183

    Employed, 182, 184

    Minnesota, 161, 164-165, 167-170, 172, 182-183, 214, 260, 358

Women of Color, 165, 169

Women Venture, 184

World Series, 9, 348

World War I, 4, 22, 66, 146

World War II, 22-23, 26-27, 66, 147, 203, 219, 266

World Wide Web, 11, 232

World Wrestling Federation, 13

Wrestling Champions, Four-time State, 371

Wynia, Ann, 167

Y2K, 13

Yankee Girl, 7

Yastrzemski, Carl, 343

Year, Driest/Wettest, 285

Young, Dr. George W., 234

Youngdahl, Luther W., 92, 131

Yudof, Mark, 12, 152

Yugoslavians, 71

Zipper, 265, 274

Zoo, Minnesota, 230

Zukerman, Pinchas, 206